BEAUTIFUL IMPERIALIST

BEAUTIFUL IMPERIALIST

CHINA PERCEIVES AMERICA, 1972–1990

David Shambaugh

PRINCETON UNIVERSITY PRESS   PRINCETON, NEW JERSEY

Copyright © 1991 by Princeton University Press
Published by Princeton University Press, 41 William Street,
Princeton, New Jersey 08540
In the United Kingdom: Princeton University Press, Oxford
All Rights Reserved

Library of Congress Cataloging-in-Publication Data
Shambaugh, David L.
Beautiful imperialist : China perceives America. 1972–1990 / David
Shambaugh.
p.   cm.
Includes indexes.
ISBN 0-691-07864-5
1. United States—Foreign public opinion, Chinese.   2. Public
opinion—China—History—20th century.   I. Title.
E183.8.C5S46   1991
973.92—dc20   91-2135   CIP

This book has been composed in Linotron Palatino

Princeton University Press books are printed
on acid-free paper, and meet the guidelines
for permanence and durability of the Committee
on Production Guidelines for Book Longevity
of the Council on Library Resources

Printed in the United States of America by
Princeton University Press, Princeton, New Jersey

10 9 8 7 6 5 4 3 2 1

For Ingrid and Christopher

Contents

Tables and Figures _____

Preface

I HAVE SPENT a decade immersed in studying Chinese perceptions of the United States. It has been an extraordinarily interesting pursuit. It has brought me an enriched understanding of my native land (especially through others' eyes) as well as an enriched understanding of the country of my professional interest. I hope this volume will interest readers as much as it has the author. Americans will no doubt find many of the Chinese Marxist interpretations of their nation both startling and illuminating. Chinese readers will no doubt find of interest what their countrymen—whom I designate "America Watchers"—have to say about the United States. Those America Watchers who have contributed the commentary I portray in this volume will, I hope, not be offended. I have done my resolute best to translate their writings and spoken words accurately, to convey properly the context of their statements, and I apologize for any inaccuracies or misstatements of fact. At the same time, some of China's America Watchers and the Chinese political elite may not find this a book "friendly to China." It was not intended to be. Scholarship is supposed to be objective. I have endeavored to be objective in my portrayals of Chinese perceptions of America and my analyses of them. If friendship is characterized by candor, then this is a "friendly" study.

Readers in both China and the United States can take heart in the principal finding that, since the Sino-American rapprochement of 1972, Chinese understanding of the United States has improved markedly, despite continued distortion and misperception. It is my belief that only through continued improvement of mutual understanding will Sino-American relations be able to attain the constructive equilibrium that has eluded both nations for so long.

London
July 1990

Acknowledgments

THIS VOLUME had its origins in a doctoral dissertation. The topic was inspired by my own interests in the role of perceptions in international relations and in Sino-American relations and received impetus from my two Ph.D. supervisors at the University of Michigan, professors Michel Oksenberg and Allen Whiting (later of the University of Arizona). I thank Professor Oksenberg for his continual push for precision and nuance, for asking the tough (and often unanswerable) questions, for his personal interest in the subject, and for his friendship. Professor Whiting has been a pacesetter in the study of perception and Chinese foreign policy, from his classic *China Crosses the Yalu* to his more recent *China Eyes Japan*. His attention to detail, subliminal arguments, and the linkage between perception and policy enriched this study immeasurably, and I am in his debt for this assistance. His personal warmth and friendship also proved crucial at several difficult stages.

The other members of my original dissertation committee at Michigan—professors Harold Jacobson, Kenneth Lieberthal, Alfred Meyer, and Martin Whyte—are also due my deep gratitude for their input to this study and contributions in and out of the classroom. Various parts of the manuscript reflect their expertise and advice.

Numerous colleagues in the China field have taken the time to read and comment on the manuscript. I owe particular thanks to Gilbert Rozman, Steven Levine, and Steven Goldstein for their painstaking care and constructive criticisms as outside reviewers. Their suggestions made turning a dissertation into a book a considerably easier task. I also thank Harry Harding, Michael Hunt, Jonathan Pollack, and Michael Yahuda, who have taken the time to read drafts and discuss the topic with me. To all I owe a great debt.

I also thank my numerous Chinese colleagues and friends who over the years have shared with me their views on the United States. Many have taken much time and, in some cases, personal risk. During various phases of the research I have been hosted in China by the International Politics Department at Peking University, the American Studies Centers at Fudan and Wuhan universities, and the Institute of American Studies and Institute of World Economics and Politics at the Chinese Academy of Social Sciences. Thanks to all concerned for making arrangements and providing hospitality.

My colleagues in the Department of Political Studies at the School of Oriental and African Studies, University of London, have endured seminar discussions on aspects of the topic and provided many useful comments for improvement of the manuscript.

No book, at least one of this nature, can reach fruition without financial support. Along the way the following bodies have contributed funds for my research on this project: the Horace H. Rackham School of Graduate Studies at the University of Michigan; the Office of Research of the United States Information Agency; the Ford Foundation; the Committee on Scholarly Communication with the People's Republic of China; and the China Exchange Scheme of the British Academy/Economic and Social Research Council of the United Kingdom. The Woodrow Wilson International Center for Scholars and the School of Oriental and African Studies both provided necessary leave time for research and writing.

At Princeton University Press, Asian Studies editor Margaret Case has been very supportive and professional in her assistance. Anita O'Brien has proven a superb copy editor and has made this a far better manuscript than was originally the case. Working with both has been a pleasure.

Last, but by no means least, I owe a deep debt to family and friends. My fellow graduate students at Michigan—particularly Scott Wong, Carrie Warra, Diane Scherer, Tom Buoye, Steve Jackson, Shen Mingming, and Iain Johnston—lent moral and intellectual support at crucial junctures. My parents, George and Genevieve Shambaugh, and my brother George E. Shambaugh III, anxiously watched the whole process and have been vital sources of support in many ways. My wife Ingrid and son Christopher have both been deprived of countless hours of a husband and father as a result of this project. This book is therefore lovingly dedicated to them.

Abbreviations

AEI	American Enterprise Institute
BIISS	Beijing Institute of International Strategic Studies
CASS	Chinese Academy of Social Sciences
CIA	Central Intelligence Agency
CIS	Center for International Studies of the State Council
CPSU	Communist Party of the Soviet Union
CSCE	Conference on Security and Cooperation in Europe
EMT	Equivalent Megatonnage
GATT	General Agreement on Tariffs and Trade
IAS	Institute of American Studies, Chinese Academy of Social Sciences
ICIR	Institute of Contemporary International Relations
IIS	Institute of International Studies
IMEMO	Institute of International Relations and World Economics, Soviet Academy of Sciences
INF	Intermediate Nuclear Force
IWEP	Institute of World Economics and Politics, Chinese Academy of Social Sciences
MAD	Mutual Assured Destruction
MFA	Ministry of Foreign Affairs
MFN	Most-Favored Nation
MOFERT	Ministry of Foreign Economic Relations and Trade
MX	Missile Experimental
NATO	North Atlantic Treaty Organization
NCNA	New China News Agency
OECD	Organization of Economic Cooperation and Development
OPIC	Overseas Private Investment Corporation
PD	Presidential Directive
PLA	People's Liberation Army
SDI	Strategic Defense Initiative
SIIS	Shanghai Institute of International Studies
SIOP	Single Integrated Operational Plan
SLBM	Submarine Launched Ballistic Missile
START	Strategic Arms Reduction Talks
TRA	Taiwan Relations Act

BEAUTIFUL IMPERIALIST

One

Introduction

IN HIS classic study *Scratches on Our Minds*, the late Harold R. Isaacs argued that Americans hold a series of dichotomous "love/hate" images of China and the Chinese.[1] This study examines the other side of the Sino-American perceptual dyad—Chinese images of the United States—and concludes that, for their part, the Chinese have held equally ambivalent sets of images of the United States. "Beautiful Imperialist," the title of this study, is a literal translation of the oft-used term "American imperialism," which nicely captures the ambivalence—admiration and denigration—that distinguishes Chinese perceptions of the United States. If one accepts the premise that underlies this study, namely, that behavior is principally a function of perception, then it can be argued that the ambivalent images that China and the United States hold of each other have had much to do with the recurring cycles of amity and enmity that have characterized Sino-American relations since the late nineteenth century.

When President Nixon arrived in Beijing in February 1972, a new era of Sino-American relations opened. After the civil war on the Chinese mainland ended, a great gulf of communication had developed between the societies of The People's Republic of China and the United States, perpetuated by the Cold War confrontation between the two governments. The first two decades following the civil war were punctuated by repeated conflict between the United States and China around China's periphery: the Korean War of 1950–1953; the Taiwan Straits Crises of 1954–1955 and 1958; and the war in Vietnam, which brought limited engagement of People's Liberation Army and United States troops in 1965. During these two decades the United States tried to "contain" "Communist China" militarily, also blocking Beijing's admission into the United Nations and enforcing a trade embargo against the People's Republic.

With Nixon's dramatic opening and historic visit to China, contact between the two societies and governments was reestablished after a twenty-three year hiatus. How did the long period of no contact, and the vitriolic anti-American propaganda waged in China during this time, affect Chinese perceptions of the United States? What im-

[1] (New York: John Day & Co., 1958).

ages of America did Chinese bring to this new phase of the relationship? How have Chinese views of the United States evolved since the Nixon visit? Is there a range of Chinese interpretations of America, and do they cluster into identifiable categories?[2] If so, how do they vary over time?

To answer these questions fully requires an examination of Chinese perceptions of the United States during the 1950s and 1960s, if not of earlier periods. This has been and is being done by others.[3] This study, therefore, examines Chinese perceptions of the United States during the period from the Nixon opening to China in 1972 to the immediate aftermath of the Tiananmen tragedy of 1989. In terms of state-to-state relations, this period encompasses extremes of amity (following the Nixon visit and the normalization of diplomatic relations in 1979) and enmity (following the Tiananmen crisis of 1989), as well as several periods of uncertainty (1977, 1980–1982), and progressive interaction (1978–1980, 1983–1988). To a certain extent the images and perceptions presented in this study parallel the fluctuating status of state-to-state relations between the two countries, but they also

[2] The distinction between "image" and "perception" is not made clear in the literature, and the two terms are usually used interchangeably. In this study "image" will be used to describe *categories* of specific articulated perceptions. The image is a mental construct that categorizes and orders disparate pieces of information and helps to shape an articulated response (perception). My distinction follows that of Allen S. Whiting: "*Image* refers to the preconceived stereotype of a nation, state, or people that is derived from a selective interpretation of history, experience, and self-image. . . . *Perception* refers to the selective cognition of statements, actions, or events attributed to the opposite party as framed and defined by the preexisting image. To use a figure of speech widely found in the literature, *image* provides the frame and the lenses through which the external world is seen or *perceived*." Allen S. Whiting, *China Eyes Japan* (Berkeley: University of California Press, 1989), p. 19.

[3] Research on Chinese images of the United States during earlier periods is currently being undertaken by Michael Hunt; see his *Images and Action: The Chinese Communist Party Confronts the United States, 1920s–1950s* (New York: Columbia University Press, forthcoming). Also see Yin Lichuan, "Chinese Perceptions of American China Policy, 1945–1990," Ph.D. dissertation, School of Oriental and African Studies, University of London, in progress; chapters by Michael Hunt, David Shambaugh, and Akira Iriye in David Shambaugh, ed., *Mutual Images and U.S.-China Relations*, Occasional Paper no. 32 of the Asia Program, Woodrow Wilson International Center for Scholars; David Shambaugh, "Anti-Americanism in the People's Republic of China," *The Annals of the American Academy of Political and Social Science*, vol. 497 (May 1988): 142–56; Jonathan D. Pollack, "Perception and Action in Chinese Foreign Policy: The Quemoy Decision," Ph.D. dissertation, University of Michigan, 1976; Tu Wei-ming, "Chinese Perceptions of America," in Robert C. Oxnam and Michel C. Oksenberg, eds., *Dragon and Eagle* (New York: Basic Books, 1978), pp. 87–106; and the chapters by Zhang Baijia, He Di, Yuan Ming, Chen Xiaolu, Wang Jisi, Steven M. Goldstein, and Jonathan D. Pollack, in Harry Harding and Yuan Ming, eds., *Sino-American Relations, 1945–1955: A Joint Reassessment of a Critical Decade* (Wilmington: Scholarly Resources, 1989).

exhibit a distinct quality of linear development from the critical and ideological to the respectful and nuanced.

Importantly, of whom do I speak when referring to "Chinese" images and perceptions? This is a study of China's "America Watchers" and their articulated perceptions of the United States.[4] An "America Watcher" is an individual whose full-time professional occupation is to study and interpret events in the United States or American foreign relations for China's concerned elite or mass public.

Because autonomous channels of information are few and the Chinese media are generally controlled, it is via China's community of America Watchers that both the leaders and the mass public receive most of their information about the United States. Thus, to a significant extent, the America Watchers serve as the interpretive prism through which information about the United States is processed before it reaches the Chinese elite and public. China's America Watchers inform the leadership by means of oral briefings and classified government channels. They inform the intelligentsia about the United States through specialized professional publications (including both books and periodicals), and the mass public through the print and broadcast media. The America Watchers are therefore critically important in determining broader "Chinese" images of the United States, and hence what national images and elite perceptions help to shape China's policies toward the United States.

China's America Watchers

America watching in China has become a growth industry, responding to the insatiable demand among the populace for knowledge about the United States. Chinese have long been fascinated by "Old Gold Mountain" (the term for San Francisco but used more generally to describe America),[5] but during the 1980s the thirst for knowledge about the United States grew at an unprecedented rate. Untold millions of Chinese tune in daily to the Voice of America, and Chinese

[4] I use the term "articulated perceptions" because it is uncertain whether the perceptions offered in this study are indeed the true cognitive beliefs of those considered. The perceptions used for this study were articulated in publications and interviews with the author; both forums are subject to manipulation for propaganda purposes.

[5] Three studies of this earlier fascination are particularly noteworthy: Michael Hunt, *The Making of a Special Relationship: The United States and China to 1914* (Columbia University Press, 1983); Chang-fang Chen, "Barbarian Paradise: Chinese Views of the United States, 1784–1911," Ph.D. dissertation, Indiana University, 1985; R. David Arkush and Leo O. Lee, eds., *Land without Ghosts: Chinese Impressions of America from the Mid-Nineteenth Century to the Present* (Berkeley: University of California Press, 1989).

bookshops are swamped by eager readers searching for translations
of American books (of which nearly a thousand were published in
China during the decade 1977–1987).[6]

Paralleling this fascination with things American among the Chinese public has been a need to know more about the inner workings
of the United States among China's leaders and throughout the
sprawling government bureaucracy. The dearth of knowledge about
China inside the American government at the time of rapprochement
was at least matched on the Chinese side. As Zhang Wenjin, a senior
America specialist who was intricately involved in the opening to the
United States, admitted when asked about the influence of America
specialists on the making of China's America policy, "Chairman Mao
and Premier Zhou actually knew very little about the United States;
they had to rely upon us. Now our leaders have much contact with
Americans in China, they read many articles and materials on the
United States, but they still need us to help interpret the United
States for them."[7]

When presidential envoy Henry Kissinger arrived at the Nanyuan
military airport south of Beijing on his July 1971 secret mission, he
was greeted by a small group of specialists on the United States that
included Huang Hua, Ji Chaozhu, Zhang Wenjin, and T'ang Wensheng (Nancy T'ang).[8] When President Nixon arrived on his historic
state visit the following February, he was met by the same group plus
Han Xu and other old America hands. This small cohort has played
an important role in guiding China's America policy since the rapprochement, and for several their involvement dates from before
1949. Huang Hua, Zhang Wenjin and Han Xu were aides-de-camp to
Zhou Enlai during the civil war and participated in both the Chongqing and Nanjing negotiations. Zhang Wenjin accompanied Zhou to
the 1954 Geneva Conference on Indochina, the first time that senior

[6] See David L. Shambaugh, *Books About America in the People's Republic of China, 1977–1987* (Washington, D.C.: United States Information Agency, 1988).

[7] Interview, Beijing, May 16, 1990.

[8] Zhang Wenjin, Nancy T'ang, and Wang Hairong had been dispatched to pick Kissinger up in Islamabad. For Kissinger's account see Henry Kissinger, *White House Years* (Boston: Little, Brown, 1979), p. 43. In an interview in Beijing on May 16, 1990, Zhang Wenjin recalled the first meeting: "We arrived in Pakistan ahead of Kissinger. We boarded the [Pakistani] aircraft first. Shortly after midnight Kissinger boarded. When he met us he was very animated and happy to see us, but his Treasury Department guards very surprised! After takeoff we talked for a while. Our discussions were not of a substantive nature; Kissinger had much preparing to do for his meetings with our leaders. After landing at Nanyuan [airport] we took him to the Diaoyutai Guest House where he met Premier Zhou Enlai a few hours later. From the start, the personal atmosphere was excellent."

American and Chinese officials had met since the revolution. Ji Chao-zhu had served at the Military Armistice Commission meetings at Panmunjom, later interpreted for Chairman Mao and other Chinese leaders in their meetings with U.S. officials, and served as the long-time number two in Washington before being appointed envoy to the United Kingdom. Huang Hua went on to a number of ambassadorial postings and later crowned his diplomatic career as China's foreign minister. Zhang Wenjin and Han Xu held high posts in the Foreign Ministry and became ambassadors to the United States. Nancy T'ang was purged along with her mentors, the Gang of Four, following Mao's death.

While this elite corps of China's leading America hands have played key roles as formulators and implementers of China's policy toward the United States since rapprochement, their numbers have expanded considerably over the last two decades. Today, China's leaders have at their disposal multiple sources of information and intelligence about the United States emanating from a sprawling community of approximately six hundred to seven hundred America Watchers spread throughout a complex civilian and military bureaucracy (see figure 1.1). Most central government and party organs (first tier) and professional research insitutes (second tier) now have large sections and staffs responsible for monitoring developments in the United States; many universities (third tier) have established American Studies centers; and a variety of national research associations (fourth tier) have been formed to bring together Americanists from different professional walks of life. In addition, several dozen New China News Agency correspondents now file regular reports from the United States in Chinese newspapers.

I have detailed this expansive community of America Watchers elsewhere.[9] Suffice it here to offer some observations about this community collectively, and subgroups among them.

Expertise among such a large cohort of specialists varies, as would be expected. It varies for a number of reasons, which include access to published data on the United States, opportunities to visit the United States, exposure to other cultures and modes of interpretation, educational training, and professional role. The potential impact of these and other variables on the actual perceptions articulated by the America Watchers is discussed in chapter 7, but brief elaboration of the professional-role variable will highlight the spectrum of

[9] See David L. Shambaugh, "China's America Watchers," *Problems of Communism* 37 (May–August 1988): 71–94. For a Chinese depiction of this community see Zi Zhong-yun, "Zhongguo de Meiguo yanjiu," *Meiguo yanjiu*, no. 1 (1987): 7–20.

Fig. 1.1 The Structure of China's America-Watching Community

First Tier

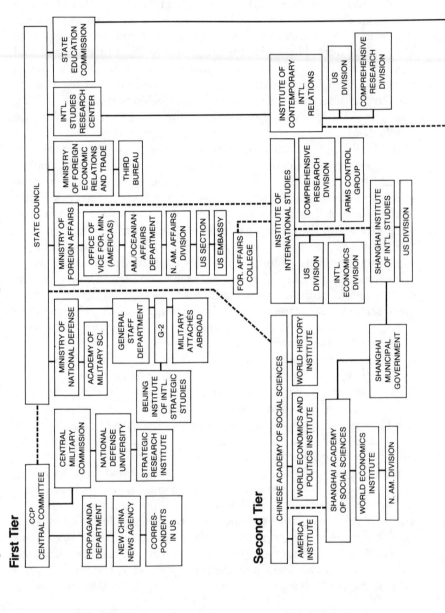

Second Tier

Third Tier

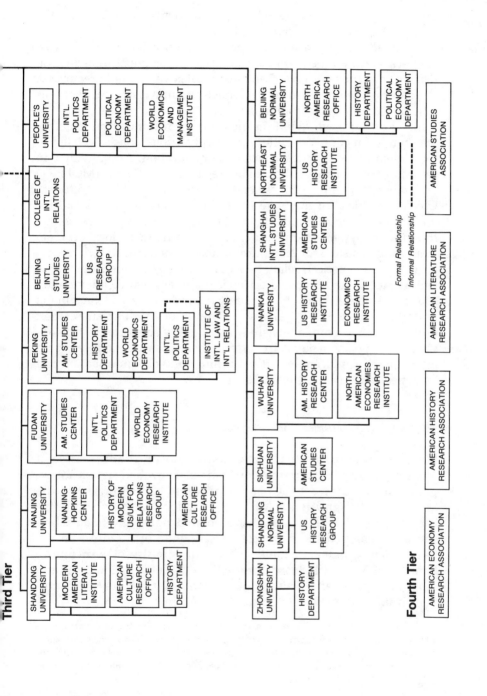

Fourth Tier

Formal Relationship ——————
Informal Relationship - - - - - - -

SHANDONG UNIVERSITY
— MODERN AMERICAN LITERAT. INSTITUTE
— AMERICAN CULTURE RESEARCH OFFICE
— HISTORY DEPARTMENT

NANJING UNIVERSITY
— NANJING-HOPKINS CENTER
— HISTORY OF MODERN US/UK FOR. RELATIONS RESEARCH GROUP
— AMERICAN CULTURE RESEARCH OFFICE

FUDAN UNIVERSITY
— AM. STUDIES CENTER
— INT'L. POLITICS DEPARTMENT
— WORLD ECONOMY RESEARCH INSTITUTE

PEKING UNIVERSITY
— AM. STUDIES CENTER
— HISTORY DEPARTMENT
— WORLD ECONOMICS DEPARTMENT
— INT'L. POLITICS DEPARTMENT
— INSTITUTE OF INT'L. LAW AND INT'L. RELATIONS

BEIJING INT'L. STUDIES UNIVERSITY
— US RESEARCH GROUP

COLLEGE OF INT'L. RELATIONS

PEOPLE'S UNIVERSITY
— INT'L. POLITICS DEPARTMENT
— POLITICAL ECONOMY DEPARTMENT
— WORLD ECONOMICS AND MANAGEMENT INSTITUTE

ZHONGSHAN UNIVERSITY
— HISTORY DEPARTMENT

SHANDONG NORMAL UNIVERSITY
— US HISTORY RESEARCH GROUP

SICHUAN UNIVERSITY
— AMERICAN STUDIES CENTER

WUHAN UNIVERSITY
— AM. HISTORY RESEARCH CENTER
— NORTH AMERICAN ECONOMIES RESEARCH INSTITUTE

NANKAI UNIVERSITY
— US HISTORY RESEARCH INSTITUTE
— ECONOMICS RESEARCH INSTITUTE

SHANGHAI INT'L. STUDIES UNIVERSITY
— AMERICAN STUDIES CENTER

NORTHEAST NORMAL UNIVERSITY
— US HISTORY RESEARCH INSTITUTE

BEIJING NORMAL UNIVERSITY
— NORTH AMERICA RESEARCH OFFICE
— HISTORY DEPARTMENT
— POLITICAL ECONOMY DEPARTMENT

AMERICAN ECONOMY RESEARCH ASSOCIATION

AMERICAN HISTORY RESEARCH ASSOCIATION

AMERICAN LITERATURE RESEARCH ASSOCIATION

AMERICAN STUDIES ASSOCIATION

different types of America Watchers and hence shed light on the range of expertise to be found in this community.

Essentially there exist four types of America Watchers. That is, America Watchers perform four different professional roles in Chinese society: those who work in the central government bureaucracy; journalists; research institute personnel; and university teachers (this schema varies slightly from figure 1.1).

Many of those who work in the central government bureaucracy are merely functionaries who implement various policies related to the United States for their concerned organization. An individual in the Ministry of Foreign Economic Relations and Trade (MOFERT) who must deal with a Chinese end-user for selling a U.S. product in China, an official of the State Educational Commission responsible for placing American students in Chinese universities, or personnel from the foreign affairs bureau of any unit who make local arrangements and translate for American visitors all perform staff duties related to Sino-American relations that require some knowledge of the United States, but because their job is not interpretative, they do not count as America Watchers. Certainly many America Watchers in the central government bureaucracy perform important implementation duties, but they simultaneously work as policy advocates, policy advisers, and policy makers. To perform these professional roles properly requires significant expertise on, and up-to-date information and intelligence about, the United States.

The Central Government Bureaucracy

Many ministries under the State Council maintain a cadre of at least ten America specialists, many of whom have now had significant exposure to the United States and Americans. Not surprisingly, the Ministry of Foreign Affairs, Ministry of National Defense and its related organs, MOFERT, and other economic, trade, and financial institutions maintain the strongest concentration of expertise on the United States. But even units such as the Ministry of Agriculture, Ministry of Nuclear Industry, or the Bank of China maintain Americanists on their staffs. This is only natural, as it reflects the institutionalization of the Sino-American relationship.[10]

[10] It was a working premise of the Carter and Reagan administrations that the creation of constituencies of Americanists throughout the Chinese bureaucracy may serve the purpose of pro-American advocacy groups within the Chinese government, which, if not arguing for policies benefiting expanded relations, would at a minimum

While it must be said that the expertise on the United States among such individuals is quite sophisticated, my own interaction with many of these individuals leads me to agree fully with a former senior American official with extensive experience in dealing with China's leading Americanists who said, "None of these individuals can put themselves in the place of a United States decision maker; they lack the sociological-anthropological training necessary for them to transcend their own system and view the United States as an American would."[11] No doubt the same assertion could be made about America's leading China specialists as well.[12]

Professional Research Institutes

America Watchers in professional research institutes perform two different professional roles. First, they perform advisory roles very similar to those in the central bureaucracy. That is, they mainly perform the professional role of intelligence analyst, but they are not directly policy advocates as their counterparts in Foreign Ministry might be. Their advisory role to policy makers, which might better be termed consultative, is essentially carried out through writing interpretive analyses of events concerning the United States and orally briefing higher-level policy makers and Chinese leaders.

America Watchers in five civilian research institutes apparently have the most regular input into the (America) policy process: the State Council's Center for International Studies (CIS); the Institute of Contemporary International Relations (ICIR), which serves China's top leadership via the CIS; the Foreign Ministry's Institute of International Studies (IIS); the Shanghai Institute of International Studies (SIIS); and the Institute of American Studies (IAS) at the Chinese Academy of Social Sciences (CASS).[13]

---

serve to better inform the generalists who make China's America policy or, at a maximum, serve to anchor the relationship bureaucratically and thus stabilize it during times of stress. Some of this argument is developed by Michel C. Oksenberg, "The Dynamics of the Sino-American Relationship," in *The China Factor: Sino-American Relations and the Global Scene*, ed. Richard H. Solomon (Englewood Cliffs: Prentice-Hall, 1981), pp. 48–80.

[11] Interview, March 29, 1985.

[12] For a discussion of America's China specialists, see the essays in David L. Shambaugh, ed., *The American Study of Contemporary China*, forthcoming.

[13] For additional details of these and other concerned organizations in the Chinese foreign policy bureaucracy, see David L. Shambaugh, "China's National Security Research Bureaucracy," *China Quarterly*, no. 110 (June 1987): 276–304; and A. Doak Bar-

The CIS is an organization similar to the U.S. National Security Council in that its main function is to coordinate research on international affairs within the Chinese government and channel it to the Chinese leadership.[14] The CIS serves not only as a transmitter of reports from lower to higher levels, but also as drafter of policy position papers. For example, China's shift away from the United States in favor of a more equidistant policy vis-à-vis the Soviet Union in 1982–83 was reportedly initiated by CIS staff.[15]

The ICIR is, in short, China's CIA. It is China's largest civilian intelligence research unit, with a research staff of three hundred. It provides the senior elite of the party and government with current intelligence and finished estimates, as well as briefing materials prior to official visits. The U.S. research division, headed by Song Baoxian, has about thirty researchers who look mainly at U.S. domestic issues, while the "comprehensive" research division focuses on U.S. foreign, defense, and strategic policies. Strategic analysts Zhou Jirong, Wang Baoqin, Qi Ya, Ren Mei, and Gu Guanfu rank among China's most astute observers of international security affairs.

The IIS, with a total research staff of approximately 175, is the Foreign Ministry's main think tank. IIS studies are sent mainly to the Ministry of Foreign Affairs, but sometimes they circulate more widely throughout the upper echelons of government. The ten staff members of the U.S. research division essentially set their own research agendas, but they also regularly contribute papers to the North American Affairs Division (*Bei-Mei shi*) of the Foreign Ministry, sometimes write biographical profiles and background papers prior to a diplomatic visit, and occasionally write specific studies requested by senior leaders.[16] Senior America Watchers at the IIS—Zhuang Qu-

---

nett, *The Making of Foreign Policy in China: Structure and Process* (Boulder: Westview Press, 1985).

[14] Interview at the State Council Center for International Studies, May 12, 1990. Founded in 1982, the center was headed by former ambassador and senior foreign policy adviser Huan Xiang until his death in 1989. Since Huan's passing and the removal of Zhao Ziyang from office (Zhao relied extensively on this and other think tanks under the State Council), by its own admission the center's influence in the Chinese foreign policy making process has declined.

[15] Interview with CIS staff member, October 17, 1984.

[16] Interviews with IIS staff, November 30, 1983; January 12, 1984; and May 18, 1990; and interviews with Foreign Ministry officials, March 25, 1983; May 17, 1990. An example of a senior leader commissioning reports from IIS staff occurred in 1984 when then-Premier Zhao Ziyang tasked senior IIS America Watcher Zhuang Qubing to write a report on the U.S. Strategic Defense Initiative (SDI) and its implications for China. A nonclassified version of this report appeared later in the institute's journal. See Zhuang Qubing, "Meiguo 'xingqiu dazhan' jihua," *Guoji wenti yanjiu*, no. 4 (1984): 24–31.

bing (retired), Pan Tongwen, Jin Junhui, Song Yimin, and Ye Ru'an—rank among the best of their profession in China.

SIIS also theoretically serves the Foreign Ministry, although its location in Shanghai gives it significant autonomy. While small in staff size, the institute produces an analytical product of high quality—which does not go unnoticed in Beijing. The State Council CIS frequently asks SIIS staff for specific papers.[17] Leading America Watchers at SIIS include Zhang Jialin and Ding Xinghao.

The Chinese Academy of Social Sciences' Institute of American Studies is, as would be expected, the central locus of expertise on the United States in China. The IAS is also the institutional home of the Chinese Association of American Studies. Founded in 1981, the IAS has a critical mass of Americanists (now totaling forty full-time researchers), most personally recruited by former director Li Shenzhi (often referred to as China's Arbatov). Li, a former aide to Zhou Enlai, drew upon his Yanjing University connections (a source of many leading Americanists) and other *guanxi* to build a high-quality scholarly institute. While scholarly research is IAS's main pursuit, leading staff members are frequently called upon to prepare reports for, or brief, China's leaders. Li himself has accompanied several of China's leaders on visits to the United States. Among its high-quality research staff, the leading Americanists at IAS include current director Zi Zhongyun, economist Chen Baosen, strategic specialists Zhang Jingyi and Wu Zhan (retired), diplomatic historians Zhang Yebai and He Di, domestic politics experts Li Miao and Zhang Yi, and U.S. society and culture specialist Dong Leshan.

America Watchers working in the above five institutes generally perform the first of the two aforementioned professional roles—intelligence analysts cum policy advisers. Their analytical products are generally nonideological, straightforward analyses of the United States. One should add to these five civilian institutes those under the military (Academy of Military Sciences, National Defense University, and Beijing Institute of International Strategic Studies), as well as a number in the trade and finance spheres, since their work is also highly policy oriented and generally non-Marxist in character.

A second, and different, professional role performed by America Watchers in research institutes is that of "establishment intellectual."

---

[17] For example, in May 1990 SIIS America Watcher Chen Peiyao was preparing a paper, at CIS's request, on the future U.S. role in NATO as a result of the political changes in Eastern Europe and the Warsaw Pact, while Ding Xinghao wrote a special report for the Central Committee on the implications of most-favored nation status for China's America policy (in which Ding argued for limited Chinese retaliation if the United States revoked MFN status). Interviews in Beijing, May 12 and 16, 1990.

This term was coined by Carol Lee Hamrin and Timothy Cheek to denote Chinese intellectuals who are

> members of the establishment, serving and operating within the governing institutions of the People's Republic. . . . As a subgroup within the ruling elite, they [have] a deep interest in perpetuating the system. . . . They play a key mediating role in coordinating a symbiotic exchange of services—an implicit social contract—between rulers and the larger intellectual elite. In this exchange the [establishment] intellectuals provide expertise and buttress the moral legitimacy of the governing group by explaining and popularizing its policies.[18]

How does being an "establishment intellectual" in a professional research institute affect China's America Watchers? Unlike their counterparts in the above-mentioned five institutes, who contribute to the policy process, the principal professional task of the second group is more theoretical and abstract in nature. That is, their job is to analyze the United States within a specific theoretical framework set down by the "establishment"—namely, Marxism-Leninism. The task of researchers in such institutes is not to write studies for policy elites, but rather to view the world through a Marxist-Leninist lens, write theoretical treatises, and hence justify policy in ideological terms.

Such is the case with research institutes affiliated with the CASS, such as the Institute of World Economy and Politics (IWEP), the Institute of World History, Institute of Modern History, Institute of Economics, Institute of Sociology, and, of course, the Institute of Marxism–Leninism–Mao Zedong Thought. Outside the CASS, several institutes within the Central Party School are also included in this category. Such institutes operate at the periphery of the America-watching community insofar as their America Watchers have broader theoretical purviews than their counterparts in policy-related institutes, but they nonetheless contribute a significant amount of the total written product of the America-watching community.

Taken together, professional research institutes in these two categories—policy- and ideology-oriented—constitute the second type of America Watchers. Numerically, they constitute the largest contingent within the America-watching community, and they are generally well-informed about the United States, even if some of their analyses are cast in doctrinaire terms.

[18] Timothy Cheek and Carol Lee Hamrim, "Introduction: Collaboration and Conflict in the Search for a New Order," in *China's Establishment Intellectuals*, ed. Carol Lee Hamrin and Timothy Cheek (Armonk: M. E. Sharpe, 1986), pp. 3–4.

Journalists

The third professional type of America Watcher is the journalist who works for the New China News Agency (NCNA). An official organ of the Propaganda Department of the Central Committee of the Communist Party, NCNA plays an extremely important role in interpreting the United States for the Chinese leadership and populace alike. NCNA has posted its correspondents in the United States since 1979 (since 1972 at the United Nations), and their reports appear daily in the Chinese print and broadcast media. This is the single most important source of information about the United States for the general public. The agency also maintains a translation staff of several thousand whose full-time job is to translate the American press. The translations are carried in *Cankao ziliao* (Reference materials) for a limited number of high officials and cadres with a "need to know," and in *Cankao xiaoxi* (Reference news) for a more general, though still restricted, readership.

Many NCNA correspondents are newcomers to America watching, but several senior correspondents are old America hands. The agency became something of a haven for these individuals during periods of political turmoil and persecution. Senior America hands such as Li Shenzhi, Peng Di, Li Miao, Chen Youwei, Li Yanning, and Zhang Haitao all took refuge at NCNA for long periods of time and, as a result, built bona fide careers as journalists while their previous careers were suspended.

In terms of professional role, many journalistic America Watchers can certainly be considered "establishment intellectuals," as their trade can be a highly propagandistic one. But, as will be seen in this study, NCNA correspondents were among the first to break free from ideological interpretations of the United States.

Universities

American studies in Chinese universities and colleges is a rapidly growing field. By virtue of faculty concentration and institutionalized programs, at least fifteen different universities and colleges can be considered part of the America-watching establishment (see figure 1.1).

The quality of America watching in universities is uneven. The majority of their analyses are highly doctrinaire, and most teaching and research takes place within the Marxist-Leninist intellectual tradition.

This is partially because there are a number of genuine Marxist-Leninists in Chinese universities, but also because university professors also play the role of "establishment intellectual." Universities in China, like the news media, are supposed to be "transmission belts" for inculcating certain state-approved knowledge and norms of behavior in their students. University professors are civil servants and do not generally have the adversarial relationship with the state that is characteristic of Western intellectuals.[19] Their job is generally to transmit and perpetuate doctrine, not to create knowledge or foster independent thinking.

Thus, much America watching in Chinese universities is generally ideological and highly doctrinaire. There are important exceptions to this rule, particularly at Peking University and Fudan University in Shanghai, but the majority of America watching academics in China toe the party line. Even when there is no party line to toe, as was the case during much of the 1980s, they continue to churn out Marxist studies of the United States.

When one considers Chinese perceptions of America, therefore, the aforementioned institutional landscape and differing professional roles must be borne in mind. America Watchers in China do not simply ply their trades individually; they must work within definite bureaucratic and intellectual confines.

These observations about the professional roles of China's America Watchers are developed at greater length in chapter 7. They are noted here to provide the reader with an institutional sense of the America Watchers who articulate the specific perceptions provided in chapters 2–6 of this study.

The Informing Literature

This is a study of the perceptual sources of Chinese foreign policy. In so doing it draws upon and joins three sets of literature in the field of comparative foreign policy: decision-making analysis; Soviet foreign policy and images of the United States; and the domestic sources of Chinese foreign policy. This informing literature also offers useful perspectives with which to view the images and perceptions offered in this study.

[19] The traditionally symbiotic relationship between universities and the state, and the intellectual and the state more broadly, is discussed in Jerome Grieder, *Intellectuals and the State in Modern China* (New York: The Free Press, 1981).

Images and Decision-Making in International Relations

Why study images? We are concerned with studying images because people's interpretations of a phenomenon do much to shape their subsequent behavior, and social scientists are fundamentally concerned with why people act as they do. As W. I. Thomas observed in 1928, "If men define situations as real, they are real in their consequences."[20] This is why we study images.

Students of international relations seek to explain the behavior of nation-states and other institutional actors. But states are not abstract entities; they are composed of human beings. Thus, to understand the foreign policy behavior of a given nation, one must comprehend the images of those concerned elites who make the policy decisions that help shape their state's actions in the international arena. These images, in turn, are the product of many stimuli, but ultimately all considerations external to the individual must be filtered through one's internal perceptual screen before one acts.

Cross-cultural images as a variable in interstate relations have been an object of study by scholars at least since ancient Greece. The classic account by Athenian historian Thucydides, the *History of the Peloponnesian War* (431–404 B.C.), is essentially a psychological analysis of the Athenian and Spartan combatants. Aside from analyzing the political causes and technical aspects of the war, Thucydides emphasized the cultural characteristics that gave rise to it. The importance of understanding the psycho-cultural bases of one's adversary in war has been a persistent theme in analyses of international relations ever since Thucydides, from Chen Shou's third-century *History of the Three Kingdoms* through Clausewitz's *On War* and more recently Waltz's *Man, the State, and War.* With the advent of the "behavioral revolution" in American social science in the 1950s and 1960s, the study of the relationship between cognition and behavior began to attract an increasing number of scholars across several disciplines. Social and cognitive psychologists led the way, but political scientists, sociologists, and historians soon followed suit.

Those who study international relations, and its subfield of comparative foreign policy, were quick to embrace the new focus on the study of perception. The study of the domestic sources of foreign policy began to assume prominence as scholars took issue with the "Realist" school of foreign policy analysis, which tended to conceive of nation-states as unitary and rational actors pursuing their national interests. Gradually over time the foreign policy behavior of states

[20] W. I. Thomas, *The Child in America* (New York: Knopf, 1928), p. 572.

increasingly came to be viewed as the product of various domestic factors acting autonomously, and in conjunction with, external stimuli.[21] As a result, the boundary between the study of comparative politics and international relations, as subdisciplines of political science, began to break down.

Of crucial importance among these domestic factors are the cognitive constructs of foreign policy decision makers. By introducing the intervening variable of the perceptual process through which a decision maker interprets stimuli before formulating a response, scholars try to look inside the "black box" of decision making by focusing on the "idiosyncratic" level of analysis. They try to explicate the intuitive belief that reality exists in the eye of the beholder, but they have found this empirically difficult. Ole Holsti, a leading scholar of perception and foreign policy, has noted that access to hard data for use in constructing and analyzing belief systems (the basis of images) is a fundamental methodological impediment: "Unlike the analyst who can index his variables with such measures as GNP per capita, arms budgets, trade figures, votes in the U.N. General Assembly, or public opinion polls, those interested in beliefs of decision makers have no yearbook to which they can turn for comparable evidence, much less quantitative data presented in standard units."[22]

Despite the methodological problems associated with constructing and analyzing belief systems, research on what in 1956 Sprout and Sprout termed the "psychological milieu" (as distinguished from the "operational milieu") of international politics has proceeded apace in the field of international relations.[23] Efforts to probe inside the "black box" of decision making has produced a voluminous number of "pretheoretical" models and case studies, but few middle-range theoretical works.[24] By placing the individual decision maker's belief system at the center of a complex network of organizational and other influences, Snyder, Bruck, and Sapin pioneered this era of foreign policy decision-making theory in general, and the consideration

[21] James Rosenau was among the first to specify this interaction in "Foreign Policy as an Issue Area," in *Domestic Sources of Foreign Policy*, ed. James Rosenau (New York: The Free Press, 1967), pp. 11–50.

[22] Ole Holsti, "Foreign Policy Viewed Cognitively," in *Structure of Decision: The Cognitive Maps of Political Elites*, ed. Robert Axelrod (Princeton: Princeton University Press, 1976), p. 35.

[23] Harold and Margeret Sprout, *Man-Milieu Relationship Hypotheses in the Context of International Politics* (Princeton: Princeton University Center for International Studies, 1956).

[24] For an explanation of this distinction see James Rosenau, "Pre-Theories and Theories of Foreign Policy," in *Approaches to Comparative and International Politics*, ed. Barry Farrell (Evanston: Northwestern University Press, 1966), pp. 27–92.

of cognitive factors in particular.[25] Others followed. As Holsti reminds us in a useful state-of-the-field survey, diversity has been the rule in this research.[26]

The individual policy maker has been the main level of analysis and central focus of this genre of studies because of the assumption that beliefs held by individuals are heterogeneous, and therefore when put into a decision-making situation the variations will become manifest. Consequently, the belief system of the individual decision maker is conceptualized as the intervening variable between the independent variable of external stimuli (information) and the dependent variable of the decisional output (policy). Thus, in one form or another, much of the comparative foreign policy literature on decision making has attempted to reconstruct individuals' belief systems and assess their impact on information processing, the articulation of a perception, the making of a policy decision, and learning from postdecision feedback. This sequence is represented in figure 1.2.

The literature on belief systems and foreign policy decision making has centered on how the elements of one's belief system interrelate. This literature has drawn heavily upon cognitive psychology. Concepts such as cognitive balance and congruity, cognitive complexity, cognitive distortion, cognitive consistency, and cognitive dissonance are some of the operative concepts in this field. If there is one core theme in this literature, it is that there is a strong tendency for people to recognize what they expect to see, and to assimilate incoming information into preexisting image structures. In psychology these

Fig. 1.2 Belief Systems and Information Processing

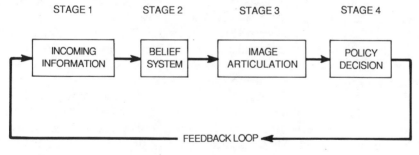

[25] Richard Snyder, H. W. Bruck, and Burton Sapin, *Foreign Policy Decision-Making: An Approach to the Study of International Politics* (Glencoe: The Free Press, 1962).

[26] Ole Holsti, "Foreign Policy Viewed Cognitively," p. 36; Also see Richard Little and Steve Smith, eds., *Belief Systems and International Relations* (Oxford: Basil Blackwell, 1988).

phenomena are known respectively as cognitive consistency and dissonance reduction. In short, people assimilate or reject information in such a way as to maximize the congruence among the cognitive elements of their belief system. To anticipate one of my principal findings, this study offers strong evidence that such is also the case among China's America Watchers. That is, more often than not, the America Watchers find in the United States what they expect to see. In essence, many of them look in search of confirmation of pre-existing images.

The effects of cognitive dissonance on foreign policy decision makers have been noted in a number of case studies, but nowhere more comprehensively than by Robert Jervis in his landmark study *Perception and Misperception in International Politics*.[27] If his study can be summarized, Jervis concludes that the strong tendency toward cognitive consistency, in all its various manifestations, leads foreign policy decision makers to misperceive their adversaries and other actors in the international arena much more often than they receive signals as they were intended. On this basis Jervis concludes that misperception often leads directly to conflict. As a result, he identifies elite images as the single most important variable in international relations. It is this premise that underlies the present study.

Soviet Foreign Policy and Images of the United States

Perhaps nowhere in the comparative foreign policy literature is the study of images better developed than in the subfield of Soviet foreign policy, particularly in Soviet-American relations. Ever since the Bolsheviks came to power in 1917, American scholars have attempted to assess the impact of Marxist-Leninist ideology on the global perspectives of Soviet elites, as well as upon domestic institutions, policies, and the populace. During the cold war, attempts to understand the mindset of Soviet foreign policy elites flourished, and Marxist-Leninist ideology assumed prominent attention as a variable in studies of the domestic sources of Soviet foreign policy. As such, ideology has been conceived of both as autonomously affecting an elite's belief system and images and as an integral component of the belief system—that is, as an independent and dependent variable respectively. It has also been conceived of as a post facto rationalization for policies pursued "rationally and efficiently."[28]

---

[27] Robert Jervis, *Perception and Misperception in International Politics* (Princeton: Princeton University Press, 1976).

[28] William Zimmerman, "What Do Scholars Know about Soviet Foreign Policy?" in

Textual exegesis of Communist "esoteric communications" has held a central place in the "Kremlinological" tradition.[29] Content analysis, both quantitative and qualitative, has often been the only way to detect policy differences among elites.[30] Leadership statements and commentary in the organs of mass media have thus long been scrutinized in the West for clues to elite cleavages and factional strife in the Soviet Union. This was particularly the case during the Stalin era when foreign analysts looked for the slightest variation in a press that remained remarkably uniform and controlled. This situation contributed greatly to the acceptance of the unitary actor model of Soviet foreign policy.

With Khrushchev's ascension to power, however, the situation changed. As the monolithic, totalitarian nature of the Stalinist regime began to erode, so too did the unitary actor paradigm. Western scholars of Soviet foreign policy discovered a changed elite and data base. The top elite—what Robert Putnam has termed the "proximate elite" (those directly involved in national policy making)—remained an important object of study, but an "influential elite" also increasingly became the unit of analysis. The latter group Putnam defines as individuals with "substantial indirect or implicit influence; those to whom decision-makers look for advice, whose opinions and interests they take into account, or from whom they fear sanctions."[31]

In analyzing domestic Soviet affairs, this changing level of analysis spurred studies of specialists,[32] occupational interest groups,[33] and "tendency analysis."[34] In analyzing Soviet foreign policy, this meant looking below the "proximate elite" level of the Politburo and Foreign Ministry to the "influential elite" level of international relations scholars and specialists. The emergence during the Khrushchev era of several specialized international relations institutes in the Soviet Academy of Sciences and other research-oriented organizations, as

Soviet Foreign Policy in a Changing World, ed. R. Laird and E. Hoffmann (New York: Aldine, 1986), p. 94.

[29] William E. Griffith, "Communist Esoteric Communications: Explication de Texte," in *Handbook of Communication*, ed. Ithiel de Sola Pool and Wilbur Schramm (Chicago: Rand McNally, 1973), pp. 512–20.

[30] For a useful overview of this literature see William deB. Mills, "Content Analysis of Communist Documents," *Studies in Comparative Communism* 18, 1 (Spring 1985): 81–92.

[31] Robert Putnam, *The Comparative Study of Political Elites* (Englewood Cliffs: Prentice Hall, 1976), p. 11.

[32] See, for example, Richard Remnek, ed., *Social Scientists and Policy Making in the USSR* (New York: Praeger, 1977).

[33] H. Gordon Skilling and Franklyn Griffiths, eds., *Interest Groups and Soviet Politics* (Princeton: Princeton University Press, 1969).

[34] Franklyn Griffiths, "A Tendency Analysis of Soviet Policy Making," in ibid.

well as their proliferating publications, provided a glimpse into the previously murky world of elite discussions on foreign policy issues.

Western scholars quickly gravitated to this level of analysis and new data base. They discovered not only more discriminating analyses than emanated from Politburo and Foreign Ministry spokesmen, but also an entire world view that fundamentally departed from previous Stalinist dogma.

In his pioneering study of this era, William Zimmerman detailed these changed Soviet "perspectives" on international relations.[35] Zimmerman found evidence in Soviet commentaries of general movement away from the simplistic, ideologically driven, and zero-sum (i.e., two-camp) assumptions characteristic of the Stalin era toward greater understanding of the complexities of international relations and increasingly empirical appraisals of the international system that paralleled Western concepts, terminology, and images. Zimmerman discovered that in Soviet commentaries the main actors in international relations had become nation-states and not the class-based world systems of capitalism and socialism. Soviet analyses of the international hierarchy were reconfigured to allow the Soviet Union equal status with the United States, with each country controlling well-defined spheres of influence. Assessments of the balance of power had passed through a cycle from "balanced distribution" to "preponderance" of power to "equilibrium," and back to a more ambiguous balance dubbed the "correlation of forces."

What is particularly relevant to this study in this literature is how Soviet elite images of the United States changed during this period. To anticipate another principal finding, the Chinese perceptions of the United States as presented in this study bear a striking similarity to those articulated in the Soviet Union during the Khrushchev era in terms of terminology used, issues debated, and conclusions reached.

The American recognition that the systematic study of Soviet elite images of the United States may yield fruitful insights into what motivates Soviet behavior toward the United States, bilaterally and mul-

---

[35] William Zimmerman, *Soviet Perspectives on International Relations, 1956–1967* (Princeton: Princeton University Press, 1969). Also see Zimmerman's "Elite Perspectives and the Explanation of Soviet Foreign Policy," *Journal of International Affairs* 24, 1 (1970): 84–98. For three more recent studies that bring Zimmerman's pioneering work forward through the 1980s and Gorbachev's "New Thinking," see Allen Lynch, *The Soviet Study of International Relations* (New York: Cambridge University Press, 1987); Margot Light, *The Soviet Theory of International Relations* (London: St. Martin's Press, 1988); and Richard K. Hermann, *Perceptions and Behavior in Soviet Foreign Policy* (Pittsburgh: University of Pittsburgh Press, 1985).

tilaterally, has resulted in an impressive body of scholarship, in both quantity and quality. As the major protagonist of the United States, the Soviet Union has received considerable attention from scholars, journalists, and government analysts.

Invariably these studies place Soviet images of the United States in the broader context of Marxist-Leninist theories of capitalist development. As a result, they all include an analysis of how the Stalinist image that the capitalist state apparatus is subordinate to the monopoly bourgeoisie eroded during the Khrushchev era. This is traced both in the general context of Soviet doctrinal assessments of imperialism and "state-monopoly capitalism" and in the particular case of the United States. The Chinese interpretation of these issues is examined in chapter 2.

Frederick Barghoorn was the first Western scholar to analyze the challenge to Stalin and his "subordination thesis" posed by Eugen Varga, the exiled Hungarian economist and director of the Institute of International Relations and World Economics (IMEMO) in Moscow.[36] Varga's heretical views (in the eyes of Stalin) not only landed him in personal disgrace, but also resulted in the closing of the institute. After Stalin's death, however, Varga was rehabilitated and the institute was reconstituted. Stalin's legacy, however, did not die easily. Stalin's "subordination thesis" and imprint upon Soviet political economists long outlived him. It was not until after Khrushchev's famous denunciation of Stalin in his "secret speech" to the Twentieth Congress of the Communist Party of the Soviet Union in 1956 that Soviet analyses of imperialism and state-monopoly capitalism began to change.

A key element in Varga's critique was the assertion that the state acts in the interests of the bourgeoisie as a whole, not solely on behalf of the financial oligarchy.[37] This, in effect, was a rejection of the Leninist-Stalinist postulate that the only goal of the state in monopoly-capitalist society is to procure greater and greater profits for the monopoly and finance oligarchy strata of the bourgeoisie. As a matter of doctrine, though, several scholars have noted that Lenin's views of the relationship between the state and monopoly bourgeoisie and financial oligarchy were more ambiguous than Stalin's.[38] While Stalin

[36] Frederick Barghoorn, "The Varga Discussion and Its Significance," *The American Slavic and East European Review* 6 (1948): 214–36.

[37] See Richard Nordahl, "The Soviet Model of Monopoly Capitalist Politics," Ph.D. dissertation, Princeton University, 1972; "Stalinist Ideology: The Case of the Stalinist Interpretation of Monopoly Capitalist Politics," *Soviet Studies* 26, 2 (April 1974): 239–59.

[38] Bob Jessop, *The Capitalist State* (New York: New York University Press, 1982); Ralph Miliband, *The State in Capitalist Society* (London: Weidenfeld and Nicolson, 1969);

perceived a unidirectional relationship of control of the former by the latter, Lenin envisioned a relationship of "coalescence" between the two.

Of particular relevance here are the marked doctrinal changes during the Khrushchev years. Zimmerman, Hough, Marantz, and others have analyzed these changes in Soviet elites' worldview, and in Soviet foreign policy more generally.[39] Analysis of Soviet perceptions of the United States also became a flourishing area of study.[40]

Martin Carnoy, *The State and Political Theory* (Princeton: Princeton University Press, 1984); G. Clark and M. Dear, *State Apparatus* (Boston: Allen and Unwin, 1984); R. Alford and R. Friedland, *Powers of Theory: Capitalism, the State, and Democracy* (Cambridge: Cambridge University Press, 1985).

[39] William Zimmerman, *Soviet Perspectives on International Relations, 1956–1967*; Jerry Hough, "The Evolution of the Soviet World View," *World Politics* 32 (July 1980): 509–30; Paul Marantz, "Prelude to Detente: Doctrinal Change under Khrushchev," *International Studies Quarterly* 19, 4 (December 1975): 501–28; Bohdan Bociurkiw, "The Post-Stalin 'Thaw' and Soviet Political Science," *Canadian Journal of Economics and Political Science* 30, 1 (February 1964): 22–48.

[40] Frederick Barghoorn, *The Soviet Image of the United States: A Study in Distortion* (New York: Harcourt, Brace, 1950); Urie Bronfenbrenner, "The Mirror Image in Soviet-American Relations: A Social Psychologist's Report," *Journal of Social Issues* (1961): 45–57; Max Beloff, "Soviet Historians and American History," in *Contemporary History in the Soviet Union*, ed. J. Keep (New York: Praeger, 1964), pp. 306–14; William Zimmerman, "Soviet Perceptions of the United States," in *Soviet Politics since Khrushchev*, ed. A. Dallin and T. Larson (Englewood Cliffs: Prentice-Hall, 1968), pp. 163–79; Paul Aron, ed., *Soviet Views of America* (White Plains: International Arts and Sciences Press, 1969); William Zimmerman, *Soviet Perspectives on International Relations, 1956–67*, especially chapter 6; Franklyn Griffiths, "Images, Politics, and Learning in Soviet Behaviour toward the United States," Ph.D. dissertation, Columbia University, 1972; Richard Mills, "One Theory in Search of Reality: The Development of United States Studies in the Soviet Union," *Political Science Quarterly* 87 (1972): 63–79; Paul Hollander, *Soviet and American Society* (New York: Oxford University Press, 1973); Robert Hansen, "Soviet Images of American Foreign Policy," Ph.D. dissertation, Princeton University, 1975; Nelson Polsby, "JFK through Russian Eyes," *Political Science Quarterly* 90, 1 (Spring 1975): 117–26; Richard Mills, "Soviet Views of the United States," *Problems of Communism* 25 (May–June 1976): 79–82; Stephen Gilbert, *Soviet Images of America* (New York: Crane and Russak, 1977); S. Frederick Starr, "The Russian View of America," *The Wilson Quarterly* (Winter 1977): 106–17; Morton Schwartz, *Soviet Perceptions of the United States* (Berkeley: University of California Press, 1978); N. Sivachev and Yakovlev, *Russia and the United States: U.S.-Soviet Relations from the Soviet Point of View* (Chicago: University of Illinois Press, 1979); William Potter, "Perception and Misperception in U.S.-Soviet Relations," *Problems of Communism* 29, 2 (1980): 68–82; S. A. Grant, *Soviet Americanists* (Washington, D.C.: USICA Research Report, 1980); John Lenczowski, *Soviet Perceptions of U.S. Foreign Policy* (Ithaca: Cornell University Press, 1982); William Taubman, *Stalin's America Policy* (New York: Norton, 1982); Neil Malcolm, "Soviet Interpretations of American Politics: A Case of Convergence?" *British Journal of Political Science* 12 (1982): 43–73; Neil Malcolm, *Soviet Political Scientists and American Politics* (New York: St. Martin's Press, 1984); Richard M. Mills, *As Moscow Sees Us: American Politics and Society in the Soviet Mindset* (New York: Oxford University Press, 1990).

These studies tell us that there is a trend over time toward increasingly complex and nonideological Soviet images of the United States. This is due not only to the development of American studies in the Soviet Union, but also to the emergence of a professional cadre of America Watchers—the Amerikanistiki. American studies was not the only area studies field to blossom during the Khrushchev era; Soviet Sinology, for example, also enjoyed a rejuvenation.[41]

All of these studies detail the altered imagery of U.S. domestic and foreign affairs resulting from the doctrinal changes in Marxism-Leninism under Khrushchev. Having abandoned the notion that a unitary and omnipotent finance oligarchy dictated U.S. domestic and foreign affairs, Soviet Amerikanistiki shifted their focus from Wall Street to Washington. They began to analyze intraexecutive branch bureaucratic politics, executive-legislative relations, and a variety of interest groups. The latter was significant because it implicitly recognized that elements outside the bourgeoisie participated in the policy process. Even analyses of the bourgeoisie became more differentiated as other regional monopoly groups appeared to challenge the old monied interests in the Northeast. Soviet Americanists discovered the U.S. middle class, and in so doing realized that they were not on the verge of revolution. They saw that, while beset by nagging problems, the U.S. economy was in no immediate danger of collapsing. Finally, they discovered "sober elements" among the U.S. "ruling circles" who favored détente with the Soviet Union.

In short, the Varga controversy and de-Stalinization had a far-reaching impact on Soviet perspectives on international relations. Soviet commentators became much less dogmatic and doctrinaire in their ideological interpretations, and they came to accept many of the methodologies popular in the West. Soviet scholarly analyses of international affairs after Stalin therefore became less of a guide to predicting Soviet behavior because of their post hoc rationalizing nature, and more of a guide to understanding the parameters of Soviet elite thinking and policy options because of the increased role of specialists in the policy process. The linkage between elite and specialist

---

[41] Gilbert Rozman, "Background," in *Soviet Studies of Premodern China*, ed. Gilbert Rozman (Ann Arbor: Michigan Monographs in Chinese Studies), pp. 7–38; Rozman, *A Mirror for Socialism: Soviet Criticisms of China* (Princeton: Princeton University Press, 1985); Robert Gates, "Soviet Sinology: An Untapped Source for Kremlin Views and Disputes Relating to Contemporary Events in China," Ph.D. dissertation, Georgetown University, 1974; Gretchen Sandles, "Soviet Images of the People's Republic of China, 1949–1979," Ph.D. dissertation, University of Michigan, 1981; Columbia University Ph.D. dissertation in progress by Elizabeth Wishnick; and Princeton University dissertation in progress by Deborah Kaple.

perceptions and foreign policy output is thus a complex reciprocal process whereby perceptions contribute to the decision-making environment in which policy is made. In other words, in the post-Stalin era the study of elite perceptions became fundamental to assessing the domestic sources of Soviet foreign policy.

Domestic Sources of Chinese Foreign Policy

Western scholarship on the domestic sources of Chinese foreign policy, including elite images and perceptions, is conspicuous by its absence. The field's laggard productivity is particularly striking in contrast to the progress made by colleagues studying the sources of Soviet foreign policy noted above. Remarkably, there are no counterpart volumes in the Chinese foreign policy literature to Zimmerman's or Hough's studies of Soviet international relations specialists and their images of the international system,[42] to Bialer's volume on the domestic sources of Soviet foreign policy,[43] or to others who have studied Soviet images of America.[44]

A. Doak Barnett's 1985 study of the Chinese foreign policy decision-making structure and process is a welcome addition to a small and dated literature.[45] This volume, taken together with a few other, shorter studies of international relations–related institutions in China,[46] has contributed to our understanding of the structure of key

[42] William Zimmerman, *Soviet Perspectives on International Relations, 1956–1967*; Jerry Hough, *The Struggle for the Third World: Soviet Debates and American Options* (Washington, D.C.: Brookings, 1986).

[43] Seweryn Bialer, *The Domestic Context of Soviet Foreign Policy*.

[44] See sources cited in note 40.

[45] Barnett, *The Making of Foreign Policy in China: Structure and Process*; Daniel Tretiak, "Who Makes Chinese Foreign Policy Today (Late 1980)," *Australian Journal of Chinese Affairs*, no. 5 (1981): 137–57; Roger Dial, "The New China News Agency and Foreign Policy in China," *The Contemporary Asia Review* 1, 1 (1977): 39–54; Donald Klein, "The Management of Foreign Affairs in Communist China," in *China: Management of a Revolutionary Society*, ed. Donald Klein (Seattle: University of Washington Press, 1971); "Peking's Evolving Ministry of Foreign Affairs," *China Quarterly* (October–December 1960); "The Men and Institutions behind Chinese Foreign Policy," in *Sino-American Relations 1949–71*, ed. Roderick MacFarquhar (New York: Praeger, 1972); Melvin Gurtov, "The Foreign Ministry and Foreign Affairs during the Cultural Revolution," *China Quarterly* (October–December 1969).

[46] Alastair I. Johnston, *China and Arms Control: Emerging Issues and Interests in the 1980s* (Ottawa: The Canadian Centre for Arms Control and Disarmament, 1986); James Huskey, "USIA Conference on PRC Research Institutes and Their Impact on Foreign Policy," United States Information Agency *Research Memorandum* (Washington, D.C., February 28, 1986); David L. Shambaugh, "A Profile of International Relations on Chinese Campuses and IR Associations and Publishing in the PRC," *China Exchange News*

organizational and individual actors who make Chinese foreign policy, but our knowledge of the roles that international relations specialists play in the decision-making process remains sketchy. We have no equivalent study of foreign policy specialists to compare with Halpern's study of economists and economic policy making in China,[47] or Lieberthal and Oksenberg's study of energy policy decision making.[48] There exist only two assessments of international relations as an academic discipline in China,[49] and a few state-of-the-field appraisals of political science.[50]

If the paucity of scholarly attention paid to decision making in Chinese foreign policy is striking, then the lack of consideration of elite images and perceptions is even more notable. This inattention is more the result of an inadequate data base than a lack of recognition by scholars that elite images and perceptions are important variables to study. Opportunities to interview Chinese policy makers and international relations specialists were virtually nil until recent years. Moreover, until the revival of professional research institutes and their publications in the post-Mao era, the documentary data base was limited to a handful of official media organs such as the *People's Daily*, *Beijing Review*, New China News Agency dispatches, and monitored radio broadcasts—all of which helped contribute to a unitary-actor model of Chinese foreign policy.

With the revival of professional research on international relations and the explosion of periodical, newspaper, and book publishing since the late 1970s, foreign analysts of China (including Chinese foreign policy) now confront a situation of bibliographic overload. The net result has been the gradual emergence of more discriminating studies based on these varied primary data, which have had the overall effect of eroding the efficacy of monolithic approaches to the

---

(June 1985): 11–17; and Shambaugh, "China's National Security Research Bureaucracy," *The China Quarterly*, no. 110 (June 1987): 276–304.

[47] Nina Halpern, "Economic Specialists and the Making of Chinese Economic Policy, 1955–1983," Ph.D. dissertation, University of Michigan, 1985.

[48] Kenneth Lieberthal and Michel Oksenberg, *Policy Making in China: Leaders, Structures, and Processes* (Princeton: Princeton University Press, 1988).

[49] Douglas P. Murray, *International Relations Research and Training in the People's Republic of China* (Stanford: Northeast Asia–United States Forum on International Policy, 1982); David L. Shambaugh and Wang Jisi, "Research on International Studies in the People's Republic of China," *PS* 27, 4 (Fall 1984): 758–64.

[50] Thomas P. Bernstein, "Political Science," in *Humanistic and Social Science Research in China*, ed. Anne Thurston and Jason Parker (New York: Social Science Research Council, 1980); Harry Harding, "Political Science," in *Science in Contemporary China*, ed. Leo Orleans (Stanford: Stanford University Press, 1980); Zhao Baoxu, *The Revival of Political Science in China* (Berkeley: Institute for East Asian Studies and Center for Chinese Studies, University of California, 1983).

study of contemporary China in all its facets. The study of the Chinese domestic economy and political scene has revealed this trend more readily than the fields of Chinese foreign and defense policy. The latter are still severely constrained by the availability of published data and by Chinese fears of infringement upon areas of national security—some of which are justified and some not because of the extraordinary scope of the Chinese definition of "state secrets." To offer but a single example relevant to those wishing to conduct research on Chinese scholarly views of international relations, as recently as mid-1984 more than half of seventy periodicals relevant to the study of Chinese foreign policy were classified *neibu* and therefore restricted to internal circulation.[51] These periodicals contain the highest quality and frankest scholarly assessments written by Chinese international relations specialists and foreign policy practitioners.

Gilbert Rozman was the first Western scholar to tap extensively into this newly available literature in his landmark book on Chinese images of the Soviet Union.[52] Rozman and Michael Ng-Quinn have also drawn on these primary data in articles.[53] Allen S. Whiting's major study of Chinese perceptions of Japan also draws on this new material, as do several studies by Jonathan Pollack and Banning Garrett and Bonnie Glaser.[54] There is much more potential research to be done, however, given the West's new access to international relations institutes, scholars, and publications in China.[55] The opportunity to

[51] See the periodical table in my "Profile of International Relations on Chinese Campuses and IR Associations and Publishing in the PRC."

[52] Gilbert Rozman, *The Chinese Debate about Soviet Socialism, 1978–1985* (Princeton: Princeton University Press, 1987).

[53] Gilbert Rozman, "China's Soviet Watchers in the 1980s: A New Era in Scholarship," *World Politics* 37, 4 (July 1985): 435–74; Michael Ng-Quinn, "International Systemic Constraints on Chinese Foreign Policy," in *Chinese Foreign Policy in the Post-Mao Era*, ed. Samuel Kim (Boulder: Westview Press, 1989), pp. 82–110.

[54] Allen S. Whiting, *China Eyes Japan*; Jonathan D. Pollack, *China's Potential as a World Power* (Santa Monica: The Rand Corporation, Report P-6524, 1980); Pollack, *The Sino-Soviet Rivalry and Chinese Security Debate* (Santa Monica: The Rand Corporation, Report R-2907-AF, 1982); Pollack, *The Lessons of Coalition Politics: Sino-American Security Relations* (Santa Monica: The Rand Corporation, Report R-3133-AF, 1984); Pollack, *Security, Strategy, and the Logic of Chinese Foreign Policy* (Berkeley: University of California Institute of East Asian Studies, 1981); Pollack, "The Korean War and Sino-American Relations," in *Sino-American Relations, 1945–1955*, ed. Harding and Yuan; Banning Garrett and Bonnie Glaser, *War and Peace: The Views from Moscow and Beijing* (Berkeley: Institute of International Studies, University of California, 1984); Garrett and Glaser, *Chinese Estimates of the U.S.-Soviet Balance of Power* (Washington, D.C.: Woodrow Wilson International Center for Scholars, Asia Program, 1988).

[55] For an excellent survey of potential areas of research drawing on these new primary data, see Michael H. Hunt and Odd Arne Westad, "The Chinese Communist

probe the thinking of this "influential elite" and juxtapose their "input" against various types of foreign policy behavioral "output" will be at the cutting edge of research in the field for some time to come. The systematic and empirical study of the domestic sources of Chinese foreign policy, including elite perceptions, should begin to proliferate. One gets the sense that the field is in a state analogous to the study of Soviet foreign policy during the Khrushchev era. Perhaps within a generation of scholarship the field of Chinese foreign policy will have true counterpart studies to those of Zimmerman, Hough, Bialer, Griffiths, and the others noted above.

These observations about the relative paucity of Western studies of the domestic sources and elite images underlying Chinese foreign policy rationale and behavior should not be misconstrued to mean that there has been a total absence of such studies. Important exceptions exist. While the main thrust of the field has focused attention on the output of Chinese foreign policy with respect to dyadic relationships, regional subsystems, and international institutions, there remains a rather substantial body of literature that attempts to explain Chinese foreign policy from the input side, including the consideration of "Chinese" images. The problem with most of this literature, however, is that it tends to proceed a priori from a unitary-actor paradigm and does not generally disaggregate "Chinese" images to distinguish between competing images of different elites. The exceptions to this rule are studies that extrapolate from domestic political factional analysis to identify foreign policy "debates" among the leadership. This genre of studies is discussed below, but first some summary comments are warranted about studies of Chinese images of the world in the unitary-actor tradition. Three main strands in this literature can be identified: traditional, normative, and rational approaches.

The traditional approach is found in the writings of historians who emphasize the continuity of Chinese historical images. Proponents of this approach argue that the most productive way to comprehend the images underlying contemporary Chinese foreign policy is to study imperial China's view of the world. This approach is exemplified in the writings of such historians as Fairbank, Mancall, Fitzgerald, Ginsberg, Feuerwerker, and others.[56] To oversimplify, these scholars tend

---

Party and International Affairs: A Field Report on New Historical Sources and Old Research Problems," *The Chinese Quarterly* 122 (June 1990): 258–72.

[56] John K. Fairbank, ed., *The Chinese World Order* (Cambridge: Harvard University Press, 1968); Fairbank, "China's Foreign Policy in Historical Perspective," *Foreign Affairs* 47, 3 (April 1969): 449–63; Mark Mancall, *China at the Center: 300 Years of Foreign Policy* (New York: The Free Press, 1984); Mancall, "The Persistence of Tradition in Chi-

to proceed from the premise of a Sinocentric tribute system. As such, China presides over a hierarchical system of peripheral states organized in concentric realms around it.[57] All such states establish tributary relationships with China on the basis of China's superiority and location at the center of this system. These scholars have naturally found this explanation to have its greatest validity in explaining China's relations with its Asian neighbors, but they have also drawn upon specific instances in China's past to explain contemporary Chinese foreign policy.

A more normative set of interpretations of Chinese images of international relations can be distinguished based on "Maoist ideology." This cohort of studies combines Mao's sinified version of Marxism-Leninism with political tactics developed during the Communists' rise to power. These studies address both Mao Zedong's personal role in policy making and the externalization of the Chairman's "thought" on Chinese images of world affairs. Scholars such as Oksenberg, Pye, and Hinton have written of the Great Helmsman's preeminent role in Chinese foreign policy making during his lifetime.[58] Other scholars, such as Gittings, Schwartz, Kim, Yahuda, Meisner, O'Leary, Tsou, and Halperin, looked to Mao's theoretical interpretations of Marxism-Leninism as the foundation of Chinese images of the world.[59] Of central importance in these studies are such concepts

---

nese Foreign Policy," *The Annals of the American Academy of Political and Social Science* 349 (September 1963): 14–26; C. P. Fitzgerald, *The Chinese View of Their Place in the World* (London: Oxford University Press, 1964); Norton Ginsberg, "On the Chinese Perception of a World Order," *China in Crisis*, volume 2, ed. Tang Tsou (Chicago: University of Chicago Press, 1968), pp. 73–92; Albert Feuerwerker, "Chinese History and the Foreign Relations of Contemporary China," *The Annals of the American Academy of Political and Social Science* 402 (July 1972): 1–14; Francois Geoffroy-Dechaume, *China Looks at the World* (London: Faber and Faber, 1967); J. Cranmer-Byng, "The Chinese View of Their Place in the World: An Historical Perspective," *China Quarterly*, no. 53 (January–March 1973): 67–79.

[57] Fairbank in particular develops this theme.

[58] Michel Oksenberg, "Mao's Policy Commitments, 1921–1976," *Problems of Communism* 25, 6 (November–December 1976): 1–26; Lucian W. Pye, "Mao Tse-tung's Leadership Style," *Political Science Quarterly* 91, 2 (Summer 1976): 219–35; Harold C. Hinton, *China's Turbulent Quest* (Bloomington: Indiana University Press, 1972).

[59] John Gittings, *The World and China, 1922–1972* (New York: Harper & Row, 1974); Gittings, "The Statesman," in *Mao Tse-tung in the Scales of History*, ed. Dick Wilson (Cambridge: Cambridge University Press, 1977), pp. 246–71; Benjamin Schwartz, *Communism and China: Ideology in Flux* (Cambridge: Harvard University Press, 1968), especially chapters 2, 4, 5, 6, 8, 10; Schwartz, "China and the West in the 'Thought of Mao Tse-tung,'" in *China in Crisis*, vol. 1, book 1 (Chicago: University of Chicago Press, 1968), pp. 365–79; Michael Yahuda, *China's Foreign Policy after Mao: Towards the End of Isolationism* (London: Macmillan, 1983), chapter 3; Maurice Meisner, *Mao's China: A History of the People's Republic* (New York: The Free Press, 1977); Greg O'Leary, *The*

as Mao's "theory of the three worlds" and "people's war," his interpretation of Lenin's theory of imperialism, his application of Hegelian dialectics to the analysis of "contradictions," combined with the more general influence of his populist, nationalist, and egalitarian impulses. In essence, these scholars explain Chinese foreign policy behavior as guided by Maoist ideology.

Yet other scholars, such as Armstrong, Van Ness, Van Slyke, and Mozingo, examine the role of "united front" tactics, as derived from Communist strategy in the Chinese civil war, in Mao's global thinking.[60] In these authors' view, the "united front" doctrine was externalized by China's dichotomous foreign policy of maintaining state-to-state relations ("united front from above") with party-to-party relations and support for insurgencies ("united front from below").

Finally, one can also discern studies of Chinese images that seek to establish the rational calculation of China's national interest. These are mainly studies of Chinese crisis management and national security behavior, such as those by Whiting, Pollack, Vertzberger, Zagoria, Gurtov and Hwang, and Ross.[61] These studies examine Chinese assessments of threat to its national security, and the effects of diplomatic signaling and misperception on conflict escalation. A related body of literature by scholars who study the Chinese military attempts to establish linkages between Chinese perceptions of international and regional security trends and outlays in the defense budget, force disposition, and the performance of the PLA in battle.[62]

Shaping of Chinese Foreign Policy (New York: St. Martin's Press, 1980); Tang Tsou and Morton Halperin, "Mao Tse-tung's Revolutionary Strategy and Peking's International Behavior," American Political Science Review 69, 1 (March 1965): 80–99.

[60] J. D. Armstrong, Revolutionary Diplomacy: Chinese Foreign Policy and the United Front Doctrine (Berkeley: University of California Press, 1977); Peter Van Ness, Revolution and Chinese Foreign Policy (Berkeley: University of California Press, 1970); Lyman Van Slyke, Enemies and Friends (Stanford: Stanford University Press, 1967); David Mozingo, Chinese Policy toward Indonesia, 1949–67 (Ithaca: Cornell University Press, 1972).

[61] Allen Whiting, China Crosses the Yalu: The Decision to Enter the Korean War (New York: Macmillan, 1960); Whiting, The Chinese Calculus of Deterrence (Ann Arbor: University of Michigan Press, 1975); Whiting, "New Light on Mao: Quemoy 1958: Mao's Miscalculations," China Quarterly, no. 62 (June 1975): 263–70; Jonathan Pollack, "Perception and Action in Chinese Foreign Policy: The Quemoy Decision," Ph.D. dissertation, University of Michigan, 1976; Yaacov Vertzberger, Misperceptions in Foreign Policymaking: The Sino-Indian Conflict, 1959–1962 (Boulder: Westview Press, 1984); Donald Zagoria, Vietnam Triangle (New York: Pegasus, 1967); Melvin Gurtov and Byong-moo Hwang, China Under Threat: The Politics of Strategy and Diplomacy (Baltimore: Johns Hopkins University Press, 1980); Robert S. Ross, The Indochina Tangle: China's Vietnam Policy, 1975–1979 (New York: Columbia University Press, 1988).

[62] See, for example, John Wilson Lewis, "China's Military Doctrines and Force Posture," in China's Quest for Independence: Policy Evolution in the 1970s, ed. Thomas Fingar (Boulder: Westview Press, 1980), pp. 147–98; John Wilson Lewis and Xue Litai, China

What this large and diverse body of literature shares in common, it seems, is that it proceeds from the assumption that China acts externally as a unitary and, in the case of the third group, essentially rational actor. On the whole, these scholars do not question the fact that a "Chinese" image of situation "X" exists, from which "Beijing's" foreign policy is derived. Most studies of this genre were written during a period when China was viewed abroad as having a certain monolithic and purposive character. Indeed, hindsight and discussions with Mao's associates have given some credibility to this paradigm.

This genre of literature did not own exclusive rights to the field. A competing group of scholars emerged during the 1970s who, owing their origins to the study of Chinese domestic politics, challenged the unitary-actor approach through the application of factional analysis. They proceeded from the recognition that since competing groups of elites could be distinguished as advocating different images of China's domestic evolution, so too must they hold differing views on foreign policy questions. The flood of new data that emerged during the Cultural Revolution, mainly in the form of Red Guard tabloids, greatly contributed to the dismantling of the totalitarian model for interpreting domestic affairs and the unitary-actor model in foreign affairs alike. Textual exegesis inherent in "Pekingological" analysis, as inherited from the "Kremlinological" tradition, became the accepted method for distinguishing differing foreign policy perceptions within the Chinese elite and high command.

Studies such as those by Ra'anan, Zagoria, Yahuda, and Gurtov and Harding detected a heated "strategic debate" within high policy councils during 1965–1966 over the implications for China of the American military escalation in Vietnam.[63] Studies by Gottlieb and

---

Builds the Bomb (Stanford: Stanford University Press, 1988); Jonathan Pollack, "Rebuilding China's Great Wall: Chinese Security in the 1980s," in *The Chinese Defense Establishment: Continuity and Change in the 1980s*, ed. Paul H. B. Godwin (Boulder: Westview Press, 1983), pp. 3–20; David L. Shambaugh, "China's Defense Industries: Indigenous and Foreign Procurement," in ibid., pp. 43–86; Paul H. B. Godwin, "Soldiers and Statesmen in Conflict: Chinese Defense and Foreign Policies in the 1980s," in *China and the World*, ed. Samuel Kim; Jonathan Pollack, *Security, Strategy, and the Logic of Chinese Foreign Policy*.

[63] Uri Ra'anan, "Peking's Foreign Policy 'Debate,' 1965–1966," in *China in Crisis*, volume 2, ed. Tang Tsou, pp. 23–72; Donald Zagoria, "The Strategic Debate in Peking," in ibid., pp. 237–68; Michael Yahuda, "Kremlinology and the Chinese Strategic Debate, 1965–66," *China Quarterly*, no. 49 (January 1972): 32–75; Melvin Gurtov and Harry Harding Jr., *The Purge of Luo Jui-ch'ing: The Politics of Chinese Strategic Planning* (Santa Monica: The Rand Corporation, Report R-548-PR, 1971). It is important to note that more recent research by economist Barry Naughton sheds new light on this debate.

Garver similarly documented debates in 1969–1970 over the opening to the United States.[64] Other scholars such as Lieberthal, Van Ness, and Oksenberg and Goldstein have discovered more nuanced perspectives within the elite on issues related to China's general opening to the outside world.[65] Yet others, such as Harding, Shirk, Fingar, Robinson, Whiting, and Lieberthal, have explored the broader interplay of domestic politics, economics, and foreign policy.[66]

While all of these studies disaggregate a unitary actor, China, to consider differing perspectives in the leadership, and hence are welcome attempts to explore images and other domestic sources of Chinese foreign policy, they nonetheless focus on the top elite. With the possible exceptions of Shirk's and Fenwick's studies of Chinese foreign trade policy,[67] none explores the bureaucratic origins of the relationship between images and policy. More important, none explores the images articulated by second-echelon international relations specialists (as opposed to elites and foreign policy practitioners) and the potential impact of these individuals and their images on policy. Finally, none explores the cognitive dynamics of Chinese elite's images.

Where, then, if anywhere, in the Chinese foreign policy literature

See Naughton, "The Third Front: Defense Industrialization in the Chinese Interior," *China Quarterly*, no. 115 (September 1988): 351–86.

[64] Thomas Gottlieb, *Chinese Foreign Policy Factionalism and the Origins of the Strategic Triangle* (Santa Monica: The Rand Corporation, Report R-1902-NA, 1977); John Garver, "Chinese Foreign Policy in 1970: The Tilt toward the Soviet Union," *China Quarterly*, no. 82 (June 1980): 214–49; Garver, *China's Decision for Rapprochement with the United States* (Boulder: Westview, 1982).

[65] Kenneth Lieberthal, "The Foreign Policy Debate in Peking as Seen Through Allegorical Articles, 1973–76," *China Quarterly*, no. 71 (September 1977): 528–54; Peter Van Ness, "Three Lines in Chinese Foreign Relations, 1950–1983: The Development Imperative," in *Three Visions of Chinese Socialism*, ed. Dorothy Solinger (Boulder: Westview Press, 1984), pp. 113–42; Michel Oksenberg and Steven Goldstein, "The Chinese Political Spectrum," *Problems of Communism* 23, 2 (March–April 1974): 1–13.

[66] Harry Harding, "The Domestic Politics of China's Global Posture, 1973–78," in *China's Quest for Independence*, ed. Thomas Fingar, pp. 93–146; Thomas Fingar, "Domestic Policy and the Quest for Independence," in ibid., pp. 25–92; Susan Shirk, "The Domestic Political Dimensions of China's Foreign Economic Relations," in *China and the World*, ed. Samuel Kim, pp. 57–81; Thomas W. Robinson, "Restructuring Chinese Foreign Policy, 1959–76: Three Episodes," in *Why Nations Realign*, ed. K. J. Holsti (London: Allen and Unwin, 1982), pp. 134–71; Allen Whiting, *Chinese Domestic Politics and Foreign Policy in the 1970s* (Ann Arbor: Center for Chinese Studies, 1979); Kenneth Lieberthal, "Domestic Politics and Foreign Policy," in *Chinese Foreign Relations in the 1980s*, ed. Harry Harding (New Haven: Yale University Press, 1985).

[67] Susan Shirk, "The Domestic Political Dimensions of China's Foreign Economic Dimensions"; Ann Fenwick, "Chinese Foreign Trade Policy and the Campaign Against Deng Xiaoping," in *China's Quest for Independence*, ed. Thomas Fingar, pp. 199–224.

are these gaps filled? With respect to the second echelon of international relations specialists there is only the pioneering work of Rozman on China's Soviet Watchers, Johnston on Chinese arms controllers, mine on national security specialists, and Whiting on China's Japan hands.[68] The study of the cognitive sources of perceptions held by Chinese foreign policy elites is virtually nonexistent. Other than Boardman's exploratory essay on possible methodological approaches to the subject,[69] the only actual study of the cognitive dynamics underlying Chinese images of external affairs is that by Bobrow, Chan, and Kringen.[70] While this volume is an important first cut at the subject matter, its findings must be questioned on the grounds of an inadequate data base. The authors tried to ascertain Chinese elite perceptions on foreign policy issues from interviews and content analysis of the Chinese media. The interviews, however, were conducted not with policy makers or specialists but with refugees in Hong Kong, and the media sample was limited to a few periodicals and monitored radio broadcasts that were aimed primarily at foreign audiences and had been translated into English. In other words, the authors' reliance on English-language sources limits the utility of their otherwise provocative findings.

It is to these bodies of literature on elite images as domestic sources of foreign policy that the present study is intended to contribute. When reading the ensuing chapters one should keep in mind that this is a study at the "individual" and "role" levels of analysis. There are indeed alternative levels of analysis at which one can analyze United States–China relations over this time period: global systemic, nation-state interactive, societal, governmental.[71]

Thus, this is a study of United States–China relations as seen through one medium—China's America Watchers and their articulated perceptions of the United States. In my view, we can only understand China's increasingly complex behavior toward the United States during this period as a function of the increasingly complex

---

[68] Gilbert Rozman, "China's Soviet Watchers in the 1980s: A New Era in Scholarship"; Alastair I. Johnston, *China and Arms Control*; David L. Shambaugh, "China's National Security Research Bureaucracy"; Allen S. Whiting, *China Eyes Japan*.

[69] Robert Boardman, "Perception Theory and the Study of Chinese Foreign Policy," in *Advancing and Contending Approaches to the Study of Chinese Foreign Policy*, ed. Robert Dial (Halifax: Dalhousie University Centre for Foreign Policy Studies, 1974), pp. 321–52.

[70] D. Bobrow, S. Chan, and J. Kringen, *Understanding Foreign Policy Decisions: The Chinese Case* (New York: Free Press, 1979).

[71] See J. David Singer, "The Level-of-Analysis Problem in International Relations," in *The International System: Theoretical Essays*, ed. Klaus Knorr and Sidney Verba (Princeton: Princeton University Press, 1961).

images the America Watchers hold and the perceptions they articulate to those policy makers who shape and guide China's America policy.

Scope of the Study

This study is primarily concerned with establishing the content and variation of perceptions of the United States as articulated by China's America Watchers over the period 1972–1990. That is, what is the substance of their articulated perceptions, what is the variation among them, and how have they evolved over time? Simply to bring to light and explicate systematically a whole body of writing and statements about one culture by the other is of intrinsic interest. When these two countries are as important on the world scene as are the United States and the People's Republic of China, making such perceptions known publicly is not of insignificant consequence. As was asserted in the previous section, behavior depends much on how one perceives and defines the environment; thus, to understand China's approach to the United States and what might be called the "inner structure" of Sino-American relations, an examination of Chinese perceptions of the United States is of vital importance.

Second, and related to the above, this study is interested in explaining the variance and evolution of perceptions over time. That is, why have they changed or, in some cases, not changed? Put another way, why do the America Watchers articulate the perceptions about the United States that they do? What are the key explanatory factors (political, diplomatic, intellectual, sociological) that shape the specific perceptions and the images that lie behind them? In other words, what linkages can be established between image formation and articulation of perceptions? Answering this second set of questions helps account for variation among individual America Watchers, cohorts of them, and as a total community.

Third, this study seeks to come to terms with the relationship between perception and policy, and the impact of the former on the latter. The reader should be forewarned that this is an extremely difficult gap to bridge empirically. After a decade of almost constant work on the subject of perceptions while observing the behavioral interactions between the United States and China, I remain as convinced as ever of the empirical difficulties involved in making categorical conclusions about the impact of China's America Watchers' perceptions of the United States on policy. The evidence simply remains too fragmentary to sustain more than informed and reasoned conjecture about the impact. This is because the broad direction of China's policy toward the United States, like Chinese foreign policy more generally, continues to be made by a handful of individual politicians at the top of the government and party apparatus. These individuals most certainly draw on the perceptions and advice of China's America-watching community, but without opportunities to interview at that most elite level of the system or to use material from party and government archives, making empirically firm the linkage between perception and policy is impossible. Nonetheless, one can make reasoned inferences about the nature and milieu of the information and advice provided to the leadership by China's America Watchers. Thus, clarifying the relationship between the input of perception and the policy output is the third main goal of this study.

Organization of the Text

These questions are pursued in five thematic chapters and the conclusion. Each covers the eighteen chronological years that are the temporal focus of this study (1972–1990), although different chapters may emphasize different years more or less intensively. Throughout the study the perceptions articulated by China's America Watchers cleave into two separate schools of images (Marxist and non-Marxist), but in examining American foreign policy a third tendency of articulation appears: traditional Chinese. These schools not only reflect the substantive differences between the major cohorts of America Watchers but also serve as convenient organizing constructs to order systematically the disparate perceptions within each chapter. Throughout the text more refined opinion groups within the two principal schools also emerge.

Chapter 2 is a chapter on ideology. In case some may believe that Marxist-Leninist ideology is dead in China,[72] it offers strong evidence to the contrary. Ideology not only remains an important legitimating tool for the Communist Party but continues to serve as a major mode of discourse and dialogue among certain intellectuals. It also continues to play an important role in the policy arena as it serves as both an explanatory and a legitimating device for justifying policy decisions made on more pragmatic grounds. This is why chapter 2 is im-

[72] Many in the West began to pronounce the "end of ideology" in China after the *People's Daily* proclaimed in a famous December 7, 1984, editorial that "We cannot expect the writings of Marx and Lenin of that time to provide solutions to all our current problems."

portant. It details internal Chinese discussions about three theoretical subjects that have important bearing on analysis of the United States: imperialism, state-monopoly capitalism, and hegemony. All three issues are of key importance to Chinese officialdom not only in terms of justifying the "superiority of the socialist system," but because they had to be reconciled with Beijing's new relations with the United States. How was it that a bastion of socialism like People's China could enter into an extensive relationship with the world's foremost imperialist, state-monopoly capitalist, and hegemonist power? Chapter 2 examines how Chinese Marxist theorists made the theoretical readjustments necessary with respect to these three issues after the opening to the United States.

Chapter 3 commences examination of perceptions of the United States per se and builds upon chapter 2's emphasis on economic change in modern imperialist systems. It looks at the America Watchers' contrasting views of the American economy, in particular their perceptions of two issues dear to the hearts of the Marxist School—monopoly capitalism and economic "crises." It concludes with a survey of the America Watchers' perceptions of the general conditions of the U.S. economy during the Carter and Reagan years.

Chapter 4 analyses the America Watchers' perceptions of American society. It finds that, not unsurprisingly, the Marxists see American society in class terms. Discussions of the American bourgeoisie, middle class, working class, and poor are considered, and an intense Chinese debate about the American proletariat's degree of "impoverishment" is uncovered. This debate is linked to the question of the potential revolutionary militancy of the American working class, which is also considered in the context of the Marxists' perspectives. The non-Marxists hold a much more dynamic view of American society that is focused less on classes and more on social phenomena. Many of the non-Marxists' writings on American society are conveyed in the forums of travelogues. Several of the more notable of these are examined, presenting a relatively integrated view of American society, as well as the Chinese media's discussion of racism and family life in the United States.

Chapter 5 leaves the economic and social "base" and examines the America Watchers' contrasting views on the political "superstructure" in the United States. Their perceptions of American politics fall into four main realms: (1) the role of monopolies and other nongovernment actors in the political process; (2) the structure and process of policy making in and among different branches of government; (3) social groupings and ideological tendencies in the general polity; and

(4) a comparative analysis of the 1972, 1976, 1980, 1984, and 1988 U.S. presidential elections.

Chapter 6 examines the America Watchers' contrasting perceptions of the conduct of American foreign policy. Their perceptions of the roles of both government and nongovernment actors in the foreign policy–making process are examined in the context of domestic politics in chapter 5; thus, the discussion in chapter 6 is limited to the "output" side of U.S. foreign policy. Perceptions of the general conduct of American foreign policy are examined in the context of U.S. policies toward the Third World, the Soviet Union, and China.

The conclusion begins by seeking to explain why the America Watchers articulate contrasting images of the United States, and it concludes with a discussion of the importance of this study's finding for Sino-American relations. I assess a series of variables that shape the America Watchers' perceptions and speculate on their relative importance, in particular the potential impact of professional role and foreign exposure, but also the influence of political, diplomatic, and cultural factors. The conclusion returns to the question posed at the outset of the introduction, namely, what are the implications of China's America Watchers' perceptions of the United States for Sino-American relations? What progress in mutual understanding has been made since the rapprochement of 1972, and what perceptual gaps remain? What is the impact of these perceptions on China's America policy?

Thus, the text that follows is organized in a "building block" approach that begins with the ideological milieu that lies behind many of the more specific perceptions examined in the case studies of chapters 3, 4, 5 and 6. Considered together, the core data chapters capture a fairly complete sample of the United States and Chinese perceptions of it. There are no doubt some missing elements that certain readers would like to know more about, but one cannot cover everything.

Finally, I reiterate that this is intentionally not a study of the behavioral dimension of Sino-American relations. Its purpose is to probe beneath the behavioral level to explore one source of that behavior—perceptions. This might be described as the "inner structure" of the relationship. The study therefore does not catalogue the evolution of the relationship over time—governmental dialogue, state visits, agreements, cooperation and discord, and so forth. That is done in many other studies. Chapter 7, the conclusion, does place the perceptions in a policy context, but those expecting a straightforward history of Sino-American relations will be disappointed.

Sources and Data

With respect to the Chinese sources used in preparing this study, I drew upon a full range of books, periodicals, newspapers, and newsletters (*tongxun*). Many were restricted-circulation (*neibu*) materials; two neibu periodicals that were particularly useful were *Shijie jingji yu zhengzhi neican* (Internal reference materials on world economics and politics), published by the Institute of World Economics and Politics at the CASS, and *Meiguo yanjiu cankao* (Reference materials for research on the United States), published by the CASS Institute of American Studies. Neibu journals, as Gilbert Rozman also discovered in his research on China's Soviet Watchers,[73] are extraordinarily valuable because they are meant for discourse among concerned specialists and elites and thus often display an analytical candor and discussion of policy issues absent in open-source (*gongkai*) journals. To some degree the same can be said for neibu books, but they are meant for circulation among a much wider Chinese audience and frequently find their way into the hands of foreign scholars. They too are used extensively in this study. I have not designated neibu sources as such in the footnotes, but their classification will be evident to the knowing reader. In addition to neibu materials, I use a full range of unclassified books, periodicals, newspapers, and other printed materials in Chinese and translation. This study brings to light much published data never before examined.

In addition to these written sources, over the course of seven years of research I formally interviewed 160 individual Chinese, of which approximately 140 are bona fide America Watchers (carrying out full-time research on the United States) while the other 20 are theorists who work on related subjects. Many were interviewed more than once, thus affording more candid and in-depth discussions resulting from familiarity with the individual and the subject. While the majority of these interviews took place in China, some were in the United States and a few in Europe. The majority of these interviews were on the record, but only in a very limited number of cases have I chosen to identify the individual concerned. The changeable political climate in China warrants the continued protection of identities.

My third data source are lecture notes taken in classes about the United States that I attended in the economics, history, law, and international politics departments at Beijing University when I was a student there from 1983 to 1985.

---

[73] Gilbert Rozman, *The Chinese Debate about Soviet Socialism, 1978–1985*; "China's Soviet Watchers in the 1980s: A New Era of Scholarship."

Central Arguments and Principal Findings

In the following chapters I present a spectrum of views on the United States presented by China's America Watchers. Throughout, these perceptions cleave into two major image clusters: Marxist and non-Marxist. The Marxist School is distinguished by interpretation of the United States using Marxist-Leninist categories of analysis and terminology. The non-Marxist School is characterized, quite simply, by non-Marxist interpretations and terminology. While there exists an intellectual coherence in the Marxist School, the non-Marxist School is notable precisely for its atheoretical, nonideological, ad hoc, and descriptive nature.

Within each school two more refined lines of analysis appear. Within the Marxist School there exists a dogmatic group that follows Stalin's analysis of capitalism, as well as a more flexible line that can be characterized as Leninist. Within the non-Marxist School one discerns "statists" whose focus of analysis is the apparatus of state, and "pluralists" who view the United States in far more variegated and pluralistic terms. The study reveals an evolution over time from the Stalinists to the pluralists, but also a continuing competition between Marxist and non-Marxist interpretations of the United States. In chapter 6 a third major opinion group is encountered in the context of American foreign policy. This group emphasizes U.S. hegemonic behavior abroad, and consequently I label them "hegemonists."

Each opinion group has its adherents in different institutions: the Marxists are primarily located in universities, the Central Party School, the Institute of World Economics and Politics of the Chinese Academy of Social Sciences (CASS), and the Shanghai Institute of International Studies. The non-Marxists are found mainly in the central government bureaucracy (particularly the Foreign Ministry), the CASS Institute of American Studies, the Institute of International Studies, the Institute of Contemporary International Relations, the New China News Agency, and military-affiliated institutes. The hegemonists cut across all of these institutions.

Based on these divisions, the central argument of this study is that professional role is the primary determinant of China's America Watchers' articulated perceptions. Other variables such as an individual's socialization, exposure to the United States, access to source materials, and cultural factors all contribute to shaping the America Watchers' perceptions of the United States, but the evidence suggests that professional role is primary.

The spectrum of perceptions of the United States articulated by

China's America Watchers as presented in this study leads one to the conclusion that, despite considerable progress, Chinese understanding of the United States remains shallow and seriously distorted. With a few exceptions, the vast majority of America Watchers in China do not understand the United States very well. The non-Marxists are best informed about the United States, but even their analyses usually lack subtlety and sophistication. The main implication of this conclusion is that a significant perceptual gap exists on the Chinese side that will continue to contribute to the fluctuating nature of Sino-American relations in the future.

Two

Ideological Foundations

WITH THE announcement in July 1971 that American envoy Henry Kissinger had paid a secret visit to Beijing, China's ideologues were put to a test. How could it be that a leading representative of "American imperialism" had been welcomed into Chairman Mao's study in the Zhongnanhai? To make matters worse, this presaged a visit by "warmonger" Nixon the next year. How could this be justified? What did it say about imperialism in general, and its American variant in particular? Had Chairman Mao changed his assessment of the imperialist threat? Was Soviet "social imperialism" now a greater threat than the traditional American variety? China's ideologues were faced with a conundrum.

It did not take a theoretical genius to figure out that China's strategic shift was stimulated by the Soviet threat. Whether or not one accepted the logic or rationale of the rapprochement, it was a fact of diplomatic life. But how was it to be justified in ideological terms?

At first, no doubt responding to cues from central authorities, the principal Chinese media organs ceased their overtly hostile attacks on the United States. In their place, more subtle references to "imperialism" appeared, which could easily be distinguished from its twin "social imperialism" (the USSR). This new pattern of references was reinforced by delegate Deng Xiaoping's speech to the Sixth Special Session of the United Nations General Assembly, which served as a precursor to Mao's own "Theory of the Three Worlds." Both superpowers now constituted the "first world," and through their bullying of others demonstrated their "hegemonic" nature.

Thus, Deng's 1974 speech at the United Nations was the first major sign of ideological revisionism in the foreign policy domain in the wake of China's turn westward. Despite the fact that the "three worlds" thesis provided the theoretical rationale for mobilizing a united front of the second and third worlds against the first world, Deng's speech offered an assessment of one superpower on the wane and the other in the ascent.[1] Under such conditions, the weaker of

[1] See Michael Yahuda, *China's Role in World Affairs* (London: Croom, Helm, 1978), p. 240.

the two could be a candidate for inclusion in the "broad united front" against the more pressing threat.

Just as Deng had opened the door to ideological revision, he was purged in the wake of the Tiananmen incident of April 1976. With his second rehabilitation from political purgatory in 1977 and his subsequent outmaneuvering of Hua Guofeng and seizure of political power by the time of the Third Plenum of the Twelfth Central Committee a year later, Deng set about to revamp China's foreign policy. This required a recasting of China's world view, and this in turn necessitated overhauling the ideological base that undergirded the policy superstructure.

With Deng back in power, China's cadre of Marxist-Leninist theorists set about reevaluating many of the operative interpretations of the United States and other capitalist countries with which China had now opened diplomatic ties. This was done in the context of specific countries such as the United States (discussed in subsequent chapters), but also in broader terms of capitalist development. In fact, as this chapter illustrates, changes in specific interpretations of the United States had to await broader doctrinal revisionism about the nature of capitalism.

Three theoretical issues in the realm of official orthodoxy figured prominently in internal Chinese debates during the 1979–1989 decade: imperialism, state-monopoly capitalism, and hegemonism. I will examine the Chinese debates on these subjects sequentially, although there is certain overlap among them. The debates about imperialism and state-monopoly capitalism were particularly intertwined with respect to the internal development of capitalist societies, while discussions about hegemony and imperialism were linked in the external domain. The debates on these three issues provide the context for, and are fundamental to, an understanding of the specific analyses by China's America Watchers of the U.S. economy, society, polity, and foreign policy. The debates on imperialism are particularly relevant to analyses of the American economy and foreign policy; debates on state-monopoly capitalism to analyses of the U.S. economy, society, and politics; and debates on hegemony underlie Chinese analyses of U.S. foreign policy.

For Marxist-Leninists the terms "imperialism" and "state-monopoly capitalism" have specific theoretical meanings in the context of the historical development of capitalism as a world system. Both terms represent concepts that are central to the Marxist-Leninist paradigm for the analysis of advanced capitalist countries. Both terms encompass theoretical constructs that deductively guide analyses of specific capitalist countries such as the United States.

For most America Watchers in the Marxist School, the United States is the world's most noteworthy example of an imperialist and state-monopoly capitalist country, and for America Watchers of both schools the United States is the most poignant example of a nation practicing a hegemonist foreign policy.

To understand fully the meaning and significance of the specific perceptions of the United States articulated by Marxist School commentators (and even many in the non-Marxist School) in the following chapters, one must therefore understand the broader theoretical background from which they are derived. Moreover, without reference to the treatment of these topics in Marxist-Leninist classics, one cannot appreciate the significance of views expressed in the Chinese polemics.

Classical Marxist-Leninist Theories of Imperialism and Monopoly Capitalism

For Marx, politics was a function of economics. Those capitalists who owned the "means of production" also monopolized political power to further their drive for profit. Marx viewed the state apparatus itself as a reflection of the balance of economic classes in society. Those elites who administer the state apparatus represent the interests of the classes who own the means of production. Marx therefore saw the political system and the state as part of the "superstructure" built upon the economic "base." He stated this base-superstructure interpretation of politics most clearly in *The German Ideology, The Civil War in France, The Poverty of Philosophy, Preface to a Contribution to a Critique of Political Economy*, and the third volume of *Das Kapital*. With the possible exception of *The Civil War in France*, where he does discuss certain conditions under which the state can play an autonomous role in political and economic life, Marx articulates the recurrent thesis throughout these works that the state is a mere instrument of class rule and political conflict is a manifestation of class struggle—be it between classes or within the ruling class. For Marx, the economic base determines the balance of political forces in the struggle for state power as well as the institutional structure of the state over which political struggle is waged. The majority of Marx's political analyses (which must be gleaned from his predominant interest in economics) focus on the various ways in which the state is used as an instrument for the exploitation of wage-labor by capitalists, or the maintenance of bourgeois class domination in the political sphere. Thus, Marx never really analyzed in any detail the actual internal workings of the capitalist state or political process. Similarly, his views of the state and politics under socialism were also never well developed.

Engels contributed little more than Marx did to analysis of the state and politics. Their co-authored *The German Ideology* and the *Communist Manifesto* go further in this subject area than any of their individual manuscripts. Following Marx's death, however, Engels did go a step further in *Anti-Dühring* by addressing the phenomenon of imperial expansion. Marx had very little to say on this subject, but Engels noted that European powers were rapidly expanding overseas in search of new markets. But Engels thought this was only a transitional phase that could not stave off the eventual collapse of capitalism after a series of increasingly severe economic crises at home. Far from arresting this process, Engels believed, the imperialist phase would only hasten its development.

Engels also went a step further than Marx in analyzing state intervention in the capitalist economy, and thus he was really the first to address the issue of "state capitalism." In discussing joint-stock companies, Engels asserted that they would fail unless the state intervened to subsidize production. He went so far as to assert that state capital would eventually dominate all productive forces in society. Engels' notions of state capitalism proved to be the departure point for ensuing analyses of imperialism.

Between 1900 and 1920 the term "imperialism" was introduced into Marxist lexicon, and a systematic theory of imperialism emerged. Three writers were primarily responsible for this: Rudolf Hilferding, Nikolai Bukharin, and Vladimir Ilyich Lenin. All three saw themselves as updating Marx to take account of an economic phenomenon that had developed since Marx's time (although he had predicted it), namely, the rise of monopoly. All three saw the emergence of monopolies as a major departure from free competitive capitalism.

The first genuinely Marxist theory of imperialism was set forth by Hilferding, an Austrian Marxist who later became a leader of the German Social Democratic Party and served as the German minister of finance in 1928–1929. In 1910 Hilferding published *Finance Capital*. His magnum opus focused on the role of banks as the catalyst in the growth of monopoly. Hilferding argued that the separation of industrial and financial (banking) capital, which was characteristic of the era of competitive capitalism, disappears in the epoch of monopoly capitalism when the two are fused together. The bulk of Hilferding's treatise was concerned with this monetary fusion, but he also discussed the effect of finance capital on class structure, the role of the state, and ideological change. He spoke of the "personal union" of "finance capital," by which he meant that industrialists and bankers are linked not only economically, but also because their personnel are interchangeable. Bankers sit on the boards of industrial firms and vice versa. Family, educational, and social ties cement the ruling class together. Hilferding therefore argued that the rise of finance capital led to the creation of a ruling bourgeoisie that, while hierarchically configured, was relatively unified under the direction of the "magnates of finance capital." This change in the structure of the ruling bourgeoisie, from divided and competitive to relatively unified, concomitantly involved a change in its relationship to the state. Hilferding suggested that the bourgeois ruling classes and the state were "integrated" and mutually dependent. For example, he expressed the view that the state provided tariff protection to gain the benefits of monopolies, while the finance oligarchy required a powerful state apparatus to promote and protect capital export and territorial expansion. Since Hilferding's book dealt mainly with the internal dynamics of the capitalist state and economy, he paid relatively little attention to these latter external manifestations.

Bukharin's analysis of imperialism proceeded directly from Hilferding's, both chronologically and thematically, but went further in examining the external dimensions of finance capital. The essential difference between the two is that where Hilferding saw one process at work (the concentration and centralization of capital), Bukharin recognized two processes. Like Hilferding, he recognized the nationalization of monopoly capital by the state, but he also paid particular attention to the internationalization of capital. Bukharin noted the growth of international interdependence, the expansion of the world economy, and the division of the world into national blocs. Bukharin saw the contradiction of these two tendencies as leading to war, the breakdown of monopoly capitalism, and revolution. In his *Imperialism and the World Economy*, Bukharin was the first Marxist theorist to assert that international cartels necessitated an international alliance of capitalists and capitalist states, despite the continued competition among them. In other words, the international monopoly bourgeoisie had a shared interest in preserving the imperialist system despite their competitive imperialist policies. Bukharin's argument, therefore, moves from imperialism as a policy to a characteristic of the world economy at a particular stage of development. This was an important and novel departure in the Marxist literature on imperialism at the time. Thus Bukharin recognized a fusion of economic and political power into one colossal state-capitalist trust that simultaneously colluded with other, similar entities in the capitalist world by in effect forming cartels, while at the same time fiercely competing for colonial annexations that often led to imperialist war.

Lenin's analysis of imperialism and politics under capitalism proceeded directly from Hilferding and Bukharin. His *Imperialism, the Highest Stage of Capitalism* has become the most famous work on imperialism in the Marxist genre. Lenin's major purpose in writing his treatise was to counter "that renegade" Kautsky's theory of "ultra imperialism," which he believed was leading the remnants of the Second International in a fallacious direction. Kautsky believed that it was possible for the imperialist powers to collude and divide their spoils internationally, thus eliminating interimperialist competition and wars. Lenin fundamentally disagreed with this view and argued that war was inevitable between imperialist states. Lenin set forth a number of characteristics in the development of capitalism during his epoch:

(1) the concentration of production and capital has developed to such a high stage that it has created monopolies which play a decisive role in economic life;

(2) the merging of bank capital with industrial capital and the creation, on the basis of this "finance capital," of a financial oligarchy;

(3) the export of capital as distinguished from the export of commodities acquires exceptional importance;

(4) the formation of international monopoly capitalist combines which share the world among themselves; and

(5) the territorial division of the whole world among the biggest capitalist powers is completed.[2]

The influence of Hilferding and Bukharin on Lenin's thinking is readily apparent, but Lenin does go incrementally further in several respects. Like Hilferding, he notes the first two characteristics, but his treatise on *Imperialism* draws attention to traders in stocks and bonds in addition to bankers and industrialists as members of the finance oligarchy. Like Bukharin, Lenin notes the internationalization of capital, but he implies that political-military forms of rivalry have supplanted economic competition among the capitalist powers. Lenin follows both by asserting that monopoly is the most distinguishing characteristic of the domestic economy in the imperialist stage of development, but he is more explicit in describing the relationship between monopolies and imperialism as an inevitable *stage* in capitalist development. For example, he states, "If it were neces-

[2] Vladimir Lenin, *Imperialism, the Highest Stage of Capitalism* (Beijing: Foreign Languages Press, 1970).

sary to give the briefest possible definition of imperialism we should
have to say that imperialism is the monopoly stage of capitalism."[3]
This stage Lenin believed to be the "highest," and last, in capitalism's development before the onset of socialist revolution. He thus
termed imperialism to be "moribund," "parasitic," and "decaying."
While asserting that the death of imperialism and monopoly capitalism as a world system was inevitable, Lenin was not specific about
when he believed the end would come, even though he implied that
it was near. Lenin's lack of specificity on this point has been a bone
of contention in Marxist circles ever since: some argue that imperialism's death is at hand, while others believe the opposite.

Lenin's lack of specificity about the precise nature of the relationship between the state and monopoly bourgeoisie has also led to
great disputes among Marxist theorists. Nowhere in *Imperialism* does
Lenin use the term "state-monopoly capitalism," although at one
point he does refer to the "national state groups of financiers."[4] To
be sure, "finance capital" (the coalescence of banking and industrial
capital) does play a central role in Lenin's analysis of imperialism, but
his discussion of state-monopoly capitalism is relegated to a minor
place in his later wartime writings (e.g., *State and Revolution*), usually
in connection with the German state's procurement of military sup-
plies. Although Lenin is therefore correctly identified by later Soviet
theorists as having inaugurated the term "state-monopoly capitalism," he was vague about its characteristics (particularly in reference
to eliminating the anarchy of production) and did not distinguish it
as a separate substage in the development of imperialism as distinct
from monopoly capitalism more generally. Lenin was content to reiterate Hilferding's nebulous assertions about the coalescence of finance capital and the state without exploring in any detail the exact
nature of this relationship, much less the specific nature and functions of the imperialist state qua state.

During the 1930s Comintern pronouncements increasingly referred
to state-monopoly capitalism. The Comintern viewed increased state
intervention in capitalist economies in the wake of the Great Depression as a final, abortive attempt to overcome the "general crisis of
capitalism." The writings of Soviet theorist Eugen Varga were indicative of this line. Writing in 1934, Varga suggested that monopoly
capitalism was turning into state-monopoly capitalism as imperialist
states sought to cope with the "Great Crisis" by launching the next,

---

[3] Ibid., p. 105.

[4] Ibid., p. 131. The term used in the Chinese translation is "national financial
groups" (*guomin caituan*); see Lie Ning, *Diguozhuyi shi zibenzhuyi de zuigao jieduan* (Beijing: Renmin chubanshe, 1974), p. 99.

and last, imperialist war.[5] The Comintern took this prognosis to heart and began preparing for global proletarian revolution, which it believed would "arise from the ashes" of this war.

In China, Mao Zedong adhered to the Comintern line. Ensconced in the caves at Yan'an, Mao wrote in 1937 that the "contradictions" between monopoly and nonmonopoly capitalism, and between colonial powers and colonies, were so sharp that imperialist war was inevitable. Further, "Lenin and Stalin have correctly explained these contradictions and correctly formulated the theory and tactics of the proletarian revolution for solving them."[6] Other than this oblique reference, Mao did not address himself to the theoretical issues of monopoly capitalism and the structure of the imperialist state during this period. Mao had a revolution to make and would just as soon leave such lofty issues to the theoretical high priests of the Comintern.

Stalin also did not express much interest in the internal workings of the capitalist state during the interwar period. In 1924, in the *Foundations of Leninism*, he referred to the "dominance of finance capital in the advanced capitalist countries . . . the omnipotence of a financial oligarchy which is the result of the domination of finance capital,"[7] but he did not use the term "state-monopoly capitalism" until after World War II. In 1952 Stalin left his indelible mark on the Marxist analysis of advanced capitalism by articulating the view in *Economic Problems of Socialism in the U.S.S.R.* that the capitalist state was subordinate to the finance capital oligarchy:

> The word "coalescence" is not appropriate. It superficially and descriptively notes the process of merging of the monopolies with the state, but it does not reveal the economic import of this process. The fact of the matter is that the merging process is not simply a process of coalescence, but the subjugation of the state machine to the monopolies. The word "coalescence" should therefore be discarded and replaced by the words "subjugation of the state machine to the monopolies."[8]

Thus, Stalin's views of the "dominance" of the finance oligarchy (1924) and the "subjugation" of the capitalist state (1952) to the mo-

---

[5] Eugen Varga, *The Great Crisis and Its Political Consequences: Economics and Politics, 1928–1934* (London: Modern Books, 1934).

[6] Mao Zedong, "On Contradiction," in *Four Essays on Philosophy* (Beijing: Foreign Languages Press, 1974).

[7] Joseph Stalin, *The Foundations of Leninism* (Beijing: Foreign Languages Press, 1977), p. 26.

[8] J. V. Stalin, *Economic Problems of Socialism in the U.S.S.R.* (Beijing: Foreign Languages Press, 1972), pp. 43–44.

nopolies are significant qualitative departures from the "fusion" and "coalescence" views expressed earlier by Hilferding and Lenin respectively, and in 1951–1952 by Varga. In the *Economic Problems of Socialism in the U.S.S.R.*, Stalin also reiterated Lenin's thesis of the inevitability of war between the imperialist powers. The postwar peace, in Stalin's view, was temporary and illusory.

After Stalin's death in 1953, his "subordination thesis" and ideas about the inevitability of war came under attack. The catalyst was the more general denunciation of Stalin by Khrushchev in his "secret speech" to the Twentieth Party Congress in 1956. Following the Congress, Soviet scholars and theoreticians published numerous studies that openly broke with the dogmatic determinism that had characterized Stalinist assessments of politics under capitalism. Instead, they asserted that state-monopoly capitalism really signaled a qualitatively new stage in the development of imperialism. This view was particularly put forward by scholars in the Institute of International Relations and World Economics (IMEMO).

Despite general agreement on this point among Soviet writers, no unitary view of the relationship between the capitalist state and monopolies emerged. To the contrary, Soviet images of capitalist politics, particularly in the United States, were widely divergent. They ranged from a continuation of crude economic determinist analyses characteristic of the Stalinist era, whereby the political superstructure is a total function of the economic base, to those who argued the primacy of politics over economics. These views proliferated in part because of the absence of a single, guiding interpretation from Khrushchev and his top theorists, but also because of the political rehabilitation of numerous international relations specialists following Stalin's death. Political economists in the economic institutes of the Soviet Academy of Sciences continued to defend Stalin's dictum that the capitalist state was subordinate to the monopolies, while members of IMEMO led the way in articulating more nuanced and pluralistic images of politics in the capitalist world. Opinions diverged among IMEMO analysts over the degree of "coalescence" of the capitalist state and large monopolies. Some, like IMEMO director Varga (who had been rehabilitated after Stalin's death), Dalin, and Arbatov (later to become director of the USA/Canada Institute), expressed the view that the capitalist state exercised substantial political autonomy from the monopolies. Others, such as Leontiev, Lenin, and Cheprakov, believed the state served the interests of the entire bourgeoisie rather than specific oligarchies because "finance capital" was itself divided and diffused.

These differences may seem like splitting hairs—or even irrelevant—to non-Marxists, but taken together these interpretations represented a qualitative breakthrough in Soviet analyses of the West. Further, as was noted in chapter 1, they provided the theoretical rationale for a total reordering of Soviet foreign policy as characterized by the "peaceful coexistence" and "détente" policies of the 1960s and 1970s respectively.

The consequence of these Soviet doctrinal revisions and de-Stalinization was felt by Marxist-Leninists around the world. In Western Europe, it influenced the tactics of nonruling Communist parties as these parties attempted to gain power through the ballot box rather than armed struggle. It also stimulated the rise of a new generation of Western European writing on state-monopoly capitalism.[9] Among Communist countries this Soviet "revisionism" was denounced by the Chinese, Albanians, and others as heresy. The Soviet policy of peaceful coexistence with the West, and the theoretical revisionism that gave rise to it, became a significant component of the Sino-Soviet split.

The Chinese Reaction

As the Soviets reverted to more fundamental and flexible Leninist assessments of monopoly capitalism, the Chinese clung to the more dogmatic and deterministic Stalinist interpretations of the "general crisis of capitalism," combined with a Trotskyite optimism about world revolution. The Chinese took the uncompromising position of the three "no peaces" (san wu he): no peaceful competition, no peaceful coexistence, and no peaceful transition to socialism. China took a particularly tough stand on the "parliamentary path to socialism" as pursued by Italian Communist Party Chairman Togliatti and other Western European Communists who thought they could seize power through the ballot box.[10]

Many of these diatribes were reportedly written at the behest of Kang Sheng,[11] whom Mao had put in charge of drafting the major polemical attacks on the Soviet Union. Beginning in 1961, Kang instructed the Institute of International Relations (Guoji Guanxi Yanjiusuo) to draft theoretical articles on the demise of imperialism to fuel

[9] For an excellent overview of this generation of theory, see Bob Jessop, *The Capitalist State* (New York: New York University Press, 1982).

[10] See, for example, "The Differences between Comrade Togliatti and Us," *Peking Review* 6, 1 (January 4, 1963), p. 4.

[11] Interview with an America Watcher knowledgeable about this period, September 18, 1986.

the polemic with the Soviets. Researchers at the institute did as they were told, but, according to one knowledgeable participant, not all were convinced of imperialism's imminent death. By 1964 some Chinese scholars in the institute were questioning Lenin's core assumptions of the moribundity of imperialism and the inevitability of imperialist war.[12] These doubts were reportedly raised internally throughout 1964–1965, but they were abruptly cut off in 1966 when the Cultural Revolution erupted. Thus, behind the uncompromising Chinese contributions to the Sino-Soviet polemics of this period and tracts such as Lin Biao's *Long Live the Victory of People's War!* lay doubts and a debate among many Chinese theorists and scholars over the accuracy of these writings.

With the end of the Cultural Revolution, Mao's death, the overthrow of the "Gang of Four," and China's opening to the outside world, Chinese interpretations of the capitalist world began to change. Chapters 3–6 examine this change in the specific context of the United States, but many of those specific images are derived from more general doctrinal reassessments of imperialism and state-monopoly capitalism. Importantly, the doctrinal breakthroughs on these questions helped provide analytical flexibility for area studies specialists like the America Watchers.

Beginning in 1978, Chinese Marxist theorists began to reopen the debates on imperialism and state-monopoly capitalism that had been aborted by the Cultural Revolution. They debated these issues among themselves in books and professional journals. These debates rapidly gained momentum and reached polemical proportions. These polemics have gone wholly unnoticed in the West to date. As will be demonstrated in subsequent chapters, these polemics have had a profound impact on analyses of specific capitalist countries.

It is important to note the close parallels between the range of opinions expressed and conclusions reached in these Chinese polemics and in those of Soviet theorists during the Khrushchev era. The Chinese were apparently unaware of the Soviet debates when they were taking place. One finds no references to the Soviet debates in the Chinese literature of the time. Xu Kui, director of the Institute of Soviet and East European Studies at CASS, indicated as much in a January 1990 interview: "We did not know much about the Varga-Stalin debates when they were taking place; only after the Sino-Soviet break did they come to our attention. Prior to that time, Stalin's *Economic Problems of Socialism in the U.S.S.R.* had a big impact on

[12] Ibid.

us."[13] This statement is questionable as several Chinese economists were resident in IMEMO both during and after the Varga-Stalin debates. As will be seen from the subsequent Chinese polemics on imperialism and state-monopoly capitalism, these individuals were instrumental in challenging and revising Stalinist dogma and advancing Vargaesque lines of argument in their stead.

The Polemic on Imperialism

It can be seen that the conditions on which Lenin developed his thesis that imperialist wars are inevitable have changed. Failure to study such profound changes in the foundation and conditions for the development of monopoly capitalist economy would make it hard to understand why since World War II no war has broken out between the developed capitalist countries in spite of this or that contradiction or clash of interest between them. . . . This shows that in any consideration of the question of war and peace in contemporary times we must work out a new scientific thesis guided by Marxism-Leninism and based on post-war historical facts, and must not adhere to the thesis propounded by Lenin before and after World War I based on the historical facts of those days; still less should we indiscriminately adopt certain viewpoints presented by Stalin in the early post-war years. . . . The situation as a whole has not turned out as Stalin predicted.[14]

When this explicit repudiation of Lenin's and Stalin's writings concerning imperialist war (as enunciated by Chen Qimao, director of the Shanghai Institute for International Studies, in a keynote speech to the Shanghai Symposium on Preserving World Peace, May 20–22, 1986) appeared in *Beijing Review* in 1986, it was the first time that the Chinese had admitted the fallibility of these theses in a public forum expressly aimed at foreigners. Such a startling public repudiation of one of the classic canons of Marxism-Leninism is not made without forethought, nor does it come about without internal debate. In this case, it had taken eight years of intense internal debate before the Chinese could admit such revisionism before the world.

The polemic on imperialism as a stage of development focused on Lenin's assertion that it was the "highest" stage of capitalism and was to be the final stage prior to the revolutionary transition to socialism. Thus, Lenin termed imperialism to be "moribund." This is

[13] Interview, CASS Institute of Soviet and East European Studies, January 11, 1990.
[14] Chen Qimao, "War and Peace: A Reappraisal," *Beijing Review* 29, 23 (June 9, 1986): 18–25.

variously referred to in Chinese as *chuisi* (moribund, dying), *fuxiu* (decaying, degenerating), *miewang* (dying out, becoming extinct), or *moluo* (declining, waning).

The question of imperialism's pending death or longevity was a troubling one for Chinese theorists who contemplated their country's new relations with the imperialist world. Chinese Marxist theorists thus began asking themselves just what Lenin meant by moribund. Just how soon was imperialism due to die? Indeed, sixty years had passed since Lenin's prediction of imperialism's pending death, yet it had not died. What did that say about the other arguments in Lenin's "theory of imperialism"? These issues were hotly debated in Chinese theoretical circles during the 1980s, but particularly between 1980 and 1983.

The imperialism polemic was not just an abstract theoretical debate; it carried concrete implications for Chinese foreign policy toward capitalist countries. It provided the post hoc theoretical rationale for a policy of accommodation and constructive exchange with the West. Those who argued that imperialism exhibited longevity promoted a policy of accommodation and exchange with imperialist countries.

The post-Mao polemic proceeded through three overlapping phases. It began in theoretical circles affiliated with the Party School and first found expression in the May 1980 issue of the CCP Central Committee theoretical journal *Hongqi* (Red flag), which published sixteen articles during the ensuing year on "theoretical questions of imperialism." These articles were then assembled for mass distribution in the volume *Lun dangdai diguozhuyi jingji* (Theories of contemporary imperialist economies).[15]

The second stage began in late 1980 and early 1981 in the social science journal of Fudan University (Shanghai) and spread to other university journals until mid-1982. Thus, university scholars joined party theorists in the polemic.

From late 1981 through 1983, the third stage in the polemic began and expanded as the debate spread to researchers in the Chinese Academy of Social Sciences, particularly the Institute of Economics and Institute of World Economics and Politics. *Jingji yanjiu* (Economics research), the journal of the Institute of Economics, convened a symposium on contemporary imperialism in 1982 and published the papers in the collected volume *Lun dangdai diguozhuyi* (Theories of

---

[15] *Hongqi* Social and International Section Editing Group, *Lun dangdai diguozhuyi jingji* (Beijing: Hongqi chubanshe, 1982).

contemporary imperialism).[16] The two journals of the Institute of World Economics and Politics—*Shijie jingji* (World economics) and *Shijie jingji yu zhengzhi neican* (Internal reference materials on world economics and politics)—and *Zhongguo shehui kexue* (Chinese social science), an organ of the academy, also contributed some key pieces. Throughout this period, university textbooks on the political economy of capitalist countries also discussed the longevity of imperialism. These texts capture the range of positions taken on the question of the pace of imperialism's pending death. A survey of twenty-three texts[17] revealed three equally held images of the death of imperialism: seven asserted that imperialism was simply dying,[18] seven stated it would die soon,[19] and eight estimated that imperialism's death is a long-term historical process.[20] One text ventured to declare that im-

[16] Jingji Yanjiu Bianjizu, *Lun dangdai diguozhuyi* (Shanghai: Renmin chubanshe, 1984).

[17] I consider this survey to be fairly comprehensive in that these texts were acquired in eleven major cities representing a geographic dispersion across China: Beijing, Tianjin, Shenyang, Shanghai, Nanjing, Guangzhou, Wuhan, Chongqing, Chengdu, Lhasa, and Urumqi. The compilers and publishing houses of these texts were equally dispersed geographically.

[18] Shandong Higher Education Political Economy Teaching and Editing Group, eds., *Zhengzhi jingjixue* (Shandong: Renmin chubanshe, 1983), p. 224; Beijing Teachers College Political Economy Editing Group, *Zhengzhi jingjixue jiaoxue cankao ziliao xuanbian* (Beijing: Beijing shifan xueyuan chubanshe, 1981), p. 209; Fu Liyuan and Wang Maogen, *Zhengzhi jingjixue* (Beijing: Beijing daxue chubanshe, 1984), p. 184; Cao Ruoxian, ed., *Zhengzhi jingjixue zixue gailun* (Beijing: Jingji kexue chubanshe, 1983), p. 69; Song Tao, ed., *Zhengzhi jingjixue* (Beijing: Renmin daxue chubanshe, 1982), pp. 248, 268; Ding Bing and Wu Shitai, *Makesi de zhengzhi jingjixue jianshi* (Sichuan: Renmin chubanshe, 1983), p. 246; Yu Guangyuan and Su Xing, *Zhengzhi jingjixue* (Beijing: Renmin chubanshe, 1978), p. 75.

[19] Sun Ru and Zhuo Zhong, eds., *Zhengzhi jingjixue jianghuo* (Beijing: Renmin chubanshe, 1978), pp. 189–90; Zhao Wanglin, ed., *Zhengzhi jingjixue yuanli* (Guangxi: Renmin chubanshe, 1984), p. 458; Sixteen Universities and Research Institutes of Southern China Political Economy Editing Group, *Zhengzhi jingjixue daxue changyong jiaocai* (Sichuan: Renmin chubanshe, 1980), pp. 448–49; Ding Wenshan et al., *Zhengzhi jingjixue* (Beijing: Zhongyang guangbo daxue chubanshe, 1983), pp. 361, 366–67; Shanghai Higher Education Institute, *Zhengzhi jingjixue* (Xinjiang: Renmin chubanshe, 1984), pp. 134–35; Song Tao, ed., *Zhengzhi jingjixue* (Beijing: Renmin chubanshe, 1983), pp. 744–50, 772–76; Political Economy Editing Group, *Jianming zhengzhi jingjixue* (Henan: Renmin chubanshe, 1979), pp. 237, 252–53.

[20] Zhao Yulin, *Zhengzhi jingjixue wenti tansuo* (Guangxi: Renmin chubanshe, 1983), p. 235; Eight Higher Education Teachers Colleges Editing Group, *Jianming zhengzhi jingjixue shi* (Henan: Renmin chubanshe, 1982), p. 402; Liu Zhilin and Lu Jidian, *Zhengzhi jingjixue* (Sichuan: Chongqing chubanshe, 1983), p. 160; Beijing University Economics Department, *Zhengzhi jingjixue jiaoyu cankao ziliao* (Beijing: Beijing daxue jingjixi, 1983), p. 81; Wang Zhenhua, *Zhengzhi jingjixue jiangshou tiyao* (Beijing: Zhongyang guangbo daxue chubanshe, 1983), p. 252; Zhong Weida, ed., *Zhengzhi jingjixue* (Jilin: Renmin chubanshe, 1981), p. 355; Zhu Shaoyun, ed., *Zhengzhi jingjixue* (Beijing: Faxian

perialism "must already be dead because of the upsurge of proletarian revolution since World War II."[21] None expressed the view that imperialism would not die. Despite important nuanced differences over the pace of imperialism's death, all accepted Lenin's basic thesis about its moribund nature.

Nor did any of the sixteen articles in *Hongqi*, the party's theoretical journal, challenge the basic correctness of Lenin's thesis. Senior party theorist Qiu Qihua contributed two key articles to the *Hongqi* forum on imperialism that directly addressed the moribund thesis. Qiu argued that Lenin's thesis was not outmoded and was entirely correct. The problem was that "certain comrades" misunderstood its essence and misinterpreted Lenin to mean that decaying (*fuxiu*) capitalism could not develop rapidly.[22] To the contrary, Qiu claimed in a companion article aptly entitled "Is Lenin's Thesis of Moribund Imperialism Decidedly Obsolete?":

> When Lenin called imperialism moribund capitalism, he did not mean that imperialism would perish immediately. . . . The world structure of imperialism will perish only in portions and one at a time. Only a little over sixty years have passed since Lenin put forward the thesis of imperialism being moribund capitalism. This is a relatively short time in the history of mankind. Judging from the trend of developments, imperialism might continue to survive for a fairly long period of time. Even so, the correctness of Lenin's thesis cannot be refuted.[23]

This view of imperialism as a long-term historical process articulated by Qiu Qihua in 1981 eventually became the accepted compromise position after two more years of debate. It offered the perfect resolution of the issue because it removed the short-term predictive determinism and provided long-term flexibility while not refuting the basic correctness of Lenin. Qiu's views, however, by no means put an end to the debate.

As the controversy spread to universities, Fudan University in Shanghai stood at the forefront. Fudan's International Politics Department and World Economy Research Institute have, since the mid-1960s, been the leading university centers in China for the study of capitalist countries. In addition, the Political Economy Department

---

chubanshe, 1983), p. 273; Li Qianheng et al., *Zhengzhi jingjixue jianming duben* (Beijing: Zhongguo qingnian chubanshe, 1980), p. 330.

[21] Yuan Xialiang and Zhao Jinxiu, *Tongsu zhengzhi jingjixue* (Sichuan: Renmin chubanshe, 1984), p. 443.

[22] Qiu Qihua, "Lun dangdai zibenzhuyi de fuxiuxing," *Hongqi*, no. 20 (1980): 36–41.

[23] Qiu Qihua, "Liening guanyu diguozhuyi chuisixing de lun duan guoshi le ma?" *Hongqi*, no. 7 (1981): 41–46.

faculty includes several specialists of Marxist political economy with national reputations. Fudan's social science journal, *Fudan daxue xuebao*, published numerous articles in 1981–1982 concerning various aspects of Lenin's theory of imperialism. Usually Chinese are reluctant to criticize each other personally in a public forum, unless an individual has been officially singled out for criticism. But the debate on the moribund nature of imperialism at Fudan took on a personal dimension.

The lead article in the debate was written by Fudan graduate student Chen Weishu. Chen's article, simply entitled "Some Viewpoints on Modern Monopoly Capitalism," argued that while imperialism had some moribund characteristics, particularly parasitic social relations (*jisheng shehui guanxi*), on the whole production had increased greatly under monopoly capitalism, especially since World War II. Based on his image of economic growth in the West, Chen concluded that imperialism was not in danger of dying anytime soon.[24]

Two issues later Yin Bocheng responded in an article entitled "A Basic Understanding of the Moribund Nature of Imperialism—A Discussion with Comrade Chen Weishu."[25] Yin directly criticized many of Chen's arguments and particularly his conclusion about the longevity of imperialism. His argument revolved around the stagnation (*tingzhi*) of investment by large monopolies in areas other than science and technology, which he felt would exacerbate economic depression and result in the eventual collapse of imperialism. But because of the new technological revolution, Yin believed that the West would be able to avoid catastrophe in the near term.

Three issues later Fudan economics professor and noted specialist on monopoly capitalism Gong Weijing staked out a third image of imperialism's demise in an article entitled "How to Understand the Moribund Nature of Imperialism—A Discussion with Comrades Chen Weishu and Yin Bocheng."[26] Gong criticized Chen for "overemphasizing the stimulation of productive forces by monopoly capitalism," and he criticized Yin for "avoiding the question of the relations of production." Instead, Gong emphasized the widening income gaps between the monopoly bourgeoisie and the proletariat in the postwar era. On this basis Gong concluded that Marx's belief that the "absolute impoverishment of the proletariat" would inexo-

[24] Chen Weishu, "Dui xiandai longduan zibenzhuyi de jidian kanfa," *Fudan daxue xuebao*, no. 3 (1981): 21–27.

[25] Yin Bocheng, "Dui diguozhuyi chuisixing de jiben renshi—he Chen Weishu tongzhi duilun," *Fudan daxue xuebao*, no. 5 (1981): 17–21.

[26] Gong Weijing, "Zenmayang renshi diguozhuyi chuisixing—yu Chen Weishu, Yin Bocheng liang tongzhi shangque," *Fudan daxue xuebao*, no. 2 (1982): 13–19.

rably lead to social revolution, and therefore the contradictions in the capitalist world were very sharp and imperialism was bound to die soon. Consequently, Gong interpreted Lenin's moribund thesis literally; imperialism would die soon.

Three issues later the debate in *Fudan daxue xuebao* came to an abrupt end with a partial recantation by Chen Weishu.[27] He did so not by abandoning his "productive forces" (*shengchanli*) argument, which he continued to defend at great length, but by accepting Gong's criticism concerning the working class. As captured in the title of his article, Chen concluded that the main manifestation of moribund imperialism is the parasitic nature of social relations between the monopoly bourgeoisie and the proletariat.

This attention to social relations and the condition of the working class in the advanced capitalist countries was not unique to the Fudan University journal. Chinese theorists had considered Marx's theory of the "pauperization of the proletariat" in tandem with Lenin's theory of imperialism since 1979. The issue at hand was whether the Western proletariat was "absolutely impoverished" (*juedui pinkunhua*), and hence on the verge of revolution, or "relatively impoverished" (*xiangdui pinkunhua*) vis-à-vis the bourgeoisie, in which case their relative material comfort precluded social uprising. Led by a series of articles in *Shijie jingji*, the journal of the Institute of World Economics and Politics at CASS, a consensus emerged around the latter position by 1983. This directly influenced the moribund-imperialism thesis, because if the material position of the capitalist proletariat was not aggravated to the point of "throwing off their chains" in revolution, then one of the key conditions of imperialism's pending death was not met. This debate on the impoverishment of the capitalist proletariat is examined at greater length in chapter 4.

In mid-1981 the Chinese Academy of Social Sciences joined the imperialism polemic with two authoritative articles in *Zhongguo shehui kexue* (Chinese social science), an organ of the academy. In "The Withering Away of Imperialism According to Lenin's Original Meaning," Jiang Xuemo, the director of Fudan University's Socialist Economics Research Office, criticized Stalin for distorting Lenin's original meaning of "moribund" to imply that the death of imperialism was at hand.[28] According to Professor Jiang, Lenin's intended meaning was that imperialism is a "very long historical process" that would only make the "transition" to socialism in hundreds, perhaps

[27] Chen Weishu, "Zai lun diguozhuyi de chuisixing zhuyao biaoxian wei jishengxing," *Fudan daxue xuebao*, no. 5 (1982): 22–29.

[28] Jiang Xuemo, "Anjiao Liening de yuanyi renshi diguozhuyi de chuisixing," *Zhongguo shehui kexue*, no. 4 (1981): 77–86.

thousands, of years! Jiang added that Lenin had based his prediction on an economic analysis while Stalin overstressed the political factors.

In a companion article, the late Huan Xiang (who among his many official positions could be said to have been Deng Xiaoping's senior foreign policy adviser) echoed the views of Jiang Xuemo:

> The basic thesis of Lenin's *Imperialism*, including the dying out of imperialism, is undoubtedly completely correct. Even today it is not yet out of date and remains a sharp weapon for us to use to research imperialism. But we must also recognize that this book was written nearly seventy years ago. History has changed and developed greatly since then, and the present situation is greatly changed from what he analyzed. Therefore, at present the question is not to defend and prove the correctness of every word of *Imperialism*. . . . I think to study the problem of imperialism and prove its trend of development (which is certainly moving in the direction of extinction and death) we must reach new conclusions on the basis of new materials, not only using the words in *Imperialism*. . . . The process of imperialism going down to its doom is rather long and may be tortuous, and it has lots of ups and downs. At present it still has a certain vitality; not only does it exist, but it can still develop somewhat. Only from a long-term and historical point of view is it declining and dying out.[29]

Jiang Xuemo and Huan Xiang therefore concurred with Qiu Qihua's earlier compromise position between the "quick death" and "no death" camps, that is, long-term death. Huan's statement that imperialism "still has a certain vitality" is an important admission and reflects his own preoccupation with the development of science and technology in the West. Given Huan Xiang's pivotal position in the Chinese foreign-policy-making establishment (then director of the State Council's Center of International Studies), his views can be taken as both theoretical windowdressing on China's newfound relations with imperialist countries and guidance for interpretation by lower-level theorists.[30]

While Huan's contribution to the debate did, in the end, emerge as the compromise interpretation of the question of moribund imperialism, it did not immediately produce either an end to the discussion or a uniform interpretation, but it did spark serious research inside the academy. In 1982 as the debate on imperialism's longevity reached its height, CASS researchers stood at the forefront.

[29] Huan Xiang, "Guanyu 'diguozhuyi chuisixing' de wenti," *Zhongguo shehui kexue*, no. 4 (1981): 89–90.

[30] For a broader exposition of Huan Xiang's worldview see Huan Xiang, *Zong-heng shijie* (Beijing: Shijie zhishi chubanshe, 1985).

Naturally, the Institute of Marxism–Leninism–Mao Zedong Thought took up the issue. The institute's maverick director, Su Shaozhi, called for more research on the issue in a speech commemorating the centenary of Marx's death:

> Although the present-day capitalist world generally suffers from sluggishness or stagnation and from serious crises (economic, political, social, cultural, etc.), it is obviously hard to say with certainty that the total collapse of capitalism is already in sight. Hence the renewal of the discussion on the "resilience of capitalism."[31]

The staff in Su's institute thus began to turn their attention from studying socialism to advanced capitalism. In summarizing debates in the institute during the early 1980s, one staff member recalled, "We concluded that what Lenin actually meant by 'moribund' was a 'trend' (chushi). When you look at capitalist countries today you can see they still have life (shengmingli). . . . Speaking frankly, taking capitalist systems as a whole, this system can meet the needs of all the people of the world."[32]

The debates in CASS also spread into more general economist circles in the academy's Institute of Economics and Institute of World Economics and Politics. During 1982–1983 the journal of each institute carried about a dozen articles on imperialism.

The articles published by the Institute of World Economics and Politics were largely carried in its neibu journal Shijie jingji yu zhengzhi neican (Internal reference materials on world economics and politics), although some appeared in its unclassified journal Shijie jingji (World economy). The former periodical provides an in-depth look at unofficial Chinese thinking about current issues in international relations and Chinese foreign policy, which Chinese are usually reticent to discuss in forums open to examination by foreigners. The journal often carries candid assessments of other countries and sensitive issues prior to official policy changes. For example, Gilbert Rozman found that Shijie jingji yu zhengzhi neican played a leading role in reassessing Soviet socialism before the "thaw" in bilateral Sino-Soviet relations in the mid-1980s.[33]

During 1982–1983 the journal published eleven articles specifically on imperialism, its moribund character, and the accuracy of Lenin's treatise. The lead article in this series was a sweeping indictment of

---

[31] Su Shaozhi, "Developing Marxism under Contemporary Conditions," in Su Shaozhi et al., Marxism in China (Nottingham: Russell Press, 1983) p. 26.

[32] Interview at Institute of Marxism–Leninism–Mao Zedong Thought, Chinese Academy of Social Sciences, May 15, 1990.

[33] Rozman, "China's Soviet Watchers in the 1980s."

Lenin's "theory of imperialism," criticizing Lenin's famous "five points" one by one.[34] First, not all monopoly capitalist countries were deemed imperialist; for example, Scandinavian countries, Canada, and Japan. "These countries are not aggressive and expansionist externally, therefore it appears that imperialism is not a scientific concept."[35] Second, it was noted that the world has not been divided by imperialist countries, but rather between the United States and Soviet Union—one imperialist and one social-imperialist. Third, while the export of capital is a notable feature of modern imperialism, in the United States—the world's leading capital exporter—capital imports actually exceed capital exports. Fourth, colonies no longer sustain imperialism as the postwar world has witnessed decolonization. Fifth, interimperialist war has not occurred; rather, modern wars primarily exist between developing countries. Thus, the author of the lead article questioned the very legitimacy of Lenin's "theory." With this general indictment for starters, ensuing articles addressed the different criteria of imperialism raised in Lenin's treatise—including his moribund thesis.

Two articles attempted a linguistic analysis of the term "moribund" in both Chinese and Russian, and both concluded that Lenin intended the term to convey the notion of "transition."[36] The term "transition" (guodu) became an important codeword for the view that imperialism's death is a "long-term historical process" (hen chang de lishi guocheng), that is, the transition of one historical stage to another. The first of these two articles, by Yang Lujun, also asserted that "capitalism still has a vitality not to be underestimated, and its death is not close at hand."[37] This provoked a strong response in a later article, which asserted that "Comrade Yang does not understand the profound scientific meaning of the word 'dying,' and his analysis is not logical or tenable."[38] Another article also took issue with the "transition thesis" by invoking Stalin's Foundations of Leninism, which asserted that "imperialism is 'dying capitalism' because

[34] Liu Xun, "Guanyu dangdai diguozhuyi de jige lilun wenti," Shijie jingji yu zhengzhi neican, no. 1 (1982): 22–30.

[35] Ibid., p. 22.

[36] Yang Lujun, "Yingdangxiao diguozhuyi 'chuisixing' de tifa," Shijie jingji yu zhengzhi neican, no. 3 (1982): 39–40; Sui Qiyan, "Yingdang jianchi 'diguozhuyi shi chuisi de zibenzhuyi' de tifa," Shijie jingji yu zhengzhi neican, no. 11 (1982): 39–40. For another advocate of the "transition thesis" see Dong Zhuangdao, "Diguozhuyi weishenma hai chichi bu si?" Shijie jingji yu zhengzhi neican, no. 3 (1982): 21–22.

[37] Yang Lujun, "Yingdangxiao diguozhuyi 'chuisixing' de tifa," p. 40.

[38] Zhang Qishan and Yu Wei, "Quxiao diguozhuyi 'chuisixing' de tifa genju kezai," Shijie jingji yu zhengzhi neican, no. 10 (1982): 30.

imperialism pushes capitalist contradictions to their summit, after which a proletarian revolution begins."[39]

While imperialism and hegemony are distinguished from one another by many Chinese theorists, one article in the series entitled "Is It Certain that All Monopoly Capitalist Countries Are Imperialist?" equated imperialism with hegemony (baquanzhuyi), defining both as the military subjugation of other states.[40] On this basis the authors stated that imperialist countries existed prior to monopoly capitalism (e.g., the Roman Empire, Napoleonic France, British Empire), and therefore they concluded that not all monopoly capitalist countries (e.g., the Scandinavian nations and Canada) are imperialist. This image provoked a direct refutation by a certain Bai Nan, who argued that Lenin's theory must be taken literally to mean that all monopoly capitalist countries are imperialist because Lenin's theory is "scientific."[41] As will be discussed below, most Chinese Marxist theorists consider imperialism to be a stage of capitalist development, while hegemony is a policy and type of behavior.

While no clear resolution of the issue of imperialism's death emerges from the articles in Shijie jingji yu zhengzhi neican, the majority argued the "transition thesis." As evidence they emphasized the boom in capitalist production in the postwar era, the continued advancement of science and technology, the growth of the middle class, and the "relative impoverishment of the proletariat." The minority insisted on a strict and literal interpretation of Lenin's use of the term "moribund." They explicitly rejected the "transition thesis," which was the cornerstone of the majority interpretation. As evidence of their position they emphasized the stagnation of productive forces under monopoly capitalism, severe economic crises, and a militant and "absolutely impoverished proletariat." Notwithstanding the detractors, and taken together with the articles in Zhongguo shehui kexue, the Academy of Social Sciences was beginning to forge a consensus in favor of a more flexible and objective interpretation of Lenin's thesis on moribund imperialism anchored on the belief that the end was not in sight.

This consensus was reinforced by the "Forum on Contemporary Imperialism" articles published during 1982–1983 in the journal of

[39] Zheng Biao, "Ye tan 'anjiao Liening de yuanyi renshi diguozhuyi de chuisixing,' " Shijie jingji yu zhengzhi neican, no. 10 (1982): 24.

[40] Liu Jirui and Li Binsheng, "Longduan zibenzhuyi guojia jiu yiding shi diguozhuyi guojia ma?" Shijie jingji yu zhengzhi neican, no. 5 (1983): 53–54.

[41] Bai Nan, "Longduan zibenzhuyi guojia jiushi diguozhuyi guojia—yu Liu Jirui, Li Binsheng liangwei tongzhi shangque," Shijie jingji yu zhengzhi neican, no. 10 (1983): 32–33, 42.

the Institute of Economics, *Jingji yanjiu*. Since its days under the direction of Sun Yefang, the Institute of Economics has a history of putting forth maverick, revisionist positions in theoretical debates of Marxist political economy.

The forum articles were assembled together in the volume *Lun dangdai diguozhuyi* (Theories of contemporary imperialism)[42] and were summed up in a review article in the September 1984 issue of *Jingji yanjiu*. The reviewer claimed that the forum participants concluded that "imperialism will not die in the world very soon . . . the era of transition from imperialism to social revolution will have to be a quite long one in which the conditions will be very complex and there will be many complications."[43] This conclusion was borne out in the forum articles. The majority of articles dealt with Lenin's five criteria of imperialism and not the question of imperialism's death per se. The three that did discuss moribund imperialism explicitly and unequivocally argued the "transition thesis" and criticized Stalin for overstressing the political superstructure to the neglect of the economic base in his *Foundations of Leninism* and *Economic Problems in the U.S.S.R.*, thus distorting Lenin's original meaning of the term "moribund."[44]

By late 1983 and early 1984 those theorists who argued the transition thesis of imperialism's long-term death had clearly garnered the dominant position in the polemic. The CASS contributions to this polemic proved crucial in helping to forge the majority position. A small group of researchers in the Economic Theory Research Office of the Institute of World Economics and Politics contributed many of the key pieces. Included among this group were several individuals who had contact with Varga's Institute of International Relations and World Economy in Moscow in the 1950s and admit to being influenced by his writings.[45] As will be seen below, these individuals also played key roles in revising the Stalinist interpretation of state-monopoly capitalism. As Li Zong, the current director of the institute (and a key contributor to the imperialism and state-monopoly capitalism polemics), recently argued, "Stalin and Mao both overestimated the rapidity of death of imperialism—for forty years it has

[42] Jingji yanjiu bianjizu, *Lun dangdai diguozhuyi* (Shanghai: Renmin chubanshe, 1984).

[43] Xi Yonglu, "Shu ping: Lun dangdai diguozhuyi," *Jingji yanjiu*, no. 9 (1984): 78–80.

[44] Li Zong, "Dangdai diguozhuyi shi gengjia fuxiu de zibenzhuyi," in Jingji yanjiu bianjizu, *Lun dangdai diguozhuyi*, pp. 1–24; Wu Jian, "Dangdai diguozhuyi rengran shi chuisi de zibenzhuyi," pp. 25–30; Hong Wenda, "Lun diguozhuyi de fuxiuxing he chuisixing," pp. 44–69.

[45] Interviews at the Institute of World Economics and Politics, Chinese Academy of Social Sciences, December 24, 1984; January 23, 1990.

been comparatively stable. We recognize it as a long period, but we also do not say that Lenin was wrong."[46]

While the polemic on imperialism's longevity peaked in 1983–1984, publications on the subject continued in academic circles through the rest of the decade. With respect to the issue of imperialism's longevity there existed a uniformity of opinion in books and articles. This uniformity adhered to the consensual opinion forged during the polemic by Huan Xiang, Qiu Qihua, and others.

The conclusions offered in Qiu Qihua's book *Xiandai longduan zibenshuyi jingji* (Modern monopoly capitalist economics) were indicative of these further discussions: "When we say that imperialism is moribund capitalism . . . it is not to say that imperialism has no strength (*liliang*). . . . From a phenomonological point of view, from a near-term perspective, from a tactical perspective, imperialism certainly still has strength and is a real tiger (*zhen laohu*); but from an intrinsic perspective, from a long-term perspective, from a strategic perspective, imperialism is decaying (*fuxiu*), is moribund (*chuisi*), and is a paper tiger."[47]

To abandon the thesis that imperialism would eventually die and give way to socialism would amount to ideological heresy and was thus impossible. Even during the height of Zhao Ziyang's power and the ideological revisionism associated with him and his advisers, to jettison one of the core tenets of Marxism-Leninism (namely, that socialism would eventually derive from, and prevail over, imperialism) would be going beyond acceptable theoretical bounds. Even Zhao's "primary stage of socialism" could not tolerate such an admission. Thus, Lenin's moribund thesis was stretched to its most flexible limit by arguing that imperialism was a "long-term historical stage" that would collapse someday in the evolution of mankind, but not in the foreseeable future.

The Polemic on State-Monopoly Capitalism

"State-monopoly capitalism" is also a fundamental concept in Chinese Marxist assessments of the United States. The concept is intertwined with that of imperialism in that it discusses the political and economic relationships derivative from the rise of monopoly in advanced capitalist countries. The term itself indicates a close relation-

[46] Interview at the Institute of World Economics and Politics, Chinese Academy of Social Sciences, May 10, 1990.

[47] Qiu Qihua, *Xiandai longduan zibenzhuyi jingji* (Beijing: Zhonggong zhongyang dangxiao chubanshe, 1987). The quotation is from pp. 360–61.

ship between the state apparatus and the monopoly bourgeoisie. The key question is, how close?

From 1978 to 1984, Chinese theoretical analyses of state-monopoly capitalism shifted away from the dogmatic Stalinist interpretation that the capitalist state was subordinate to, and directly controlled by, the large monopolies and finance oligarchy. This shift was gradual. It evolved through roughly four overlapping phases (see table 2.1) in which incrementally different sets of perceptions of the relationship between the capitalist state and monopoly bourgeoisie were articulated. Exceptions exist, of course, but generally these phases and perceptions can be summarized as follows.

Between 1978 and 1980, as during the Maoist era, the "subordination thesis" reigned supreme. This perspective not only is explicitly argued in context but is also easily recognized by the use of the terms *congshu* (subordinate), *kongzhi* (control or domination), *zhangwo* (control or have direct command), *caozong* (manipulate), and *zhipei diwei* (controlling, dominant, or governing position).[48] The terms *gongju* (tool, instrument) and *fuwu* (serve) are slight variations of the subordination thesis, for example, "the state is an instrument of class rule" or "the state serves the monopoly bourgeoisie."

During 1980–1981 this view came under attack by those who felt that it was too mechanical and rigidly dogmatic. In place of the subordination thesis, these theorists argued for a more literal and orthodox interpretation of Lenin's postulate that the finance oligarchy and state were "unified." This view usually found expression in the terms *lianhe* (unite, ally, unify, combine, join together) and *jiehe* (joint or join together). This perspective was argued equally, and frequently together, with the subordination thesis during 1980–1981.

During 1982–1983, the third phase, the unification thesis began to achieve prominence over the subordination thesis, but with a slight difference. The degree of tightness of the "close relationship" (*miqie*

Table 2.1
Stages of the State-Monopoly Capitalism Polemic

	Years	Perspective
Stage 1	1978–1980	Subordination thesis exclusive
Stage 2	1980–1981	Subordination and coalescence theses coexist
Stage 3	1982–1983	Coalescence thesis dominant
Stage 4	1983–1984	Monopoly competition and state autonomy argued

---

[48] All translations are from the standard *Han-Ying cidian* (A Chinese-English dictionary) (Beijing: Shangwu yinshuguan, 1981).

guanxi) between the monopoly bourgeoisie and the state was qualified to imply a separateness between these entities. The state and monopoly bourgeoisie were portrayed as unitary, but distinct, entities that were "coalesced." Instead of *lianhe* and *jiehe*, the terms *ronghe* (coalesce, merge, fuse, mix together) and *yinxiang* (to influence or affect) appeared more frequently. This terminology connotes a more ambiguous, albeit intertwined, relationship between the capitalist state and monopolies. The utility of this perspective for Chinese theorists lay precisely in its ambiguity. That is, they did not need to spell out the exact nature of the relationship between the state and monopoly bourgeoisie.

During 1983, studies of the monopoly bourgeoisie in specific capitalist countries increased significantly. Upon close examination, Chinese researchers discovered that the monopoly bourgeoisie did not act in concert with the capitalist state but rather was internally divided and highly competitive. Various monopoly financial groups (*longduan caituan*) competed fiercely with each other in the economic marketplace and vied for government influence.

Having disaggregated the monopoly bourgeoisie, some analysts began in 1984 to examine the capitalist state as an autonomous entity. They recognized that there are competing forces within the state apparatus, but they also asserted that the state enjoys a significant degree of autonomy and independence (*duli*) from the monopoly bourgeoisie.

Thus, in the span of six years, Chinese theoreticians' images had evolved—in four progressive stages—from the belief that the capitalist state was completely subordinate to the monopoly bourgeoisie to the view that it exhibited autonomy. This doctrinal change had far-reaching implications, as will be seen in subsequent chapters, because the conclusion that the state is an autonomous economic and political actor opened the door to the analysis of the market economy and intragovernmental bureaucratic politics. Moreover, once the monopoly bourgeoisie is no longer seen as unitary and omnipotent, but rather as divided and competitive, analysis of other actors in a pluralistic policy process is possible. Nonmonopoly classes—particularly the middle class—are recognized as participants in the capitalist economy and bourgeois political system and are not just "impoverished" proletarians waiting to overthrow their monopoly capitalist overlords. Finally, the channels of economic and political participation are viewed as multiple, including interest groups and political parties. Even elections are no longer deemed irrelevant exercises that benefit only the bourgeoisie.

In short, a simple dichotomous bourgeoisie-proletarian model of capitalist society was altered to take into account a greater multiplicity of actors and processes. Importantly, all of this was done in the name of Lenin. By invoking Lenin's more flexible interpretations of these questions rather than Stalin's more dogmatic views, revisionist Chinese Marxist theorists had actually engineered important theoretical and analytical departures from Marxism-Leninism—all in the name of Marxism-Leninism!

The following summary examines in more detail how the "subordination" image gave way to images of "unification/coalescence," "monopoly fragmentation," and "state autonomy." By and large, the discussion of the polemic on state-monopoly capitalism excludes references to specific capitalist countries, in part because the polemic was waged among Marxist political economists and theoreticians, not area specialists. The dialogue was frequently of an abstract theoretical nature, and little specific evidence was marshaled to bolster a priori assertions.

The Subordination Thesis

The subordination thesis was most clearly articulated in university journals and textbooks. Of the twenty-three political economy texts noted above in the context of the imperialism polemic, twenty used terminology that conveyed the subordination thesis (seven exclusively, thirteen together with the unification thesis, while only three articulated the unification thesis alone). This is not surprising insofar as these texts are the basic propaganda tools for indoctrinating university students and teaching Marxist theory to cadres. Their organization and content are quite uniform. Their purpose is to convey the "correct" definitions and interpretations as deemed appropriate by the relevant authorities.

Who are these authorities, and what is "correct"? Many of these texts contained wording identical, or remarkably similar, to that in the *Concise Dictionary of Political Economy* edited by noted economist Xu Dixin. This handy reference aid provides "correct" definitions of 1,297 phenomena in the political-economy universe, including the following:

Financial group (*caituan*): In the imperialist stage of development, the main capitalist countries' economies, politics, cultural and social life, and other aspects are all under the domination (*zhipei*) of large financial groups.

Financial oligarchy (*jinrong guatou*): Imperialist countries are under the control (*zhangwo*) of finance capital which manipulates (*caozong*) the national economic lifelines. In practice state power is controlled (*kongzhi*) by monopoly capitalists and monopoly capital groups. The rule of the financial oligarchy is one of the most basic characteristics of imperialism. . . . State political power becomes the ruling tool (*gongju*) of the finance oligarchy. On the one hand, they influence (*yinxiang*) the domestic and foreign policies of government for the benefit of the monopoly capitalists. On the other hand, they place bourgeois political parties under their control (*kongzhi*), and dispatch their agents to enter government, parliament, and other major organizations to directly control (*zhijie zhangwo*) the state apparatus.

State-monopoly capitalism (*guojia longduan zibenzhuyi*): Monopoly organizations and state political power are united together (*jiehe qilai*). . . . The monopoly organizations manipulate (*caozong*) and use (*yong*) the state apparatus in all aspects of national economic life to increase their individual wealth and monopoly rule, to carry out foreign expansion, etc.[49]

University textbooks for political science courses also tend to take these definitions as their reference points in discussing the political systems of capitalist/imperialist countries. For example, the basic text used for the introductory course on "Capitalist Countries' Constitutions and Political Systems" in the Peking University Law Department during the 1983 fall term had this to say:

Governments are organized to express the interests of the ruling classes through the state apparatus. . . . The purpose of bourgeois political parties is to perpetuate their class rule, to manipulate (*caozong*) elections, control (*kongzhi*) the parliament, and control the government. . . . Under conditions of capitalist societies' moribund reactionary life, pressure groups and monopoly financial groups control society, political power, economy, etc. . . . The largest types of pressure groups are under the control of monopoly financial groups. . . . The American president, for example, is under the control of the monopoly bourgeoisie, and he is their highest representative.[50]

The text used for the introductory undergraduate course on "Political Systems of Capitalist Countries" in the International Politics Department at Peking University during the 1984 spring term similarly stated:

The state is an instrument of class rule. . . . Bourgeois democratic systems are an expression of the way the bourgeois class executes its political rule.

[49] Xu Dixin, ed., *Jianming zhengzhi jingjixue zidian* (Beijing: Renmin chubanshe, 1984), pp. 222–23, 315–16, 301.

[50] Luo Haocai and Wu Xieying, *Zibenzhuyi guojia de xianfa he zhengzhi zhidu* (Beijing: Beijing daxue chubanshe, 1983), pp. 251, 129, 144, 149–50, 231, 230, and 281.

The bourgeois class writes the constitution, makes the laws, and establishes a parliamentary system to serve its interests, etc.[51]

The subordination thesis also finds expression in university journals. A classic exposition is provided by Fudan University professor Gong Weijing (who also took a hardline position on imperialism's death) in the *Nankai daxue xuebao* (Nankai University study journal):

> The main manifestation of the capitalist era is that the private monopoly bourgeoisie controls state political power. . . . We recognize that the monopoly bourgeoisie places its agents in positions of state power and uses important organizations to control policy decisions, and moreover uses these policy decisions to serve the monopoly bourgeoisie. This is to say that in the relationship between the state and the monopoly bourgeoisie, the latter is predominant. They directly control and use the state apparatus; moreover, the state is subordinate (*congshu*) to them and serves them.[52]

While Gong and other commentators articulate the classic subordination thesis by using the unambiguous terminology of "control," others employ the softer verb "serve" (*fuwu*), for example, "the state serves the monopolies." This linguistic variation is more ambiguous, but the result is roughly the same. Chen Weishu, for example, uses this term in an article in the journal *Shijie jingji* (World economics): "In essence it can be seen that the state is in the service of monopoly organizations. From the existing situation it can be seen that private monopoly organizations occupy the dominant position."[53]

The Unification Thesis

The use of the term "serve" was, however, challenged by defenders of the unification/coalescence thesis. They argued from the Leninist perspective for a looser definition of the relationship between monopolies and the state, that is, one of unification and/or coalescence. In juxtaposition to the university personnel who were the predominant defenders of the subordination thesis, the "unification" commentators were drawn largely from the Academy of Social Sciences.

One of the earliest articles to distinguish between the subordina-

[51] Yang Baihua and Song Changgu, *Zibenzhuyi guojia zhengzhi zhidu* (Beijing: Shijie zhishi chubanshe, 1984), pp. 4, 21.

[52] Gong Weijing, "Guanliao longduan zichanjieji zai ziben diguozhuyi guojia buzhan tongzhi diwei," *Nankai daxue xuebao*, no. 5 (1980): 17, 22.

[53] Chen Weishu, "Guanyu guojia longduan zibenzhuyi jieduan de ruogan wenti," *Shijie jingji*, no. 3 (1979): 39.

tion and unification theses appeared in *Shijie jingji*, the journal of the Institute of World Economics and Politics. In "State Monopoly Capitalism Is a New Stage in the Development of Monopoly Capitalism," writing under the pseudonym Cai Peitian, then institute director Pu Shan politely begged to differ with the use of the verb "serve":

> I think that it is fully necessary to emphasize that the state organs serve (*fuwu*) monopoly organizations, but it is not proper to replace "merger" (*ronghe*) and "unification" (*jiehe*) of monopoly capital with this kind of wording because the concept of "merger" and "unification" is more plentiful and deeper. It not only includes the meaning that the state serves the monopoly organizations, but it also expresses most concisely the new effect of the state interfering directly in the economy, and it represents the reality of the transformation of finance-monopoly capital into state-monopoly capital. The question is whether monopoly capital is capable of preserving its rule without the state's direct interference in the economy, not that the state monopoly preserves private monopoly or vice versa. . . . We recognize that a state-monopoly bourgeoisie exists, and it is precisely that state political power and the monopoly bourgeoisie are closely merged together (*miqie ronghe zai yiqi*), and this then becomes a bureaucrat-monopoly bourgeoisie. . . . In the period of ordinary monopoly the state is still the representative of the entire monopoly bourgeoisie, but in the period of state-monopoly capitalism the state becomes the representative of the bureaucrat-monopoly bourgeoisie. . . . The system of government of state-monopoly capitalism then becomes a fascist autocracy (*faxisi zhuanzheng*). Under this kind of system the rule of the bureaucrat-monopoly bourgeoisie cannot be concealed.[54]

This perspective was refuted by some subordination thesis commentators. Chen Qiren, professor of political economy in Fudan University's International Politics Department and one of China's leading theorists of imperialism, also wrestled with the semantic problems of the subordination thesis and concluded that "serves" was the most apt term. In his important book on the subject, *Diguozhuyi lilun yanjiu* (Research on theories of imperialism), Chen explained his rationale:

> Concerning the essence of state-monopoly capitalism, the majority of Soviet economists use the wording "unification" (*jiehe*) or "coalescence" (*ronghe*) in describing the relationship between state political power and the monopolies. . . . Our country's economists have discussed this prob-

[54] Cai Peitian, "Guojia longduan zibenzhuyi shi longduan zibenzhuyi fazhan de xin jieduan," *Shijie jingji*, no. 4 (1978): 33, 35.

lem repeatedly. . . . Because these two terms are not precise enough, the wording "the state organs serve the monopoly organizations" (*guojia jiguan fuwu longduan zuzhi*) is increasingly able to eliminate this shortcoming.[55]

When asked in 1983 why he felt the terminology of the unification thesis was inadequate, Professor Chen opined that it did not adequately express the "informal control" (*bu zhengshi de kongzhi*) that the monopolies exercise over the state in state-monopoly capitalism.[56] In 1984 Professor Chen went to the United States for a year of research at Princeton University. By the time he returned to China, his thinking had reverted to the subordination thesis. In 1985 he completed a major study of contemporary imperialism in which he states categorically, "A handful (*yixiaocuo*) of the biggest monopoly capitalists control (*zhangwo*) total political power."[57]

While Chen's first veiled and then not-so-veiled defense of the subordination thesis was typical of university-based specialists, others were more explicit. In a book entitled *Liening de "Diguozhuyilun" he dangdai zibenzhuyi* (Lenin's theory of imperialism and contemporary capitalism), three Sichuan University professors of political economy asserted:

> The state safeguards the total benefits of the entire monopoly capitalist class. . . . It serves the dominant class in the capacities of the pure organs of state power—army, police, judiciary, bureaucracy, etc.—to safeguard the personal assets of the capitalist class, to suppress the resistance of the proletariat, and to consolidate the domination of the capitalist class.[58]

Despite the almost unswerving defense of the subordination thesis by university scholars, they were increasingly isolated by the rising tide of "coalescence" commentary emerging from party and government think tanks. Several of the articles in the CCP Central Committee-sponsored "Forum on Economic Problems of Imperialism" carried in *Hongqi* during 1980–1981 drew attention to the "personal union of big capitalists and government officials," which was central to Hilferding's and Lenin's unification thesis. One article in the *Hongqi* series claimed:

[55] Chen Qiren, *Diguozhuyi lilun yanjiu* (Shanghai: Renmin chubanshe, 1984), pp. 104–5.

[56] Interview at Fudan University, July 6, 1983.

[57] Chen Qiren, *Diguozhuyi jingji yu zhengzhi gailun* (Shanghai: Fudan daxue chubanshe, 1986), p. 211.

[58] Wang Maoxing et al., *Liening de "Diguozhuyilun" he dangdai zibenzhuyi* (Sichuan: Renmin chubanshe, 1982), pp. 188–227.

Formerly monopoly capitalists themselves seldom appeared on the political stage. They relied principally on their managers or agents as their representatives. However, after the [Second World] War, many of the oligarchs found that if they themselves did not personally take charge of the authority of the state, the problems confronting them could hardly be solved. Consequently, some of the monopoly capitalists, while searching for managers, had to climb onto the political stage themselves. . . . It indicates a new development in postwar state-monopoly capitalism.[59]

By late 1981 the polemic had clearly spread to professional research institutes that championed the unification thesis and were willing to go further. Pu Shan's (also known as Cai Peitian) aforementioned discussion in *Shijie jingji* of direct state "interference" in the national economy was a harbinger of later analyses by members of the Institute of World Economics and Politics, Institute of Economics, and other CASS area studies institutes. As the researchers began to study the actual relations of ownership (*suoyouzhi guanxi*) in Western countries, they expressed the view that nationalization of private monopoly industries had become prevalent in Western Europe, Japan, Canada, and the United States. This was an important conceptual breakthrough for such analysis because it implied that the state was an autonomous economic actor. This recognition remained implicit in the writings of CASS staff during 1981 and 1982, but it was not until 1983–1984 that they were willing to assert openly the "relative independence" of the state.

Thus, at first, CASS researchers recognized the autonomy of the state within the context of the unification thesis. This is made clear, for example, in a collaborative work by researchers in the Institute of World Economics and Politics (IWEP), edited by then director and leading theorist Qiu Qihua and written for use as a text in the Central Party School: "The state directly controls (*zhijie zhangwo*) monopoly capital; nationalized monopoly capital and private monopoly capital are thereby unified (*jiehe*)."[60] Thus, in Qiu's inverted thinking it was not the monopolies that controlled the state, but the other way around! In this way Qiu believed that a new form of coalescence had appeared. This view also became a core theme of three other influential books written by the same group of senior IWEP researchers, which included Qian Junrui, Pu Shan, Qiu Qihua, Wang Shouhai,

[59] Tao Dayong, "Zhanhou diguozhuyi guojia jinrong ziben de pengzhang jiqi bianhua," *Hongqi*, no. 19 (1981): 47–48.

[60] Qiu Qihua et al., *Xiandai longduan zibenzhuyi jingji* (Beijing: Zhonggong zhongyang dangxiao chubanshe, 1982), p. 42.

Wang Huaining, Zheng Weimin, Wang Dejun, Chen Dezhao, Li Zong, Lo Chengxi, Jiang Chunzi, Yu Kexing, and others.[61]

This group of IWEP researchers formed the critical mass of political economists and theorists who spearheaded the move away from doctrinaire Stalinist interpretations of capitalist economies and imperialism toward more orthodox Leninist perspectives. Interviews with seven of these individuals confirmed, without exception, their adherence to the unification thesis interpretation of the relationship between the capitalist state and monopolies.[62] As one such researcher succinctly put it, "the unification thesis captures the relative independence which the state enjoys in economic life; the term 'control' is too Stalinist!"[63] Another leading member of this group concurred: "Lenin used the term *ronghe* (coalesce) to describe this relationship for a reason."[64]

After more than a decade of thinking about and writing on the subject, Qiu Qihua reflected his summary views of the state-monopoly relationship in 1990:

> In class terms, the leaders of these countries represent monopoly-financial (*caituan*) interests. But the government does not simply follow the wishes of the *caituan*. This is not factual. The government is not passive. It coordinates the interests of the big *caituan* in order to meet its needs. The state personifies monopoly capital. It has an interest in maintaining the capitalist system as a whole. You can sometimes say that one minister or another represents a specific *caituan*, but not on the whole. You must have a dialectical mind to understand the relationship between the state and the *caituan*. They restrain each other and intrude on each other. . . . The definition of state-monopoly capitalism is the merger (*jiehe*) of the state and monopoly capital.[65]

The CASS Institute of Economics staff also played a key role in the state-monopoly capitalism polemic. Some of them, however, rejected not only Stalinist interpretations, but Leninist ones as well. They went beyond the unification thesis to analyze the specific composition of monopoly groups in the advanced capitalist countries. These

[61] Qian Junrui, ed., *Zibenzhuyi yu shehuizhuyi zonghetan* (Beijing: Shijie zhishi chubanshe, 1983); Fan Kang, ed., *Zibenzhuyi xingshuai shi* (Beijing: Beijing chubanshe, 1984); Wang Huaining, ed., *Shijie jingji yu zhengzhi gailun* (Beijing: Shijie zhishi chubanshe, 1989).

[62] Interviews with CASS Institute of World Economics and Politics staff, October 20, 1983; October 25, 1983; October 20, 1984; December 10, 1984; December 24, 1984; May 25, 1985; January 11, 1990; May 9, 1990.

[63] Interview at the CASS Institute of World Economics and Politics, May 25, 1985.

[64] Interview at the CASS Institute of World Economics and Politics, May 10, 1990.

[65] Interview with Qiu Qihua at the Central Party School, May 17, 1990.

researchers discovered intense competition within an internally divided monopoly bourgeoisie, thus staking out a third distinct image of state-monopoly capitalism. This was reflected in the "Forum on Contemporary Imperialism" articles carried in the Institute's journal *Jingji yanjiu*. The lead article in this series, for example, stated categorically:

> For the purpose of improving their own competitive position in the fierce struggle for the dominant position, the important monopoly groups all strive to control the state apparatus. The state becomes the target of open struggle between these important monopoly groups, which inevitably increases the close unification of the interests of the state and monopoly capital.[66]

Several other forum articles reiterated the view that the increased nationalization of industries by the capitalist state since the Second World War did signify that state-monopoly capitalism was a qualitatively distinct and new stage in capitalism's general development,[67] whereby the state intervened in the economy to protect the interests of the monopolies.[68]

The CASS area studies institutes—the Japan Institute, America Institute, West European Institute—have been the major contributors to studies of the structural and functional fragmentation of monopolies in the advanced capitalist countries. These institutes have published numerous studies of various aspects of specific capitalist economies. Both monopoly and nonmonopoly actors, in both the public and private sectors, have been examined. Significant among these is the state (i.e., government) itself. These analysts recognize that the capitalist state is not a monolithic entity, but that power and authority are geographically dispersed and institutionally devolved. In so doing, they go beyond the unificationists' recognition of the state acting as an autonomous entity under conditions of coalescence with the monopolies. Instead, they are more explicit about the state's independence as an economic and political actor. As a result, they expend their analytical energy examining the internal functioning of

[66] Qiu Qihua et al., "Lun yiban longduan zibenzhuyi zhuanbian wei guojia longduan zibenzhuyi," *Jingji yanjiu*, no. 11 (1981): 54.

[67] Gan Dangshan, "Cong suoyouzhi kan guojia longduan zibenzhuyi," in *Lun dangdai diguozhuyi*, pp. 131–47; Zhang Youwen and Chu Baoyi, "Lun zibenzhuyi fazhan de xin jieduan," pp. 148–61; Gong Weijing, "Guojia longduan zibenzhuyi shi zibenzhuyi fazhan de 'xin jieduan' ma?," pp. 162–77.

[68] Liu Yonghui, "Shi lun longduan duiyu diguozhuyi jingji fazhan shuangzhong zuoyong," *Jingji yanjiu*, no. 4 (1981): 69.

the state apparatus. This fourth view of the state's independent role, in the case of the United States, is evident in the next two chapters.

The area studies institutes were not the only ones in CASS to recognize explicitly the independence of the capitalist state. Even Su Shaozhi, the director of the Institute of Marxism–Leninism–Mao Zedong Thought, was able to proclaim in 1983 that

> The contemporary capitalist state plays the role of protecting the organism of society and ensuring the entire process of expanded reproduction. Such a state is at once a capitalist state and one independent of the various strata of the capitalist class. The emergence of such a kind of modern state makes it necessary to reappraise Lenin's thesis of the state being purely an instrument for exploiting the oppressed classes. And in the developed capitalist countries it is no longer necessary for the socialist revolution to smash the existing state machine. . . . Confronted as we are with the new characteristics of the contemporary capitalist state, we should undoubtedly pay adequate attention to the question of how the Communist parties in different countries ought to explore, in the light of actual realities in their own countries, the specific roads of the socialist revolution there.[69]

Coming as it did from one of China's leading and most maverick Marxist theorists, such an analysis is extremely significant not only on theoretical grounds, because of its explicit repudiation of Lenin's analysis of the capitalist state, but also on policy grounds, because of the implications for China's relations with other Communist parties. Su's references elsewhere in this speech to Gramsci, Marcuse, Althusser, Giddens, Dahrendorf, and others reveal that some Chinese Marxists were beginning to examine some of the post-Stalinist theories of the state written in Europe and the United States that had so influenced the tactics of European Communist parties to seek political power through democratic means, including power-sharing with "bourgeois" parties.

Even though the Chinese Communist Party has argued since the Sino-Soviet split for "independent paths to socialism," Chinese Marxist theorists have displayed remarkable ignorance of the writings of European Marxists despite their professed interest in "Eurocommunism." Except for this speech by Su Shaozhi, Chinese theorists appear totally unaware of Western theories of the state—Marxist or otherwise. I have found no evidence of the works of Poulantzas, Miliband, Gramsci, and so forth in translation or referred to in Chinese theoretical writings. Nor does the work of Domhoff, Mill, or other neo-Marxist American elite theorists appear in Chinese

---

[69] Su Shaozhi, "Developing Marxism under Contemporary Conditions," pp. 28–29.

publications. Indeed, a graduate seminar on "Theories of Imperialism" in the International Politics Department at Beijing University during 1984 did not introduce any of these theorists and only touched on Galtung's dependency theory as something worthy of "further investigation." Until Su Shaozhi's speech on the centenary of Marx's death, Chinese theorists were busy regurgitating only the Soviet classics.

Thus, in the polemic on state-monopoly capitalism, Chinese Marxist theorists articulated four distinct views: subordination, unification/coalescence, monopoly fragmentation, and state autonomy. The data for the latter are extensive and are found in analyses of various capitalist countries. The analyses of state autonomy in the United States are evidenced in the following chapters.

Perspectives on the Polemics

What has been seen in the polemics on both imperialism and state-monopoly capitalism is more of an evolution of views than competing groups staking out unchangeable positions. To be sure, certain contributors to these debates stuck hard to their positions, but as a community these analysts exhibited a learning curve. Their views evolved in stages that frequently overlapped. While there was a clear evolution of views over time, it would not be accurate to conclude that these debates reflected zero-sum rejections of one interpretation by another. Different views coexist, even though the center of theoretical gravity shifted over time (see table 2.2).

Some interesting institutional affiliations of the contributors to these polemics have also been noted, and here one senses more competing perspectives than an evolution. In both polemics it was clear that the Stalinist perspective was articulated by a combination of university-based and some senior party theorists. This was a determinist perspective. On the longevity of imperialism this cohort argued imperialism's imminent death. For them, "moribund" was taken literally. Similarly, this cohort argued the Stalinist subordination thesis in the state-monopoly capitalism polemic. They took the view that the working class in imperialist countries was "absolutely impoverished" and ready to throw off its chains and rise up in revolution.

The other main opinion group to emerge from these polemics was a Leninist one. By invoking Lenin, and in some cases explicitly rebuking Stalin, this group argued for doctrinal flexibility. Their perspective is that imperialism and imperialist countries are here to stay as they noted imperialism's continued "life" and "strength." But in

Table 2.2
Differences in Stalinist and Leninist Opinion Groups

Issue	Stalinists	Leninists
Moribund imperialism	Imminent death	Longevity, slow death
State-monopoly relationship	Subordination thesis	Unification thesis
Impoverishment of proletariat	Absolute impoverishment	Relative impoverishment
Institutions	Universities, Central Party School	CASS institutes

recognizing this, these theorists could not offer the heretical view that Lenin's sacrosanct theory of imperialism was wrong or outdated. Rather, they cloaked their analyses of imperialism in Lenin's theory. They similarly argued the thesis of "relative impoverishment" of the proletariat and the rise of the middle class. With respect to state-monopoly capitalism the Leninists primarily argued the "unification/coalescence" thesis (again citing Lenin), although some went much further to argue monopoly fragmentation and state autonomy. These latter perspectives will become more apparent in subsequent chapters.

The Leninist opinion group was institutionally anchored in the Chinese Academy of Social Sciences, particularly the Institute of World Economics and Politics, but important contributions came from the Institute of Economics and Institute of Marxism–Leninism–Mao Zedong Thought. These institutes at CASS were instrumental in forging consensus and revisionist views that eventually held the day in Chinese Marxist theoretical circles, despite some recalcitrant holdouts in the universities.

The significance of the victory of the Leninists in these two polemics should be viewed not only in the context of these two issues, but also in the fact that they introduced analytical flexibility in their analyses of the state vis-à-vis the monopoly bourgeoisie that, in turn, permitted area studies specialists like the America Watchers to argue state autonomy. As will be seen in chapter 5, the America Watchers disaggregate the state apparatus to study bureaucratic politics. This would also have been impossible under previously prevailing conditions of the subordination thesis. Similarly, the recognition that the science and technological revolution had helped stave off imperialism's collapse, and that repeated economic crises were not leading ipso facto to Stalin's "general crisis of capitalism," but rather that the capitalist economy demonstrated resiliency, also permitted area studies economists to examine the inner workings of capitalism much more closely. In foreign policy terms, the recognition that war was no longer inevitable between capitalist states was another marked departure from both Leninism and Stalinism.

Finally, the polemics on imperialism and state-monopoly capitalism offered the ideological rationale for China's opening to the West. They offered the justification for a policy of peaceful coexistence rather than intractable class struggle between two opposed systems. As long as imperialism continued to show signs of "life" and the capitalist state was no longer controlled by the monopoly bourgeoisie, it was not ideological capitulationism to deal with imperialist states.

Chinese Concepts of Hegemony

The term "hegemony" (baquanzhuyi) in the Chinese lexicon goes far back into Chinese history. In modern times, the term has become particularly pronounced in Chinese assessments of international affairs during the post-Mao era. It was first used in 1968 to criticize the Soviet invasion of Czechoslovakia and the "Brezhnev Doctrine." Thereafter, hegemony became the codeword to refer to Soviet foreign policy. Prior to the Czech invasion the Soviet Union had been variously referred to as "social-imperialist" (socialist in word, imperialist in deed) or "revisionist." As one of China's leading specialists on the Soviet Union put it,

> "Revisionism" was used to describe ideological deviation, countries whose leaders departed from the socialist road; "social-imperialism" was originally used by Lenin in his criticism of the Second International, but we used it to refer to Soviet policies of oppression (yapo) and interference (ganshe) in the internal affairs of other countries. By the early 1970s we began to fuse (ronghe) social-imperialism together with hegemonism.[70]

Thus, throughout the decade of the 1970s when one saw the term hegemonism or hegemonist in the Chinese press, it was reasonably sure to refer to the Soviet Union.[71] Beginning in the 1980s, however, Chinese commentators began to use the term to refer to American foreign policy as well (see chapter 6).

[70] Interview at the CASS Institute of Soviet and East European Studies, May 7, 1990.
[71] In 1978–1979 the term "regional hegemonist" also began to appear with reference to Vietnam and Cuba.

How do Chinese define hegemonism? Virtually all references in Chinese writings on international affairs define the term in the context of one or another nation's foreign policy. Unlike the polemics on imperialism and state-monopoly capitalism where extensive debates took place over definitional issues, such is not the case with hegemony. Almost all references are contextual. Therefore, to ascertain how the Chinese define hegemony and the philosophical and historical origins of the concept in Chinese thought, I interviewed a number of Chinese historians, philosophers, and scholars of literature, politics, and international relations.

Definitions of Hegemony

Scholars at the CASS Institute of Soviet and East European Studies defined hegemonism as "A country that imposes its will onto another sovereign country, so that the policies of country Y will serve the interests of country X. There are cultural, military, economic, political, and ideological means of hegemony."[72] An America Watcher at the CASS Institute of American Studies said, "I define hegemonism as interference in internal affairs, but it may also be considered as expansionism. Hegemony is when a country imposes its system, ideas, and way of life upon other countries. Imperialism refers to capitalist countries while hegemonism refers to countries regardless of system."[73]

A scholar in the International Politics Department at People's University reflected,

> Many people use the term hegemony, but few define it. In China when we use this term we mean big countries that try to control or interfere in smaller acountries. Many scholars mix up imperialism and hegemony. We do not know if it is a system or a policy. Before the 1980s we thought it was a system, like Soviet social-imperialism. We now define hegemony as a policy. For example, in the past when we called the United States imperialist we meant the system; today we use hegemony to describe its foreign policy.[74]

A leading international relations theorist at the CASS Institute of World Economics and Politics defined hegemony as "oppressing other countries politically, controlling them economically, subjecting

[72] Interview at the CASS Institute of Soviet and East European Studies, May 7, 1990.

[73] Interview at CASS Institute of American Studies, May 7, 1990.

[74] Interview at the Department of International Politics, People's University, May 11, 1990.

them to big-power chauvinism, and intimidation by military power. In short, it is power politics." His colleague added, "Hegemony is a policy, not a system, not a stage. It requires an expansionist mentality. Only when real communism is realized, with no classes and no states, will there be no hegemony. The current unequal international order is a hegemonic one."[75]

Analysts at the Institute of Contemporary International Relations also stressed the imposition of one's will as the defining quality of hegemonism. Said one, "Hegemony means imposing one's own will on others in order to seek privilege in international affairs. In the past, seeking hegemony was mainly demonstrated in gunboat diplomacy. Gunboat diplomacy was military hegemony, but I think that this was a means to the end of political hegemony. For the past century China has been subjected to hegemonism, so when the term is used today all Chinese know what it means." His colleague disagreed: "I see no difference between old and new forms of hegemonism in its essence. Although the means have changed, hegemonism is a comprehensive concept of military, ideological, political, and ideological intrusion."[76]

What do Chinese scholars see as the sources of hegemonism? An analyst at the Beijing Institute for International Strategic Studies noted three criteria for qualifying as a hegemonist: (1) strong military power; (2) a traditional nature of aggression toward others; (3) the big bullying the small.[77] An America Watcher at the Institute of American Studies opined that "Desire for power is most important. Big powers inevitably become expansionist and hegemonist."[78]

Thus, a range of definitions of hegemony is offered by Chinese international affairs specialists in a variety of research institutes. The common denominator is the strong imposing their will on the weak. Several analysts mentioned interference in internal affairs as the sine qua non of hegemony. Many noted military subjugation as the key manifestation, but several also noted nonmilitary means. Can a nation still be considered hegemonist if it does not use military means to control others? Most would agree that nonforceful means of control are equally effective (and less noticeable), but in the case of the Soviet Union one scholar at the Institute of Contemporary International Relations confessed, "Since the 1960s we said the Soviet Union was hegemonist because it invaded countries. But since the withdrawal from Afghanistan the Soviets have publicly recognized mis-

[75] Interviews at CASS Institute of World Economics and Politics, May 10, 1990.
[76] Interviews at the Institute of Contemporary International Relations, May 17, 1990.
[77] Interview at the Beijing Institute for International Strategic Studies, May 9, 1990.
[78] Interview at CASS Institute of American Studies, May 7, 1990.

takes, and thus they have stopped a policy of hegemony. We can now say they are no longer hegemonist!"[79]

Hegemony and China's Worldview

While some made explicit China's history of being subjected to hegemonist aggression, all would agree with that viewpoint. The "century of humiliation" is indelibly etched on the psyches of most Chinese and, importantly, serves as the most fundamental of all reference points in modern China's worldview. Therefore, the reason Chinese analysts of international affairs use hegemony as a key element in their analyses is directly linked to modern China's own historical experience. Not being able to rule their own country after centuries of relative insulation had a traumatic effect on generations of modern Chinese. It is no accident that when Chairman Mao proclaimed the founding of the People's Republic on October 1, 1949, his first words were, "The Chinese people have stood up!" There certainly exists a potentially large propaganda windfall to be gained from other developing countries who have similarly been subjected to outside aggression, colonialism, and neocolonialism, but the importance of this element in the Chinese worldview is genuine and not to be underestimated.

The Chinese are among the most vocal proponents of the doctrine of state sovereignty on the world stage today and have real difficulty coming to terms with the realities of the interdependent world of the late twentieth century. One gets the sense that China wishes the world would return to the Westfalian state system of reified sovereignty found in sixteenth-century Europe.[80] One sees the notion of immutable state sovereignty expressed in many Chinese foreign policy pronouncments, not the least of which are the hallowed "Five Principles of Peaceful Coexistence."

Thus, the use of hegemony has its roots in China's modern historical experience, and not only in Chinese analysts' perception of world affairs. The history of the concept of hegemony in Chinese thought, however, far predates the Soviet invasion of Czechoslovakia or the "century of humiliation." It literally dates from the Spring and Autumn period of 722 to 481 B.C.

The character ba (霸), which is the root of the term for hegemony

[79] Interview at Institute of Contemporary International Relations, May 17, 1990.

[80] For an elaboration of this theme and how it relates to Chinese concepts of imperialism and hegemony see my "The Soviet Influence on the Chinese Worldview," *The Australian Journal of Chinese Affairs*, forthcoming.

(baquanzhuyi), stems from traditional Chinese political thought and appears in a variety of ancient historical records. Baquanzhuyi comes from baquan, literally, the "powerful ruler." But baquan derives from badao, to rule by force. Since the Warring States period (468–221 B.C.), badao has usually been juxtaposed against wangdao (benevolent rule) in Chinese thought.[81]

While linguistically derivative, contemporary uses of hegemony and the earliest uses of the term are not conceptually the same. Initially, ba did not have a derogatory connotation. Only after the Warring States did it assume a negative meaning.

During the Spring and Autumn period, when the Zhou dynasty was declining, ba was used to refer to the leaders of the major feudal states that, in times of dynastic decline, intervened to stabilize the empire, resist foreign invasion, and maintain order within its borders.[82] Thus, the use of force to unify the empire was thought legitimate. In the Analects, Confucius (551–479 B.C.) referred positively to the five hegemons (wu ba) by praising Guanzhong, the leader of the Qi state: "Without Guanzhong the Chinese nation would not have survived." Confucius also wrote that a good hegemon combined the necessary use of force with benevolence (renyi).

Mencius (c. 372–289 B.C.), a leading Confucian disciple, disagreed with the Master. Mencius criticized Guanzhong (and Confucius's praise of him) as a mere hegemonic feudal lord (bazhu) who ruled only through might. In this context Mencius was the first to distinguish rule by force (badao) from benevolent rule (which he variously referred to as renyi, wangdao, and renzheng) and hence coined the wangdao/badao distinction. It was Mencius who developed the notion of humane government in early Chinese political thought. "The people turn to a humane ruler as water flows downward or wild beasts take to the wilderness. Win the people's hearts, and the Mandate of Heaven will be yours," said Mencius.

Later the Legalists, particularly Han Feizi (died c. 233 B.C.), praised ba and the use of force as a legitimate means to unify China and in so doing fused it with rule through law. To pursue ba was to pursue fa(zhi) or law. The neo-Confucianists (with whom the Legalists were debating how to unify and rule China) would have none of it. For

---

[81] The following discussion on ba is particularly informed by interviews conducted at the CASS Institute of Philosophy, May 10, 1990, and the CASS Institute of History, May 11, 1990. I also wish to thank Deborah Porter for her assistance in tracing the literary origins of ba.

[82] Thus, the first references to ba are to be found in the Zuozhuan. For an English translation see Burton Watson, The Tso Chuan: Selections from China's Oldest Narrative History (New York: Columbia University Press, 1989).

them, benevolence (*wangdao*) was the only legitimate method of unification and rule. This they defined in terms of morality (*de*) and principle/rites (*li*). It had nothing to do with artificial constructs like law.

In associating hegemony (*ba*) with law (*fa*), the Legalists also invoked punishment (*xing*) as the legitimate use of force. This concept is also to be found in ancient Chinese writings on just or "righteous" war (*yizhan*).[83] Several military texts (*bingfa*) from the Warring States period discuss the hegemon's role in carrying out a just war against an errant and unrighteous feudal lord. Perception of unbenevolent and immoral rule, of which there were a number of criteria, is therefore the basis of waging a just war. In this context, the use of hegemonic force is thought entirely legitimate.

Thus, the concept of hegemony dates to early Chinese history and thought and has to do with concepts of proper governance. After the Warring States and down through the ages, to resort to force or coercion was thought profoundly illegitimate and tyrannical.

This philosophical background therefore underlies Chinese analyses of contemporary international relations. Today Chinese frequently use the idiom *heng xing badao*, to act as a tyrant and lord it over another,[84] or simply *baquanzhuyi* when referring to the superpowers or other "regional hegemonists." This will become operational in chapter 6 when we examine Chinese perceptions of American foreign policy, but it is important to establish the philosophical and linguistic origins of the term here in order to understand fully the broader role that the concept of hegemony plays in China's world view.

Summary

The Chinese concepts of imperialism, state-monopoly capitalism, and hegemony examined in this chapter together form the ideological base upon which many specific Chinese analyses of the American superstructure are derived. This chapter traced discussions and subtle debates in the sphere of ideological orthodoxy related to the Chinese Marxist understanding of the capitalist world. In the cases of imperialism and state-monopoly capitalism there were important analytical departures from a dogmatic Stalinist past and a redressing of orthodox theory to accompany changes in Chinese government pol-

---

[83] I am indebted to Alastair I. Johnston for sharing with me his research findings on this subject, which derive from his broader study of Chinese strategic culture.

[84] *Han-Ying chengyu he changyong ci* (Gansu: Renmin chubanshe, 1979), p. 207.

icy. While significant departures in Chinese terms, it is important to note that Chinese Marxist thought (at least in these two cases) does not join, engage, or contribute to a more general body of international Marxist thought. There has been much work of a fairly sophisticated theoretical nature done on the questions of imperialism and state-monopoly capitalism in Europe, Latin America, the United States, and the Soviet Union over the past two decades, but Chinese Marxists show no awareness of this literature and instead are busy regurgitating debates that took place in the Soviet Union thirty-five to forty years ago.

In the case of hegemony, Chinese international affairs specialists remain conceptually rooted even more distantly in their nation's past. The concept of hegemony has operational meanings in the contemporary world, but it philosophically derives from ancient Chinese concepts of governance. The world of the late twentieth century is no longer reducible to mere *wangdao/badao* terms.

With these ideological foundations in mind, the chapters that follow will consider how these concepts become operational in the context of China's America Watchers' perceptions of the United States.

Three

The American Economy

OF ALL ASPECTS of the United States, the economy commands the greatest attention among China's America Watchers. A larger cadre focus on this aspect than on any other, and, in sheer volume, analyses of the American economy dominate Chinese publications about the United States. This chapter taps into this vast literature by exploring the Marxists' and non-Marxists' contrasting perceptions of four aspects of the American economy. The first two best capture the Marxist critique, while the latter two are of primary concern to the non-Marxists.

First, I will examine images of American monopoly capitalism and state-monopoly capitalism. This subject is fundamental to the Marxists' perceptions of American economic and political life. Chapter 5 will explore the impact of monopolies on American political life; the discussion here will thus include only the evolution of American monopolies over time and their relationship to the American economy.

Second, I will discuss the Marxists' images of "crises" in the American economy. The concept of economic crises (*jingji weiji*) holds particular significance in Marxist political economy because it is such crises that supposedly strain the capitalist economy to its breaking point, exacerbating social tensions and thus stimulating a social revolution led by the proletariat to overthrow the capitalist system. Marxists have long held that each "partial" crisis would inexorably lead the capitalist economy in question progressively closer to a "general crisis," at which point revolution would take place. From 1979 to 1982 Chinese Marxists waged a heated debate among themselves over the question of why the repeated crises that had afflicted the American economy had not brought about its collapse. The participants in this debate divided into two camps—Stalinist and Leninist. I will examine the respective positions of each group and note the interpretation that emerged triumphant.

Third, I will look at the America Watchers' interpretations of the U.S. economy during the Carter administration. During this period, the non-Marxists began to emerge as a distinct school of interpretation. They began to use the print media and professional scholarly publications to articulate their views. The non-Marxists' primary interest lies in interpreting current events, and they do so in a largely atheoretical manner that presents the facts to their readership—be it the mass public or top leadership—in a straightforward manner. This does not mean that their commentaries are not negative or critical; indeed, most of them are. Their analyses of various facets of Carter administration policies that attempted to deal with "stagflation," high interest rates, and the like are critical in tone and substance but nonideological in presentation. This section therefore examines this commentary on a range of economic issues confronting the United States during the Carter years.

Fourth, I will do the same for the Reagan administration. By the time President Reagan assumed office—the Chinese term it "mounting the throne" (shangtai)—the U.S. economy was entering a severe recession, which would only worsen. Would Reagan have any new formulas for setting the economy right? The non-Marxists were fascinated with the "economic recovery program" that Reagan announced soon after taking office, but they were particularly intrigued by the "supply-side" economic theories that underlay this program. They devoted much ink to analyzing this program and its theoretical underpinnings. The non-Marxists concluded that the economic future of the United States was not too bright despite the economy's strong rebound from recession. One development in particular could change this, however: the "new technological revolution." Here one begins to see evidence of the one issue that the Chinese have long admired about the United States—advanced science and technology.

Taken together, the America Watchers' perspectives on these four issues offer a fairly comprehensive assessment of their perceptions of the American economy.

Marxist Perspectives on the American Economy I: Monopoly and State-Monopoly Capitalism in the United States

The vast majority of the Marxist School of China's America Watchers are in agreement that monopoly capitalism in the United States began with the rapid industrialization of the late nineteenth century. They also believe that state-monopoly capitalism can be dated from the New Deal when the government directly intervened in the economy, although many think that it accelerated greatly during and since World War II with the advent of the military-industrial complex. Thus, according to these analysts, the United States practiced "free capitalism" (ziyou zibenzhuyi) for the first century of its existence, has been a "monopoly capitalist" nation for the last century, and a "state-monopoly capitalist" country for the last sixty years.

These are important benchmarks for distinguishing broad stages during the last century of American economic development. Within these stages, however, the Marxists have noted substantial change in the composition and strength of individual monopoly financial groups (*longduan caituan*) and in the evolving relationship between these groups and the U.S. government. The vast majority of Chinese writings on these stages are concerned with the post–World War II period of state-monopoly capitalism. Only a handful of analyses deal with the transition from "free capitalism" to monopoly capitalism in the late nineteenth century and the evolution of the latter during the early twentieth century.

The Rise of Monopoly Capitalism in America

The American economy was depicted as dominated by agriculture and small, light-industrial enterprises before the Civil War. Markets were competitive, capital and property ownership was decentralized, transportation and communications were primitive, and so forth. According to many Chinese historians, the United States was in a pre-industrial stage of development, a "free capitalist" stage of unregulated barter and unexploitative relations of production.[1]

The Civil War changed all this. In the Chinese view, it fundamentally altered the nature of the U.S. economy by spurring an industrial revolution. Munitions and war materiel were needed. The armies of North and South needed not only cannon fodder, but cannons. Ships made of iron were built for the first time. Raw materials were mined and processed into metals, agriculture became mechanized, and so on.

The Civil War marked not only the expansion and initial industrialization (*gongyehua*) of the American economy, but, more important from a Marxist perspective, also the advent of the centralization (*jizhong*) of ownership of the means of production.[2] Property holdings,

---

[1] For typical expositions of this view and description of the pre–Civil War U.S. economy, see Huang Shaoxiang, *Meiguo jiaoshi jianbian* (Beijing: Renmin chubanshe, 1979), chapter 4; Luo Ruihua, *Meiguo nanbei zhanzheng* (Beijing: Shangwu yinshuguan, 1973), chapter 2; Liu Zuochang, *Meiguo neizhanshi* (Beijing: Renmin chubanshe, 1978), chapter 2.

[2] In Chinese the term *jizhong* (which is a basic term used throughout this literature and the discussion in this chapter) translates as both concentration and centralization. I therefore use the English terms interchangeably.

capital, and equipment began to be monopolized by a relatively small number of families, which also gained controlling interest in banks. As the economy began to make the transition from light to heavy industry, the American class structure accordingly changed from one dominated by the petty bourgeoisie to the monopoly bourgeoisie.

The transition to monopoly capitalism was thus the process of concentration of the productive forces and capital stimulated by rapid industrialization during the last three decades of the nineteenth century. A standard study of world economic history edited by two leading economists at the CASS lists three main causes for this high degree of concentration: (1) the ability of American industry to develop and adapt the newest technological innovations to production, and thereby expand productive enterprises; (2) fierce competition that eliminated inefficient producers; and (3) the advent of capitalist "economic crises" beginning in 1873, which hit small enterprises the hardest and stimulated the process of "big fish eating small fish" (da yu chi xiao yu), that is, takeovers.[3]

This process of capital concentration primarily took the form of mergers (hebing) and trusts (tuolasi). Chinese analysts use these terms interchangeably to mean generally the combination of firms to reduce competition through monopoly. The first trust formed was the Rockefellers' Standard Oil Corporation of America (Meifu Shiyou Gongsi), which "controlled" 90 percent of the U.S. oil industry. Oil was not the only commodity dominated by trusts. By 1888 seven companies "dominated" the mining of soft coal, and more than 80 percent of liquor production was "controlled" by the "whiskey trust."[4] In 1890 the U.S. Congress passed the Sherman Anti-Trust Act, but it was seen as having little effect on slowing down the formation of large trusts. In fact, in his study Meiguo longduan ziben jizhong (The centralization of American monopoly capital), Fudan University professor and noted Marxist America Watcher Gong Weijing points out that the year 1899 witnessed a greater number of mergers than any other until the late 1960s.[5]

By the turn of the century nearly every major American industry was "controlled" by a trust. In 1899, 440 trusts accounted for two-thirds of the total production of industrial products, and one-third of all banking capital was in the hands of seven families. On this basis, CASS America Watchers Fan Kang and Song Zexing concluded that

[3] Fan Kang and Song Zexing, eds., Waiguo jingjishi, vol. 2 (Beijing: Renmin chubanshe, 1982), p. 49.

[4] Ibid., p. 50.

[5] Gong Weijing, Meiguo longduan ziben jizhong (Beijing: Renmin chubanshe, 1986), pp. 8–9.

"by the time the nineteenth century changed to the twentieth, trusts had already established themselves as the dominant force in American economic life."[6]

The corporate concentration of production and capital continued during the first two decades of the twentieth century. More trusts were formed that were dominated by families such as Morgan in railroads, Du Pont in chemicals, and Ford and Chrysler in automobiles. When the American Railroad Corporation (which was owned by the Morgan family) took over several smaller railway companies in 1901 it became America's largest trust, surpassing the Rockefellers in total financial holdings.

But the Morgans and Rockefellers were not alone. Fan Kang and Song Zexing argued that "by the early twentieth century eight big financial groups not only 'dominated' the entire domestic economy, but also manipulated the government, controlled the entire national political life, and decided the nation's domestic and foreign policies." As seen in chapter 2 (and will again be apparent in chapter 5), this determinist position is an example of the orthodox Stalinist camp within the Marxist School of America Watchers, that is, the monopoly financial groups "control" the economic and political life of the nation. The "eight big financial groups" to which the authors refer, and their principal holdings, are given in table 3.1.[7]

These eight groups began to amass their wealth and holdings during the late 1800s and would continue as the dominant monopolies during the first half of the twentieth century. Their lifeblood was industry, but their financial holdings in banks increased greatly during

Table 3.1
Holdings of U.S. Monopoly Financial Groups

Financial Group	Principal Holdings
Morgan	Railroads, banking
Rockefeller	Oil, gas, banking
Kuhn-Loeb	Railroads, banking
Du Pont	Munitions, chemicals, automobiles
Mellon	Aluminium, coal, railroads, banking
Cleveland	Iron ore, metallurgy, machinery
Chicago	Banking, iron and steel, oil, agricultural equipment, railroads
Boston	Banking, textiles, shoes, fruit, light industry

Source: Fan Kang and Song Zexing, *Waiguo jingjishi*, p. 51.

[6] Fan Kang and Song Zexing, *Waiguo jingjishi*, p. 51.
[7] Ibid., p. 56.

the first decade of the twentieth century. Each caituan was composed of several magnates and tycoons. One American historian at Beijing Normal University estimated that altogether sixty families constituted the "ruling financial oligarchy."[8]

It is this combination of industrial and banking capital that Hilferding, Lenin, and others referred to as "finance capital"—a key ingredient in making the United States an "imperialist" country around this time. In addition to the formation of monopolies and finance capital, the other key indicator of America's imperialist character was economic expansion overseas. The falling rate of profit due to a shrinking domestic market forced the monopolies—and the governments they controlled—to expand overseas in search of new markets and higher profits. In their study of the U.S. economy CASS economists Fan Kang and Song Zexing note that the decade of the 1880s was the first time that more capital flowed out of the United States than into it.[9] This trend would continue for a century.

With the rapid formation of monopolies, the fusing of industrial and bank capital, and economic expansion abroad, the United States now possessed all the attributes of a classic imperialist power according to the Leninist definition in *Imperialism, the Highest Stage of Capitalism*. It was only a matter of time before the United States would clash militarily over conflicting economic interests with other imperialist powers.

This came in 1898. China's America Watchers of the Marxist persuasion agree with Fan and Song that "the world's first colonial imperialist war—the Spanish-American War—was started by the United States."[10] The United States started the war, according to historian Huang Shaoxiang, "because the American monopoly capitalist groups wanted to seize a huge sum of profits." Most of this imperial aggression was directed against Latin America and the Philippines, but according to Professor Huang it also caused the United States to step up its economic expansion in China under the pretext of the Open Door Policy whereby the United States cooperated with European powers to "divide" China.[11]

The First World War was the second example of an interimperialist war. According to Professor Huang's standard text on American history, while European imperialist powers (England, France, Germany, Russia) started the war and the United States initially took a "neutral" position, American monopoly capitalists eventually maneu-

---

[8] Huang Annian, *Ershishiji Meiguoshi* (Hebei: Renmin chubanshe, 1989), p. 48.

[9] Fan Kang and Song Zexing, *Waiguo jingjishi*, p. 63.

[10] Ibid., p. 68.

[11] Huang Shaoxiang, *Meiguo jiaoshi jianbian*, pp. 357, 360.

vered the United States into the war for three reasons: to improve military capability; because of "contradictions" with the European imperialist powers; and because the U.S. economy was stagnating and the heavy industrial sector—particularly steel and munitions—needed a boost.[12] Historian Huang Annian concurs and argues that American neutrality was merely a convenient way of buying time while the "monopolists' war industries" geared up.[13]

The First World War served the monopolists' purposes well. Industrial production in America's heartland boomed, thus benefiting the Cleveland, Chicago, and Morgan financial groups. Du Pont became a major producer of munitions, including chemical weapons. Overall industrial production rose during the war years by 32 percent, but the war-related industries (steel, munitions, chemicals, vehicles, shipbuilding) grew at rates of 70–90 percent.[14]

Not only did the increased production fill the caituan coffers, but the war also stimulated further centralization of monopoly capital. The capital holdings of the one hundred largest family-held corporations in the United States increased by 59 percent during the war years.[15] The grip of the monopoly capitalists on the overall economy had tightened.

The war also stimulated further overseas investment by American monopolists. The export of U.S. capital overseas between 1914 and 1919 doubled from $35 million to $70 million.[16]

All in all, the war had been a tremendous boon to the American monopoly capitalists. But no sooner was the war over than the U.S. economy was hit by another economic "crisis" in 1920–1921. The entire economy contracted. The industries that had boomed during the war years now suffered heavy drops in production: iron minus 74 percent, steel minus 77 percent, munitions minus 69 percent, chemicals minus 50 percent.[17] Inflation rose and wages dropped. America's economic crisis triggered a worldwide recession, but it was brief. By 1923 output levels had been restored to their prewar levels, and growth continued throughout the decade. Monopolists reaped ever larger profits.

Then came the crash of the stock market in 1929 and the ensuing Great Depression. Whereas the previous ten economic crises that the American economy had endured were "intermediate" (zhong), this

[12] Ibid., pp. 434–35.

[13] Huang Annian, Ershishiji Meiguoshi, p. 97.

[14] Fan Kang and Song Zexing, Waiguo jingjishi, p. 69.

[15] Gong Weijing, Meiguo longduan ziben jizhong, p. 22.

[16] Ibid., p. 21; Fan Kang and Song Zexing, Waiguo jingjishi, p. 71.

[17] Fan Kang and Song Zexing, Waiguo jingjishi, 3:33.

one was "comprehensive" (*zhengger*). Total industrial production during the five-year crisis (1929–1933) dropped 55.6 percent to the output levels of 1905–1906; agricultural production dropped by 60 percent; eighty-six thousand businesses went bankrupt; workers' wages plummeted 35–40 percent; and more than thirteen million families were unemployed.[18]

This was the worst crisis the capitalist world had ever faced. Monopoly capitalism itself, as a system, was threatened. Drastic measures were called for.

The answer was Roosevelt's New Deal. There is no doubt among Marxist School commentators that the New Deal was a plot hatched by the monopoly bourgeoisie in an attempt to regain their lost holdings. The America Watchers have written much about the New Deal; I will confine my discussion to the mainstream interpretation exemplified by New Deal specialist and Wuhan University historian Liu Xuyi.

The historical significance of the New Deal, according to Professor Liu, is that the United States began the transition from a "monopoly capitalist" economy to a "state-monopoly capitalist" economy. Hoover attempted to deal with this crisis as previous presidents had, that is, through a policy of noninterference by government in the private-sector economy, which was dominated by the monopoly capitalists.[19] Roosevelt's defeat of Hoover in the 1932 election, however, revealed a public mandate for state interference in the domestic economy.

Roosevelt's New Deal policies for the first time directly involved the federal government in banking, industry, agriculture, public works, social welfare, labor markets, and so forth. The overconcentration of capital was to be prevented through instituting a progressive tax system. At face value the New Deal appeared to strike a blow at monopoly capitalism, but in the long term it benefited the entire bourgeoisie, oligarchs included. Roosevelt recognized not only the severe plight of the U.S. economy, but also the threat that rising proletarian militancy potentially posed to the whole capitalist system. The Communist Party had doubled its membership during the Depression, and strikes were becoming more common. In conclusion, Professor Liu does admit that the New Deal did "improve the situation of the middle and petty bourgeoisie and to some extent alleviated class struggle in America, but it also rescued American monopoly capitalism from its hopeless situation."[20]

[18] Ibid., p. 47.

[19] Liu Xuyi, "Luosifu 'Xin Zheng' de lishi diwei," *Shijie lishi*, no. 2 (1983): p. 46.

[20] Ibid., p. 50. For an extensive discussion of workers' movements throughout

According to the Marxists, the U.S. economy enjoyed sustained growth during the mid-1930s, but—as is predictable according to the Marxist law of uneven economic development—a new economic crisis was inevitable. Such a crisis hit the economy during 1937–1938. While another "general crisis" was feared, it proved "partial," although its effects lingered until the end of the decade.

The American monopoly capitalists were confounded. Would they never enjoy the good old days again? What had rescued them from the economic doldrums before? War was again the answer.

The Second World War was, according to the Marxists, the third imperialist war in world history. It pitted some imperialists against others, that is, the "democratic capitalist countries" versus "fascist capitalist countries."[21] Both types of states practiced state-monopoly capitalism. The Marxists' reasoning is that all of the imperialist combatants had expansionist designs, especially the fascist capitalists, but it was the monopoly capitalist class in each imperialist country that pushed their respective states to join the war as a means of maximizing their economic gain.

The Marxists are in general agreement that in the United States, which belonged to the former camp, World War II inaugurated an entirely new stage in the development of state-monopoly capitalism. Thereafter, according to historian Huang Shaoxiang, monopoly capital and the state apparatus were "inseparable" (jinmi).[22] Professor Huang's use of this term is not casual. It reflects a conscious depiction of the relationship between the state and monopolies. Elsewhere in her book she prefers to use stronger terms that connote Stalin's subordination thesis.

The Transition from Monopoly to State-Monopoly Capitalism

Chinese writings on state-monopoly capitalism in the United States are voluminous. Indeed, whole symposia have been held to discuss the subject, such as the one convened by the American Economy Research Association of China in Anhui Province in 1982. This meeting resulted in the definitive volume Meiguo guojia longduan zibenzhuyi yu jingji weiji (American state-monopoly capitalism and economic cri-

American history, including this period, see Professor Liu's "Meiguo longduan zibenzhuyi fazhanshi yu Ma-Liezhuyi," Shehui kexue, no. 2 (1984): 76–80.

[21] Liu Xuyi, "Luosifu 'Xin Zheng' de lishi diwei," p. 51.

[22] Huang Shaoxiang, Meiguo jiaoshi jianbian, p. 616.

ses).[23] While the lead article in this volume, which is usually meant
to have the definitive say on a subject, did echo the unification thesis
that was becoming dominant in China at the time, it also staked out
a third scenario: the trend toward nationalization of private enterprises (*guoyouhua siqiye*) by the state in the 1960s and 1970s had actually reversed Stalin's subordination thesis to the point where the
state may now "control" the monopolies in the United States rather
than vice-versa![24] This view put forward by economist Qiu Qihua,
then the director of the Institute of World Economics and Politics at
the CASS, accords with his views examined in the previous chapter.
For Qiu, it was not the power of monopolies that was of concern in
imperialist countries, but the power of the state. Others at the conference argued that this may indeed represent a new form of state-
monopoly capitalism, but it was far more prevalent in Europe and
Japan than in the United States.[25] Still, of major significance in this
collected volume is the fact that—without exception—the authors all
accepted and articulated the unification thesis in their papers—that
is, that the state and monopolies are "coalesced."

Such unanimity had not always been the case. There had existed a
clear cleavage—and a good deal of confusion—in the America Watchers' writings on the relationship between the U.S. government and
monopoly capital in the late 1970s and early 1980s. Some clearly articulated the subordination thesis, others the unification thesis, and
still others—for reasons of confusion or ideological safety—came
down on neither side of the debate by using the terminology of both
theses. Since this material is so voluminous, perhaps the best way to
sample the material and, at the same time, identify the authors' articulated images is to tabulate many of the more important contributions to the debate, as I have done in table 3.2.

If one examines the work unit (*danwei*) of each individual, the data
reveal that university-based America Watchers have a much greater
propensity to argue the subordination thesis, while those in the
Academy of Social Sciences' Institute of World Economics and Politics led the way in arguing the unification and state-control theses.

What led the Marxists to the conclusion that American monopolies

---

[23] "Lunwenji" bianjizu bian, *Meiguo guojia longduan zibenzhuyi yu jingji weiji* (Beijing:
Shangwu yinshuguan, 1984).

[24] Qiu Qihua, "Guojia longduan zibenzhuyi de jiben xingtai jichi zai Meiguo de jiben
biaoxian," in ibid., pp. 1–14.

[25] See, in particular, Liu Yunlin et al., "Meiguo he Xi-Ou zhuyao guojia de guojia
longduan zibenzhuyi duibi fenxi," in ibid, pp. 91–101; Tong Fuquan, "Congyu Xi-Ou
he Riben de bijiao yanjiu kan Meiguo guojia longduan zibenzhuyi de jiben tiaozheng,"
in ibid, pp. 102–11.

Table 3.2
Images of Relationship Between Monopolies and the State

America Watcher	Unification	Subordination	State Control
Qiu Qihua[a]			X
Li Ningshen[b]	X		
Lin Shichang[b]	X		
Wang Huaining[c]	X		
Yang Weichi[d]	X		
Gan Dangshan[e]		X	X
Zhang Youwen[f]	X		
Chu Baoyi[f,g]	X		
Gong Weijing[h]	X	X	X
Huang Shaoxiang[i]		X	
Chen Weishu[j]	X		
Jia Ping[k]	X		
Cui Wei[l]	X	X	

[a] Qiu Qihua, "Guojia longduan zibenzhuyi de jiben xingtai jichi zai Meiguo de jiben biaoxian," in ibid., pp. 1–14.

[b] Li Ningshen and Lin Shichang, "Meiguoxing guojia longduan zibenzhuyi jichi fazhan," in ibid., pp. 15–28.

[c] Wang Huaining, "Dui Meiguo guojia longduan zibenzhuyi yidian yijian," in ibid., pp. 51–60.

[d] Yang Weichi, "Meiguo guojia longduan zibenzhuyi de fazhan," in ibid., pp. 82–90.

[e] Gan Dangshan, "Cong suoyouzhi kan guojia longduan zibenzhuyi," in Jingji yanjiu bianjizu, Lun dangdai diguozhuyi (Shanghai: Renmin chubanshe, 1984), pp. 131–47, argues the state control thesis. In an earlier article he argues the subordination thesis, "Zhanhou Meiguo longduan caituan de fazhan," Shijie jingji, no. 6 (1980): 25–39, 45.

[f] Zhang Youwen and Chu Baoyi, "Lun zibenzhuyi fazhan de xin jieduan," in Meiguo guojia longduan zibenzhuyi yu jingji weiji, pp. 148–61.

[g] Chu Baoyi, ed., Dangdai Meiguo jingji (Beijing: Zhongguo caizheng jingji chubanshe, 1981), chap. 1.

[h] Gong Weijing, Meiguo longduan ziben jizhong. On pp. 204–11 of this book Professor Gong argues all three positions, as he did in his earlier article "Guanliao longduan zichanjieji zai ziben diguozhuyi guojia buzhan tongzhi diwei," Nankai daxue xuebao, no. 5 (1980): 17, 22. In other articles he only articulates the unification thesis: "Xiandai longduan ziben jizhong de xin jieduan," Shijie jingji, no. 7 (1985): 3–9; "Zhanhou Meiguo longduan ziben jizhong de tedian," Shijie jingji, no. 2 (1980): 20–30. In a chapter he prepared for a collected volume, Professor Gong exclusively argues the subordination thesis; see Chu Baoyi, ed., Dangdai Meiguo jingji, chap. 12.

[i] Huang Shaoxiang, Meiguo jiaoshi jianbian, p. 616.

[j] Chen Weishu, "Guanyu guojia longduan zibenzhuyi jieduan de ruogan wenti," Shijie jingji, no. 3 (1979): 39–45.

[k] Jia Ping, "Dui guojia longduan zibenzhuyi fazhan de yidian kanfa," Shijie jingji, no. 3 (1979): 46–47.

[l] Cui Wei, "Meiguo junshi-gongye zongheti yu guojia longduan zibenzhuyi," Shijie jingji, no. 8 (1980): 23–29.

Table 3.2 (*cont.*)

America Watcher	Unification	Subordination	State Control
Zhang Fan[m]	X		
Zheng Yin[n]	X		
Zhu Jingyao[o]	X		
Liu Xuyi[p]	X		
Qian Junrui[q]	X		
Huang Su[r]	X		
Zhang Qichen[s]	X	X	
Tong Fuquan[t]	X	X	
Hu Guocheng[u]	X		
Yang Huijun[v]	X		
Zheng Weimin[w]	X		
Cai Peitian[x]	X	X	
Li Zong[y]	X	X	
Ye Kuilin[z]	X		
Hong Wenda[aa]	X		

[m] Zhang Fan, "Zhanhou Meiguo yinghang longduan ziben yu gongye longduan ziben de ronghe," *Shijie jingji*, no. 7 (1980): 1–9.

[n] Zheng Yin, "Meiguo guojia suoyouzhi jigou he fazhan qushi," *Shijie jingji*, no. 6 (1981): 22–28.

[o] Zhu Jingyao, "Zhanhou Meiguo longduan ziben de jingguan duoyanghua he hunhe lianhe gongsi," *Wuhan daxue xuebao*, nos. 2–3 (1980): 3–10, 49–55.

[p] Liu Xuyi, "Meiguo longduan zibenzhuyi yu Ma-Liezhuyi," *Lanzhou daxue xuebao*, no. 3 (1984): 45–56.

[q] Qian Junrui, "Guanyu Meiguo jingji de jige wenti," *Shijie zhishi*, no. 5 (1981): 2–9.

[r] Huang Su, "Lun siren longduan ziben dui guojia de yilai," *Shijie jingji*, no. 6 (1981): 16–21; Huang Su and Qin Guoqiao, "Meiguo guojia longduan zibenzhuyi de tedian jichi fazhan chengdu," *Shijie jingji*, no. 4 (1983): 63–68.

[s] Zhang Qichen, "Guojia longduan zibenzhuyi zai zhanhou de fazhan," *Shijie jingji*, no. 6 (1981): 11–15.

[t] Tong Fuquan, "Guojia longduan zibenzhuyi jingji ganyu de xin bianhua," *Shijie jingji*, no. 1 (1986): 24–27.

[u] Hu Guocheng, "Lun Meiguo jingji zhidu xiang guojia longduan zibenzhuyi de zhuanbian," *Shijie jingji*, no. 5 (1985): 13–23.

[v] Yang Huijun, "Lun Ou-Mei guojia longduan zibenzhuyi fazhan de fenxi he tedian," *Shijieshi yanjiu dongtai*, no. 4 (1985): 21–26.

[w] Zheng Weimin, "Guojia longduan ziben guoji lianhe de xin fazhan," *Fudan daxue xuebao*, no. 4 (1980): 15–20.

[x] Cai Peitian, "Guojia longduan zibenzhuyi shi longduan zibenzhuyi fazhan de xin jieduan," *Shijie jingji*, no. 4 (1978): 31–36. Cai Peitian is a pseudonym for Pu Shan.

[y] Li Zong, "Guojia longduan zibenzhuyi shi longduan zibenzhuyi fazhan de xin jieduan," *Shijie jingji*, no. 1 (1978): 17–22.

[z] Ye Kuilin, "Zhanhou guojia longduan zibenzhuyi de fazhan he zuoyong," *Liaoning daxue xuebao*, no. 3 (1982): 24–26.

[aa] Fudan daxue zibenzhuyi guojia jingji yanjiusuo bian, *Meiguo longduan caituan* (Shanghai: Renmin chubanshe, 1977), pp. 45–68.

Table 3.2 (*cont.*)

America Watcher	Unification	Subordination	State Control
Zhang Jialin[bb]	X		
Xu Xinli[cc]	X		
Teng Weizao[dd]	X		
Song Jiqing[ee]	X		

[bb] Shanghai guoji wenti yanjiusuo, *Xiandai Meiguo jingji wenti jianlun* (Shanghai: Renmin chubanshe, 1981), chap. 3. Of his many articles on U.S. monopoly capital financial groups this is the only one in which Mr. Zhang explicitly discusses the relationship between caituan and the state. In his other articles he is more concerned with the internal composition of caituan and their relation to each other.

[cc] Ibid., chap. 4.

[dd] Nankai daxue zhengzhi-jingjixi jingji yanjiusuo bianzhe, *Longduan—caituan—da gongsi* (Beijing: Renmin chubanshe, 1974), pp. 60–61.

[ee] Chu Baoyi, ed., *Dangdai Meiguojingji*, chap. 13.

do not "control" the apparatus of state? Basically this conclusion is based on their analyses of the changing relationships within and between the U.S. caituan over time. In short, the subordination thesis was based on the view of a unitary monopoly capitalist class in America, that is, the leading monopolists all colluded with one another to maximize their profits, and the U.S. government acted on behalf of the entire monopoly bourgeois class. Once the Marxist School of America Watchers discovered that there was intense competition—not collusion—among individual monopoly groups, that new groups were replacing old ones, and that the government tended to favor policies that benefited certain groups over others, then the Marxists reverted to the unification thesis, which could better account for this more complex situation and the ambiguous relationship between monopolies and the state.

According to the Marxists, then, just what has been the nature of change among American monopoly financial groups in the postwar era? Here again one encounters a large data set of voluminous Chinese writings on this subject. I will draw upon a small sample from these analyses to summarize the main conclusions of the Marxists. These conclusions can be summarized under two general headings: changes in the capital concentration among caituan, and changes in the relative financial strength among caituan. The latter is obviously a function of the former, but each raises different subissues, so they can be treated as analytically distinct.

The Marxists seem to identify five significant changes in capital concentration among American monopoly financial groups in the postwar era:

1. Capital is increasingly concentrated.
2. Capital holdings are increasingly diversified.
3. Interpenetration of caituan has increased.
4. The role of bank capital has increased.
5. State-monopoly capitalism has increased.

I shall examine each in turn.

First, the Marxists assert that the concentration of capital among caituan has reached an unprecedentedly high level in the postwar era. In his book on capital concentration in the United States, Gong Weijing presents a table summarizing, over time, the "comparative percentage of total capital assets of the two hundred largest manufacturing companies in the United States" (see table 3.3).

How is it that one hundred firms have come to dominate nearly half of all corporate assets, and 60 percent are in the hands of the two hundred largest firms? In a word, through mergers.

Zhang Jialin of the Shanghai Institute of International Studies, arguably China's leading authority on American caituan, claims that the "high tide" of mergers has passed through three phases in postwar America.[26] The first phase lasted from the mid to late 1950s when more than 3,000 enterprises merged. The second phase lasted from 1966 to 1970 when 8,000 more merged. The third phase began in 1978 and continued through the time Zhang published his article in 1980. During 1978 alone, Zhang counted 2,106 mergers totaling more than $34 billion in assets.

Zhang also noticed another trend in corporate mergers, which he identified as "one of the most important features of the current concentration of production and capital in the United States"—namely, "conglomerate mergers" (*zonghexing hebing*). Zhang defines these as

Table 3.3
Capital Assets of Major American Corporations

	1950	1955	1960	1965	1970	1975	1980
100 largest corporations	39.7	44.3	46.4	46.5	48.5	45.0	46.8
200 largest corporations	47.7	53.1	56.3	56.7	60.4	57.5	59.7

Source: Gong Weijing, *Meiguo longduan ziben jizhong*, p. 41.

[26] Zhang Jialin, "Meiguo longduan caituan shili he zuhe de ruogan bianhua," *Shijie jingji*, no. 9 (1980): 23–24.

the "merging of different trades and professions."[27] This is an extremely significant development, Zhang argues, because caituan "no longer dominate" only one or a few industries, but rather diversify their holdings.

Diversified capital holdings among caituan are therefore the second main trend the Marxists notice about changes in postwar capital concentration in the United States. They argue that the two are not mutually exclusive and contradictory. That is, the caituan have diversified their investments while amassing greater aggregate capital holdings. Monopoly capitalists have diversified, Zhang argues, because they "realize that a diversified enterprise is more economical, more effective, and more profitable than a single-product enterprise."[28] Zhang gives the example of Litton Industries which, before 1954, was only a small firm producing electronic tubes. After a succession of mergers, by 1980 Litton owned some one hundred small companies that produce over ten thousand products ranging from aircraft carriers to medical instruments.

Litton Industries is not exceptional. Zhang argues that the majority of America's largest corporations—such as Exxon, General Motors, General Electric, ITT, IBM, and Boeing—have all become conglomerates. As a result of the diversification of investment of corporations under their control, American caituan are less easily defined by specialization of production. For example, the Morgan caituan—whose holdings used to be concentrated in steel and railways—now has significant holdings in the following industries: oil, electronics, automobile, armaments, aircraft, atomic energy, and so forth.[29] Similarly, the Rockefeller caituan has diversified from oil into coal, chemicals, electronics, airlines, atomic energy, armaments, foodstuffs, and the service sector. The Du Pont caituan, while maintaining the chemical industry as its raison d'être, has expanded into the automobile industry, development of weapons systems, and the service sector. The Chicago caituan, which used to depend solely on agriculture and retail commerce, now has "great strength in oil, steel, and sophisticated weapons."[30] The Mellon caituan has moved from oil and aluminum to atomic energy and the service sector. All caituan have become heavily involved in banking.

Diversified capital investments have given rise to the third noticeable trend: the interpenetration among caituan. During the prewar years caituan were recognizable not only by the family that controlled

[27] Ibid.
[28] Ibid., p. 24.
[29] Shanghai guoji wenti yanjiusuo, *Xiandai Meiguo jingji wenti jianlun*, p. 103.
[30] Ibid.

them or the geographical region they dominated, but also because their capital holdings were concentrated in one or a few industries. The diversification of investment in the postwar years has made caituan much less distinct as familial, regional, or financial entities. Single families no longer hold the majority of stock in single-product companies, investments are national and increasingly international, and above all the caituan have increasingly invested in each other's capital stock. This has resulted in a high level of interpenetration among monopoly financial groups.

Take, for example, the two largest caituan—Rockefeller and Morgan. According to Zhang Jialin, "since the mid-1970s they have infiltrated each other and mixed up their interests. There are no longer intense struggles between the two groups, and their demarcation line is gradually fading."[31] In another article Zhang uses Exxon, IBM, Mobil Oil, Gulf Oil, Du Pont, and Ford Motor Company as leading examples of corporations that were once dominated by a single caituan but are now controlled by many. Zhang also points to the practice of concurrently appointing the same individuals to boards of directors of different corporations as "an important way" for caituan to penetrate each other.[32]

This raises the fourth trend in the evolution of postwar American caituan: the increasingly close relationship between banking and industrial capital, and the increasing dominance of the former over the latter. Long ago Hilferding and Lenin pointed to the tendency of bank and industrial capital to merge in the era of monopoly capitalism to form "finance capital." The Marxists now assert that, in the postwar era, it has reached epidemic proportions. "Financial institutions (particularly commercial banks) are now the nucleus (hexin) of monopoly financial groups." To get around laws proscribing direct investment by commercial banks in nonfinancial enterprises, the banks have relied on a variety of trust funds as a method to "exercise control over enterprises and corporations."[33] This can be accomplished by holding a relatively small number of shares in a corporation, even 1–2 percent of shares that carry voting rights. By the late 1960s, Zhang argues in this article, nearly half the number of total shares carrying voting rights on the stock market were owned by banks via trust funds. Morgan Guaranty Trust, First National Citi-

[31] Zhang Jialin, "Dongbu caituan de xin zuhe," *Shijie jingji daobao*, August 1, 1983, p. 5.

[32] Shanghai guoji wenti yanjiusuo, *Xiandai Meiguo jingji wenti jianlun*, p. 103.

[33] Zhang Jialin, "Meiguo longduan caituan shili he zuhe de ruogan bianhua," pp. 23–24.

bank, Bankers Trust, and Chase Manhattan respectively were the largest shareholders.

The final trend contributing to capital concentration among caituan is increased government intervention in the economy, particularly via the military-industrial complex. Cui Wei, a professor at Beijing Normal University and long-time member of the Marxist School of America Watchers, defines the military-industrial complex as "a complex system composed of government military organizations, big monopoly military companies, research institutes that are responsible for developing military technology, and mass organizations that are related to military activities (the first two parts form the core of the complex)."[34]

The military-industrial complex contributed a great deal to accelerating state-monopoly capitalism in the United States, and greatly stimulated capital concentration in the hands of the leading caituan. Throughout the postwar era the fifty largest defense contractors have garnered more than half of the Pentagon's total military orders.[35] The Marxists argue that war has long been a stimulant to the American economy and that, in search of ever-increasing profits, the military-industrial complex has been the driving force behind the arms race with the Soviet Union, has fueled conflicts worldwide, and has made the United States fight one war after another.

Moreover, the American economy has become militarized. According to Xu Xinli of the Shanghai Institute of International Studies, in the United States one in five laborers (20 percent of the entire workforce), five thousand towns, seventy-six industrial centers, twenty-two thousand main contractors, and more than one hundred thousand minor contractors work for military-related production.[36] All of this has turned the United States into the "world's largest armaments manufacturer."[37]

Taken together, these five main themes emerge from the Marxists' writings about changes in capital concentration in America during the post–World War II period. In brief, the capital holdings of the leading monopoly financial groups have become more concentrated, diversified, interpenetrated, dominated by banks, and integrated into the military-industrial complex. These are trends that have affected the caituan overall.

[34] Cui Wei, "Meiguo junshi-gongye zongheti yu guojia longduan zibenzhuyi," *Shijie jingji*, no. 8 (1980): 27.

[35] Ibid., p. 25.

[36] Shanghai guoji wenti yanjiusuo, *Xiandai Meiguo jingji wenti jianlun*, pp. 123, 134.

[37] Huang Su and Qin Guoqiao, "Meiguo guojia longduan zibenzhuyi de tedian jichi fazhan chengdu," p. 66.

How have these trends affected the relative balance of financial power among them? To assess the relative strength of different caituan, one must have an accurate estimate of the assets of each, claims veteran caituan-watcher Zhang Jialin. Zhang bemoans the fact that today this is no easy task, for three principal reasons:

> First, the shareholders of many American corporations register their share certificates in the name of their consignee so as to conceal the real background of the monopoly groups. Second, the infiltration among the monopoly groups is very high, many enterprises are jointly controlled by two or more monopoly groups, and the members of the board of directors hail from different monopoly groups. Thus, the interrelationship of the groups is very complicated and it is very difficult to judge which monopoly groups a certain enterprise is subordinate to and to verify the accuracy of the actual strength of each monopoly group in a certain enterprise. Third, the U.S. government has never published formal data concerning the relative strength of monopoly groups and the background of the enterprises.[38]

Notwithstanding such data problems in their research, the Marxists continually attempt to gauge the shifting positions of different American caituan.

One significant change in the postwar era has been the enlargement of the "eight big monopoly financial groups" (*ba da caituan*) to ten principal groups. The Kuhn-Loeb caituan ceased to exist after the war (because its principal holdings were bought out by the Rockefeller caituan), while three new groups arose: the Citibank, California, and Texas caituan. In a 1980 article on the postwar development of U.S. monopoly financial groups, Fudan University Professor Gan Dangshan presents the data summarizing changes in the proportion of total monopoly assets and the resulting rank order of each caituan (table 3.4).[39]

From this table one gains a sense of changes in the pecking order of American caituan as estimated by the Marxists. This is the standard order given by most Marxists. Since their estimates are usually based on a 1974 standard study by Fudan University's Capitalist Countries Economic Research Institute,[40] there is little variance in their writings in terms of the rank order and shifting strength of the caituan. Unfortunately, with the important exception of Zhang Jialin of the Shanghai Institute of International Studies, the Marxists have not produced a comprehensive study of changes in relative strength

---

[38] Zhang Jialin, "Meiguo longduan caituan shili he zuhe de ruogan bianhua," p. 24.

[39] Gan Dangshan, "Zhanhou Meiguo longduan caituan de fazhan," *Shijie jingji*, no. 6 (1980): 25.

[40] Fudan daxue zibenzhuyi guojia jingji yanjiusuo, *Meiguo longduan caituan.*

Table 3.4

Relative Strength of U.S. Monopoly Financial Groups

Monopoly Financial Group	1935		1948		1960		1974	
	%	Rank	%	Rank	%	Rank	%	Rank
Rockefeller	10.8	3	21.7	2	25.8	2	26.4	1
Morgan	49.5	1	45.0	1	29.3	1	24.1	2
California	—	—	—	—	12.8	3	13.4	3
Citibank	—	—	—	—	5.6	6	10.3	4
Chicago	7.0	4	7.5	4	7.3	4	9.6	5
Boston	2.8	7	4.9	6	4.0	9	4.5	6
Mellon	5.5	5	4.7	7	4.5	7	3.6	7
Texas	—	—	—	—	—	—	3.0	8
Du Pont	4.3	6	5.3	5	6.3	5	2.7	9
Cleveland	2.3	8	2.5	8	4.4	8	2.5	10
Kuhn-Loeb	17.8	2	8.4	3	—	—	—	—

Source: Gan Dangshan, "Zhanhou Meiguo longduan caituan de fazhan," p. 25.

of caituan in the 1980s, so most writers continue to base their analyses on earlier data. Zhang, however, believed as of 1980–1981 that the Chicago caituan had become subordinate to the Morgan and Rockefeller groups, that the Morgan and Citibank caituan had merged, and that the Boston and Cleveland caituan had essentially become extinct.[41]

The Marxists go to great lengths to determine the holdings of each caituan. Again, Zhang Jialin has probably done the most extensive research in this area. Table 3.5, a run-down of the holdings of the "eight big caituan," is taken from Zhang's research.[42]

This kind of detailed work tracing the linkages in American monopoly capital is typical of an enormous body of Chinese analysis over the last thirty years. In literally hundreds of books and articles, not a single page or sentence ever explicitly questioned the a priori assumption that monopoly financial groups actually exist in the United States or other capitalist countries.

Occasionally, fragmentary evidence would appear indicating that there was internal debate over the declining role of monopoly financial groups, but it was usually coupled with a tough rejoinder that

[41] Zhang Jialin, "Meiguo longduan caituan shili he zuhe de ruogan bianhua"; Shanghai guoji wenti yanjiusuo, Xiandai Meiguo jingji wenti jianlun, chapter 3. There are, of course, numerous other sources to consult detailing these holdings. Primary among them are Meiguo longduan caituan and Nankai daxue zhengzhi-jingjixi shijie jingji jiaoyanshi, Zhanhou diguozhuyi jingji jige wenti (Tianjin: Renmin chubanshe, 1975), pp. 3–31.

[42] Zhang Jialin, "Meiguo longduan caituan shili zuhe de ruogan bianhua."

Table 3.5
Principal Holdings of U.S. Monopoly Financial Groups

Financial Group	Principal Holdings
Morgan Group	Morgan Guaranty Trust Company, J. P. Morgan & Company, Morgan-Stanley, First National Citibank, Chemical Bank, Manufacturers Hanover Trust, Bankers Trust, Northwest Bank & Company, American Express, Travelers Insurance, Prudential Life Insurance, New York Life Insurance, Connecticut General Life Insurance, Westinghouse Electric Corporation, Lockheed Aircraft Corp., Textron Corp., Goodyear Tire & Rubber Corp., United Airlines, Sears & Roebuck, IBM, General Electric, ITT, U.S. Steel, Union Carbide, Continental Oil, Union Oil of California, Coca-Cola, Pepsico, Chrysler Corp., Pan Am, Burlington Northern, Sante Fe Industrial, Southern Railway, Norfolk & Western Railway, AT&T, PG&E, K-Mart, Union Department Stores
Rockefeller Group	Chase Manhattan Bank, First Chicago, First National Citibank, New York Bank, First Boston, Metropolitan Life Insurance, Equitable Life Insurance, Exxon Corp., Standard Oil of Indiana, Raytheon, American Electric Power, Eastern Airlines, Commonwealth Edison, Texas Utilities, AT&T, ITT, Chrysler Corp., Goldman Sachs, Lehman Brothers
California Group	Bank of America, Security Pacific National Bank, Wells Fargo, Georgia Pacific, Lockheed, General Dynamics, Standard Oil of California, Getty Oil, Western Oil, Litton Industries, Crocker National Bank, Occidental Petroleum, Hughes Aircraft, Georgia-Pacific, PG&E
Citibank Group	Citicorp, First National Citibank, First Bank System, Atlantic Richfield Corp., Caterpillar Tractor, Eastman Kodak, Phillips Petroleum, United Technologies, Xerox Corp., Boeing Aircraft, 3M Corp., Bendix Corp., Grumman Aircraft, J.C. Penney
Chicago Group	Illinois Continental National Bank, Northern Trust Company, First Chicago Corp., Texaco, Standard Oil of Indiana, Bethlehem Steel, U.S. Steel, Florida Light & Power, Delta Airlines
Du Pont Group	Du Pont Chemical Corporation, General Motors, National Bank of Detroit, American Express, Mobil Oil, Texaco, Goodyear Tire & Rubber, Security Pacific Corp., Mid-South Public Utilities, Detroit Edison

Table 3.5 (*cont.*)

Mellon Group	Mellon National Bank, Carnegie-Mellon University, Gulf Oil, First National Bank of Boston, Kennecott Copper Corp., U.S. Steel
Texas Group	First National Bank of Dallas, Republican National Bank of Dallas, First National City Bank of Houston, Tenneco, International Harvester, LTV, Safeway Stores Inc., Texas Instruments, Getty Oil

Source: Zhang Jialin, "Meiguo longduan caituan shili he zuhe de ruogan bianhua."

such was not the case. In 1981, for example, the director of the CASS Institute of World Economics and Politics stated in an article (following his return from a research trip to the United States):

> Some people believe that new developments in financial institutions have weakened the role of monopoly capital. For example, the dispersal of large company stock shares seems to have reduced the controlling authority of monopoly capital. This is not, in fact, the case. Stock dispersal is nothing more than a major way in which monopoly capital raises funds, expands capital, and increases profits. . . . Another example given is that with the expansion of the authority of managerial personnel, the control of monopoly capital seems to decline. This is also not a fact. The fact is that in large financial institutions and large companies, the owners and the managers are becoming increasingly melded into a single entity. . . . It is true, however, that after the war large groups of new capitalists entered the financial groups, bringing about the gradual dilution of the family nature of the financial groups and making them more social in nature. Members of the financial groups gradually became better educated, with the original capitalists studying and mastering science and technology to become people possessing specialized knowledge, and a new group of administrators, managers, engineers, and lawyers also entered the financial groups to become new capitalists.[43]

Thus, to openly question the existence of caituan, or to assert that their influence was declining, was too risky a step for members of the Marxist School of America Watchers to take even in the more liberal post-Mao intellectual climate.

Then in the first issue of *Guoji wenti yanjiu* (International studies) in 1986, Zhang Jialin, who had done more than any other single individual to promote the study of American monopoly capitalist finan-

[43] Qian Junrui, "Guanyu Meiguo jingji de jige wenti: Fu-Mei jinxue guangan," *Shijie jingji*, no. 3 (1981): 5–6.

cial groups, published an article under the appropriate title "Meiguo longduan caituan chuxian zhongda bianhua" (A major change appears in American monopoly financial groups), which proclaimed the disintegration (*jieti*) of American caituan. In his article Zhang asserted:

> Since the war, financial groups as a type of monopoly capitalist domination have continually declined. By the 1980s, it was already apparent that mutual contention among monopoly financial groups no longer existed in America. . . . Individual monopoly financial groups as a unit of the finance capital social structure *no longer exist.* . . . In the 1980s, there is no longer enough sufficiently factual evidence to support the claim that these mutually competitive monopoly financial groups exist.[44]

How could Zhang come to this startling conclusion after years of not only asserting the existence of caituan and analyzing them in excruciating detail, but also arguing that they were the key motive force behind the entirety of American politics and economy? Why the sudden change?

This change in Zhang's thinking was influenced by a year he spent as an exchange scholar in the United States during 1983–1984. By his own admission it produced a change in degree, not the total rejection of caituan that he proclaimed in his 1986 article. When asked in May 1985, after his return from the United States, whether his views of monopoly financial groups had changed during his time in the United States Zhang replied, "Now I believe that there is influence (*yingxiang*), not control (*kongzhi*), of government by the financial groups."[45]

Actually, kernels of Zhang's conclusion that caituan no longer exist can be found in his earlier writings. Buried in two of his earlier articles is the sentence "American monopoly financial groups are in the process of disintegration and reorganization."[46] As early as 1983—in an obscure article that served as the basis of his 1986 article—Zhang stated flatly that "recently it is apparent that the eight and ten big financial groups *do not exist.*"[47] And, as seen earlier in his 1980 *Shijie jingji* article, Zhang had reservations about whether the Chicago and Cleveland caituan still existed. While these are indications that

---

[44] Zhang Jialin, "Meiguo longduan caituan chuxian zhongda bianhua," *Guoji wenti yanjiu*, no. 1 (1986): pp. 23–30, 53. The quotation is from pp. 23–24.

[45] Interview at the Shanghai Institute of International Studies, May 14, 1985.

[46] Zhang Jialin, "Meiguo longduan caituan shili he zuhe de ruogan bianhua," p. 30; Shanghai guoji wenti yanjiusuo, *Xiandai Meiguo jingji wenti jianlun*, p. 109.

[47] Zhang Jialin, "Meiguo longduan caituan chuxian zhongda bianhua," *Shijie jingji daobao*, July 25, 1983, p. 4.

Zhang's thinking was changing, he did not elaborate the reasons for his startling conclusion until his 1986 article. His principal reasons were four.

First, Zhang does not think that regional caituan ever really existed because, on the one hand, the main eastern and midwestern groups have long had holdings outside of their regions, while on the other hand the "western" and "southern" caituan were never able to truly establish control over their geographical regions. The Bank of America did have large holdings in California, but not in other western states. In Texas, the largest forty-two corporations had to rely on banks outside of the state for 80 percent of their financial support. Zhang had long argued that the locus of U.S. financial power had not shifted to the Sun Belt (*yangguang didai*), as had many of his colleagues, but remained with the eastern caituan—particularly on Wall Street. In his 1980 *Shijie jingji* article, for example, Zhang stated, "The allegation of 'power shifting' is inaccurate. According to analysis of various data and materials, the western and southern financial groups by and large have to hang onto the coattails of the eastern financial groups, and American political and economic power is still under control of the latter."[48] Here Zhang was not necessarily saying that the eastern caituan was in control, but that the southern and western groups—including the Texas and California groups—could not sustain themselves.

Second, drawing upon his earlier argument that expanded production has led to the extensive diversification (*duoyanghua*) of capital holdings among caituan, on the one hand, and mergers, on the other, Zhang argues that this thorough interpenetration has made it impossible to distinguish distinct financial groups any longer.

Third, Zhang argues that because of the decentralization of stock holdings, voting rights are always changing, and it is therefore impossible to recognize caituan control because of this fluid situation. Further, banks can no longer control enterprises because of these interdependent stock holdings. Companies now control companies, and small shareholders even play a role. The result is that "financial organs" and enterprises have become less interdependent (*yicun*). Thus a key component of "finance capital" has disappeared.

Fourth, so many banks and companies now draw their earnings from overseas investments, and are thus integrated into an international financial community, that their identity as domestic Ameri-

[48] See, for example, Fan Kang, "Meiguo nanbu fazhan he zibenzhuyi maodun kuochang," *Renmin ribao*, June 15, 1977, p. 6; Zhang Jialin, "Meiguo longduan caituan shili he zuhe de ruogan bianhua," p. 28.

can—and familial or region-specific—financial groups is no longer apparent. But Zhang argued that the internationalization of the American economy has led to severe "contradictions" between those monopoly capitalists (mainly in the east) who garner a large share of their earnings abroad, and those in the interior who remain oriented toward the domestic market.

In conclusion, Zhang argues that while caituan have disintegrated and no longer exist per se, finance capital still has a "significant influence" (*zhongda yingxiang*) on the American economy. "A few finance capital organs still have an 'advantageous position' (*youyue diwei*) to influence the economy because they have 'money capital' (*huobi ziben*), particularly 'loan consortiums' (*daikuan yingtuan*)."[49]

A year after Zhang's stunning article appeared in *Guoji wenti yanjiu* he elaborated his maverick views on the changed nature of caituan and other features of the U.S. economy in a book appropriately titled *Bianhua zhongde Meiguo jingji* (The changing American economy).[50] In this volume Zhang made his case for a thorough reevaluation of the state of the U.S. economy. In this book Zhang breaks with his Marxist, and even many non-Marxist, colleagues who predict gloom and doom for the U.S. economy. In addition to reiterating his new views on the nonexistence of caituan, Zhang offers seven other reasons for reevaluating the U.S. economy: (1) the rapid development of high technology enterprises; (2) the increased importance of the service sector; (3) specialization of agricultural production; (4) the revival of small business; (5) the growth of new industry in the South and West and the retooling of traditional industries in the Northeast and Midwest; (6) the international character of the U.S. economy; and (7) the apparent ability to whip stagflation. On the basis of these indicators, Zhang's prognosis for the U.S. economy was considerably more upbeat than the majority of his colleagues'.

When considered in the context of Zhang's gradual transformation from classical Marxist political economist to his rejection of many of the assumptions and conclusions that were once accepted a priori, his publications of 1986–1987 are remarkable departures from prevailing orthodoxy. Needless to say, many other long-serving members of the Marxist School of America Watchers were not so willing to accept Zhang's heretical views.

Soon after his book was published, it received a less-than-flattering review in *Shijie jingji*, the leading journal of the profession and

---

[49] Zhang Jialin, "Meiguo longduan caituan chuxian zhongda bianhua," *Guoji wenti yanjiu*, p. 28.

[50] Zhang Jialin, *Bianhua zhongde Meiguo jingji* (Shanghai: Xueshu chubanshe, 1987).

mouthpiece of the revisionist economists and theoreticians at the CASS Institute of World Economics and Politics.[51] Evidently Zhang's views even went beyond the permissible boundaries of IWEP. It is one thing to induce flexibility of interpretation into existing ortho- doxy as long as it does not challenge the core corpus of thought; it is quite another to reject fundamental assumptions as Zhang had done. The September 1988 issue of *Shijie jingji* also published a stinging re- buke of Zhang's thesis on the "withering away" (*xiaowang*) of caituan in America by Fudan University caituan specialist Gong Weijing (who figured prominently in the state-monopoly capitalism de- bates).[52] Invoking Marx's law of capital accumulation, Gong argued the opposite case from Zhang. Rather than the diversification of stock holdings and interpenetration among caituan, Gong argued that mo- nopolies in the United States were more wealthy and powerful than ever. How did Zhang respond to this rebuke? "I decided not to re- spond to his article since he does not have any evidence to support his view and all he used were outdated materials. Besides, he has never been to the United States."[53] Although these were the only published criticisms of Zhang Jialin's revisionist views, many other caituan experts interviewed in 1990 explicitly disassociated them- selves from Zhang's interpretations. As for Zhang himself, he contin- ues his research in the United States and remains more convinced than ever that caituan no longer exist in the United States.

Marxist Perspectives on the U.S. Economy II: The Debate on Economic Crises

In addition to monopoly and state-monopoly capitalism, the other major component of the Marxists' interpretation of the failing state of the American economy is the concept of economic crisis (*jingji weiji*). This term is expressed frequently in the literature and is fundamental to Marxist perspectives of capitalist economies. The concept is some- what similar to the Keynesian notion of the business cycle but also carries broader implications in Marxist-Leninist political economy. Marx argued that capitalist economies overproduce certain types of goods. He termed this tendency the "anarchy" of capitalist produc- tion. This being the case, Marx argued, denied the "bourgeois" no-

[51] Chu Yukun, "Meiguo jingji shi gudingshang Yingguo de laolu?" *Shijie jingji*, no. 12 (1987): 87–89.

[52] Gong Weijing, "Qianlun Meiguo longduan caituan de xiaowang," *Shijie jingji*, no. 9 (1988): 37–43.

[53] Personal communication, June 12, 1990.

tion of a natural equilibrium point (and price) between supply and demand. Rather, production and consumption are in constant disproportion, and this "anarchy" causes repeated economic "crises." Each crisis further increases the capitalist's need to extract greater amounts of "surplus value" from the laboring classes, thus further impoverishing the proletariat until they have no alternative but to revolt.

For the Marxist School of America Watchers there exist many attendant issues related to economic crises in capitalist countries such as the United States, but here I will only consider one fundamental issue: why have the frequent crises that afflict the American economy not led to its collapse? Why have the "partial" crises noted originally by Marx and Engels not led to the "general crisis of capitalism" foreseen by Stalin? Since the U.S. economy has not collapsed as predicted, what implications does this have for Marxist theories of capitalist economic crises?

These have been troubling questions for the Marxists to answer. Beginning in 1979 and continuing into the early 1980s, many Chinese economists attempted to come to grips with these theoretical dilemmas. As with several other controversial debates related to imperialism and state-monopoly capitalism (see chapter 2), the CASS Institute of World Economics and Politics led the way in reevaluating these issues "under new historical conditions." For example, the institute convened a meeting of more than eighty specialists on April 19–21, 1979, to discuss economic crises.[54] The institute's journal, *Shijie jingji*, was the principal publication reflecting these discussions, although the Institute of Economics' journal *Jingji yanjiu* also contributed several significant articles to the discussion. The American Economy Research Association also served as a key forum of debate, particularly at the 1979 and 1982 annual meetings.

Prior to 1979, academic writings on economic crises in capitalist countries painted a uniform Stalinist picture of economies on the verge of collapse.[55] Most of these writings were by university scholars whose main reference point was *Das Kapital* and other theoretical

---

[54] See "Benkan bianjibu zhangkai guanyu zibenzhuyi jingji weiji wenti de zuotanhui," *Shijie jingji*, no. 5 (1979): 73.

[55] See, for example, Beijing daxue shijie jingji zhuanye jingji weiji yanjiu xiaozu, *Zibenzhuyi jingji weiji* (Beijing: Renmin chubanshe, 1975); Nanjing daxue Ma-Liezhuyi jiaoyanshi zhengzhi-jingji xuezu, *Zibenzhuyi jingji weiji* (Beijing: Renmin chubanshe, 1975); Nankai daxue lishixi shijieshi zhuanye, *Zibenzhuyi shijie jingji weiji shihua* (Beijing: Shangwu yinshuguan, 1976); Nankai daxue zhengzhi-jingjixuexi yu jingji yanjiusuo, *Jingji weiji wenti jianghua* (Beijing: Renmin chubanshe, 1975); Beijing shifan daxue zhengzhi-jingjixuexi, *Jingji weiji zhishi* (Beijing: Renmin chubanshe, 1975).

Marxist works. They treated U.S. economic crises in a reductionist manner as only one example of the "general crisis" facing the capitalist world. Two books dealt exclusively with American economic crises.[56] All of these publications portrayed the American economy as beset by stagnant production, high levels of inflation and unemployment, increased capital concentration, a working class that was increasingly impoverished, and so on. Each economic crisis was deemed to be more severe than the previous one.[57] The "general crisis of capitalism" put forth by Stalin's 1952 *Economic Problems of Socialism in the U.S.S.R.* was being realized. Revolution in America could not be far away. Such was the standard prognosis of the American economy by academic economists prior to 1979.

By 1979, however, university scholars no longer dominated the discussion of capitalist economic crises. Professional economists, returning from Cultural Revolution oblivion to work in CASS and other institutions, joined the dialogue. Their perspectives were noticeably different from those of their university colleagues. While they by no means argued a single position on economic crises in the United States, they were in general agreement that Stalin's thesis of a general crisis was no longer applicable to the capitalist world—if it ever was in the first place. They reached this important determination through research on four key aspects of U.S. economic crises: the nature, intensity, duration, and number of economic crises in postwar America. These four aspects are analytically distinct but interrelated.

There were basically two opinion groups among the Marxists concerning the nature of economic crises in the United States. The first group took the position that all crises since World War II have been "periodic" or "cyclical" (*zhouqixing*). The second group argued that some crises have been "intermediate" (*zhongjianxing*). Participants in the debate themselves recognized these distinctions and used these terms to identify where their colleagues stood.[58]

Those who believe that postwar economic crises have been of the cyclical variety argued that not only has production dropped and un-

[56] Wuhan daxue jingjixi Bei-Mei jingji yanjiushi, *Zhanhou Meiguo jingji weiji* (Beijing: Renmin chubanshe, 1976); *Zhanhou Meiguo diliuci jingji weiji* (Beijing: Shangwu yinshuguan, 1978).

[57] See, for example, Beijing daxue shijie jingji zhuanye jingji weiji wenti yanjiu xiaozu, "Zhanhou zui yanzhong de zibenzhuyi shijie jingji weiji," *Beijing daxue xuebao*, no. 1 (1975): 77–84.

[58] A useful summary of these positions can be found in the editorial "Guanyu dangdai zibenzhuyi jingji ruogan lilun wenti de taolun zongshu," *Jingji yanjiu*, no. 7 (1984): 77–78.

employment risen, but such crises have become more frequent and longer in duration since World War II,[59] more extensive as they affect the entire U.S. economy,[60] and increasingly intense in their general impact on society.[61] They believe that cyclical crises will inexorably lead to the "general crisis" (zong weiji) that brings the total collapse of the capitalist system. The key underlying presumption of this school is a linear one derivative from the Marxist-Leninist stage-theory of history. That is, each crisis is progressively more intense and brings the system closer to its inevitable collapse.

Those who argued that some postwar economic crises were of the "intermediate" type do not accept this premise. They adopt a more dynamic view. While they too believe that economic crises will afflict the capitalist system until it eventually collapses, they see this as a long-term historical process fraught with fluctuation. As seen in chapter 2, this belief is central to the Leninist conclusion that American imperialism is in no danger of "dying" soon. This group of economists believe that intermediate crises are irregular in their frequency and shorter in duration,[62] affect only limited sectors of the national economy,[63] do not necessarily spread to other countries in the capitalist world,[64] and are not increasingly intense in their impact.[65]

The second opinion group holds that the United States is able to

[59] Zhou Maorong, "Lun zhanhou Meiguo de jingji weiji pinfanhua he zhouqi suo-duan wenti," Shijie jingji, no. 9 (1979): 8–13; Lin Dahui, "Zibenzhuyi guojia jingji zhouqi jincheng de tongqi guilu zai zhanhou de fugui," Shijie jingji, no. 8 (1983): 20–26; Shen Huasong, "Lun changqi boyun," Shijie jingji, no. 8 (1983): 27–33.

[60] Liu Songyao, "Luelun zhongjianxing weiji wenti," Shijie jingji, no. 10 (1980): 74–75; Li Sidi, "Zhanhou Meiguo jingji weiji he zhouqi de tedian," in Lunwen bianjibu, Meiguo jingji taolunhui lunwenji (Beijing: Shangwu yinshuguan, 1981), pp. 33–42.

[61] See, for example, Wu Dakun, "Lun zhanhou Meiguo jingji weiji yu jingji zhouqi de xinghuo," Shijie jingji, no. 11 (1979): 20–25; "Zhanhou zibenzhuyi shijie de jingji weiji yu jingji zhouqi de wuzhi tichu," Jingji yanjiu, no. 1 (1983).

[62] See, for example, Chen Qiren, "Dui 'lun zhanhou Meiguo jingji weiji zhouqi de xingzhi' yi wen de zhiyi," Shijie jingji, no. 6 (1980): 19–24; Zhou Jianping, "Zhanhou zibenzhuyi jingji weiji xin tedian jichi xingcheng yuanyin," Jingji yanjiu, no. 10 (1982); Yao Tinggang, "Zhanhou Meiguo de jingji weiji he zhouqi wenti," in Lunwen bian-jizu, Meiguo jingji taolunhui lunwenji, pp. 23–32.

[63] See, for example, Hong Junyan, ed., Dangdai Meiguo jingji (Beijing: Shishi chu-banshe, 1985), pp. 206–12; Wang Huaining, "Dangqian zibenzhuyi shijie jingji weiji wenti," Jingji yanjiu, no. 3 (1983).

[64] See, for example, Xue Boying, "Guanyu 'zhongjian weiji' de jidian zhiyi," Shijie jingji, no. 3 (1982): 39–47; Wu Jixian, "Guanyu zhanhou zibenzhuyi jingji weiji he zhouqi de jige wenti," Shijie jingji, no. 1 (1981): 1–7.

[65] See, for example, Liu Diyuan, "Meiguo zhanhou diliuci jingji weiji tong sanshi-niandai da jingji weiji de duibi fenxi," Shijie jingji, no. 1 (1980): 14–21; Benkan bianjibu, "Guanyu dangqian Meiguo jingji weiji xingtai de taolun," Shijie jingji, no. 10 (1979): 20–23.

recover from intermediate crises through government intervention in the economy. The various monetary and fiscal tools available to the government allow it to renew fixed capital investment (*guding ziben touzi*), which is the key to recovery. Deficit financing, lowering interest rates, and increasing military outlays are seen as common tactics employed by the government to overcome intermediate crises. Moreover, they believe that since 1970 venture capitalists (*maoxian zibenjia*) will take risks to invest during times of crisis. All of these permit the renewal of fixed capital which, according to Marx, is the basis of recovery.

The different criteria employed by the Marxists to distinguish between cyclical and intermediate economic crises determine the number of crises they think the United States has undergone. The degree of drop in production and rise in unemployment, duration, extensiveness of impact on the entire economy, impact on other countries, and ability to renew fixed capital investment are the operative criteria used to judge the type of economic crisis. Some Marxists select only one of these criteria, but most are more comprehensive. People's University professor and leading Marxist economist Wu Dakun, for example, is primarily concerned with fixed capital:

> There are different views on these crises at home and abroad. Some people hold that some of these crises were intermediate rather than periodic crises. I personally believe that they were periodic because, according to Marx, all crises related to the renewal of fixed capital are periodic ones. If they are not related to the renewal of fixed capital, then they can be called "partial crises" or "intermediate crises." Since all the crises in the United States after the war coincided with decreased investment in fixed capital, they should be called periodic crises.[66]

Professor Wu is a long-time analyst of American economic crises and is staunchly in the Stalinist camp of the Marxist School. He has been predicting the imminent collapse of the U.S. capitalist system and social revolution in America ever since Stalin made the same prediction in 1952. His views were the object of direct rebuttal by his colleagues during the 1979–1984 polemics on imperialism, state-monopoly capitalism, economic crises, and the impoverishment of the proletariat. Even Professor Chen Qiren of Fudan University, who is no moderate on these questions, had to take issue openly with his senior colleague.[67] So, while Wu Dakun's views are not typical, they

[66] Wu Dakun, "Jianlun zhanhou Meiguo jingji weiji tedian," *Hongqi*, no. 8 (1980): 45–48.

[67] Chen Qiren, "Dui 'lun zhanhou Meiguo jingji weiji ji jingji zhouqi de xingzhi' yiwen de zhiyi."

do illustrate how one prominent analyst arrives at his conclusions about how to label the postwar economic crises in the United States.

The Marxists are in basic agreement on the number of crises that have afflicted the American economy, even though they differ on the severity and exact duration of each crisis, and hence whether it was a "periodic" or "intermediate" crisis. According to most accounts there were twenty-nine crises between 1857 and 1980, seven since the Second World War. For example, an authoritative table that appeared in *Shijie jingji*, the journal of the CASS Institute of World Economics and Politics, stated these twenty-nine crises were as follows:

June 1857–December 1858	August 1918–March 1919
October 1860–June 1861	January 1920–July 1921
April 1865–December 1867	May 1923–July 1924
June 1869–December 1870	October 1926–November 1927
October 1873–March 1879	August 1929–March 1933
March 1882–April 1885	May 1937–June 1938
March 1887–April 1888	February 1945–October 1945
July 1890–May 1891	November 1948–October 1949
January 1893–June 1894	July 1953–May 1954
December 1895–June 1897	August 1957–April 1958
June 1899–December 1900	April 1960–February 1961
September 1902–August 1904	December 1969–November 1970
May 1907–June 1908	November 1973–March 1975
January 1910–January 1912	January 1980–July 1980.[68]
January 1913–December 1914	

Other, more recent sources list the last crisis as lasting until 1982.[69]

The Stalinist camp of the Marxist School thus argued that all postwar economic crises in the United States are cyclical, and each brings the American economy closer to collapse. By 1982, however, the Leninist camp had concluded that of the seven postwar crises that had hit the U.S. economy, three—1953–1954, 1960–1961, and 1980–1982— were intermediate crises, while the other four crises have been of the cyclical variety. This is confirmed in a 1984 article in *Jingji yanjiu* summarizing the debate.[70] This estimate by the Leninists led them to the conclusion that American economic crises are irregular in their frequency, scope, duration, and intensity, ergo they do not inexorably lead to a general crisis and collapse of the system.

[68] "Meiguo jingji weiji tongji ziliao," *Shijie jingji*, no. 3 (1982): 77.

[69] See, for example, Hong Junyan, ed., *Dangdai Meiguo jingji* (Beijing: Shishi chubanshe, 1985), p. 207.

[70] "Guanyu dangdai zibenzhuyi jingji ruogan lilun wenti de taolunhui," *Jingji yanjiu*, p. 77.

Perspectives

Thus, in this debate over economic crises one sees again—as seen previously on monopoly capitalism and imperialism—a group of analysts who remain very much in the tradition of Marxist-Leninist political economy but have moved away from the dogmatic and deterministic analysis characteristic of the late Stalin era. These America Watchers remain in the Marxist School by virtue of their commitment to Marxist-Leninist categories of analysis and therefore do not belong to the non-Marxist School. By staking out a more flexible position within the Marxist School, however, these "Leninists" gradually eclipsed the "Stalinist" camp. By 1982 their interpretations were predominant.

There remains an entirely different school of analysis of the American economy, a school of America Watchers who do not employ Marxist-Leninist categories of analysis but rather analyze their subject matter using terminology common in the United States. This is the non-Marxist School. Their largely atheoretical analyses are not derived from an explicit analytical framework but are eclectic and descriptive.

The non-Marxists are to be found in different institutions from the Marxists. Universities remain the private preserve of the Marxists. Most non-Marxists who study the American economy work for the New China News Agency, CASS America Institute, Institute of International Studies, and Institute of Contemporary International Relations. Some work for the CASS Institute of World Economics and Politics and Shanghai Institute of International Studies.

It is important to note that the non-Marxists are not necessarily more positive than the Marxists about the prospects for the American economy. They too write of many negative aspects afflicting the U.S. economy. As Xu Dixin, one of China's leading economists, put it, "American economic life is characterized by high prices, high wages, high debts, high taxes, and high consumption."[71] But the non-Marxists' analyses are more concrete and less influenced by ideological considerations. Moreover, the timeframe of non-Marxists' analyses tends to be more immediate; they are mainly concerned with interpreting current and recent events.

These tendencies will become apparent by examining the non-Marxists' analyses of the U.S. economy during the Carter and Reagan administrations. Since the non-Marxists did not really begin to emerge from political oblivion until after the downfall of the Gang of

[71] Xu Dixin, "Meiguo jingji zouma guanhua," *Beijing ribao*, March 28, 1980.

Four in 1976, analyses of the U.S. economy during the Nixon and Ford administrations were relatively scant. Those analyses that did appear in the press and a few existing scholarly journals were dominated by the Marxists. Following the downfall of the Gang of Four, however, a number of popular media and professional publications appeared that provided the non-Marxists with a publishing outlet. Thus, the periods of the Carter and Reagan administrations offer the best opportunity to tap into the vast emerging literature written by the non-Marxists.

Non-Marxist Perspectives on the American Economy I:
The Carter Years

From the non-Marxists' perspective, the three greatest economic problems facing the Carter administration were "stagflation," the energy crisis, and the declining value of the dollar. Their analyses concentrated on these issues and the efforts undertaken by the Carter administration to overcome them.

While "stagnant production" (*shengchan tingzhi*) had long been a central feature of recessions in the United States, this was now combined with a new phenomenon during the recession that greeted the Carter administration when it took office—inflation. The United States had known inflation to be a common feature of economic life throughout the post-Depression era, but it usually accompanied the expansive phase of the business cycle. Never before had Americans known stagnation and inflation simultaneously. New China News Agency correspondents (then based at the United Nations) tracked this "two-headed monster" of "stagflation" (*zhizhang*) throughout 1976, as they had during the peak of the 1974–1975 recession. Their dispatches kept their readership abreast of the latest Commerce Department statistics on housing starts, steel production, layoffs, wholesale and retail price increases, and so forth.[72]

In the opinion of these correspondents, the Carter administration's proposed remedy for stagflation was traditional Keynesianism—a prescription that had repeatedly proven itself ineffective in the past and would do so again. Carter's advisers believed that a proper mix of monetary and fiscal instruments could pull the economy out of its

[72] See, for example, "NCNA: United States Still in Economic Crisis," *FBIS-CHI*, May 24, 1976, A10; "NCNA: U.S. Harassed by Economic Difficulties," *FBIS-CHI*, August 25, 1976, A8; "NCNA: U.S. Economy Again Becomes Stagnant," *FBIS-CHI*, October 22, 1976, A3; "NCNA: U.S. Economy Experiences Another Gloomy Year," *FBIS-CHI*, December 14, 1976, A1.

doldrums. Accordingly, upon entering office in January 1977 President Carter submitted a revised version of President Ford's budget to Congress, a so-called economic stimulus package. This package intended to stimulate the economy through a combination of decreased taxes and increased government expenditure.[73]

This budget was supposed to work in tandem with a more liberal monetary policy at the Federal Reserve aimed at bringing down interest rates and increasing consumer spending and corporate investment. Federal Reserve Chairman Burns grudgingly went along with Carter's plan, but at the same time he directly criticized the Carter administration's "short-sighted" policies. In a *People's Daily* article author Gu Jin agreed with the thrust of Burns's criticism:

> Burns was not worrying unnecessarily over the danger of U.S. inflation. First, the increase in the amount of money in circulation has been too fast over the past six months, far exceeding the Federal Reserve's maximum guideline. This alone is enough to spur a new round of inflation. Second, without exception, the series of economic plans and laws proposed by the Carter administration all have the side effect of accelerating inflation. The energy law, the farm subsidy law, the law for raising the minimum wage, and the basketful of plans for stimulating the economy all tend to spur inflation. These conditions compelled Burns, who has the responsibility to stabilize the nation's finances, to increase his vigilance.[74]

In a paper delivered to the 1979 annual meeting of the China American Economy Research Association, economist Ge Qi analyzed the Carter administration's monetary policy and argued that the 1977 M_1 growth rate of 7.9 percent and M_2 rate of 9.8 percent were highly inflationary, and that the 1978 growth rates of 7.3 percent and 8.5 percent, respectively, were no better.[75] Even a strict tightening of money in circulation to nearly zero growth during 1979 could not slow the inflation rate.

In another *People's Daily* article in the spring of 1979, reporter Gu Jin noted that the United States was in the anomalous position of soaring prices alongside overstocked inventories. Mr. Gu claimed that excessive stockpiling by consumers and producers alike had produced "sham prosperity."[76] This situation, he opined in April of that

---

[73] "NCNA: Carter Presents Budget; Economy Still a Problem," *FBIS-CHI*, February 25, 1977, A5.

[74] Gu Jin, "It Is Difficult to Be Reserve Board Chairman," *FBIS-CHI*, November 30, 1977, A4.

[75] Ge Qi, "Kaisisizhuyi he Meiguo Kate zhengfu de jingji zhengce," in Lunwenji bianjizu, *Meiguo jingji taolunhui lunwenji*, pp. 147–55.

[76] Gu Jin, "The Mystery of Feeling Worried When Hearing Good News," *FBIS-CHI*, April 25, 1979, B2.

year, would inevitably lead to another recession. By July he was sure of his forecast. In another *People's Daily* article, Gu cited the dramatic downturn of key economic indicators during the second quarter: GNP dropped 3.3 percent, domestic retail sales dropped 4 percent, real personal earnings dropped 3 percent, auto sales dropped 20 percent, and inflation rose 13.4 percent.[77] He attributed these trends primarily to the stricter monetary policy pursued by the Federal Reserve since the fourth quarter of 1978.

Other Chinese correspondents in the United States also sounded the alarm of a looming recession, but they tended to blame the shrinking oil supply and attendant price increases as the catalyst. Yu Enguang, another NCNA reporter based in Washington, identified skyrocketing oil prices as having a ripple effect on the entire U.S. economy. The iron and steel, building, chemical, mining, agriculture, tourism, retail commerce, transportation, and other sectors had all "been thrown into confusion as a result of the oil shortage."[78]

Wang Fei, a third *People's Daily* correspondent in the United States, foresaw a structural shift taking place in the U.S. economy with the "traditional industries" in the Northeast and Midwest being hit hardest by the pending recession, while the "new electronics industry and aircraft industry in the Southwest and West will not be greatly affected." Based on the belief that this recession would affect some economic sectors more intensely than others, Wang ventured to guess that "it is likely that in the future the U.S. economy will recover with difficulty from its spasmodic cramps, and the revival after a recession will be a tired and slow one in a state of what the Americans call 'stagflation.'"[79]

One of the more dire assessments of the 1979 recession was offered by Chu Baoyi, a senior specialist on the American economy at the Shanghai Academy of Social Sciences Institute of World Economy. In the popular magazine *Shijie zhishi*, Chu argued that the 1979 recession was not necessarily a new development but was in fact a continuation of the 1974–1975 crisis from which the American economy had never fully recovered.[80] The alarming statistics of the first two quarters of 1979, he argued, were indicative of a more intense round of

[77] Gu Jin, "The United States Faces a New Economic Crisis," *FBIS-CHI*, August 7, 1979, B1.

[78] Yu Enguang, "The U.S. Economy Faces the Threat of Recession," *FBIS-CHI*, July 18, 1979, B1.

[79] Wang Fei, "The United States Enters Another Economic Recession," *FBIS-CHI*, August 29, 1979, B4–5.

[80] Chu Baoyi, "Yijiuqijiunian Meiguo jingji zhanwang," *Shijie jingji*, no. 4 (1979): 21–22.

the on-going recession. He thought the prospects for America's economic future were bleak, and the chances of recovery slight.

As the economic downturn of 1979 gained momentum in 1980, the Chinese press and professional economics journals debated the severity of the looming recession. Economists at the Academy of Social Sciences were of divided opinion on the nature and timing of the "economic crisis." CASS and other concerned organs convened a special symposium from November 29 to December 4, 1980, to discuss "the recent economic crisis" in the United States and other Western countries. Several of the papers concerning the United States were published in a special section of the lead issue of the 1981 *Shijie jingji*.[81] Some of these discussions were examined above. Basically, these articles debated whether the "crisis" began in 1979 or 1980, whether it had ended during 1980 or would continue, whether it was an economic crisis or recession (*jingji shuaitui*), and whether it was an intermediate or cyclical crisis.

Concerning the timing of the recession, two economists from the International Trade Research Institute of the Foreign Trade Ministry argued that the U.S. economy entered a crisis in April 1979 but had emerged by August 1980.[82] Conversely, Zheng Weimin and Chu Yukun of the CASS Institute of World Economics and Politics argued that the crisis did not begin until early 1980 and had not yet concluded.[83] Yao Tinggang of the Shanghai Institute of International Studies argued that the crisis affected only certain sectors of the U.S. economy.[84] Xiong Xingmei of the Nankai University Economics Research Institute argued that the crisis was not a "temporary recession" but a full-blown economic crisis.[85]

The uncertainty over the scope and duration of the economic downturn expressed by these professional economists was echoed by NCNA correspondents in the United States during the last half of 1980. Based on a careful analysis of Commerce Department statistics, Wang Fei predicted a "new cycle of inflation and recession" well into

[81] "Xifang guojia de jingji weiji ji jingji xingshi wenti taolunhui zai Beijing juxing," *Shijie jingji*, no. 1 (1981): 21; "Guanyu Meiguo zuijin zheici jingji weiji de taolun," *Shijie jingji*, no. 1 (1981): 11–21.

[82] Yang Ximeng and Ye Qixiang, "Meiguo guan yijiuqijiunian siyue kaishile xin de jingji weiji, yu yijiubalingnian bayue zouchu weiji," *Shijie jingji*, no. 1 (1981): 11–13.

[83] Zheng Weimin, "Zheici jingji weiji de kaishi shijian shi zai yijiubalingnian chu," *Shijie jingji*, no. 1 (1981): 13–14; Chu Yukun, "Meiguo zheici jingji weiji ji haizai fazhan zhong," *Shijie jingji*, no. 1 (1981): 19–21.

[84] Yao Tinggang, "Meiguo yijiubalingnian weiji shi yici zhongjianxing weiji," *Shijie jingji*, no. 1 (1981): 17–19.

[85] Xiong Xingmei, "Bushi jingji shuaitui, shi jingji weiji," *Shijie jingji*, no. 1 (1981): 14–15.

1981.[86] In a year-end summary Yu Enguang, citing a variety of American economic forecasts, came to the same conclusion.[87]

The annual *Yearbook of World Economy* published by the CASS Institute of World Economics and Politics came to a more positive conclusion about the outlook for the U.S. economy during 1980. Cao Meiyi, the author of the section on the American economy, concluded that a slight trend in new growth and fixed capital investment during the final two quarters of 1979 and early 1980 indicated a recovery (*huifu*).[88]

One CASS economist attempted to look beyond the immediate recession at hand in 1979 and 1980 by predicting the evolution of the entire American economy during the coming decade of the 1980s. Luo Chengxi, who studied economics under Milton Friedman at the University of Chicago in the 1940s, offered a gloomy prognosis. The U.S. economy during the 1980s would be characterized by accelerated inflation; the inability of science and technology to renew dying industrial sectors; dramatically increased public and private debt; a decline in purchasing power; a continuing high trade deficit and poor balance of payments; the declining value of the dollar; gradual industrial growth averaging about 2.9 percent; steady levels of unemployment hovering around 6 percent; a leveling off of the energy crisis; an increase in the military budget of 5 percent; and an overall growth rate of 2.7 percent for GNP.[89]

The economic woes of 1979–1980 brought on by skyrocketing oil prices and spiraling inflation plunged the Carter administration, and Carter himself, into a "crisis of confidence" (*xinxin weiji*). This period is best captured in the restricted-circulation volume *Jimi Kate zai baigong* (Jimmy Carter in the White House).[90] Written by Zhang Haitao, then NCNA bureau chief at the United Nations, this 1,300-page magnum opus is an almost day-by-day chronicle of the four years of the Carter presidency. In chapter 12 the author traces the growing frustration in the Carter White House during 1979, which compelled the president to appear repeatedly before the nation and Congress with one policy initiative after another in a vain attempt to regain their confidence and finally drove him into seclusion at Camp David to

[86] Wang Fei, "Has the U.S. Economic Recession Ended?" *FBIS-CHI*, October 1, 1980, B1–2.

[87] Yu Enguang, "Yearender: U.S. in Economic Throes," *FBIS-CHI*, December 30, 1980, B4–5.

[88] Cao Meiyi, "Meiguo," *Shijie jingji nianjian 1981* (Beijing: Zhongguo shehui kexue chubanshe, 1982), pp. 602–24.

[89] Luo Chengxi, "Bashiniandai de Meiguo jingji," *Shijie jingji*, no. 4 (1980): 24–35.

[90] Zhang Haitao, *Jimi Kate zai baigong* (Chengdu: Sichuan renmin chubanshe, 1982).

reassess his presidency. Attempts to regain the political initiative through the Vienna and Tokyo summits were futile. Zhang writes of how the public had lost faith in Carter and how members of his administration, grope as they might, had no solutions. All in all, Zhang Haitao captured the frustrated atmosphere in America at the time, which led to a bitter election campaign within the Democratic Party and the eventual election of Republican Ronald Reagan in 1980.

Non-Marxist Perspectives on the American Economy II: The Reagan Years

By the time President Reagan assumed office in 1981, the recession had intensified, and the non-Marxists' commentaries were uniformly pessimistic and critical. They remained intrigued, however, by the novel ideas advocated by the "supply-side school" (*gongying xuepai*) and its influence on the Reagan administration's economic policy—"Reaganomics" (*Ligen jingjixue*). Curiosity, though, did not equate with optimism. While they conscientiously studied the policies associated with supply-side theories and clearly presented this information to their readership in China, the non-Marxists remained highly dubious of Reagan's proposed plans for economic recovery. Even when the economy recovered after 1982, Reaganomics did not earn their explicit praise, even though they displayed a slightly more positive attitude toward the U.S. economy on the whole. By the time Reagan left office they were still not impressed, arguing that the U.S. economy was hobbled by the "four highs" and "two lows" (*sigao liangdi*): high financial deficit, high trade deficit, high liabilities, high interest rates, low inflation, and low economic expansion.[91] Although the non-Marxists do not employ ideological constructs to analyze the U.S. economy, their gloomy assessments of its general condition were not all that different from many of the Marxists'.

Theories of supply-side economics were as new to the America Watchers as to the American public when President Reagan took office. They had previously written of Milton Friedman and the "monetarist school" (*huobi xuepai*),[92] but their knowledge of non-Keynesian economics was sketchy at best. It took the election of Reagan and the attention given by the American press to his unorthodox plan for economic recovery (*jingji fuxing jihua*) to attract the America Watch-

[91] See, for example, Shi Min, "Meiguo jingji qianjing antan," *Shijie jingji*, no. 2 (1987): 7–13.

[92] See, for example, "Miertun Fuolideman," *Shijie jingji*, no. 6 (1979): 76.

ers' attention. George Bush's charge during the primaries that Reagan practiced "voodoo economics" (*fudoujiao jingjixue*) was the first indication that something new was in the offing, but it was really not until President Reagan gave his first State of the Union address that the non-Marxists focused their attention on his plan for economic recovery and its theoretical underpinnings. This speech served as the catalyst for numerous articles on the subject over the next few years.

The *People's Daily* was the first publication to introduce Chinese readers to the concept of supply-side economics. A week before President Reagan fully unveiled his economic recovery plan in the State of the Union address, correspondent Zhang Zhenya presaged how most of the Chinese media would subsequently treat it—a straightforward depiction of the elements of the plan and its theoretical underpinnings coupled with a negative assessment of its chances to solve the problems plaguing the U.S. economy. Zhang's article was even reluctant to grant that supply-side policies were really new.

Apropos of this, Zhang titled his article "Old Wine in a New Bottle." In it he argued that the supply-siders had stolen elements from several other sources, including "Say's law" of the eighteenth century, which asserts that the productive process itself will always provide producers in capitalist society with enough purchasing power to keep supply and demand in basic equilibrium. Moreover, the idea of tax cuts stimulating private investment and depressing government expenditure as put forward by Arthur Laffer were, Zhang argued, basic to Adam Smith's idea that overtaxing would reduce the amount of taxable goods and hence reduce government expenditure, as well as Keynes's idea of reducing taxes to stimulate demand. Based on the fact that he did not see much new in supply-side economics, Zhang concluded that "be it Keynesianism or supply-side economics, it is very difficult to fundamentally cure the chronic malady of the U.S. economy."[93]

People's Daily correspondent Wang Fei dutifully reported the contents of President Reagan's speech before Congress on February 18, in which he unveiled his three-hundred-page "Program for Economic Recovery." Wang found the essence of this plan to be "three cuts and one stabilization": drastic cuts in the federal budget, drastic cuts in individual and corporate taxes, drastic cuts in government regulations on business, and the formulation of a stable monetary policy. He disagreed with his colleague Zhang Zhenya by using laudatory language to describe this plan. For example,

[93] Zhang Zhenya, "Old Wine in a New Bottle—Introducing the U.S. Supply-Side Economics," *FBIS-CHI*, February 17, 1981, B1.

It signifies a fundamental break from the economic thinking and policies of successive U.S. administrations since President Franklin Roosevelt implemented the New Deal. It will have a far-reaching influence on future economic and political life in the United States and on people's welfare. . . . Reagan's three master strokes show great resolution and are very forceful. The scope of the program surpasses any similar program undertaken by all previous presidents since the war.[94]

A fortnight later Wang Fei ran another article in the *People's Daily* introducing readers to leading supply-siders Jude Wanniski, Arthur Laffer, David Stockman, Jack Kemp, and others. Wang also distinguished between the basic tenets of Keynesianism and the supply-side school:

The Keynesian theory chiefly emphasizes the demand side of the economy. It maintains that the increase in total demand in society will stimulate economic growth and that demand creates its own production. It favors government intervention to regulate the economy. According to this theory, during an economic slump, the government can provide impetus to production by reducing taxes and increasing its spending. In this way the people will have more money in hand with which to buy goods and services. When the economy overheats, the government can keep inflation from worsening by tightening monetary control and increasing taxes. . . . Contrary to the Keynesian theory, the supply-side theory emphasizes that the best way to promote economic growth is to stimulate the supply (production) side of the economy rather than to enlarge the consumption side. To stimulate production, the most important measure is to cut taxes so as to increase the income and profits of individuals and enterprises. In this way, they will save more, invest more, work more, and produce more. When production goes up, government income from taxation will increase, unemployment will drop, deficits will disappear, and inflation will slacken. The supply-siders are strongly opposed to government intervention in economic matters, thinking that the less government control the better. In their opinion, everything should be solved through free competition between private businesses and decided by the market.[95]

I quote Wang Fei at such length because it is one of the most concise expositions of the differences between the two schools offered by the America Watchers. Many others analyze different aspects and the pros and cons of the theories, as well as the specifics of the Rea-

[94] Wang Fei, "President Reagan's Economic Recovery Program," *FBIS-CHI*, February 24, 1981, B1–2.

[95] Wang Fei, "The Rise of Supply-Siders in the United States," *FBIS-CHI*, March 11, 1981, B1–2.

gan plan, but this is one of the earliest and clearest descriptions presented to the mass Chinese public.

As if to temper Wang Fei's rather upbeat assessments, however, two days later the *People's Daily* ran another article that came to the sobering conclusion that, "Although the intensification of anarchist production and free competition can bring about temporary 'prosperity,' it will eventually lead to an economic crisis. The U.S. supply-side economists can never explain and conceal this point, no matter how hard they try."[96]

As 1981 progressed, the Chinese media kept tabs on the U.S. economy and how the Reagan plan was progressing. Other media organs and economists at CASS began to supplement the analyses offered by NCNA correspondents. An article by a CASS economist in *Zhongguo qingnian bao* (China youth news) in March argued that as long as Reagan called for increased military expenditure it would necessitate deficit financing, and the resultant high debt would undermine the tax-cut and money-supply components of Reagan's recovery plan.[97]

Another article in the May issue of *Ban yue tan* (Semimonthly talks) (a publication aimed at "workers, peasants, and youth" according to its editors[98]) assessed the constituencies—pro and con—who were "engaged in an acute struggle over the direction and extent of Reagan's program concerning cutting federal expenditures":

> The majority of newly established industrial and financial groups in the western and southern part of the United States favor Reagan's program; the financial groups in the Northeast oppose cutting assistance to old industries; the farmers in the Midwest and West warn the administration that subsidies cannot be reduced for agriculture, and many mass organizations in the society are worried that social welfare will be infringed upon. Labor circles and certain black leaders oppose Reagan's program.[99]

In the May and June 1981 issues of *Shijie jingji*, CASS economists took their first crack at assessing the prospects of Reagan's plan and the supply-side economics. They offered negative assessments of each and argued their cases from a Marxist-Leninist theoretical orientation. Li Zong, who had been vice-director and senior researcher of capitalist economies since the institute's earliest days in the

[96] Gu Jin, "A Prescription Which Is Yet to Prove Its Efficiency—Commentary on U.S. President's 'Program for Economic Recovery,' " *FBIS-CHI*, March 16, 1981, B1.

[97] Yu Kexing, "The United States Is a Rich Country, but Why Has It Incurred So Much National Debt?" *FBIS-CHI*, March 23, 1981, B4–5.

[98] Interview at the New China News Agency, July 19, 1985.

[99] Zhong Yuling, "Ligen de jingji fuxing jihua," *Ban yue tan*, no. 10 (1981): 58–59.

1950s,[100] thought Reagan's plan of "returning to the 'golden age' of the 1950s and 1960s" to be futile. He reasoned that state-monopoly capitalism had developed to such a high extent in the United States since the New Deal that it was impossible to deregulate the economy as Reagan intended and, moreover, that the "intense contradictions" (*zhongzhong maodun*) of the capitalist mode of production would force the Reagan administration to abandon its plan.[101]

In an article on "The Background of the Rise of Conservative Economic Thinking in Western Countries and the Historical Destiny of Such Thinking," Qiu Qihua, Zheng Weimin, and Yang Deming (leading Marxist economists in the economic theory research section of the CASS Institute of World Economics and Politics) were equally pessimistic about the chances of monetarism and supply-side policies rescuing the American and British economies from their doldrums. Together with Keynesianism they would all fail to "overcome stagflation" or "restore prosperity" and would eventually be "swept into the garbage heap of history" (*bei saojin lishi de lajidui*).[102] As usual, Qiu left no doubt where he stood.

Three issues later, the *Shijie jingji* editorial board took the unusual step of publishing a rebuttal to the article from a student in Fudan University's World Economics Department. The student took direct issue with the conclusion of the prestigious CASS economists:

> The 1980s will be a decade when the Western countries will face comprehensive readjustment, it is the decade of the rise of conservative economic thinking. The rise of conservative economic thinking is the direct result of the stagnation, inflation, and decline the Western countries have known during the 1970s, and the 1980s will also be the decade when Western economies will probably be able to extricate themselves (*keneng baituo*) from stagnation, inflation, and decline and get on the road to fulfilling their aspirations.[103]

[100] The institute existed in embryonic form as the international economics statistics office (*guoji jingji tongjishi*) under the State Planning Commission from the mid-1950s until 1958 when it was transferred to the Economics Research Institute of the Academy of Sciences' Philosophy and Social Science Division. In 1964, on the order of Chairman Mao and Premier Zhou Enlai, it was established as an independent institute. Interview with America Watcher, June 25, 1987. Li Zong became institute director in 1988, succeeding Pu Shan.

[101] Li Zong, "Cong zhanhou Meiguo zhengfu ganyu jingji de shixian kan Ligen zhengfu de jingji zhengce," *Shijie jingji*, no. 5 (1981): 67–73.

[102] Qiu Qihua et al., "Lun xifang baoshouzhuyi jingji sikao xingqi de beijing jichi lishi mingyun," *Shijie jingji*, no. 6 (1981): 5–10.

[103] Yang Lujun, "Guanyu baoshouzhuyi jingji sichao jichi zai Ying-Mei de shiyan: jianyu Qiu Qihua deng tongzhi shangque," *Shijie jingji*, no. 9 (1981): 36–41. The quotation is from p. 41.

With this optimistic assessment, *Shijie jingji* closed discussion of the Reagan economic recovery plan for the remainder of 1981.

The media continued to chart the progress of the plan and state of the economy through the fall. In October the newsmagazine *Shijie zhishi* published a very negative assessment of Reagan's recovery plan. In it the authors ripped apart each of the four main components of Reagan's plan. The entire program was but a "plan to rob the poor and aid the rich" (*jiepin jifu de jihua*). They asserted that the tax reduction plan will benefit only "middle and upper class households," only big companies will benefit from the relaxation of government regulations while worker safety and environmental protection will suffer, the bulk of cuts in government expenditures will fall on social welfare outlays while increased military spending will enable munition manufacturers to reap huge profits, and so forth.[104]

Year-end reviews in the *People's Daily* also presented gloomy forecasts for the recovery plan.[105] All claimed that the United States was in a recession (*shuaitui*) by year's end, inflation and stagnant production continued, the federal deficit increased, interest rates remained high, unemployment had not fallen, sales had slumped badly during the last two quarters, bankruptcies of medium-size industries were on the rise, and there was no apparent end in sight. As the article by noted American economy specialist Xue Boying concluded, "Faced with this grim economic reality, more and more people are doubtful whether it is possible to carry out the principles of 'Reaganomics' from beginning to end."[106] On these pessimistic notes, the Chinese media closed their coverage of the American economy during President Reagan's first year in office.

The year 1982 was not a good one for the U.S. economy. The recession bottomed out, and unemployment, inflation, interest rates, and government debt all soared. Accordingly, the Chinese media duly reported these negative indicators; their assessments of the Reagan recovery plan were equally pessimistic. During 1982 the non-Marxists' coverage of the American economy expanded from publishing in the mainstream popular media to a number of more specialized professional publications. In large part this reflects the re-

[104] Li Zhiyi and Yang Shu'ao, "Ligen zhengfu de jingji yaofang," *Shijie zhishi*, no. 20 (1981): 8–11.

[105] Gu Jin, "The American Economy and the Reagan Administration's Counterstrategy," *FBIS-CHI*, December 14, 1981, B1–2; Yuan Xianlu, "Viewing the Chronic U.S. Economic Malady from Its Unemployment Rate," *FBIS-CHI*, December 30, 1981, B2–3; Xue Boying, "The Many Difficulties of 'Reaganomics,' " *FBIS-CHI*, December 28, 1981, B4–5.

[106] Xue Boying, "The Many Difficulties of 'Reaganomics,' " B5.

constitution of research institutes and reestablishment of these publishing channels at this time.

In January 1982 a new journal of importance appeared. *Xiandai guoji guanxi* (Contemporary international relations) was the first "open" (*gongkai*) and unclassified publication of the Institute of Contemporary International Relations (ICIR), the main civilian current intelligence analysis unit serving China's top leadership and central government. The issue carried several articles on various aspects of the United States. Among them was "An Analysis of President Reagan's 'Economic Recovery Plan.' "[107] After sketching out the basic elements of the recovery plan as stated in Reagan's February 18, 1981, speech to Congress and supply-side theories of macroeconomic management, the author noted three sources of domestic opposition to the Reagan plan.

The first source of opposition was said to be the "liberal faction of the Democratic Party" (*minzhudangnei ziyoupai*), which "represented the interests of the unemployed, energy conservationists, and small enterprises." The second source of opposition is state and local governments, because they stand to lose revenue-sharing monies from the federal government, especially in the areas of public transportation and unemployment compensation. Third, the working class stood to lose from the Reagan plan, particularly "laborers, the elderly, poor people, middle-income people, and the handicapped." These groups, the author argued, would not go down without a fight. "The congressional black caucus, more than 150 trade unions, civil rights and other social groups had already begun to establish an alliance."[108]

In March 1982 an article in the journal of the Foreign Ministry's Institute of International Studies cited foreign opposition to the Reagan plan on the basis of excessively high interest rates and the soaring value of the dollar. The author argued that these developments would "damage relations with American allies, possibly reducing their military expenditures and hence undermining the entire NATO strategy."[109]

As the recession deepened during the summer of 1982, two articles by researchers in the CASS Institute of World Economics and Politics focused on high interest rates as prolonging the recession and preventing implementation of the Reagan plan because they stifled in-

[107] Mei Ying, "Ligen 'jingji fuxing jihua' fenxi," *Xiandai guoji guanxi*, no. 1 (1982): 25–28.

[108] Ibid., p. 28.

[109] Xie Yao, "Dui Meiyuan de jinkuang jichi fazhan qushi de yixie fenxi," *Guoji wenti yanjiu*, no. 2 (1982): 31–38. The quotation is from p. 38.

vestment. One article claimed that the entire "reindustrialization" (*zai gongyehua*) strategy was predicated on channeling investment into new industries (*xinxing gongye*), and unless the prime rate dropped below 10 percent this would be impossible.[110] Another pinpointed high interest rates as the prime cause of the recession.[111]

By the fall of 1982 some non-Marxists were ringing the death knell of the supply-siders. One *People's Daily* article wrote a premature obituary for the supply-siders, saying that the tax cut passed by Congress a year earlier had failed to generate new investment as anticipated because of high deficits and interest rates. The author closed with the query, "Since the old Keynesian methods do not work, and the new toy of the supply-siders shed its luster as soon as it came on stage, what other wonderful medicines do bourgeois economists have up their sleeves?"[112] Zhang Jialin of the Shanghai Institute of International Studies agreed that the supply-side policies were failing and were on the verge of defeat by a coalition of some "traditional conservatives, liberals, governors, union leaders, workers, and minorities."[113] One year-end summary in the *People's Daily* proclaimed the Reagan economic recovery plan a "failure,"[114] while another foresaw a continuation into 1983 of the "worst economic crisis since the war."[115]

Press commentaries during January 1983 predicted not only a wellspring of opposition arising among "industrial, commercial, and financial circles" to get the Reagan administration to "thoroughly change its budget and tax revenue policies,"[116] but also that Reagan's reputation was seriously suffering. As a Beijing radio broadcast put it:

> As the economic situation worsens, more and more people have lost confidence in 'Reaganomics' advocated by Reagan when he assumed office. Some conservatives who helped Reagan with his presidential campaign

[110] Tong Fuquan, "Meiguo de 'zai gongyehua' zhanlue," *Shijie jingji*, no. 7 (1982): 59–62.

[111] He Kewen, " 'Ligen jingjixue' qianjin," *Shijie jingji*, no. 8 (1982): 57–58.

[112] Yuan Xianlu, "The Rise and Fall of the Supply-Side Group," *FBIS-CHI*, September 3, 1982, B2.

[113] Zhang Jialin, "Gongying xuepai lilun he Meiguo dangqian de jingji xianshi," *Guoji wenti yanjiu*, no. 3 (1982): 19.

[114] Yu Enguang, "Most Serious Postwar Recession in the U.S.," *FBIS-CHI*, December 27, 1982, B5.

[115] Zhang Zhenya, "U.S. Economic Prospects This Year," *FBIS-CHI*, January 6, 1983, B2–3.

[116] Unattributed report, "U.S. Industrial and Commercial Circles, Unable to Tolerate Reagan's Economic Policy, Will Publish Advertisements Openly Calling on Reagan to Change the Course," *FBIS-CHI*, January 18, 1983, B4–5.

have resigned their government jobs and others claim to 'keep distance' from him. A recent Gallup poll shows that fifty percent of those polled disapprove of the way Reagan has handled economic and other problems in the past two years. They hold that Reagan's performance is worse than Carter's, Nixon's, and Kennedy's in the first two years of their presidencies. . . . A review of Reagan's presidency over the past two years shows that he has few achievements to brag about, but that his record of failures is outstanding.[117]

The Institute of Contemporary International Relations' *Xiandai guoji guanxi* ran another article in January reporting dissension in the ranks of the Reagan adminstration caused by the inability to generate new investment and spur a recovery with supply-side policies. The supply-siders were reportedly under sharp attack, and their only hope was a partial return to Keynesian deficit-financing practices of increased taxation and looser monetary policies.[118] Veteran America Watcher Chen Dezhao of the CASS Institute of World Economics and Politics reported in *Guoji wenti yanjiu* the growing trade and fiscal frictions among the United States, Japan, and Western Europe caused by Reagan's obstinate policies and the continuing American recession.[119]

Similarly, an article by two Shanghai scholars in the February *Shijie jingji* rhetorically titled "Keynesianism Doesn't Work Anymore in the United States?" also argued that a partial return to traditional Keynesian tools was necessary.[120] The February issue also carried excerpts of papers presented at a special symposium on the current status of the world economy in December 1982 attended by many of China's leading experts on the American economy.[121] Many of them compared the 1982 recession to the Great Depression and without exception offered dire prognoses for the future of Reaganomics.[122]

In March Chen Baosen, director of the U.S. economy section of the

[117] Li Changjiu and Zhang Yuanting, "The U.S. Economy Lacks the Strength to Rise Again and the Reagan Administration Walks with Difficulty," *FBIS-CHI*, January 31, 1983, B3–4.

[118] Yan Shan and Ke Juhan, "Ping 'Ligen jingjixue,' " *Xiandai guoji guanxi*, no. 3 (1983): 17–22.

[119] Chen Dezhao, "Qishiniandai yilai de Mei-Ou-Ri jingji guanxi," *Guoji wenti yanjiu*, no. 1 (1983): 44–50.

[120] Li Xiang and Li Yinfeng, "Kaisisizhuyi zai Meiguo wanquan shiling le ma?" *Shijie jingji*, no. 2 (1983): 59–63.

[121] "Zai benbao bianjibu xingban de shijie jingji xingshi taolunhui shang de bufen fayin zhaiyao," ibid., pp. 9–58.

[122] See in particular the contributions by Teng Weizao, Li Zong, Xue Boying, Hong Junyan, Tao Dayong, Gan Dangshan, Yao Tinggang, Huang Su'an, Lin Shuzhong, Yu Kexing, Ye Qixiang, and Liu Changjiu.

CASS America Institute and one of China's leading specialists on the American economy, published an article in the *People's Daily* criticizing the "inherent contradictions in Reaganomics." He claimed that the Reagan administration was at a crossroads; it must change its economic philosophy as well as its methods. "President Reagan tries to use the economic philosophy of the eighteenth century to solve the economic problems of the end of the twentieth century," Chen claimed. However, he did see a ray of hope for economic recovery: "Judging by all signs at the present stage of the economic cycle, it is possible for the U.S. economy to rebound sooner or later this year." And on what basis did Chen make this judgment? "The only way left to ease the economic crisis is the implementation of a new technical revolution."[123] This theme gained currency among some non-Marxists over the following two years.

By mid-1983 the U.S. economy was showing signs of slight recovery. Noted international affairs expert Huan Xiang attributed the upturn to several factors: controlling the inflation rate through a looser monetary policy, falling worldwide energy prices, and a high business demand to restock inventories. While Huan thought that budget deficits and unemployment would remain high, he believed that the United States had turned the corner and would experience sustained growth for "the next two or three years."[124] Others, including the late and renowned economist Qian Junrui, believed that a large increase in foreign investment in the United States was a major contributing factor to the turnaround.[125]

The rapidity of recovery during the last two quarters of 1983 stunned many Chinese observers. In his year-end review, *People's Daily* correspondent Zhang Zhenya reported that the GNP growth rate had been restored to its prerecession level, interest rates were beginning to drop, prices were stabilizing, consumer income was increasing, investment was up, unemployment was down, inventories were replenished, and economic vitality was being restored.[126] According to these non-Marxists, the prospects for 1984 were brighter.

Not all analysts were as optimistic. Zhang Liang argued in the *People's Daily* that the Reagan administration's "blueprint" (*lantu*) was overly optimistic: GNP could not grow at 4.5 percent, unemployment

---

[123] Chen Baosen, "Reaganomics Hobbled by Reality," *FBIS-CHI*, March 7, 1983, B3–4.

[124] "Huan Xiang lun shijie jingji xingshi," *Shijie jingji daobao*, October 8, 1983, p. 4.

[125] Qian Junrui, "Shijie jingji qianjing," *Shijie jingji daobao*, January 2, 1984, p. 2; Zhang Yunlin, "Waiguo dui Meiguo zhijie touzi de zengzhang qushi," *Shijie jingji*, no. 12 (1983): 51–56.

[126] Zhang Zhenya, "U.S. Economic Upturn," *FBIS-CHI*, December 27, 1983, B5–6.

could not fall to 7.8 percent, inflation could not be kept to 5 percent, and interest rates would not fall to 8.5 percent.[127] His NCNA colleague Yu Enguang agreed.[128]

Institute of International Studies analyst Xie Yao was also guarded in his estimate of the prospects for recovery. In a lengthy analysis in his institute's journal, Xie distinguished among the short, medium, and long-term prospects. He thought the recovery would "lose its momentum" in 1984 (the short term), and that a "structural crisis" would "haunt" the U.S. economy in the medium-term (through the late 1980s), that is, the "major basic industries are not competitive enough on the international market." He argued, however, that the recession was causing the U.S. economy to undergo a basic structural reorientation. This was being caused by the "new technical revolution," which, over the long term, would transform the American economy into the postindustrial era. Hence, his prognosis for long-term recovery (mid-1990s) was brighter. This notwithstanding, Xie still concluded that the long-term recovery may be "aborted" (zhongduan) by several "unfavorable factors"—notably high budget deficits—which could spark another crisis. If this happened, he concluded, "the next cyclical economic crisis is most likely to be very serious, and would probably become the biggest since World War II."[129]

Despite these cautious predictions, the non-Marxists still had to address the issue of what brought about the recovery. Had Reagan stuck to his guns and was it the supply-side inspired program that had finally borne fruit? Or had the Reagan administration compromised on its original package?

Among others, Tong Fuquan of the CASS Institute of World Economics and Politics examined this issue and concluded the latter to be the case.[130] Tong argued in May 1984 that both political and economic considerations forced President Reagan to compromise during the second half of 1982. The political considerations were twofold: to improve relations with Congress and support Republicans' chances in the mid-term election. The economic considerations were that the inflation rate and federal deficit remained high, and that traditional

[127] Zhang Liang, "Ligen zhengfu de jingji 'lantu' yu xianshi," Renmin ribao, January 8, 1984, p. 3.
[128] See Yu Enguang, "Meiguo jingji de qunian he jinnian," Shijie jingji daobao, January 6, 1984, p. 2.
[129] Xie Yao, "Meiguo jingji de huisheng jichi qianjing," Guoji wenti yanjiu, no. 2 (1984): 1–10. The quotations are from pp. 7 and 10.
[130] Tong Fuquan, "Ligen jingji zhengce de bianhua jichi dui Meiguo jingji de xingxiang," Shijie jingji, no. 5 (1984): 62–66.

Keynesian methods to stimulate demand must be used in tandem with supply-side policies. Thus, deficit financing through increasing the money supply and government expenditures in nondefense spending were central in spurring the 1983 recovery. President Reagan therefore proved himself to be a pragmatist, which resulted in "better cooperation between the two parties" (*liangdang hezuo*).

The year 1984 was also a presidential election year. Recognizing that Americans "vote their pocketbook," as the election approached, many non-Marxists focused their attention on the influence of the economy on President Reagan's chances for reelection. Many of these analyses are examined in chapter 6. I will note just one representative analysis here.

Zhao Gui, then of the CASS America Institute, argued in August that two contradictory economic trends would determine the election.[131] On the one hand, the "misery index" (*tongku zhishu*) had risen during the first Reagan term, and this made the working class well-disposed toward the Democratic Party. On the other hand, real disposable per capita income (*renjun shiji ke zhipei shouru*) had risen for the middle and upper classes, which favored Reagan's chances for reelection. He predicted the latter would win out over the former. Many postelection analyses followed this line of reasoning in explaining Reagan's victory.

Buoyed by his sweeping election victory and a flourishing economy, President Reagan laid out his plans for his second term and the "second American revolution" in his February 1985 State of the Union address. This ambitious goal caught the attention of several America Watchers—who were not as optimistic as the president. While many grudgingly admitted that the economic turnaround had exceeded their expectations and that the chances for continued growth were good, they still could not bring themselves to agree with Reagan's long-term optimism. For example,

> It can be said that the potential achievements of Reagan's second term cannot surpass those of his first term, and in the near future the leadership of the American economy may continue to grow and American economic strength may rise a step higher, but America will never be able to recover the hegemonistic position it enjoyed in the early period after the war. His [Reagan's] call for a "second American revolution" and "greatness" will be very difficult to realize; moreover, his successors will not be able to achieve it either.[132]

[131] Zhao Gui, "Cong jingji zhuangkuang kan Meiguo jinnian daxuan," *Meiguo yanjiu cankao ziliao*, no. 8 (1984): 2–4.

[132] Li Changjiu, "Ping Ligen de Meiguo diersi geming," *Shijie jingji*, no. 4 (1985): 16.

Others were also dubious. Analysts of the Institute of Contemporary International Relations wrote that, in the long term, all would rest on solving the "high deficit problem" (*gao chizi wenti*),[133] but in the short term high interest rates would constrain further economic growth.[134] The United States may have licked "stagflation," but high unemployment and a large deficit were the price to be paid.[135] The dubious distinction of having become the world's largest capital-importing and debtor nation was seen as yet another sign of the relative declining status of the United States in the world economy.[136] The rising protectionist sentiment, as exemplified by the Jenkins bill to restrict textile imports (which was deemed potentially "unfriendly to China"), was also viewed as a bad sign for American competitiveness in the world market.[137] Others pointed to the dislocations caused by structural shifts in the American economy, such as the decline of basic industries[138] and family farming.[139] Still others noted that the United States had passed from being a creditor to a debtor nation for the first time in its history.[140] Most non-Marxist commentators argued that such fundamental structural problems would long plague the U.S. economy and thus prevent Reagan from realizing his dream.

The only possible escape route for the American economy was through the new "technological revolution" (*xin jixu geming*). Beginning in 1985 the non-Marxists exhibited great fascination with this development in the West. Their writings demonstrate familiarity with Daniel Bell's writings on "postindustrial society," Brzezinski's "technetronic era," Naisbitt's "megatrends," and Toffler's "third wave." In fact, then Communist Party General Secretary Hu Yaobang personally ordered Toffler's book required reading for the Central Committee.

[133] Ke Juhan, "Meiguo daxuanhou de jingji zhengce qushi jichi qianjing," *Shijie jingji*, no. 1 (1985): 33–36.

[134] Ke Juhan and Liang Yunian, "Meiguo gao lilu wenti de xingcheng chi yingxiang," *Xiandai guoji guanxi*, no. 8 (1985): 37–43.

[135] See, for example, Liu Chuanyan, "Cong 'tingzhi pengzhang' dao 'gao shiye gao chizi,' " *Shijie jingji*, no. 12 (1985): 1–8.

[136] Zheng Weimin and Huang Eryong, "Meiguo—zuidade ziben touruguo he zuida zhaiwuguo," *Meiguo yanjiu*, no. 4 (1987): 91–108.

[137] See, for example, Wei Bo, "The 'Jenkins Bill' and Jenkins," *FBIS-CHI*, December 6, 1985, B1.

[138] Chen Hongyou, "Meiguo jingji xiabannian hui zouxiang shuaitui ma?" *Shijie zhishi*, no. 17 (1985): 20–21.

[139] Gao Yingdong, "Riyi yanzhong de Meiguo nongye weiji," *Shijie zhishi*, no. 9 (1985): 15; Li Gongchuo, "Ping Meiguo de nongye weiji he Ligen de xin nongye zhengce," *Shijie jingji*, no. 7 (1985): 60–64.

[140] Cao Meiyi, "Meiguo you zhaiquanguo xiang zhaifuguo zhuanbian de fenxi," *Shijie jingji*, no. 11 (1985): 15–20.

From September 16 to 21, 1985, the CASS Institute of World Economics and Politics convened a special symposium on the new technological revolution.[141] Many papers were presented, some of which dealt specifically with new technological developments in the United States. Typical of these was a paper by non-Marxist convert Zhang Jialin of the Shanghai Institute of International Studies. Zhang analyzed the key components of the new technological revolution in the United States and its potential impact on economic and social development.[142] He identified four main "realms" of new technological development: (1) miniaturized electronic technology; (2) biological technology; (3) the data processing industry; (4) fiber optic communications. Next Zhang identified four "main economic and social manifestations" of these developments. First, the traditional "sunset industries" (xiyang gongye) would have to be "transformed" and their workers retrained. Second, management has to be "modernized" with more input from labor. Third, the development of the service sector has to be accelerated. Fourth, "home life" has to change to take advantage of the computer age. Zhang believed that all of these changes would require fundamental adjustments in the way Americans work and live, but that, if successfully managed, the U.S. economy could avert a "new decline."

It is clear from these and other analyses that the non-Marxists recognized that the Western world was entering a new era of economic development as a result of new developments in high technologies. They recognized the importance of this new era to be potentially as profound as the impact of the industrial revolution one century earlier.[143] As far as the United States was concerned, the new technological revolution forced the America Watchers to recognize begrudgingly the capacity for innovation and renewal of American capitalism. For example, Dong Leshan of the CASS America Institute argued that while furthering the concentration of capital in the hands of the monopoly caituan in the United States, the new technological revolution had in fact created a new class of technological experts (keji zhuanjia), facilitated the replacement of old industries by new ones, lessened the impact of economic crises, and in general been a major stimulus to rejuvenating American capitalism.[144]

[141] Xin jixu geming yu shijie jingji yanjiuban jiyao, "Conglun shijie xin jixu geming, changtan dui geguo de yingxiang," Shijie jingji, no. 12 (1985): 26–31.

[142] Zhang Jialin, "Meiguo gao jixu gongye de fazhan ji mianlin de wenti," pp. 10–11.

[143] See, for example, Lu Hengjun, Shijie xin jixu geming jianghua (Heilongjiang: Renmin chubanshe, 1984), chapter 1.

[144] Dong Leshan, "Meiguo de keji jinbu yu zibenzhuyi de fazhan," Meiguo yanjiu, no. 4 (1987): 109–19.

Despite recognizing the potential importance of the "new technological revolution," the non-Marxist America Watchers were in uniform agreement that "Reaganomics" had been a failure. Reagan's departure from office (the Chinese term is "dismounting the throne," *xiatai*) was an occasion for many America Watchers to evaluate his record. The economists did note the decline in the inflation and unemployment rates, but they argued that the combination of high fiscal and trade deficits, high interest rates, bankruptcies and industrial closures, "structural unemployment," declining rate of output, and other maladies more than offset any cosmetic gains from Reaganomics.[145] This general diagnosis of the chronic condition of the U.S. economy also sparked a number of articles about America's relative declining position in the international economy.[146] President George Bush was thought to inherit an insurmountable number of problems on the economic front that no new or old formulas could resolve.[147]

Summary

By way of summation, one may observe that for all their criticisms and doubts, the non-Marxists hold grudging admiration for the resiliency of the American economy. As has been seen, they certainly believe that the U.S. economy is beset with fundamental problems unique to advanced capitalism that cannot be resolved in the long run by any type of new economic theories or policies. They certainly did not credit the supply-siders for the recovery from the 1980–1982 recession. Nonetheless, following the 1983 recovery, the tone of their analyses did shift from near-total negativism to ambivalence or moderate positivism.

As stated at the outset of this chapter, the non-Marxists are not necessarily more positive than the Marxists in their assessments of the U.S. economy, but they are less ideological in the way they argue their positions. This is what distinguishes them from the Marxist America Watchers. Marxist-Leninist orthodoxy ipso facto leads ana-

[145] See, for example, Xue Boying, " 'Ligen jingjixue' de gaiguan lunding," *Shijie jingji*, no. 12 (1988): 19–26; Chen Baosen, "Ping Ligen shidai de Meiguo jingji," *Shijie jingji*, no. 8 (1988): 1–9; Du Xiuping, "Ping Lingen jingjixue de 'geming,' " *Shijie jingji*, no. 3 (1986): 58–63.

[146] See, for example, Li Changru, "Meiguo jingji shili diwei de bianhua," *Shijie jingji*, no. 9 (1987): 1–11; Shi Min, "Meiguo jingji diwei shuailuo de zhengjie," *Shijie jingji*, no. 12 (1987): 52–58.

[147] Yu Kexing, "Meiguo jingji xingwei de huigu yu zhanwang," *Shijie jingji*, no. 4 (1989): 7–11.

lysts in this school to examine certain indicators and questions, such as worker impoverishment, monopoly capitalism, and economic crises. This orthodoxy guides not only the objects of analysis but also the conclusions to be drawn from investigation. The Marxists proceed in a deductive manner; Marx says X or Lenin says Y, ergo this must be the case in the United States. Thus, the Marxists proceed on this basis to marshall evidence to sustain the a priori theories.

The non-Marxist economists, on the other hand, proceed in an inductive manner. They are not political economists but real economists whose evidence is more empirical and statistical. This difference leads the non-Marxists to ask different questions, explore different areas of the U.S. economy, but not necessarily arrive at different answers than the Marxist School. The fact that the Marxists and non-Marxists find themselves in essential agreement about the weaknesses of the American economy is an important finding. They have traveled different routes but have arrived at a similar destination. Some are simply eclectic in their analyses, combining both Marxist and non-Marxist analyses. This is the case, for example, with Chen Baosen, chief of the U.S. economy research section at the CASS America Institute. In 1988 Chen published his 950-page magnum opus *Meiguo jingji yu zhengfu zhengce: cong Luosifuo dao Ligen* (The American economy and government policy: From Roosevelt to Reagan).[148] For all of its detailed economic analysis, Chen's study remains heavily influenced by Marxist analysis. Combining both schools of analysis, Chen comes to the general conclusion that despite the tremendous productivity of the American economy and extensive government intervention to assist the development of different sectors, American economic and financial power remains dominated by and benefits the monopoly caituan while class differences and "social contradictions" (*shehui maodun*) have only become accentuated over time. Based on a variety of indicators, Chen agrees with his colleagues in both schools that the American economy is in irreversible decline.

Thus, in sum, China's America Watchers' perceptions of the U.S. economy are characterized by different modes of investigation, but their conclusions are quite similar. Beneath the wealthy and modern exterior lies an imbalanced and deeply flawed economy, and—as will be seen in the next chapter—a society ridden with "contradictions."

[148] Chen Baosen, *Meiguo jingji yu zhengfu zhengce: cong Luosifuo dao Ligen* (Beijing: Shijie zhishi chubanshe, 1988). For reviews of Chen's book see Xu Jingzhi, "Cong xinzheng dao Ligen jingjixue," *Meiguo yanjiu*, no. 1 (1989): 149–56; Jin Dongsheng, "Dui bange shiji yilai Meiguo jingji fazhan ji zhengfu ganshe de xitong yanjiu," *Shijie jingji*, no. 9 (1989): 87–89.

Four

American Society

THERE EXISTS a long tradition of travelogue writing by Chinese who visit America. From the mid-nineteenth century through the mid-twentieth century, Chinese who crossed the Pacific as students and scholars, laborers, government emissaries, immigrants, or to visit relatives often committed their impressions to print. These historical writings were notable for the ambivalent images of American society they portrayed. Respect for American industrial and technological prowess was typically mixed with depictions of a society beset by immorality, inequality, and racism. The collection of selected Chinese writings on American society excerpted by R. David Arkush and Leo O. Lee records many of these themes,[1] as do the earlier works of Michael Hunt and Chang-fang Chen.[2]

Arkush and Lee also point to several subsidiary themes and observations prevalent in earlier travelogue writing on American society: the politeness, religiosity, energy, and individualism of Americans. They further note that interpersonal relations of Americans have long been particularly perplexing and troubling to Chinese observers. Americans' demonstrative displays of affection and anger, the shallowness of emotional ties with others (when contrasted with the binding obligations of Chinese *guanxi*), the seeming loneliness of family life and the disparate character of the nuclear family, rugged individualism, and the physical, social, and professional mobility of most Americans have all made several generations of Chinese observers uncomfortable because they contrast so sharply with the nature of their own society.[3]

As will be seen in this chapter, many of these themes are also apparent in latter-day Chinese writings on American society. Some of the negative perceptions have been accentuated by the Marxist-Leninist imagery that overlays much of the post-1949 writing, but this

[1] R. David Arkush and Leo O. Lee, eds., *Land Without Ghosts: Chinese Impressions of America from the Mid-Nineteenth Century to the Present.*

[2] Michael Hunt, *The Making of a Special Relationship: The United States and China to 1914*; Chang-fang Chen, *Barbarian Paradise: Chinese Views of the United States, 1784–1911.* Also see the Ph.D. dissertation (in progress) by Kevin Scott Wong of the University of Michigan's Department of History.

[3] Arkush and Lee, *Land Without Ghosts*, pp. 1–12.

orthodoxy has also brought new class-based analysis to light. Today's non-Marxist writing continues to note many of the ambivalent themes noted by their ancestors. Both schools of interpretation reflect a renewed intrigue with American society, but also an essential distaste for much of American life. Writings of both schools are peppered with vignettes on crime and violence, drug addiction, prostitution and pornography, vagrancy, youth counterculture, social alienation, the breakdown of the nuclear family, and so on. This negativism is sometimes balanced by protestations of experienced "Sino-American friendship," but the basic portrayal of American society offered Chinese readers is overwhelmingly critical and negative. To no small extent this is due to the fact that many of these portrayals are to be found in official or semi-official organs of the Chinese Communist Party—which has a vested interest in casting capitalist American society in the worst light possible so as to buttress its own legitimacy. In fact, many begin with the rejoinder, "Many young people in China consider America a paradise," and then proceed to indicate this not to be the case. Thus, many of the perceptions set forth in this chapter must be seen in light of the Communist Party's struggle for legitimacy and the crisis of alienation that grips much of the Chinese population. This post–Cultural Revolution alienation has been coupled with intense interest in the West.

Chinese interest in—and writings about—American society therefore continues, and the essential perceptual ambivalence endures. While many observations of American society are contextually contained in writings on the U.S. economy and polity, this chapter will draw on a set of writings exclusively devoted to contemporary American society. Some of these come in the traditional form of travelogues, while others are to be found in general surveys (*gaikuang*) of America. Altogether I have identified 34 books published about American society between 1977 and 1987.[4] Chinese readers have, in addition, at least 60 translated books on American society and 258 translations of American literature about America that were published during this period. The periodical literature is, of course, even more prolific.

As in other chapters, I will proceed sequentially to consider Marxist and then non-Marxist perceptions followed by some summary comments. Each section contains several subsections about substrata and phenomena in American society. This schema accurately portrays the division of analytical types, but in the case of American society several of the themes noted above cut across both categories. Discussions of the underside of American society are hardly peculiar

---

[4] See my *Books on America in the People's Republic of China*, pp. 28–32.

to a Marxist worldview; they strike most Chinese, many foreigners, and even Americans alike.

Marxist Perspectives on American Society: Classes and Class Struggle

Basic to a Marxist understanding of society—especially capitalist—are class relations. The United States—in the eyes of Chinese Marxist commentators—is a society beset by marked social stratification, extreme economic inequalities, and all the attendant social maladies associated with "parasitic capitalism" developed to the extreme. Social ills—of which the United States no doubt has many—are usually attributed (explicitly or implicitly) to the tyranny of the bourgeoisie. The United States is portrayed as a land of social inequity, often times juxtaposed against the socialist paradise to be found in China.

From the Chinese Marxist perspective, therefore, the United States represents the antithesis of the type of society that the Chinese Communist Party is trying to build. Political campaigns in China against "spiritual pollution" and "bourgeois liberalization" during the 1980s are testimony to this fact. Writings in official publications about American society thus serve the negative function of indoctrinating Chinese readers against the United States rather than the positive function of educating them about the United States, pro and con. This is not, however, to denigrate the sincerity of Chinese Marxist analyses of U.S. society. The criticisms that follow in this section are deeply held and strongly felt by most of the writers concerned. For them, the United States is not only a bad place, but a country that epitomizes the struggle between the social systems of socialism and capitalism. The United States represents to them what could await a non-Communist China (or what the CCP saved Guomindang China from becoming), and the "powerful weapon of Marxism–Leninism–Mao Zedong Thought" clearly explains what has gone wrong in America.

With respect to class relations, Chinese writings on American society essentially reflect a quadripartite division of classes: the bourgeoisie (*zichanjieji*), middle class (*zhongjieji*), working class (*gongrenjieji*), and poor (*pingkunjieji*).

The Bourgeoisie

Chapters 3 and 5 provide a detailed discussion of American monopoly financial groups (caituan), which comprise the principal element of the American bourgeoisie in the Marxists' eyes. To recapitulate, the Marxists offer the reductionist argument that financial groups exert dominant influence over the entirety of American economic and social life. The reader is therefore referred to chapters 3 and 5 for discussion of the composition, nature, and ways in which these caituan exert their dominance over American economic and political life respectively. The discussion here is confined to some general descriptions of the American bourgeoisie.

How large is the American bourgeoisie, and what is its nature? The basic handbook on the United States compiled by members of the Fudan University International Politics Department Capitalist Countries Teaching and Research Office states that there are more than ten million millionaires in the United States. All are members of regional or familial caituan, and collectively they "control" (kongzhi) all banking, commerce, light and heavy industry, public utilities, communications and transportation, and science and technology.[5]

American economy specialist Chen Baosen argues that any discussion of the American bourgeoisie must be more inclusive than merely millionaires. One measure of membership in the bourgeoisie, Chen argues, is someone who employs others. Chen cites 1984 U.S. statistics from the Presidential Small Business Report that there are 113,526,000 employers in the United States.[6] But Chen goes on to say that there are also other measures of the bourgeoisie, and by very definition a bourgeois is someone who owns property. Chen cites figures of 59,390,000 property-owning Americans. Another measure, according to Chen, is per capita income. By this standard, he writes that the American bourgeoisie can be classified into four categories according to personal income: 0.5 percent as "super rich" (chaoji fuhu), 0.5 percent as "very rich" (feichang fuhu), 9.0 percent as "rich" (fuhu), and 90 percent as "ordinary" (putong) bourgeois households. The "ordinary" bourgeois households possess 65.1 percent of private wealth in the United States while the other 10 percent own 34.9 percent of personal wealth. Chen goes on to lament this concentration of wealth in America: the 0.5 percent "super rich" having an average income of $6.82 million, the 0.5 percent "very rich" averaging $1.79 million, the "rich" $397,000, and the "ordinary" bourgeoisie $39,584.

By various measures, then, Chen Baosen depicts an extensive American bourgeoisie that has accumulated considerable personal wealth. It is interesting to note the "ordinary" category in Chen's

[5] Fudan daxue guoji zhengzhixi zibenzhuyi guojia zhengzhi jiaoyanshi, eds., *Meiguo* (Shanghai: Cishu chubanshe, 1982), pp. 227, 228.

[6] Chen Baosen, *Meiguo jingji yu zhengfu zhengce*, p. 600.

schema. This is important because it points up the new Chinese recognition of the rise of the American middle class.

The Middle Class

The middle class is now recognized by most Chinese observers as a valid depiction of a substrata within the bourgeoisie. Until the 1980s this was not the case, as a simple dichotomous bourgeois-proletarian schema prevailed. As Chinese began to visit the United States, however, they discovered that American society was not so simply demarcated. As will be seen below, after exposure to the West, Chinese Marxists engaged in a sharp debate over the degree of "impoverishment" of the proletariat. To anticipate one outcome of the debate, it was concluded that a significant number of the working class had moved up the class ladder to join the middle class.

What is the middle class? According to one typical report in *Guangming ribao* in 1980, "The middle class is a social class that comprises quite a large number of people in American society. It actually includes individuals and families with middle-level income, and this mostly includes small enterprise owners, small farmers, small businessmen, ordinary executives and middle and high-ranking employees, doctors, teachers, engineers, and other professionals and technicians in the higher income bracket."[7] The article goes on to categorize 76 percent of Americans as middle class, with incomes ranging from $8,000 (below which is the poverty line) to $50,000. After detailing for readers just who constitutes the American middle class, the bulk of the article is devoted to a discussion of the triple burden on the middle class of economic stagflation, increased taxes, and rising prices during the 1970s. The resulting drop in real income resulted, according to the author, in the following:

> Many housewives must go out to work to maintain the previous standard of living. Some of them who cannot really afford houses in the suburbs have to make do with repairing old houses in the downtown area. Some have been feeling the burden of sending their children to private colleges. Some are forced to do away with vacations abroad or travel within the United States. Some have to reduce their savings or acquire more loans. Some resort to sewing their own clothes, planting their own vegetables, and other means to save on expenses.[8]

[7] Dong Mei, "The Condition and Ideological Trend of the Middle Class in the United States," *Guangming ribao*, May 24, 1980, *JPRS* 75962, June 30, 1980, p. 30.
[8] Ibid., p. 31.

The article describes the progressive tax structure in the United States and its impact on the middle class, the impact of high interest rates, the growing debts of middle-class Americans, and the increased number of bankruptcies and small business and farm foreclosures. On the basis of these financial burdens, the author correctly points to the political appeal of the Reaganite Republican platform of that election year. Many middle-class Americans saw hope, Dong Mei argues, in the Reagan economic program and appeal to "national pride and patriotism."[9]

While most America Watchers, including the Marxists, came to accept the distinction of the middle class as a separate element of the American bourgeoisie, discussion of the middle class was not without dissenting opinions. The 1983 "spiritual pollution" campaign in China triggered a wave of Marxist articles criticizing Western society. Among them were several attacking the notion of a nonexploitative middle class. One typical article in an internal-circulation journal of the Academy of Social Sciences argued that even those who were not members of the "big bourgeoisie" still "clipped coupons" and lived off the surplus value of the working class, and thus they had to be considered part of the bourgeoisie and party to its exploitation.[10]

The Working Class

By far the bulk of Chinese Marxist writing on American class relations relates, not unexpectedly, to the status of the proletariat. Two issues in particular dominate discussion: the relative "impoverishment" and relative militancy of the proletariat in the class struggle with the bourgeoisie. Chinese Marxist theory—at least of the Maoist variety—held that the American proletariat was "absolutely" impoverished and thus imbued with revolutionary militancy and on the verge of rising up to "throw off its chains." Mao's own writings and official propaganda both portrayed these images during the period of Sino-American estrangement. Old habits die hard, and it was not until the mid-1980s that China's America Watchers apparently concluded that the United States was not on the verge of a socialist revolution led by an aroused proletariat.

How did they arrive at this conclusion? In short, firsthand exposure to the United States together with more general de-Maoification

[9] Ibid., p. 32.

[10] Huo Shitao, "Shilun zhongchanjieji," *Shijie jingji yu zhengzhi neican*, no. 6 (1984): 32–36, 19.

in China combined to offer a thorough reassessment of the status of the American working class. Crucial to this reassessment was the lively debate waged among Marxist theorists in China during the late 1970s and early 1980s over the relative "impoverishment" of the proletariat in Western countries—but primarily in the United States. Discussions of the militancy of the working class continued throughout the same period.

THE DEBATE ON THE "IMPOVERISHMENT OF THE PROLETARIAT"

Like the polemics of imperialism and state-monopoly capitalism examined in chapter 2, the debate on the impoverishment of the proletariat was waged among Marxist theorists who specialized in capitalist systems, and the critical mass of debate was located in the Capitalist Countries' Research Office of the Institute of World Economics and Politics at the Chinese Academy of Social Sciences. The institute's journal *Shijie jingji* was a principal national forum for the debate and outlet for CASS's more maverick theorists. Marxist scholars from other institutes and universities also contributed significantly to the dialogue, but the IWEP was the epicenter of debate.

Also, as in the imperialism and state-monopoly capitalism polemics, theoretical innovation came in subtle shifts by degree in argument rather than the wholesale jettisoning of existing orthodoxy. Thus, the issue of debate was not whether the American proletariat was impoverished (because to challenge this Marxist maxim would be considered too heterodox), but whether the proletariat was "absolutely" or "relatively" impoverished. "Absolute impoverishment" (*juedui pingkunhua*) suggested that the capitalist system was thoroughly exploitative and had driven the working class into such a state of poverty that their revolutionary potential was very high. "Relative impoverishment" (*xiangdui pingkunhua*), on the other hand, suggested that standards of living for the proletariat were not so dire, and indeed the working class had enjoyed the fruits of postwar economic expansion and thus had a stake in upholding—not overthrowing—the capitalist system. These were the lines of debate.

The debate began in earnest in late 1978 and early 1979 following a conference on the subject convened by Fudan University in October 1978. Fudan University's International Politics Department, Political Economy Department, and World Economy Research Institute had since 1964 been assigned by the central government the task of being the national center (among universities) for the study of capitalist countries' economies, societies, polities, and foreign policies, while Peking University was told to concentrate on the developing world, and People's University on the socialist world.[11] The conference was attended by seventy "theoretical workers" (*lilun gongzuozhe*) from more than thirty concerned institutions from across China.[12] The official report on the conference also alleges that economists at the Institute of International Relations had begun to discuss the issue of the condition of the capitalist proletariat in 1963, but these discussions had been terminated by the Gang of Four. This is interesting in that it was at this institute (an intelligence forerunner to the current Institute of Contemporary International Relations, then under the direction of Kang Sheng and the Investigation Department of the Communist Party) where challenges to Stalinist orthodoxy with respect to imperialism and state-monopoly capitalism were first raised—also to be curtailed by the Gang of Four and the Cultural Revolution (see chapter 2). At any rate, with the Gang arrested, Mao and Kang Sheng dead, and many "theoretical workers" rehabilitated from Cultural Revolution May 7th Cadre Schools, debate began anew.

Division of opinion at the Fudan conference on the impoverishment of the proletariat reportedly divided along three lines.[13] The first group apparently argued that "historical conditions can change" and that "an absolutely impoverished working class no longer exists (*bu cunzai*) in the main capitalist countries." On this basis, the first group argued that Marx's theory of the impoverishment of the proletariat was not a "law" (*guilu*). The second school of opinion argued the opposite; not only did "absolute impoverishment" continue to exist in all (*dou cunzai*) capitalist countries, but the gap between capitalists and proletarians had widened (*hougou*) so that the average worker was worse off than ever! On this basis, they argued, Marx's theory was a "scientific law." The third group, in a true compromise tradition, opined that the term "absolute impoverishment" could be interpreted in either a narrow or broad sense (*xiayi* versus *kuangyi*). In a narrow sense there is no denying that the material condition of the capitalist working class has improved markedly, but in a broad sense "it cannot be denied" that impoverishment frequently exists (*jingchang cunzai*). If viewed in this sense, the third group argued that Marx's theory was sustained as a "law."

These three lines of argument from the Fudan conference essentially framed the parameters of the debate over the next four years. The latter position, which became known as the "relative impover-

---

[11] For the evolution of this policy decision and its consequences see my and Wang Jisi's "International Studies in the People's Republic of China."

[12] Lin Zhenjin, "Taolun zibenzhuyi zhidu xia wuchanjieji," *Shijie jingji*, no. 1 (1979): p. 69.

[13] As described in the report on the conference, ibid.

ishment" position, eventually prevailed. This kind of compromise—revision without rejection—permitted Chinese Marxist theorists to explore the middle class and look more closely at the nature of the proletariat's material and political condition, all the while maintaining allegiance to Marxist orthodoxy. Like the debates on the longevity of imperialism and the relationship of the state to monopolies, which opened the doors to more detailed and revisionist interpretations, this too was an important theoretical breakthrough.

But all was not decided at the Fudan meeting. Several years of continued debate ensued over the status of the proletariat's degree of impoverishment and potential revolutionary militancy. With respect to the impoverishment issue, the first issue of *Shijie jingji* in 1979 sparked continued debate by running a series of articles excerpted from the Fudan conference. Interestingly, as in the polemics on imperialism and state-monopoly capitalism, those articles that took the dogmatic position on the absolute impoverishment of the capitalist proletariat cited Stalin and Soviet scholarly writings of the late Stalin era (1952–1953) as proof of their ideological correctness,[14] while those that took the heretical and compromise positions both invoked Lenin's *Selected Works* to bolster their arguments.[15] This was the way to pay tribute to the orthodoxy while in fact undermining it.

With the Fudan conference over, the maverick Marxist theorists at CASS's IWEP set about pressing their case for the "relative impoverishment" of the bourgeoisie. By doing so they were arguing that advanced capitalism was not as evil as it had been made out to be by the Maoists, and implicitly that there was something to learn from the status of capitalist workers. When considered together with the judgment that imperialism (i.e., advanced capitalism) was not in danger of collapsing soon, and that the state exhibited substantial autonomy from the monopoly bourgeoisie, to argue that the working class under advanced capitalism was not really impoverished (and hence not on the verge of revolution) was tantamount to the rejection

[14] See Jiang Xuemo, "Jue dui pingkunhua shi jianduan de chuxian de xianxiang, bushi jingji guilu," *Shijie jingji*, no. 1 (1979): 61; Wang Jialin, "Youshi juedui pingkunhua shi yitiao zibenzhuyi de jingji guilu," ibid., pp. 61–62.

[15] For those who argue the "relative impoverishment" position, see Xiang Xiaofei, "Buneng yong shenghuo shuiping bi guoqu e'hua lai jieshi juedui pingkunhua," ibid., pp. 62–63; and Li Chenglin, "Zai fada de zibenzhuyi guojiazhong bu cunzai juedui pingkunhua, wuchanjieji pingkunhua zhuyao de biaoxian wei xiangdui pingkunhua," ibid., pp. 63–64. For the compromise position, see Yang Shiwang, "Juedui pingkunhua you 'xiayi' he 'kuangyi' de liangzhong geyi, shi youshi er bushi shizhong cunzai de xianxiang," ibid., pp. 65–66; and Du Houwen, "Zai liangzhong geyi de juedui pingkunhuazhong, kuangyi de juedui pingkunhua shi jingchang de xianxiang," ibid., pp. 66–67.

of three of the key tenets of Marxist orthodoxy on capitalism. All three revisionist positions helped justify China's diplomatic opening to the West, thus offering further evidence that in the post-Mao era ideology came to play a post hoc rationalizing role for policy decisions based on other pragmatic criteria.

The CASS Institute of World Economics and Politics had one built-in advantage in all three polemics, namely, that it published the key journals in China for discussion of such topics (*Shijie jingji* and *Shijie jingji yu zhengzhi neican*). In the case of the "impoverishment of the proletariat" debate, *Shijie jingji* began to publish numerous articles advocating the "relative impoverishment" position. The second issue of *Shijie jingji* in 1979 published an article on foreign scholarly discussions on the impoverishment issue.[16] Without exception, all citations were drawn from the Soviet Academy of Sciences' Institute of Economics during the Khrushchev era. As witnessed in chapter 2, this was the period when many Chinese economists (now at CASS's IWEP) were resident in Varga's institute and were exposed to the de-Stalinization taking place there. Thus there is further evidence that Chinese Marxist discussions of the early post-Mao era closely paralleled those in the Soviet Union under Khrushchev, and that the Chinese discussions were directly influenced by the Sino-Soviet scholarly exchange of that era. The same issue of *Shijie jingji* also published several reference tables on wages of workers in selected capitalist countries during the postwar era that clearly show the inexorable increase in the standard of living over time.[17]

Throughout the remainder of 1979, articles were published that enumerated the problems facing capitalist workers as a result of stagflation, industrial layoffs, and so on, but still took the point of view that their impoverishment was "relative."[18] One article devoted specifically to the status of worker impoverishment in the United States, written by former Milton Friedman student Luo Chengxi (a senior economist at the IWEP), took note of the improved standard of living for American workers throughout the economic boom years of the 1950s and 1960s, but it also dwelt at length on the "underclass" and welfare state in America.[19]

[16] Luo Pihong and Lin Zhengan. "Guowai xueshujie guanyu zibenzhuyi zhidu xia wuchanjieji pingkunhua wenti de taolun," *Shijie jingji*, no. 2 (1979): 66–68.

[17] "Zhuyao zibenzhuyi guojia gongrenjieji de jingji gaikuang," *Shijie jingji*, no. 12 (1979): 78–80.

[18] See, for example, Lin Baipeng, "Pingkunhua lilun yu zhanhou zibenzhuyi guojiazhong wuchanjieji de diwei he gaikuang," *Shijie jingji*, no. 8 (1979): 30–35, 18; Shi Min, Lin Zhengan, and Liu Shihua, "Zhanhou fada zibenzhuyi guojia gongrenjieji de xiaofei zengchang yu pingkun," *Shijie jingji*, no. 11 (1979).

[19] Luo Chengxi, "Dierce shijie dazhanhou Meiguo wuchanjieji de juedui pingkunhua," *Shijie jingji*, no. 5 (1979): 24–31.

The 1979–1982 economic recession in the United States helped sustain Chinese attention on the condition of the working class into the early 1980s. Much of this attention focused on perceived worker militancy.

CLASS STRUGGLE AND THE REVOLUTIONARY POTENTIAL
OF THE PROLETARIAT

Chinese Marxist writings on the militancy of the American proletariat and potential for revolution in the United States were nothing new. Since the Yan'an period, Chairman Mao had written of both, particularly with reference to the "black liberation movement" (*heiren jiefang yundong*).[20] The Sino-American estrangement after 1949 only accelerated such writings. They perhaps reached a zenith during the 1960s as the militant Cultural Revolution in China coincided with the antiwar movement and race riots in the United States. It may seem absurd for Americans to consider that their nation was on the verge of a violent socialist revolution during the tumultuous days of 1968–1969, but that is precisely what the Chinese propaganda machine was predicting at the time. With the Sino-American rapprochement, such articles disappeared from the Chinese press almost overnight. This is not to say that reporting on proletarian militancy ceased, but it was toned down considerably and devoted almost exclusively to coverage of strikes and the trade union movement.

The years 1976, 1977, and 1978 were considered banner years for American proletarian militancy. In 1976 the Chinese press reported on strikes of automobile workers, rubber workers, coal miners, public utility workers, truck drivers, school teachers, nurses, and so on.[21] One commentary concluded that "The American workers have displayed militant unity in their strike struggles this year. . . . The militancy shown by the rank-and-file organizations in this year's mass movement has given new impetus to the workers' struggle."[22] In mid-1977 New China News Agency reported that "The U.S. working class movement shows a new upsurge in militancy this year. A mounting succession of strikes have flared up in protest against ruth-

[20] See, for example, Mao Zedong, "Zhichi Meiguo heiren fandui diguozhuyi zhongzu qishide zhengyi douzheng de shengming," *Renmin ribao*, August 9, 1963; Mao Zedong, "Zhichi Meiguo heiren kangbao douzheng de shengming," *Renmin ribao*, April 17, 1968.

[21] See, for example, Mei Ping, "New Developments in the Struggle Waged by Workers on Strike in Western Countries," Peking Domestic Service, August 10, 1976, *FBIS-CHI*, August 12, 1976, A1–2.

[22] "U.S. Workers Showing Increasing Militancy," *Xinhuashe*, October 11, 1976, *FBIS-CHI*, October 14, 1976, A2–3.

less exploitation and oppression by the monopolists and their agents.
. . . The working class is intensifying its fight because capitalist exploitation is becoming more ruthless in the United States. . . . Ruthless exploitation and oppression serves only to enhance the class awareness of the American workers to carry on their movement with increasing momentum."[23] A year-end commentary declared, "The American working class and laboring people have carried out widespread struggles against exploitation and oppression by the monopoly capitalist class in 1977,"[24] while another added, "While opposing the monopoly capitalists, the masses of U.S. workers have also clearly directed their struggle against a few union leaders who are agents of the bourgeoisie in the workers' movement."[25]

Such comments about labor unions are not atypical. A 1978 commentary opined with reference to the coal miners strike, "What is noteworthy is that the struggle between the workers and the union leaders has also intensified, breaking the control of the union leaders."[26] An article on the history and role of American labor unions in *Shijie zhishi* in 1980 argued that U.S. unions had long since been coopted by the bourgeoisie and were, in fact, conduits for buying the political complacency of the American proletariat.[27]

The capitalist also buys the complacency of the working class through increased wages and fringe benefits. Said an article in the *Worker's Daily*: "Under the capitalist system the income of workers does not increase automatically with the development of production because of the insatiable greed of the capitalist for profits. The working class therefore relies on struggle against the capitalist to force a readjustment of their wages and fringe benefits to numb the class consciousness of workers so that the social order can be stabilized and the capitalist system of exploitation maintained."[28]

The social welfare system is similarly viewed as a capitalist trick. As Marxist America Watcher Yao Tinggang noted in a 1982 article in *Hongqi* (Red flag), "When adopting widespread social welfare poli-

---

[23] "Strikes Increase as U.S. Workers Show New Militancy," *Xinhuashe*, July 18, 1977, *FBIS-CHI*, July 20, 1977, A3–5.

[24] "NCNA Reports Labor Problems in U.S.," *Xinhuashe*, 31 December 1977, *FBIS-CHI*, 5 January 1978, A4.

[25] No author, "The U.S. Working Class Is Advancing Amid Struggle," Peking Domestic Service, February 27, 1978, *FBIS-CHI*, March 3, 1978, A3.

[26] "U.S. Workers Wage Heroic Struggle Against Monopoly Capital," *Xinhuashe*, April 28, 1978, *FBIS-CHI*, April 28, 1978, A3.

[27] Dong Mei, "Meiguode gonghui he gongren yundong," *Shijie zhishi*, no. 9 (1980): 9–11.

[28] Sun Shangqing, "Correctly Look at the Life of American Workers," *Gongren ribao*, March 11, 1980, JPRS 75457, April 8, 1980, p. 1.

cies, the monopoly capitalist class does not proceed from a sense of benevolence, but aims at mitigating class contradictions and consolidating its rule. . . . Implementation of the social welfare system is necessary for the monopoly capitalist class to grab higher monopoly profits and to maintain its class interests."[29] Social security is viewed as a particular form of capitalist profit-mongering. An article in *Shijie zhishi* in 1981 claimed that the social security system is another form of extracting surplus value in that workers are forced to pay into the scheme over the years while the bourgeois state and capitalist bankers invest and earn interest from workers' earnings.[30]

After 1980 one notices a marked drop-off of Chinese Marxist writing on the American proletariat in the press and scholarly journals. That which exists relates primarily to strikes[31] or labor unions.[32] One notable exception was Professor Liu Xuyi, a specialist on American history at Wuhan University and secretary-general of the American History Research Association. Professor Liu, who probably has no peer as a Marxist historian of the United States in China (except perhaps Huang Shaoxiang), was prolific throughout this period. Many of his journal articles were edited and appear in Liu's 1987 volume *Dangqian Meiguo zongtong yu shehui* (The contemporary American presidency and society).[33] This book is, in short, a history of class struggle in America. Professor Liu sees ever-heightening class tensions, ever-increasing proletarian militancy, unceasing exploitation and oppression by the monopoly bourgeoisie, the fallacy of the welfare state, but a bright future for the United States once the socialist sun finally dawns on its shores. Of the latter prospect Professor Liu has no doubt.

Professor Liu must, however, be considered a virtual minority of one. Most Marxists in China have come to realize that America is not

[29] Yao Tinggang, "Analysis of the Social Welfare System in Developed Capitalist Countries," *Hongqi*, no. 6 (1982), *JPRS* 80980, June 4, 1982, p. 80.

[30] Mei Zheng, "Cong Meiguo kan zibenzhuyi guojia de shehui fuli zhidu," *Shijie zhishi*, no. 13 (1981): 15–17.

[31] See, for example, Zhou Li, "Zhanhou zhuyao zibenzhuyi guojia bagong yundong de fazhan jichi jingji genyuan," *Shijie jingji*, no. 4 (1982): 23–28; Huang Su'an, "The Influence of the Protracted Economic Recession and Crisis of the West on the Working Class," *Hongqi*, no. 16 (1983), *JPRS*, October 5, 1983, pp. 78–85; Zhou Tong, "Yinianlai shijie gongren douzheng," *Renmin ribao*, April 30, 1984.

[32] See, for example, Zhang Yunting, "Dangqian Meiguo gonghui yundong de dongxiang he wenti," *Shijie jingji yu zhengzhi neican*, no. 9 (1983): 49–52; Chen Bolin, "The Current State of the Labor Movement in the United States," *Gongren ribao*, January 12, 1982, *FBIS-CHI*, February 4, 1982, B3–4; Zhang Youlun, "Meiguo gongren yundong he shehuizhuyi de fazhan," *Meiguo yanjiu*, no. 4 (1987): 120–36.

[33] Liu Xuyi, *Dangqian Meiguo zongtong yu shehui: xiandai Meiguo shehui fazhan jianshi* (Hebei: Renmin chubanshe, 1987).

ripe for revolution. Despite the continued sustenance of the Marxist paradigm for interpreting the American economy, society, polity, and foreign policy—as seen in this study—and the generally dire state that this cohort of America Watchers perceive the United States to be in, they still do not arrive at the conclusion that ergo revolution is at hand. Thus, during the course of the 1980s, Chinese Marxist writing about proletarian militancy in the United States declined in general, and discussion of revolutionary potential disappeared altogether.

The Poor

Poverty in American society draws considerable attention from China's America Watchers, Marxist and non-Marxist alike. Their writings portray the fact that a whole class of destitute Americans exists below the working class.

The plight of America's homeless draws particular attention. Chinese newspaper readers often read dispatches about the homeless, and Chinese television airs visual images of vagrants in American cities. *People's Daily's* Washington, D.C., correspondent Yuan Xianlu decided to investigate the problem by visiting soup kitchens and shelters in the capital. His report concluded:

> The growing number of vagrants is naturally linked with the deterioration of economic conditions in America. The large number of homeless young and adult Negroes is a result of the protracted unemployment rate of the Negroes. The noticeable increase of homeless women reflects the ever-aggravating family and social issues of the country. Large groups of cheap housing have also been torn down to make way for luxury dwellings. The rent becomes ever-higher, and the number of houses that the poor can afford dwindles more and more. Isn't it an irony that the prosperity of society is pushing more and more people into the tragic circumstance of becoming homeless?[34]

Yuan's exploration into American poverty also took him into Appalachia and the South where he discovered that the collapse of family farming and the seasonal migrant fruit pickers had led to an upsurge of vagrancy in Sun Belt cities. He also found what he described as the "employed poor" who live above the official poverty line but can-

[34] Yuan Xianlu, "Poverty in America," *Renmin ribao*, January 5–6, 1982, *JPRS* 80051, February 8, 1982, p. 10. For a discussion of abandoned children, child prostitutes, and "street urchins," see Li Gu, "Meiguo jietou de liulanger," *Shijie zhishi*, no. 21 (1983): 11.

not afford food, adequate housing, medical care, or clothing, yet "have televisions, washing machines, and refrigerators, and some even have cars." This led Yuan to conclude that "America's poverty is concealed behind a 'rose-colored curtain.' "[35]

Other reports focused on what another *People's Daily* correspondent labeled the "mockery" of the United States being the world's largest agricultural producer while so many go hungry.[36] Reagan administration cutbacks of food stamps and nutrition allowances were criticized.[37]

America's poor, in short, fit easily into the Marxist image of capitalist society. They form the bottom tier of the four-level class pyramid perceived by the Marxist America Watchers. The non-Marxists, on the other hand, do not envision American society in class terms as much as a kind of social melting pot. To be sure, as will be seen in the following section, they criticize many aspects of American society. But theirs is a more dynamic and inclusive image that takes account of a greater variety of social actors and processes.

Non-Marxist Perspectives on American Society: The Melting Pot

Travelogues are probably the most poignant example of the non-Marxist perspective on America. They are frequently referred to in Chinese by the proverb "viewing flowers from horseback" (*zuoma guanhua*), meaning a quick and superficial glance at a land.

Travelogues come in two principal forms. The first form are articles carried in newspapers or popular journals that record the general impressions of the author after a trip to the United States. The second form—books—are certainly more lengthy and somewhat more analytical in nature. Both forms essay on a wide variety of observed phenomena in American society and culture.

Two salient characteristics stand out about this particular type of commentary on the United States. First, the recorded impressions are highly experiential and anecdotal. That is, the impressions of Chinese visiting America tend to be much more profoundly influenced by personal experiences than by what they read or are told. This may have much to do with the highly personalistic nature of Chinese so-

[35] Yuan Xianlu, "Poverty in America," p. 11.

[36] See, for example, Zhang Liang, "The Crisis of Farm 'Surplus' and the Phenomenon of Hunger," *Renmin ribao*, January 28, 1983, *FBIS-CHI*, February 3, 1983, B5–6.

[37] Zhang Liang, "More People in the United States Are Living Below the Poverty Line," *Renmin ribao*, August 5, 1983, *FBIS-CHI*, August 9, 1983, B7–8.

ciety: the importance of personal relationships (*guanxi*), the close
proximity in which Chinese live and the concomitant lack of broader
spatial perspective, and the general preference for the experiential
over the intellectual. The second characteristic is somewhat related
and to be expected of any traveler, namely, the tendency to compare
the foreign country in question with one's homeland. This is done
both implicitly and explicitly. Implicit cultural categories of interpretation order and categorize what is being perceived, while explicit
comparisons are frequently offered. Travelogues therefore often say
more about the perceiver than the perceived. The perceptual baggage
that the traveler carries with him or her profoundly shapes the experience had in a foreign land. Both of these proclivities thus exhibit
a kind of mirror imagery in the ways in which Chinese visitors perceive and portray the United States in travelogue writing.

   This section draws upon both travelogue writing as well as the
more standard journalistic and scholarly interpretations used
throughout this study. First I will sample the post-1972 travelogue
writings. These provide a random yet integrated view of the United
States. Second, I will draw on more specialized writings to explore
two topics about which much is written: racism and American family
life.

Chinese Travelogues about the United States

Soon after President Nixon's historic visit to China in 1972, the American Society of Newspaper Editors invited a delegation of Chinese
journalists to tour the United States. The Chinese Journalists' Delegation visited ten cities in eight states, covering eight thousand miles,
during May–June 1973. Their itinerary included visits to the White
House (where they were received by President Nixon), corporate
boardrooms, the New York Stock Exchange, historical sites, factories,
farms, and of course newspaper offices. It was the first glimpse mainland Chinese had had of the United States in over twenty years.
Their visit also provided Chinese readers an initial firsthand account
of the Beautiful Imperialist. The delegation included representatives
of many Chinese publications: Xinhua News Agency, the *People's
Daily*, *Guangming ribao*, the Shanghai daily *Wen hui bao*, the Guangzhou daily *Nanfang ribao*, and the English-language *Peking Review* and
China Reconstructs. The *People's Daily* correspondents on the delegation regretted that there was not more contact with American workers but claimed to be impressed by the tour and the "American peo-

ple's deep friendship for the Chinese people."[38] Their report also noted that they were impressed by the effect of piecework to raise labor productivity, the extroversion of Americans (particularly children), and the intense interest in China that they encountered everywhere. They also commented about "the many problems of American society—inflation, crimes, drugs, pollution, racial discrimination, and the wide gap between rich and poor." The *Guangming ribao* correspondent also noted the interest in Chinese socialism that the Americans whom they met exhibited and the general evocations of friendship and curiosity.[39] The *Peking Review* writer-editor Wang Xi also commented on these two experiences but noted the prevalence of narcotic addiction, "social ferment," and the threat of unemployment. On the latter she noted:

> Quite a number of the nine million university students in the United States are haunted by the threat of unemployment. But every day the media, the papers, radio and television, feed the young with tales of the poor becoming rich. We ourselves heard more than once such talk that the American system provides opportunities for the ordinary guy as well as for the rich. However the words of a young technician bared the essence of this propaganda. "It's a kind of drug, it's opium," he said.[40]

In the autumn of 1978, as the diplomatic normalization accords were being secretly negotiated in both capitals, a second Chinese journalists' delegation visited the United States. This delegation's itinerary was also varied. Their printed observations, however, were more penetrating and less prone to hyperbole about "Sino-American friendship." Some members were impressed by the popularization of science,[41] while others were awed by the modernity of communications and transportation—particularly the frequency with which Americans travel by airplanes and automobiles.[42] The most perceptive observations, however, were recorded by journalist, philoso-

[38] "People's Daily Correspondents Describe U.S. Visit," *FBIS-CHI*, August 6, 1973, A4–6. This report is excerpted from the August 4, 1973, *Renmin ribao* as transmitted by *Xinhuashe* on the same day.

[39] Zhang Zhanghai, "Notes on Journey to the U.S.," *Guangming ribao*, July 27, 1973, as carried in *Ta kung pao* (Hong Kong), August 2, 1973, p. 14.

[40] Wang Xi, "From Manhattan to Honolulu: A Trip through the USA," *Peking Review*, September 7, 1973, pp. 43–45. The quotation is from p. 45.

[41] Yang Yumei, "Observations on the Popularization of Science in the United States," *Renmin ribao*, October 6, 1978, *JPRS* 72423, December 13, 1978, pp. 12–16.

[42] Li Yanning, "U.S. Civil Aviation, Railroad, and Inland River Shipping Operations," *Renmin ribao*, November 1, 1978, pp. 29–33; "Automobiles and Highways in the United States," *Renmin ribao*, November 3, 1978, pp. 34–36.

pher, and pundit Wang Ruoshui. Many of Wang's observations are worth recalling.[43]

Wang was initially struck by U.S. skyscrapers. He thought them impressive structures at first, but then he came to realize (referring to New York City) that these "tall buildings blocked out the sunlight. It was as though the pedestrians were in a dark valley. Men looked even smaller, as though they were crowded in by these monsters of capitalism." Traffic order also impressed Wang. Unlike China, vehicles stayed in their lane, stopped at traffic lights and for pedestrians, and rarely sounded their horns. "The Americans felt it was an insult to have a driver honk at them." The abundance of automobiles (and resulting gasoline consumption) astounded Wang, as it did his colleagues. The service sector also left an impression: plentiful goods in the shops, courteous service personnel, and the custom of tipping. "In some cases tips were even given in bathrooms!" Wang observed. The generally clean state of American cities (except New York) was another positive impression; "clean streets and few flies." Automation also left a deep impression on Wang. He was impressed by self-operating elevators, vending machines, subway farecard machines, automatic change machines, and the overall reduction in manual labor in factories. The number of public parks and museums with the "careful preservation" of cultural relics further impressed him.

What bothered Wang about the United States? On the negative side of the ledger, he noted crime, poverty, drugs, religion, outward appearances, and the level of tension among working people. The threat of crime was brought home to him during a taxi ride in Detroit where he witnessed the bullet-proof glass between driver and passenger. Wang was also taken for a drive in New York on upper Broadway, through Harlem, and into Brooklyn where he witnessed "many impoverished houses" and prostitution. The drug problem was apparently impressed on Wang by the Chinese Embassy in Washington, which hosted the delegation for a special screening of *The Man with the Golden Arm*—lest they return to China with misguided notions about capitalist America! The prevalence of religion Wang found particularly puzzling. He was surprised to find a bible in every hotel room, to learn that Americans judged their president by religious standards, and to witness "the big swindler from South Korea" Reverend Sun Myung Moon. The only answer Wang could arrive at to explain the prevalence of religion in the United States was that "religion was still so powerful that the ruling class needed it and

[43] Wang Ruoshui, "A Glance at the United States," *Renmin ribao*, October 17–19, 1978, pp. 17–28. The following quotations are all drawn from this three-part series.

that men still could not master their own destinies." Some American living habits he also found odd. When referring to Americans' dress, Wang observed they were "excessive in their outlandish and bizarre costumes." Finally, he found that Americans were extremely "energetic and tense" while working, but "when they play, they play." These were among Wang Ruoshui's initial impressions of the United States.

These two journalistic delegations provide a flavor of some of the early travelogue accounts of the United States following the Sino-American rapprochement. Articles written by individual travelers represent another category of travelogue writing.

The Chinese investigative journalist and social critic Liu Binyan spent part of the 1982–1983 academic year with the International Writers Program at the University of Iowa. Liu published several of his observations on the United States, based on his stay in Iowa City, in the *People's Daily*.[44] The physical order and landscape of Iowa City was the first thing that struck Liu. All the houses were so neat and tidy on separate plots of land, yet each having an individual character that Liu reckoned reflected the personality of the owners. "I felt as if I had slipped into a colorful cartoon world," he wrote. Liu was amused by the number of pet dogs. He commented that he rarely saw pregnant women in public. Child-rearing practices also intrigued Liu Binyan. The emphasis on creating individual personalities, giving children their own bedrooms and belongings, paying them allowances for spending, and smothering them in material items were notable characteristics of the midwestern middle-class families Liu encountered.

Chen Yi, who had a long career in the People's Liberation Army's General Political Department and then headed the Propaganda Department of the Shanghai Communist Party during the early 1980s, visited the United States in 1988 and published his reflections in the now defunct *Shijie jingji daobao*.[45] The plentiful range of consumer items stunned Chen Yi, but not as much as the prices. "I saw some goods in American stores, such as shoes, that were selling for $90–$100 but in China can be bought for 40–50 yuan. Women's dresses selling for $160 can be bought in China for at most 100 yuan. I couldn't see much difference in style or quality, so why can't our

---

[44] See, for example, Liu Binyan, "America—Broad and Narrow," *Renmin ribao*, February 28, 1983, *FBIS-CHI*, March 8, 1983, B1–4. Curiously, he omits recollections of his year in the United States in his biography *A Higher Kind of Loyalty* (New York: Random House, 1990).

[45] Chen Yi, "Random Thoughts on Visiting the United States," *Shijie jingji daobao*, March 13, 1989, *JPRS CAR-89-047*, May 17, 1989, pp. 2–9.

goods get on the U.S. market?" Chen wondered. He praised American initiative and hard work, ecology, the telephone system, technology, and democracy. His criticism was reserved for crime, drug use, and homosexuality.

Wu Dakun, a specialist on the American economy at People's University, had distinctly negative impressions of the United States during his visit in 1980. He singled out exorbitant prices, pornography, racial discrimination, youth unemployment, and homosexuality as social maladies of the United States.[46]

Another traveler, Chen Xiaohui, a secondary school teacher from Hangzhou, visited her siblings in Pennsylvania. Madame Chen was so put off by the United States that she returned to China early and committed her impressions to print in the *People's Daily*.[47] Chen began her article by criticizing the "double burden" of high taxes and high prices on Americans. Her brother, a college professor, was apparently having a difficult time making ends meet. The "frantic" lifestyle of Americans also bothered Chen: "During my three and a half months in America I saw people rushing around incessantly making a living." Care for the aged (or lack thereof) particularly upset Chen. She related the story of her brother, who once shared a hospital room with an "old man who died because of wrong medication administered by the nurse." Even more distressing to Chen was the fact that the old man's family would not consider filing a malpractice suit because of the prohibitive cost: "Money is more important than the old man's life and all moral principles can be ignored!" In general Chen found social relations among Americans to be "mercenary." She also criticized racism and unemployment. Finally, her socialist sensibilities had been offended to the point that she decided to return home to the "socialist motherland . . . where there is security for my basic living."

This account illustrates a persistent subtheme in much of the travelogue writing about American society, namely, the uncertainty of life in the United States. To many Chinese, the United States seems a Darwinian jungle. Competition, and mobility in the workplace and in people's personal lives, fuel this perception. Life's uncertainty and the unpredictability of job, of relationships, and so forth raise fear of *luan* (disorder) in the minds of visiting Chinese—the worst fate to befall the social order in China.[48] Chinese fear of disorder and uncertainty leads them to have difficulty grasping the positive value Amer-

[46] Wu Dakun, "Meiguo de jingji he shehui," *Shijie zhishi*, no. 13 (1980): 6-9.

[47] Chen Xiaohui, "Why I Advanced My Return from the Visit to America," *Renmin ribao*, January 11, 1982, *JPRS* 80051, February 8, 1982, pp. 13–15.

[48] Lucian Pye's writings are particularly germane on this point.

icans attach to individuality, competition, and mobility. Thus, they tend to misinterpret key dimensions of the dynamism of American society.

Another form of newspaper travelogue is from the Chinese-American who decides (or is commissioned) to write an article for a Chinese publication. These generally take a negative tone and try to dissuade Chinese readers from having an exaggerated sense of the United States as some kind of paradise. Many are targeted at Chinese youth. Perhaps the best-known examples of this medium are the 1980–1985 "Letters from America" written by Chinese-American writer Yu Lihua and published in the *People's Daily*. Yu's initial "letter" in April 1980 was distinctly critical of life in the United States:

> Based on my more than twenty years of living in the United States, I say to the friends who want to come out that they should never have the illusion that the United States is heaven, nor should they believe the rumors that they hear and think that the United States is a place where any problem can be solved. To those friends who are not coming out now, I would like to say that they should never have any sentiments of worship toward the West, especially the United States, as a result of incorrect and exaggerated reports. Despite its advanced industry and abundant supplies, the United States has many slums in its large cities, and there are frequent reports about people dying of starvation and cold. There are also many people who live on potatoes.[49]

This initial "letter" provoked an outpouring of mail from young Chinese readers. On popular demand, Yu Lihua acquiesced to write a second series in 1985, which was considerably more upbeat.[50] In these "letters" Yu notes that relations between the sexes are less promiscuous, more equal, and youth are "self-reliant, independent, and industrious."

Another example is the Chinese-American Zhao Haosheng. In one article Zhao criticized the "high-consumption habits" and extravagant lifestyle of Americans, "phony democracy," drug addiction, the cost of college education, the inequality of income, and parking tickets.[51]

Books are the other principal outlet of travelogue writing in China.

---

[49] Yu Lihua, "My Experience in the United States," *Renmin ribao*, April 20, 1980, *FBIS-CHI*, April 22, 1980, B1.

[50] These are compared in James L. Huskey, *"Letters From America," 1980–1985: Images of the U.S. for China's Youth* (Washington, D.C.: U.S. Information Agency Research Memorandum, 1985).

[51] Zhao Haosheng, "A Talk about the United States," *Xin shiqi*, no. 1 (1979), *JPRS* 76257, August 20, 1980, pp. 1–7.

One of the most notable Chinese travelogues of America was written by the eminent anthropologist Fei Xiaotong. Fei visited the United States twice during the 1940s and published perceptive volumes in Chinese.[52] In 1979 he returned to the United States after an interlude of more than thirty years and published his impressions.[53] Fei's 1979 visit was brief, a whirlwind one-month trip with a high-powered delegation from the Chinese Academy of Social Sciences. His impressions related mostly to comparisons from the 1940s. He was particularly struck by the elements of modern society: the automobile culture, the mobility of Americans, the wonders of electronic communications, the abundance of foodstuffs and consumer durables. But as an anthropologist Fei had a keen eye for social problems. He wrote of the impersonal nature of Americans, the fleeting nature of friendships. He wrote of the "crisis of faith" (*xinxin weiji*) gripping society (before Jimmy Carter did). He wrote of the continuing underclass of blacks and other minorities, including Chinese-Americans. He also wrote of the decayed inner cities and poor South. But, on the whole, Fei's account offered grudging admiration for the United States, and he more than once expressed his astonishment at the progress made since the war.

Zhang Haitao was posted to the United Nations as chief of the New China News Agency bureau in 1972. He has published two travelogues: *America: Viewing Flowers from Horseback* and *I Discuss America*.[54] The first volume was very descriptive, explaining to readers American history, geography, organization, and so forth. The text was arranged geographically, moving from east to west, relating encounters and observations from Zhang's travels across the country in virtual diary format. New York he portrays as a vibrant city. Zhang apparently spent a lot of time at cocktail receptions, and he records several of his conversations. He describes his visits to Wall Street, the *New York Times*, Harlem, and people's homes. In an interesting section he describes the mafia (*heishoudang*, literally, the "black hand party") and its control of retail commerce, banking, and the illicit drug, prostitution, and pornography trade. Washington, D.C., receives a straightforward description of the U.S. government and national monuments. The Midwest impressed Zhang because he had the chance to interview factory workers in Detroit and Chicago, vis-

---

[52] Fei Xiaotong, *Chufang Meiguo* (Beijing: Sanlian, 1945); *Meiguoren de xingshi* (Beijing: Sanlian, 1947).

[53] Fei Xiaotong, *Fang Mei lue ying* (Beijing: Sanlian, 1980). These three books have been published together as Fei Xiaotong, *Meiguo yu meiguoren* (Beijing: Sanlian, 1985).

[54] Zhang Haitao, *Meiguo zuoma guanhua ji* (Shanghai: Renmin chubanshe, 1980), and *Wo shuo Meiguo* (Beijing: Beijing chubanshe, 1987).

ited farms in Illinois and Iowa, rode a paddleboat down the Mississippi River, and generally enjoyed the open spaces. The Sun Belt states impressed Zhang from a commercial and technological standpoint. He visited aircraft factories, oil fields, universities, and research institutes. His comments on the western United States spoke of the natural beauty but also the economic dynamism of the region. On the whole, Zhang's first book is positive in tone and accurate in what it describes.

This cannot be said of his second book *I Discuss America*, which is written in the Marxist-Leninist style characteristic of Zhang's series on American presidents. It attacks American freedom, democracy, and human rights in the first seventeen chapters and then, after some praise of American technological prowess, continues with an essentially Marxist interpretation of capitalism in the United States.

Other travelogues include two written by exchange students on student life and their experiences,[55] and one based on visiting relatives.[56] These accounts are practical introductions to living in the United States: how to shop, get a driver's license, rent an apartment, order food in restaurants, find Chinese groceries, get plugged into the local Chinese community, use libraries, find part-time employment, and so on. Some of the vignettes depicted are quite humorous.

But of all the travelogues, perhaps the two best known are Liu Zongren's *Two Years in the Melting Pot* and Wang Zuomin's *The American Kaleidoscope*.[57] They are different in nature in that Liu came to the United States as an exchange scholar and later decided to commit his experiences to print, while Wang came for the expressed purpose of writing a book about the country. Both writers worked for Foreign Languages Press in Beijing. Wang's is the more serious attempt of the two, but both are rich in observations. Since both have been translated into English, Americans would find in them interesting perspectives on their society. One commonality in their separate experiences is the importance of members of the U.S.-China People's Friendship Association in facilitating their exposure. Frequent reference is made by both authors to the "friends" they made in USCPFA.

Liu Zongren had a difficult time adjusting to America. From his initial discomfort residing in an upper-middle-class home in Chicago's northern suburbs to the end of his stay in the inner city, Liu felt

---

[55] Zhuang Chenli, *Cong daxue xiaoyuan kan Meiguo* (Shanghai: Renmin chubanshe, 1987); Chen Jiyu, *Meiguo minjian jianmian* (Anhui: Wenyi chubanshe, 1986).

[56] Wang Wei, *Meiguo tanqin jishi* (Sichuan: Xinhua chubanshe, 1984).

[57] Liu Zongren, *Two Years in the Melting Pot* (San Francisco: China Books and Periodicals, 1984); Wang Zuomin, *The American Kaleidoscope* (Beijing: New World Press, 1986). Both books have Chinese versions.

like a fish out of water. As he prepared to return to China, Liu commented, "Home now meant much more than just my wife and our son. It also meant the life I was born into, the surroundings and environment that looked Chinese, the people with whom I shared a culture, and the job at my office which I had, in the past, sometimes resented. I longed for them all." What had brought Liu to this state of mind? It began with alienation from and disgust with middle-class life. It was the affluence that bothered Liu most. This was summed up in one vignette about Christmas. As Liu helped his host family unpack "dozens" of boxes of ornaments to decorate the Christmas tree, he came upon "one big carton that contained a hundred eggnog cups, brought out for use only once a year at their Christmas party. I found this amazing. For several years I had wanted to buy just four stemmed glasses so we would not have to drink wine from tea cups."

Eventually, this middle-class affluence convinced Liu to move into the city of Chicago and rent a house together with some other visiting Chinese (it is common for mainland Chinese in the United States to reside together rather than living with American families and thus integrating themselves into American society). This move brought more problems and unusual experiences: an uncooperative landlord who would not fix the furnace during the winter, repair plumbing, or exterminate rats; street crime; racism; grocery shopping; and so forth. Liu became more and more insular, spending time at home for fear of venturing out. He passed his time in front of the television: "By the time I had been in Chicago for five months, I calculated that I had logged 750 hours of TV time." Eventually Liu began to venture out and visit other parts of the United States. By the time of his departure he had sampled other locales and walks of life, but he left with an uneasiness about life in America.

Wang Zuomin's *American Kaleidoscope* also contains much experiential narrative, but it shows greater perspective. She had been brought to the United States and funded by major U.S. corporations in order to write a book to introduce the United States to Chinese readers. She traveled coast-to-coast visiting all sectors of American society. Her summary impressions on the positive side include the hard-working diligence of Americans; their love of life; the democratic tradition; the informality of life and friendliness of Americans; the emphasis on personal independence; the philanthropic spirit; higher education; transportation and communication systems; creativity and the continual search for new and better ways of doing things; and the value that apparently all Chinese envy about the United States—technology. On the negative side, Wang criticizes the lack of care for the aged; the cost of health care; the threat of unemployment; crime, prostitution, drug use, and pornography; poverty; class polarization; and treatment of minorities.

Thus, travelogues present to the Chinese reader a relatively integrated view of American society not found in most news reports or scholarly writings. It is also an easily digestible genre for average citizens (*laobaixing*); they are able to relate to the discussion better than to more sterile analyses, and they tend (rightly) to view travelogues as less prone to censorship and the propaganda purposes of the authorities. There is no lack, however, of writing on American society of a non-Marxist nature in the Chinese print media. Much of this clusters around two principal issues that appear to be of particular concern: racism and family life.

Race and Racism

During the Maoist era and its immediate aftermath, the plight of minorities in the United States was viewed mainly in the context of their need for "liberation" from capitalist tyranny. Whole books were published on the subject.[58] As one 1976 NCNA dispatch succinctly put it, "Through unremitting struggles, many U.S. minority people are increasingly aware that struggle against racial persecution is linked with the struggle of the whole U.S. working class for liberation. The monopoly capitalist system is the root cause of racial oppression."[59]

Since the late Maoist era, Chinese commentary on race and racism in the United States has shifted from the political to the analytical. For example, during the Maoist era Martin Luther King, Jr., was not generally seen as a positive political force because he advocated nonviolence and did not profess a broader socialist solution to the plight of U.S. minorities. But during the 1980s King enjoyed something of a "rehabilitation" in China. The designation of King's birthday as a holiday marked an outpouring of articles on King's life. The *People's Daily* praised his contributions to the advancement of minority rights.[60] Another article, by CASS America specialist Li Daokui (who has probably investigated King's life more than any other Chinese scholar), traced his life and career in detail and introduced Chinese

[58] Zhongguo renmin jiefang jun 52977 budui lilunzu he Nankai daxue lishixi Meiguoshi yanjiushi ji 1972 ju bufen gong-nong-bing xueyuan, *Meiguo heiren jiefang yundong jianshi* (Shandong: Renmin chubanshe, 1977).

[59] NCNA Correspondent, "U.S. Minorities Fighting On," *Xinhuashe*, December 27, 1976, *FBIS-CHI*, December 29, 1976, A11.

[60] Jing Xianfa, "Dream and Reality," *Renmin ribao*, January 16, 1986, *FBIS-CHI*, January 22, 1986, B1.

readers for the first time to King's philosophy and entourage, the NAACP and Southern Christian Leadership Conference, the Rosa Parks incident, the Selma marches, and so on.[61] Li also discussed the harassment of King by J. Edgar Hoover and the FBI.

The other racial subject that drew Chinese attention during the 1980s was the Klu Klux Klan and the general resurgence of overt racial harassment. The 1979 Greensboro incident where Klan members and neo-Nazis opened fire on anti-Klan demonstrators, killing four and wounding ten, only to be acquitted by a white jury of shooting in self-defense, focused attention on this element in American society.[62] Subsequent articles on the Klan examined its activities and social base in American society. One Chinese journalist reported on a Klan guerrilla training base in Alabama where violent tactics were taught.[63] Another *People's Daily* report claimed that "Among the Klansmen are Congressmen, ranking officials, and other big shots. Because they can get operating funds from big capitalists, they dare to break the law and do all kinds of unscrupulous things."[64]

Family Life in America

Much of the commentary on American family life has to do with the breakdown of the nuclear family. Chinese observers are surprised at the amount of cohabitation and divorce.[65] Family violence—wife beating, child abuse, parent beating, homicide—also attracts attention.[66] Others comment on the increased conservatism in American families and return to traditional values and morality during the 1980s.[67]

Most of the commentary on American families focuses on youth.

[61] Li Daokui, " 'Zhengqu zhengyi erdui de zhihui': xiao mading lude jinmushi," *Meiguo yanjiu*, no. 1 (1987): 143–59.

[62] See Wang Fei, "New Tide of Racism in the United States," *Renmin ribao*, January 9, 1981, *FBIS-CHI*, January 12, 1981, B2–3.

[63] Zi Ban, "New Violence of the 'Invisible Empire'—The Ku Klux Klan in the United States Is On the Rampage Again," *Guangming ribao*, May 27, 1981, *FBIS-CHI*, June 25, 1981, B1–3.

[64] "Racial Discrimination and the Ku Klux Klan in the United States," *Renmin ribao*, March 7, 1981, *FBIS-CHI*, March 12, 1981, B5.

[65] See, for example, Jin Feng, "A Preliminary Inquiry into American Society—Part II," *Renmin ribao*, July 20, 1979, *JPRS* 74012, August 15, 1979, pp. 3–4.

[66] Ibid., and Jiang Jilong, "Family Violence in the United States," *Gongren ribao*, April 8, 1979, *FBIS-CHI*, April 24, 1979, B2.

[67] Much of this writing is sampled in the next chapter but see, for example, Liu Xuyi and Hu Jinpin, "Meiguo xinyoupai chutan," *Meiguo yanjiu*, no. 4 (1988): 114–34.

A few scholarly articles have examined the hippie and New Left movements of the 1960s. In one article, Wen Yang of the CASS America Institute introduced Chinese readers to the Beat Generation, the sexual revolution, Woodstock, Haight-Ashbury, LSD, the Jefferson Airplane, the Love Generation, Abbie Hoffman, Hunter S. Thompson, Bob Dylan, "dropping out," motorcycle gangs, and other symbols of the 1960s.[68] In a companion article on the New Left, Wen Yang discussed the Free Student Movement, SDS, the Weather Underground, the 1968 Democratic Convention, and a host of campus upheavals.[69]

Yet other articles discuss aberrant youth. John Hinckley received much media attention in China. Leading NCNA correspondent Peng Di found Hinckley to be typical of American youth and the embodiment of the demented nature of American society: "From the fragments gathered about the young life of this youth Hinckley, people can more or less get a picture of the ills of American society."[70] America Watcher Chen Youwei wrote a similar article about the 1982 Washington Monument sniper Paul Kendrick, an unemployed Vietnam veteran.[71]

These examples no doubt appeal to Communist Party Propaganda Department cadres and editors as they portray American youth as victims of their system. There are no assassins, snipers, or mass murderers in Chinese society.

Summary

This chapter has examined a variety of perceptions of American society. The Marxists see the United States as one would expect—from a class perspective. Their image is a conflictual one. They perceive a tyrannical bourgeoisie, an indulgent middle class, an exploited and militant working class, and a downtrodden poor. They have debated the status of "impoverishment" of the proletariat; as discussed, they apparently no longer believe that the American working class is "ab-

[68] Wen Yang, "Fan zhuliu wenhua de ya wenhua qun," *Meiguo yanjiu*, no. 4 (1988): 95–112.

[69] Wen Yang, "Meiguo liushiniandai de 'xin zoupai' yundong," *Meiguo yanjiu*, no. 3 (1988): 105–24.

[70] Peng Di, "The Youth of Hinckley," *Xinhuashe*, April 17, 1981, *FBIS-CHI*, April 20, 1981, B5.

[71] Chen Youwei, "A Memory Which Is Sad to Recall," *Renmin ribao*, November 30, 1982, *JPRS*, December 15, 1982, pp. 1–2.

solutely impoverished" and on the verge of "throwing off their chains" to rise up in revolution.

A variety of travelogue and more specialized writing from the non-Marxist perspective has also been discussed. Much of the travelogue writing is experiential and anecdotal (as one might expect), and individual experiences did much to shape the writers' broader views of the United States. These travelers' impressions were varied, but one salient theme stood out—ambivalence. There was much to admire about American society (industriousness and creativity, friendliness, technology, and modernity in most respects), but also much that troubled Chinese observers (crime, racism, the cost of living, and the general unpredictability of American life).

This theme of ambivalence weaves throughout the perceptions examined in this study. The United States produces contradictory feelings for most Chinese. This is beautifully captured in an article written by NCNA Washington bureau chief and long-time America Watcher Li Yanning in 1984 entitled "America—A Country Full of Contradictions":

> This country's education is so developed . . . on the other hand 26 million Americans are illiterate or semiliterate. . . . America's science and technology is so advanced . . . on the other hand religious superstitution is so prevalent in this country that during their race the presidential candidates of the two parties each had to vow solemnly that he was a good Christian. . . . On the one hand, there is a large number of unemployed persons in America; . . . on the other hand, every year as many as a million foreigners try by every means to migrate to America. . . . America's medical profession is so advanced; on the other hand the cost of medical treatment is so expensive . . . that if a person needs an operation it is better for him to spend the money on the airfare to Europe and go into hospital there. . . . Americans put a lot of stress on keeping fit; . . . on the other hand, so many people become addicted to drugs and do not hesitate to destroy themselves. . . . America is a country that is particular about its legal system; . . . on the other hand, there are so many people who are able, after they commit a crime, to escape the law's punishment.[72]

[72] Li Yanning, "America—A Country Full of Contradictions," *Huanqiu*, no. 12 (1984), *JPRS* CPS-85-018, February 27, 1985, pp. 1–2.

Five

The American Polity

THE STUDY of American politics in China has, like other aspects of American studies, undergone considerable change since the Sino-American rapprochement. This chapter will discuss the evolution from a myopic preoccupation with how monopoly capitalists control the U.S. government in the 1970s to a more nuanced and reasonably sophisticated understanding of political pluralism in America in the 1980s and 1990s. There has been an evolution from the former to the latter over time, but also a stubborn resistance of the Marxist interpretation of politics under capitalism. That is, one sees both an evolution of analytical emphases and the continued coexistence of the Marxist and non-Marxist schools of analysis. The two schools find some common ground in their analyses of the importance of nongovernmental actors in the political process. The evolution of analysis passes roughly through four sequential stages, from the Stalinist "subordination thesis" to the Leninist "unification thesis" to a "statist" perspective that emphasizes the inner workings of the U.S. federal government, and finally to a "pluralist" paradigm that takes account of a wide range of actors and processes on the American political stage.

The reasons for this evolution of analysis are several. First, and foremost, the impact of direct exposure to the United States is apparent. The political realities discovered by the America Watchers after firsthand exposure to the United States made many of them question, refine, and, in some cases, reject their previous one-dimensional approach to American politics in favor of a more multifaceted and accurate understanding of American political pluralism. These discoveries paralleled the realizations about the American economy and society seen in the previous two chapters.

Second, parallel to physical exposure was an increased access to documentary materials on the mechanics of policy making in the federal government, Congress, and at the state and local levels. This factor resulted in increased inductive, empirical analyses rather than the deductive, reductionist analyses characteristic of the prenormalization era.

Third, changes in the Chinese intellectual milieu made it possible for the America Watchers not only literally to discover democracy and pluralism, but to be permitted to write about it as well. The general political climate in China during the 1980s was conducive to the intellectual exploration and discussion of other political systems, but more specifically the reinterpretation of some core canons of Marxist-Leninist orthodoxy permitted formerly heretical views to be aired. In the context of studying American politics, the polemics on imperialism and state-monopoly capitalism discussed in chapter 2 were crucial openings for the Chinese area studies specialists to examine the inner workings of democratic political systems. Quite simply, without the theoretical breakthroughs seen in chapter 2 that the capitalist state could act independently of the monopoly bourgeoisie and that monopolists were divided and competitive, the statist and pluralist perspectives apparent in this chapter would not have been possible, or at least would have been delayed in their appearance. Once it was argued that the state exhibits independence of action from the ruling class, the door was opened to analysis of the bureaucratic functioning of the state apparatus itself, as well as the various political influences—governmental and nongovernmental—upon the state. Thus, this chapter must be viewed against the backdrop of the ideological polemics examined in chapter 2.

As in previous chapters, this one is organized to contrast Marxist and non-Marxist perspectives on American politics, focusing on the actors and processes that each school deems relevant to explaining how politics in America functions. This includes consideration of the role of monopolies, the executive branch, Congress, state and local government, and nongovernment actors (interest groups, foundations, think tanks, political action committees, and so forth). I then consider the America Watchers' interpretations of the American electorate and electoral system by examining Chinese domestic coverage of five U.S. presidential campaigns from 1972 through 1988. The chapter concludes with a brief comparison of the alternate models and explanations of American politics offered by China's America Watchers.

Marxist Perspectives on American Politics

For all Marxist School analysts, the key actors in U.S. domestic politics are monopoly financial groups (*longduan caituan*). All other political actors, especially the state, are perceived to be manipulated by these groups.

Marxist historians in China have gone to great lengths to date and trace the rise of these groups in American economic and political life.[1] While they are in general agreement that these groups have come to play the dominant role in American politics, historians disagree as to when this became the defining characteristic of American political life. This subject was a central object of debate at the 1979–1983 meetings of the China American History Research Association.[2]

The disagreement is exemplified in the writings of two of China's most noted American historians, Huang Shaoxiang and Liu Xuyi. Huang, a senior researcher at the CASS Institute of World History, argues in her standard textbook *Meiguo tongshi jianbian* (A concise history of the United States) that the United States passed from the free competitive capitalist stage to the monopoly capitalist stage in the late nineteenth century but did not make the full transition to state-monopoly capitalism until the Second World War, when the state and the monopoly-controlled defense industries pooled their resources for the war effort. On this basis, Huang further argues that while monopoly financial groups did not assume a "controlling position" in American politics until after World War II, they have exerted "influence" on domestic politics and foreign policy since the Spanish-American War of 1898.[3] In a 1985 interview Huang defended her explicit use of the subordination thesis and argued that "American political parties are tools in the hands of the monopoly bourgeoisie, and there is no real difference between the two major parties."[4]

Liu Xuyi, professor of history and director of the U.S. History Research Center at Wuhan University, also argues the subordination thesis in print and in person. But he disagrees with Huang over timing. He dates the "domination" of American politics by monopoly financial groups from the New Deal, when, in his estimation, the United States became a state-monopoly capitalist country (having been imperialist and monopoly capitalist since the Spanish-American War of 1898) due to the unprecedented state intervention in the pri-

---

[1] The *Index of American History Papers and Reference Materials*, for example, lists twenty-six articles on the subject between 1979 and 1981 alone. See Sichuan daxue lishixi Meiguoshizu bian, *Meiguoshi lunwen ziliao suoyin* (Wuhan: Meiguoshi yanjiuhui, 1983), pp. 29–30.

[2] This has been confirmed by several conference participants, the *Bulletin* of the association (*Zhongguo Meiguoshi yanjiuhui tongbao*), the two conference volumes resulting from these meetings (*Meiguoshi lunwenji*), and Hao Guiyuan, "1979–82 guonei Meiguoshi yanjiu gaishu," *Shijie lishi dongtai*, no. 10 (1983): 10–17.

[3] Huang Shaoxiang, *Meiguo tongshi jianbian* (Beijing: Renmin chubanshe, 1979); see chapter 7 and pp. 662–64 in particular.

[4] Interview at the Institute of World History of the Chinese Academy of Social Sciences, May 7, 1985.

vate economy following the Great Depression.[5] As was seen in chapter 3, Professor Liu argues that Roosevelt undertook the New Deal at the explicit behest of Morgan, Mellon, Rockefeller, and other magnates in order to recover their lost profits. This is clearly an image of subordination of the state to monopolists. Professor Liu qualifies this image somewhat by agreeing with Huang that the state-monopoly merger was sealed over the munitions industry during World War II, but he differs in his dating of the monopoly control of government from the time of the New Deal.

Professor Liu's view seems to be the dominant one among historians of the United States in China. It will be interesting to see if this is the view adopted in the definitive multivolume *History of the United States*, sponsored by the American History Research Association, of which Professor Liu is secretary-general and main editor. The production schedule for this series was pushed back several times during the late 1980s for both technical and political reasons, and as of 1991 no volumes had yet appeared. Professor Liu's perspectives on state-monopoly capitalism are certainly evident in the "Series on Modern American History," a set of monographs edited by Professor Liu that covers every administration from Roosevelt through Nixon. The volume on Eisenhower and modern Republicanism, written by Han Tie (one of Professor Liu's former graduate students), makes the argument that all administrations since the New Deal have been so politically beholden to monopoly capital that they cannot implement economic policies that run counter to the financial interests of the monopolies.[6] Professor Han further argues that Republicans in particular have had to abandon their laissez-faire inclinations in the interest of preserving the state-monopoly capitalist system.

Probably the classic work on the subject of monopoly capitalism is five-hundred page *Meiguo longduan caituan* (American monopoly financial groups), first published in 1977 with an updated and revised edition published in 1987.[7] This work by several leading members of Fudan University's Research Institute on the Economies of Capitalist Countries (Yu Kaixiang, Hong Wenda, Jiang Zehong, Gong Weijing,

[5] Interview with Liu Xuyi at Wuhan University, October 26, 1984, and Liu Xuyi, "Meiguo longduan zibenzhuyi yu Ma-Liezhuyi," *Lanzhou daxue xuebao*, no. 3 (1984): 45–56; "Luosifu 'xin zheng' de dishi diwei," *Shijie lishi*, no. 2 (1983): 44–55; and "Meiguo longduan zibenzhuyi fazhan shi yu Ma-Liezhuyi," *Shehui kexue*, no. 2 (1984): 76–80.

[6] Han Tie, *Aisenhaoweier de xiandai gonghedangzhuyi* (Wuhan: Wuhan daxue chubanshe, 1984).

[7] Fudan daxue zibenzhuyi guojia jingji yanjiusuo bian, *Meiguo longduan caituan*, 1st ed. (Shanghai: Renmin chubanshe, 1977); 2d ed. edited by Gong Weijing and Gan Dangshan, 1987.

Gan Dangshan, Chen Qiren, Zheng Lizhi, and others) remains the most comprehensive and systematic exposition of the Marxists' position in general, and the subordination thesis in particular.

The authors argue that the "control of the U.S. government apparatus" and "domination of political power" by caituan is essentially accomplished through manipulating the "bourgeois" parties and elections and then appointing government officials who directly represent the interests of specific monopoly groups. According to the authors, every president and his cabinet since 1945 have represented one or more of these financial consortia.[8] Before the Second World War these groups tended to be familial, interconnected, and concentrated in the northeastern United States, giving rise to a straightforward "Wall Street rules Washington" model of American politics. Since 1945, however, these groups have become regionally dispersed, more competitive, and less dominated by families.

For example, President Truman and several key members of his administration (secretaries Burns, Marshall, Acheson, and Johnson) were thought beholden to the Morgan financial group. Defense secretaries Forrestal and Lovett were deemed representatives of the Dillon and Du Pont groups respectively.

While President Eisenhower personally owed his "main" (*zhuyao*) loyalties to the Morgan group and also "certainly had connections" (*yiding you guanxi*) to the Rockefeller group, the Republican Party was "dominated" (*zhangwo*) by the Chicago caituan during the late 1940s and 1950s. Eisenhower's cabinet members, however, had more wide-ranging backgrounds. Secretary of State Dulles was a Rockefeller man, while defense secretaries McCloy and Gates represented the Morgan group. Others in the Eisenhower administration represented regional groups. Christian Herter, who replaced Dulles, came from the Boston financial group, while treasury secretaries George Humphrey and Robert O. Anderson represented the Cleveland and Texas caituan respectively.

John F. Kennedy "combined" the support of the Boston and Rockefeller groups. Secretary of State Rusk owed his allegiance to the Rockefellers, Secretary of Defense McNamara to the Ford Motor group and Midwest "war industrialists," while Secretary of the Treasury Douglas Dillon personified the Dillon-Reed caituan.

President Johnson was at first allied with his native Texas caituan, but later "drew close to" (*kaolong*) the eastern groups. Johnson's election in 1964 was "the first time that someone outside the eastern financial groups became president." But Johnson too had to compro-

---

[8] Ibid. (1st ed.), pp. 88–89.

mise with the eastern caituan. He retained Dean Rusk from the original Kennedy administration and replaced McNamara with Clark Clifford, an "agent" of the Rockefellers. Douglas Dillon's successors at Treasury represented the New York investment houses of Goldman Sachs and the Lehman Brothers.

Nixon's ascendance to the presidency represented the increased importance of the western caituan, especially the Bank of America and the "West Coast war industries clique." The authors attribute Nixon's resignation following the Watergate affair not to his violation of the Constitution, social contract, or the people's trust, but to the fact that "the economic base of his political power infringed upon (*weifan*) the interests of the Wall Street oligarchy."[9] Monopoly groups frequently put American presidents in office but, according to the authors, this was the first example of a caituan removing one from office. Secretaries of State Rogers and Kissinger were the only representatives of the eastern groups (both Rockefeller) in Nixon's administration, while all others came from the Texas or California groups.

Gerald Ford altered the balance somewhat by including more members from the "Midwest commodities clique" in the domestic policy arena, such as Donald Rumsfeld, George Shultz, and William Simon. But Rockefeller "henchmen" Kissinger and Schlesinger continued to dominate the foreign and defense policies of the Ford administration.

Jimmy Carter personally represented "new southern banking and commercial interests," but in forming his cabinet he "fused together" (*ronghe*) representatives from the southern caituan with others from the Rockefeller caituan (Mondale, Vance, Brzezinski). Carter's joining of the Rockefeller-backed Trilateral Commission in 1973 was proof positive that he personally was their "agent" in the White House.

Ronald Reagan, like Nixon, represented the western caituan, but the "most conservative elements" (*zui baoshou fenzi*) within it. Reagan made token gestures to the eastern caituan interests by appointing eight cabinet officers with ties to Rockefeller, Morgan, or Du Pont, but his key advisers (Weinberger, Clark, and later Shultz) all had business ties to western financial interests.

As seen in chapter 3, the majority of Marxist School commentators now relatively play down familial caituan connections and instead stress regional groupings, especially the rise of southern and western economic and political power in the United States. The fact that the last six presidents are not from the east, and five (Johnson, Nixon, Carter, Reagan, Bush) hail from the Sun Belt, is proof, they say, of

[9] Ibid., p. 51 (1st ed.), p. 92 (2d ed.).

the increased devolution of financial and political power among the monopoly bourgeoisie. Wall Street no longer rules Washington exclusively. Southern bankers, Texas oil barons, California defense industrialists, Sun Belt high-technology magnates, and midwestern commodities traders now more than hold their own against Wall Street financiers and traditional eastern monied interests.

One of the most detailed and interesting expositions of the devolved political power of regional financial groups is to be found in Cao Shaolian's textbook *Meiguo zhengzhi zhidu shi* (History of the American political system).[10] Professor Cao traces the changing representation of caituan in various administrations over time. He breaks the financial groups up into four regions: Northeast, Midwest, South, and West. He then analyzes the internal composition of each and their impact on various administrations. With respect to political influence, Professor Cao rank orders them as follows (political influence and financial portfolios do not always covary equally in his scheme of things).

Throughout the twentieth century the Rockefeller caituan has had the greatest influence, with literally every administration beholden to it in some degree. Presidents McKinley, Harding, Eisenhower, Kennedy, and Johnson were all thought to have won their elections because of Rockefeller support, and the personal presence of Nelson Rockefeller in the Ford administration personified this influence. The Rockefeller Foundation, Council on Foreign Relations, and Trilateral Commission were created by the Rockefellers as means for transmitting their personnel and policies to government. Examples abound, including Henry Kissinger and Zbigniew Brzezinski.

The political influence of the Morgan financial group has been only slightly less than the Rockefellers' and, in fact, was dominant prior to the Eisenhower years. The Morgan group allegedly dominated the conservative faction of the Republican Party. Their influence was greatest in the Grant, Cleveland, Theodore Roosevelt, Wilson, Coolidge, Hoover, and Eisenhower administrations.

The Mellon financial group has been closely tied to the Republican Party. Andrew Mellon himself personified his group's influence by being secretary of the treasury for eleven consecutive years through the Harding, Coolidge, and Hoover administrations. Through several cabinet members, Mellon also exerted influence on the McKinley and Eisenhower administrations.

---

[10] Cao Shaolian, *Meiguo zhengzhi zhidu shi* (Gansu: Renmin chubanshe, 1984), especially chapter 9. Professor Cao is now emeritus from the Wuhan University History and Law departments.

The Du Pont financial group was strongest during the Truman and Eisenhower years, although through its control of General Motors it influenced the defense policies of many administrations. The First National City Bank of New York (now Citicorp) exerted its influence through Senator Henry Jackson and writer Walter Lippmann. The Kuhn-Loeb financial group's influence peaked during the Truman years, after which time it was controlled by the Rockefeller caituan.

The Boston financial group's influence was greatest during the Theodore Roosevelt, Harding, Eisenhower, and Kennedy administrations. Its interests and influence have always been greatest with respect to Latin American policy, where it has multiple investments. For example, the overthrow of Guatemalan President Arbenz was carried out by the Central Intelligence Agency on behalf of the United Fruit Company, which was controlled by the First National Bank of Boston.

The Ford financial group has placed its representatives in the Truman, Eisenhower, Kennedy, and Johnson administrations. The influence of the Brown Brothers–Harriman financial group has been most vividly represented by the various positions that W. Averill Harriman held over the years under presidents from both parties. Similarly, Douglas Dillon represented Dillon-Reed's interests in the Kennedy administration, but this group also placed its "henchmen" in the Truman and Nixon cabinets and White House staff.

With the brief exception of Gerald Ford's administration, the midwestern financial groups' influence was greatest between the two world wars, especially during the Taft and Hoover administrations. The Chicago, Detroit, and Cleveland caituan are the main power centers in the Midwest, but as the financial strength of the midwestern industrial belt has declined, so too has its political clout.

The southern financial group is centered in Georgia and Texas. The Carter and Johnson administrations best exemplify the rise of the political muscle that has accompanied the growth of southern oil, gas, chemical, munitions, high-technology, and banking sectors. Despite bringing many southerners to Washington, ultimately both Johnson and Carter had to accommodate the northeastern caituan. Professor Cao claims, for example, that Johnson's appointment of the Bundy brothers, Clark Clifford, and others was an attempt to appease the northeastern caituan, but in the end he was kept from running for reelection in 1968 because of the opposition of the northeastern groups. Carter's appointment of many members of the Trilateral Commission to key positions in his administration revealed his deference to David Rockefeller, but, like Johnson, he fell from power because he lacked their full support.

The western financial group is concentrated in California, with branches in Arizona, Colorado, and Washington. Its economic strength lies in banking, the defense industries, mining, and high technology. The Nixon and Reagan administrations exemplify the fundamental realignment in economic and political power to the western caituan, Cao argues, although both also had to make certain concessions to the powerful eastern groups.

Therefore, except for the interlude of Gerald Ford, Professor Cao argues in his standard textbook (published in the midst of the Reagan term), the story of American politics during the last twenty-five years is one of the rise of the southern and western financial groups, and the corresponding decline in influence of the midwestern and northeastern monopolies. Many other Marxist America Watchers agree with him.

However, Zhang Jialin of the Shanghai Institute of International Studies—probably China's leading caituan expert—disagrees that the southern and western financial groups have become dominant in American politics. While acknowledging the devolution of monopoly holdings from the Northeast and Midwest to the South and West, Zhang maintained in 1981 that in politics the eastern financial groups—particularly Morgan, Rockefeller, and Citibank—remained dominant precisely because they had penetrated and coopted the financial holdings and political base of other regional caituan.[11] No president, he then argued, could be elected without the support of the northeastern groups. Johnson, Nixon, Ford, Carter, and Reagan all had to accommodate themselves to the wishes of the eastern financial groups. Presidential candidates require the support of the eastern groups not only to be elected, but also to stay in power.

Like many other America Watchers, Zhang argued that the Watergate incident was whipped up by the media organs of the eastern financial group after Nixon began to give greater consideration to the financial interests of western and southern groups, and placed more of their representatives in policy-making positions, during his second term.[12] It is interesting to note that this explanation is not too different from Nixon's own explanation at the time that he had long been a victim of the eastern establishment and media, dating at least since his 1960 loss to John F. Kennedy.

---

[11] Shanghai guoji wenti yanjiusuo bian, *Xiandai Meiguo jingji wenti jianlun* (Shanghai: Renmin chubanshe, 1981). As seen in chapter 3, it is the interpenetration of monopoly financial groups that largely convinced Zhang to write in his landmark 1986 article that caituan had ceased to exist in the United States. See Zhang Jialin, "Meiguo longduan caituan chuxian zhong da bianhua."

[12] *Xiandai Meiguo jingji wenti jielun*, p. 116.

Monopoly influence on American politics also finds expression in other specialized analyses, where U.S. administrations are thought to be controlled by caituan. This is evident, for example, in the twin studies on Richard Nixon and Jimmy Carter in the White House by Zhang Haitao, the former NCNA United Nations bureau chief during the 1970s.[13] After completing his tour at the United Nations Zhang returned to join the staff of the Institute of World History at CASS and embarked on a four-volume series on American presidents from Kennedy through Carter (the Kennedy and Johnson volumes have yet to appear).

The Nixon volume forcefully argues the case that Nixon was the chief representative of the California bourgeoisie's "thinly veiled anti-Communist clique" (*lugu fangong jituan*). Nixon performed this role thoroughout his congressional career, and his ascent to the White House "consolidated the western capital financial cliques' control (*kongzhi*) of federal power (*lianbang zhengquan*)."[14] Once in office Nixon pursued strategies to reward his benefactors, both in policy and personnel. His cabinet and White House staff were composed of many "West Coast militarists," and his "Asia first" policy was meant to benefit both financiers and military industrialists.[15] Ultimately, however, Zhang argues that these favoritist policies proved Nixon's undoing as his policies of détente with the Soviet Union offended his anti-Communist backers, the "Year of Europe" and winding down of the war in Vietnam alienated West Coast financial and industrial interests, and the Rockefeller caituan gained greater influence via Kissinger, Haig, and others. The Watergate affair was, according to Zhang, engineered by the offended financial groups.

Zhang's Carter volume explores in great detail the linkages among various components of the "Sun Belt financial group," the "Texas petroleum clique," the Rockefeller caituan, and members of the Carter administration. The "Georgia Gang" triumvirate of Lance, Jordan, and Powell represented the financial interests of the Sun Belt high-technology, Peach Street banking, and Texas petroleum consortia, while Brzezinski, Vance, Mondale, Shulman, and other administration members who belonged to the Trilateral Commission implemented a foreign policy on behalf of David Rockefeller. President Carter personified both caituan. The "Lance Affair" represented a clash of the two caituan, with Wall Street prevailing over the "Georgia Gang." The challenge to Carter inside the Democratic Party from

---

[13] Zhang Haitao, *Jimi Kate zai baigong* (Sichuan: Renmin chubanshe, 1982); *Nikesong zai baigong* (Beijing: Shijie zhishi chubanshe, 1990).

[14] *Nikesong zai baigong*, p. 63.

[15] Ibid., chapter 4.

Edward Kennedy further revealed the disenchantment with him by the old monied interests in the Northeast.

These four books by Gong Weijing and Gan Dangshan, Cao Shaolian, and Zhang Haitao are illustrative of an enormous body of writing on American caituan and their influence on the U.S. government. Other Marxist School interpretations of American politics are to be found in the periodical press, although this is also where the bulk of non-Marxist commentaries appear. As seen in chapter 3, these analyses concentrate on realignments in the financial strength of the ten main caituan: Rockefeller, Morgan, California, Citibank, Chicago, Boston, Mellon, Texas, Du Pont, and Cleveland (listed in order of financial holdings as of 1975).[16] In addition to the rise of Sun Belt groups, many of the Marxists note the increased "interpenetration" of these groups during the last twenty years. As noted earlier, this is a principal theme in Zhang Jialin's writings that led him to conclude, in the end, that caituan per se no longer exist in the United States.[17]

Thus, Marxist School America Watchers' perceptions of American politics, like those of their economist colleagues, concentrate not surprisingly on the monopoly financial groups (caituan) and the various ways that they exert influence on the U.S. government and American political life. Their's is a conspiratorial view of American politics. Profit drives politics. All significant politicians and political actors are somehow backed by, and beholden to, monopoly interests. As will be seen later in this chapter, it is in the realm of nongovernmental political actors that the Marxists and non-Marxists find common ground, although the non-Marxists'objects and methods of analysis are generally different.

Non-Marxist Perspectives on American Politics

Beginning in the 1980s a second distinguishable school of analysis began to appear with reference to American politics—the non-Marxists. The non-Marxist School is primarily distinguished by two factors: their nonideological interpretations of U.S. politics, and the scope of political actors considered. The non-Marxists do share an interest in the role of nongovernmental actors with the Marxists, but

[16] See, for example, Gan Dangshan, "Zhanhou Meiguo longduan caituan de fazhan," *Shijie jingji*, no. 6 (1980): 25–35; Zhang Jialin, "Meiguo longduan caituan shili he zuhe de ruogan bianhua," *Shijie jingji*, no. 9 (1980): 23–30; Zhang Jialin, "Dongbu caituan de xin zuhe," *Shijie jingji daobao*, August 1, 1983, p. 5; Zhang Jialin, "Meiguo longduan caituan chuxian zhong da bianhua," *Shijie jingji daobao*, July 25, 1983, p. 4.

[17] Zhang Jialin, "Meiguo longduan caituan chuxian zhong da bianhua."

they cast their analytical net more broadly to consider political actors in both state and society.

Accordingly, within the non-Marxist School two further lines of analysis can be identified. The first focuses attention on Congress, various interest groups, trends in American political thought, and general societal influences on the policy process in the United States. This group essentially articulates a "pluralist" model of American politics. While the pluralists study a wide range of political actors in the American political arena, the U.S. federal government—particularly the executive branch—is the principal political actor in the estimation of the other large cohort of non-Marxists, which can appropriately be designated as "statists." As their chief concern is the state apparatus, these America Watchers write about both the structure and process of the American federal government.

The Statists

The statists primarily adopt a structural approach that introduces their readers to the key positions and organizations in the executive branch by describing their mandated functions. They have written numerous books and articles on the presidency,[18] the vice-presidency,[19] the White House staff,[20] the National Security Council,[21] Department of State,[22] the interagency Crisis Management Committee,[23] National Security Agency,[24] Central Intelligence Agency,[25] and so

[18] See, for example, Yang Baikui and Yang Ming, Meiguo zongtong jichi xuanju (Beijing: Zhongguo shehui kexue chubanshe, 1985); Zhao Haosheng, Manhua Meiguo zongtong xuanju (Beijing: Zhongguo qingnian chubanshe, 1980); Zhong Huo, "Tantan Meiguo de zongtong," Shijie zhishi, no. 6 (1979): 12–14; and Le Shan, "Manhua baigong, zongtong, neige," Shijie zhishi, no. 2 (1981): 12–13.

[19] See, for example, Shi Chaoxun, "Qiantan Meiguo fuzongtong," Shijie zhishi, no. 9 (1981): 16–17; Zhou Lan, "Meiguo zongtong yu fuzongtong," Renmin ribao, November 5, 1980, p. 7.

[20] See, for example, Chen Qihui, "Baigong santou de quanli," Huanqiu, no. 8 (1981): 4–5.

[21] "Meiguo guojia anquan weiyuanhui," Shijie zhishi, no. 17 (1979): 14.

[22] See, for example, Jie Fu, "Meiguo guowuyuan he guowuqing," Shijie zhishi, no. 13 (1980): 5, 9.

[23] Le Shan, "Storm in Washington," Renmin ribao, March 30, 1981, in FBIS-CHI, March 31, 1981, B2; "The Crisis Management Team and Crises," Renmin ribao, March 28, 1981, FBIS-CHI, February 10, 1983, B4.

[24] Hui (name as given), "A Labyrinth Is Still a Labyrinth," Renmin ribao, February 6, 1983, FBIS-CHI, February 10, 1983, B4.

[25] See, for example, Yan Li, "Meiguo zhongyang qingbaoju neimu," Shijie zhishi, no. 13 (1981): 28–29; Yu Enguang, "Meiguo zhongyang qingbaoju de yichang fengbuo,"

forth. Textbooks and handbooks on the United States also contain detailed information on the cabinet and executive branch agencies, the civil service system, Congress, and state and local government.[26] There exists a very large body of literature on these subjects. Much of it is written by NCNA journalists and professional research institute staff.

According to most statists, the president reigns supreme. They see him as final arbiter of competing interests, policy initiator, appointer of personnel throughout the executive branch, commander-in-chief of the armed forces, and ultimate maker of foreign policy. Many statists hold an omnipotent image of the president that overestimates his real command and control.[27] Few recognize the constraints placed on the president by the separation of powers,[28] although (as will be seen below) Congress is becoming an object of increased interest among some America Watchers.

Chinese commentators sometimes write of the personal character of American presidents (competence, trustworthiness, honesty, etc.), perhaps because of the Chinese traditional respect for honorable officials and strong yet benevolent rulers (ba-wang lingdao). Chinese often seem to value strength more than benevolence in evaluating American presidents.

Former President Nixon is an illustrative case in point. Despite harsh criticism of his duplicity in domestic and foreign policies at home, Nixon was still warmly welcomed in China many times since his unceremonious resignation. As noted above, the moral implications of Watergate escaped most Chinese. As Chairman Mao reportedly told a former American official, "Watergate! What reason is that to get rid of a president?"[29]

Renmin ribao, August 7, 1981, p. 7; and Yang Yongyi, "Zhongyang qingbaoju yu Meiguo waijiao zhengce," *Meiguo yanjiu*, no. 3 (1989): 38–57.

[26] See, for example, Fudan daxue zibenzhuyi guojia jingji yanjiusuo bian, *Meiguo zhengfu jigou* (Shanghai: Renmin chubanshe, 1972); Fudan daxue guoji zhengzhixi zibenzhuyi guojia zhengzhi yanjiushi bianxie, *Meiguo: geguo shouce congshu* (Shanghai: Cishu chubanshe, 1981); Jiang Qiantian and Chen Zhigang, *Ying-Mei gaikuang* (Shanghai: Waiyu jiaoyu chubanshe, 1984); and Yang Baihua, "Meiguo de wenguan zhidu," in *Zhengfu jigou he ganbu zhidu gaige wenti lunwenxuan*, ed. Tang Jianbian (Beijing: Renmin chubanshe, 1984), pp. 312–25.

[27] This perspective is certainly evident in the only book-length treatment of the American presidency published in recent years in China. This study was written by two members of the CASS Political Science Institute. See Yang Baikui and Yang Ming, *Meiguo zongtong jiqi xuanju* (Beijing: Zhongguo shehui kexue chubanshe, 1985).

[28] Li Daokui of the CASS America Institute is an exception to this rule. See, for example, his "Shilun Meiguo xianfa de xianquan yuanze," *Meiguo yanjiu*, no. 4 (1987): 7–17.

[29] Interview, February 1985.

Many Chinese viewed President Carter as more benevolent than strong, despite having normalized diplomatic relations with China. This was due both to Carter's perceived impotence in the face of the Iran crisis and Soviet advances in the Third World, and to the post-normalization Taiwan Relations Act, which the Chinese thought was a betrayal of the spirit and letter of the normalization accords.

President Reagan was generally respected from the strength perspective, but not as a benevolent ruler. Not only were his administration's policies routinely criticized, but his character was also occasionally maligned. A biography of Reagan by an America Watcher at the Institute of Contemporary International Relations, entitled *Cong mingxing dao zongtong* (From movie star to president), criticized him as a racist, ardent anti-Communist (who as director of the Screen Actors Guild was responsible for ruining many professional careers during the rage of McCarthyism), puppet of the monopoly bourgeoisie, being indifferent to the plight of the poor and oppressed, and so on.[30]

The vice-president is also seen as an important political actor (his importance is often assessed as greater than many Americans would consider). The America Watchers consider Truman, Nixon, Johnson, Mondale, and Bush to have been the most influential vice-presidents of the postwar era. President Reagan's appointment of Vice-President Bush as chairman of the "crisis management committee" in 1981 was seen as a particularly significant enhancement of vice-presidential power.[31]

Not only do the statists examine the pinnacle of executive power—the president and vice-president—but they elaborate the executive branch structure and also pay attention to the policy-making process. They are fixated with bureaucratic in-fighting, trying to identify factions and personal and institutional rivalries. Chinese analysts of the American political scene seem quite at home with this type of analysis, here again perhaps reflecting mirror imagery in the way they view their own country's politics. For most of the statists, competing interests are reconciled, issues resolved, and decisions made in the American government primarily through intergovernmental factional strife. This is a conflict model of the political process, albeit within the context of clearly defined institutional roles.

As a result, the statists primarily take account of the bureaucratic channels of policy input into the political process. Some believe that

[30] Hu Jiang, *Cong mingxing dao zongtong: Luoneide Ligen* (Beijing: Shijie zhishi chubanshe, 1982).

[31] See note 23.

policy is made solely in the professional bureaucracy, while others believe that the president is the most important decision maker.[32] One America Watcher dismissed Congress's role in the process as "peripheral": "Congress never makes decisions, it only restrains them."[33] Another leading America Watcher at the Institute of Contemporary International Relations used the analogy of a circle to describe the U.S. foreign policy-making process: members of the National Security Council form the circle's core, with the bureaucracy, Congress, and think tanks on the periphery.[34] For the most part, the statists have an executive branch–centric view of the policy process. They perceive the federal bureaucracy as having an autonomous and powerful status.[35]

Pursuant to their fixation on the executive branch, the statists employ factional analysis. NCNA correspondents posted in Washington keep close track of the fluctuating status of key administration members. While such analyses were occasionally evident in previous administrations, they became much more frequent during the Reagan years. Relationships and the division of labor among members of the first-term Reagan White House staff absorbed the attention of many an America Watcher. What was the relative power of the White House "troika" (sanjutou), or the "three big heads" (san da tou) of Meese, Baker, and Deaver? Was Meese really as inept as he seemed? Could the California caituan really trust Bush and Baker since they represented the interests of the Texas oil clique? Would Reagan disown his "surrogate son" Deaver? These were typical questions posed by an America Watcher at the CASS's Institute of World Economics and Politics.[36] Ren Yi concluded that Meese enjoyed the greatest power among the three, but because of his ineptitude in foreign affairs and thirst for power he was undercut by Baker, Deaver, Clark, and the secretaries of state and defense. Because of Baker's ties to Bush and the Texas oil clique, however, his influence would always be proscribed by Meese, Deaver, and other representatives of the

---

[32] Interviews at the Institute of Contemporary International Relations, October 14, 1983, and the International Politics Department of Fudan University, July 21, 1983.

[33] Interview at the Institute of International Studies, November 20, 1983.

[34] Interview at the Institute of Contemporary International Relations, November 4, 1983.

[35] One of the most explicit examples of this perspective is Jin Canrong, "Jian xin Meiguo lianbang xingzheng jigou de zhengzhi diwei," Meiguo yanjiu, no. 2 (1988): 58–83.

[36] Ren Yi, "Baigong de neibu douzheng ji Ligen de lingdao zuofeng," Shijie jingji yu zhengzhi neican, no. 12 (1982): 17–20. For similar analyses see Chen Weishi, "Ligen zhengfu de quanshi renwu," Ban yue tan, no. 15 (1982): 60–62; and Chen Qihui, "Baigong sanzhutou de quanshi," Huanqiu, no. 8 (1981): 4–5.

California financial group. Despite his personal fondness for Deaver, Reagan would eventually have to fire him, because through his management of personnel and document flow to the president, Deaver had managed to alienate every cabinet member and other important officials.

The statists also closely monitored the resignations of Richard Allen, Alexander Haig, William Clark, and others from the Reagan administration. While the Marxists viewed these resignations as manifestations of rivalries and conflicts of interest between caituan, the non-Marxists usually identified disputes over substantive policy issues as the reason for resignation. Whether the policy disputes are the symptom or the cause of political conflict is not always made clear. That is, sometimes institutional rivalries are deemed the root cause, such as the State Department–National Security Council and State–Defense Department rivalries, which resulted in the Allen and Haig resignations respectively.[37] Personal rivalries (Haig-Weinberger, Shultz-Weinberger, Meese-Baker, Stockman-Regan, MacFarlane-Shultz) were also seen as a source of factional conflict, but as one leading America Watcher put it, "personalities have a lot to do with intra–executive branch struggles, but ultimately policy questions and institutional rivalries play the most important roles."[38]

The statists also recognize opinion groups in addition to personal rivalries and factions. America Watchers in the CASS Institute of World Economics and Politics believe that "isolationists" have long competed with "internationalists" for control of U.S. foreign policy,[39] but other analysts—like Zhuang Qubing of the Institute of International Studies—have identified numerous other opinion groups that contend for control of administration foreign policy: "hawks" versus "doves," "super hawks" versus "moderate pacifists," "moderate conservatives" versus "ultraconservatives," "moderate careerists" versus "faithful followers," the "California clique," the "Harvard fac-

[37] See "A Major Change in the White House Staff," *Renmin ribao*, January 5, 1982, *JPRS, China: Political, Military, and Sociological Affairs*, January 19, 1982; "Reagan Demands Haig and Allen Stop Bickering," *Renmin ribao*, November 7, 1981, *FBIS-CHI*, November 9, 1981; Zhuang Qubing, "Heige xiatai shuominle shenma?" *Shijie zhishi*, no. 14 (1982): 4–6; Fang Min, "Weishenma Heige xiatai?" *Renmin ribao*, July 3, 1982, p. 7; Yang Wenke, "Why Haig, the White House's Great Gatekeeper, Resigned," *Heilongjiang ribao*, June 29, 1982, *FBIS-CHI*, July 12, 1982. William Clark's resignation as NSC adviser was also seen as a result of the State-NSC rivalry; see Zhou Guochang, "Weishenma Kelake likai baigong?" *Yangcheng wanbao*, October 19, 1983, p. 4.

[38] Interview at the Institute of International Studies, January 12, 1985.

[39] Jin Yingzhong, "Qiansi Meiguo de suowei 'guojizhuyi,' " *Shijie jingji yu zhengzhi neican*, no. 10 (1982): 11–14.

tion," and the "middle-of-the-road faction."[40] The statists also identify factions in the economic policy arena. The "supply-side faction" has been extensively analyzed by specialists at the Shanghai Institute of International Studies, Institute of Contemporary International Relations, and CASS's America Institute, Institute of World Economics and Politics, and Institute of Economics.[41] In the battle over controlling federal budget deficits, one America Watcher identified four competing factions: (1) the "fiscal conservatives," who comprise industrialists and the "principal Republican faction" in Congress; (2) "Democrats indulging in technology," who comprise "new generation liberals"; (3) "traditional liberals," who are led by Senator Kennedy and "other staunch Democrats"; and (4) "Reagan's conservative faction," led by his "economic brain trust."[42]

Some America Watchers have also begun to apply Western decision-making theories to the study of American executive branch policy making. For example, a 1984 Master's thesis from the International Politics Department at Beijing University surveyed the applicability of game theory, cybernetic theory, interest group theory, and bureaucratic politics theories to the study of U.S. foreign policy decision making.[43] The author concluded that bureaucratic politics has the greatest explanatory value. Another study examined the use of social science theories and social scientists in U.S. government decision making. It found the existence of an "interactive triangle" among social scientists in government, universities, and think tanks.[44]

[40] Zhuang Qubing, "Meiguo yingpai yu gezipai," *Shijie zhishi*, no. 13 (1980): 4; Zhuang Qubing, "Cong duiwai shiwu kan Ligen zhengfu de neibu fenzheng," *Shijie zhishi*, no. 7 (1982): 5–6.

[41] Zhang Jialin, *Gongyingxuepai* (Beijing: Jingji kexue chubanshe, 1984); Zhang Jialin, "Gongyingxuepai lilun he Meiguo dangqian de jingji xianshi," *Guoji wenti yanjiu*, no. 3 (1982): 10–15; Mei Jing, "Ligen 'jingji fuxing jihua' pouxi," *Xiandai guoji guanxi*, no. 1 (1982): 25–28; Yan Shan and Ke Juhan, "Ping 'Ligen jingjixue,' " *Xiandai guoji guanxi*, no. 3 (1983): 18–22; Fu Yincai, "Dangdai zichanjieji jingjixue zhong de 'xin zhidu xuepai,' " *Shijie jingji*, no. 9 (1980): 71–77; Yang Deming, "Fulidemuo de jingji xueshuo he huobizhuyi de lishi gedong," *Shijie jingji*, no. 10 (1980): 65–74; Chen Baosen, "Reaganomics Hobbled By Reality," *Renmin ribao*, March 2, 1983, *FBIS-CHI*, March 7, 1983, B1; Qiu Qihua, Zheng Weimin, and Yang Deming, "Lun xifang baoshouzhuyi jingji sichao xingqi de Beijing jiqi lishi gedong," *Shijie jingji*, no. 6 (1981); Huang Fanzhang, "Gongyingxuepai yu Ligen jingji zhengce," *Shijie jingji*, no. 9 (1982): 1–8; and Ge Qi, "Kaiensezhuyi, huobixuepai he gongyingxuepai," *Shehui kexue*, no. 3 (1980): 43–46.

[42] Wang Jiangang, "Ligen de jingji sixiangku," *Jingji ribao*, March 29–30, 1983, p. 4.

[43] Li Yuanchao, "Juece lilun jichi zai Meiguo duiwai zhengce fenxi zhong de zuoyong," Master's Thesis, Beijing University, April 20, 1984.

[44] Zhang Xiang, "Meiguo shehui kexuejia zai zhengfu juece guocheng zhong de zuoyong," *Zhengzhi yu falu*, no. 3 (1984): 77–79.

Thus, the statists are learning their analytical way around the corridors of power in the White House and throughout the executive branch. In the process they attempt to identify "friendly" and "unfriendly" elements with respect to China policy. They also build on this type of analysis—particularly factional analysis—to try to cultivate and manipulate certain administration members in U.S.-China relations. In the end, though, I believe there is a good deal of mirror imagery at work in the statists' views of American politics. That is, power is concentrated at the top of the Chinese political system, and factions are prevalent in the Zhongnanhai (Beijing's equivalent of the White House and Kremlin), and thus there is a certain degree of intellectual compatibility in transposing this mode of analysis onto politics in Washington, D.C. There exists, however, another opinion group among non-Marxist America Watchers who argue that understanding American politics is not quite so simple.

The Pluralists

As distinct from the statists, the pluralist cohort of non-Marxist America Watchers cast their net more broadly than the federal government. This is by no means to say that the executive branch is not an important political actor in their estimation, as indeed it is, but the pluralists tend to concentrate more attention on the Congress, on nongovernmental actors, and on the political dispositions of the electorate. Said one leading America Watcher at the Institute of International Studies, "I must take into account the president and his staff, bureaucratic politics in the executive branch, Congress, interest groups, financial groups, and the people's interests."[45]

Many of the pluralists have also come to accept the liberal-conservative distinction in analyzing American politics. This dichotomous mode of analysis began to appear regularly in Chinese writings about the United States after Ronald Reagan's 1980 election victory. Chinese analysts began to recognize philosophical and programmatic differences between liberals and conservatives, Democrats and Republicans. They further began to distinguish between types of liberals and conservatives, recognizing cleavages within these two groupings.

In this context, the pluralists were interested in whether President Reagan's election signified a fundamental shift in the American electorate, domestic politics, and foreign policy. They argued that liber-

[45] Interview at the Institute of International Studies, July 21, 1985.

alism and liberals had assumed the prominent place in U.S. politics after the New Deal. Despite Republican presidents during the half century between Roosevelt and Reagan, there is a basic consensus in the pluralists' writings that liberal policies existed during this era. That is, they recognized that central to liberal politics is legitimate government intervention in society and the economy, albeit often at the behest of monopoly financial groups.[46]

The pluralists recognized that this liberal consensus eroded during the 1970s. America Watchers at the Institute of International Studies have argued that when it became apparent that liberal programs could not resolve the repetitive "economic crises" of capitalism and stimulate the economy, and that federal government intervention into private life was meeting opposition, "new liberals" appeared on the political scene to challenge the "traditional liberals."[47] But even with adjustments within the liberal camp, a true soul searching and questioning of traditional liberal values was seen among New Deal Democrats. Some observers noted that a group of "new conservatives" had also appeared on the American political scene who generally agreed with liberal policies to promote domestic social welfare but favored a much stronger defense posture vis-à-vis the Soviet Union and a more "interventionist" foreign policy in general.[48] Other analysts of the New Right (xinyoupai) strongly diagreed that this new group were essentially Jacksonian liberals in conservative clothing. Tracing their origins to the most extreme "rightist" elements in America, some argued that neoconservatism presaged a dangerous trend in the United States.[49] More traditional conservatives, however, were seen as rejecting the economic and social interventionism of the federal government altogether, as embodied in the New Deal and Great Society programs respectively.[50]

Most pluralists thus agree that the turn toward conservatism in the

[46] Guo Changlin, "Meiguo de ziyoupai he baoshoupai," Shijie zhishi, no. 4 (1981): 13–14.

[47] Pan Tongwen, "Meiguo de ziyoupai jiqi zhengce sixiang yanbian," Guoji wenti yanjiu, no. 3 (1984): 8–11; Hu Zhengqing, "The Conservative Marxist Tide and Its Background in the United States," Guangming ribao, July 19, 1980, FBIS-CHI, August 5, 1980, B1.

[48] Dong Mei, "Meiguo de 'xin baoshoupai,' " Guangming ribao, January 24, 1983, p. 3; Guo Qinggan, "Meiguo 'xin baoshoupai' tong Ligen zai waijiao zhengce shangde fenxi," Shijie jingji yu zhengzhi neican, no. 7 (1983): 35–38.

[49] See, for example, Liu Xuyi and Han Jinping, "Meiguo xinyoupai chutan," Meiguo yanjiu, no. 4 (1988): 113–34.

[50] Chen Qianguang, "Bashiniandai de Meiguo baoshou sichao," Guowai shehui kexue, no. 7 (1981): 21–25; Geng Huichang, "Meiguo zhengzhi tong youzhuan jiang chixu bashiniandai," Shijie jingji yu zhengzhi neican, no. 3 (1982): 39–41.

1980s, as exemplified in the 1980 and 1984 elections, represented a fundamental shift in the American political spectrum. Whether the transition from liberalism to conservatism of the American body politic would be decisive was not as clear. As one leading America Watcher put it in 1985, "The conservative movement is certainly predominant now and will probably remain that way for a while, but it cannot be said that there is a clear demarcation between the liberal and conservative eras, or that one has thoroughly replaced the other. Evidence of liberalism will remain apparent in domestic social policy and foreign policy for some time."[51] Jia Hao, a specialist in U.S. politics at the Shanghai Institute of International Studies, disagreed with this view and thought the rise of conservatism to be a more permanent fixture on the U.S. political landscape. He maintained that the conservatives had forged a "new political alliance" among themselves that was well-financed, disciplined, and likely to dominate American politics for years to come.[52] Jia claimed that this political alliance (*zhengzhi lianmeng*) was composed of five types of conservatives: the Old Right, Moderate Conservatives, New Conservatives, the New Right, and the Religious Right. These groups have penetrated both parties (although their main power base is in the Republican Party), have the backing of all major monopoly financial groups, have support among the middle and petty bourgeoisie, have established political action committees to promote their causes, and have a comprehensive agenda in both domestic and foreign policy.

Not content with merely analyzing the shifting liberal versus conservative proclivities of the electorate, one America Watcher at the CASS's America Institute has probed deeper into the philosophical origins of liberalism and conservatism in America. As a member of the first group of Chinese exchange students to study in the United States in 1979, Wen Yang returned to China four years later with a degree in American studies from Georgetown University. His writings reveal a breadth of background and depth of understanding unique among America Watchers. Although still in his early thirties, Wen Yang is already one of China's most perceptive analysts of the United States. I examined some of his views of various aspects of American society in the previous chapter. His writings on liberalism and conservatism are sprinkled with references to Tocqueville, John C. Calhoun, Adam Smith, Edmund Burke, Thomas Paine, Benjamin Franklin, Thomas Jefferson, Robert La Follette, Cotton Mather, Wil-

---

[51] Interview at the Institute of International Studies, July 21, 1985.

[52] Jia Hao, *Shilun Meiguo baoshoupai "zhengzhi lianmeng"* (Shanghai: Shanghai guoji wenti yanjiusuo, shuoshi lunwen, January 1984).

liam Sumner, and such latter-day writers as Daniel Boorstin, Louis Hartz, Richard Hofstadter, Daniel Bell, Irving Kristol, Nathan Glazer, Peter Steinfels, Clinton Rossiter, and Seymour Martin Lipset.

In the 1980s Wen Yang was most concerned with the historical and philosophical origins of American conservatism, and from this basis he proceeds to analyze contemporary conservatism. He concludes, therefore, that the "new conservatives" are not really "new" in terms of the underlying philosophy of their programs because their emphasis on individual liberties and laissez-faire economics is, in fact, classic Liberalism as derived from England.[53] Wen Yang perceives an ongoing struggle in American political philosophy between the "rugged individualism" derived from the pioneering spirit and "cooperative individualism," which has its roots in the European social contract and Leviathan state. In a discussion of equality and liberty in the United States, he expressed the view that this dichotomy accounts for the basic polarization in American politics between laissez-faire conservatives who stress liberty and state-interventionist liberals who emphasize equality.[54]

Within the conservative camp, Wen Yang sees four kinds of conservatives in the general populace and three types of conservative politicians.[55] In society at large, there exist "temperamental conservatives" who have an "instinctive attitude of opposition" (*bennengde fandui taidu*); "possessive conservatives" who oppose social change merely because they want to protect their social status, reputation, power, property, and other personal interests; "practical conservatives" who approve of policies that promote social change only if it benefits their interests as a class or as individuals; and "philosophical conservatives" who advocate conservative social change for purely ideological reasons. Among American politicians there are "ultraconservatives" (*jiduan baoshouzhuyizhe*) who mainly represent the upper and middle classes and unremittingly oppose all forms of the welfare state, "moderate conservatives" (*zhongjian baoshouzhuyizhe*) who guard against expansion of the welfare state and state interference in the private sector, and "liberal conservatives" (*ziyou baoshouzhuyizhe*)

[53] Wen Yang, "Meiguo ziyouzhuyi de yanbian," *Meiguo yanjiu cankao ziliao*, no. 10 (1985): 17–26; "Xin baoshouzhuyizhe: gaibian Meiguo zhengzhi de ren," *Meiguo yanjiu cankao ziliao*, no. 1 (1985): 28–32.

[54] Wen Yang, "Meiguoren jiazhi guan qiantan pingdeng, ziyou," *Meiguo yanjiu cankao ziliao*, no. 6 (1986): 28–38.

[55] Wen Yang, "Hewei Meiguo de 'baoshouzhuyi,' " I, *Meiguo yanjiu cankao ziliao*, no. 5 (1985): 18–26; "Hewei Meiguo de 'xin baoshouzhuyi,' " II, *Meiguo yanjiu cankao ziliao*, no. 6 (1985): 22–30.

who seek to guide social and economic change through the selected use of government regulatory agencies and law.

Wen Yang perceives that the rise of conservatism in the 1980s caused a profound identity crisis among liberals. This can be seen, he feels, among all generations, in the community, in the media, and even in the liberal-dominated universities.[56]

Wen Yang's colleague Zhang Yi, also a young specialist on American politics at the CASS's Institute of American Studies, shares the view that liberalism is on the wane and the American political landscape has been fundamentally transformed by the "Reagan revolution." In an article reviewing the Reagan years and estimating its potential lasting impact, Zhang Yi made a number of astute observations and predictions.[57] He first identified three components of the conservatism that propeled Reagan to electoral victory: "economic conservatism," which became manifest in "antigovernment" sentiment; social and moral conservatism, which was reflected mainly in popular sentiment against the breakup of the nuclear family, drug use, abortion, crime, premarital sex, and homosexuality; and foreign policy conservatism, which could "restore pride" to America and keep it "Number One" internationally. Zhang Yi argued that even before "Irangate" (Yilanmen), the "Reagan revolution" had been accomplished in these three spheres of conservatism. Not only had Reagan been able to implement his conservative platform, but he had moved the entire American political spectrum to the right. This could be seen, for example, in the conservative legislation that passed Congress, and also in the reorientation of the Democratic Party, which, Zhang argued, had made a notable "shift to the right" (bianyou). This reflected a geographical shift of power within the Democratic Party from the "Frost Belt" to the "Sun Belt." Zhang further argued that the conservative upswing could be seen in the increased attraction of organizations like the John Birch Society, Young Americans for Freedom, The Heritage Foundation, the Liberty Federation (formerly the Moral Majority), The Philadelphia Society, Congressional Club, National Political Action Committee, and The Conservative Caucus, and intellectuals like William Buckley, Jr., Irving Kristol, Martin Lipset, Daniel Bell, Norman Podhoretz, and George Will. Increased conservatism in the electorate was also indicated by increased voter turnout. How will the conservative movement cope without Reagan at the helm? Zhang Yi perceived a "Rea-

---

[56] See, for example, Wen Yang, "Meiguoren dui ziyouzhuyi de ziwo zhiyi," *Meiguo yanjiu*, no. 4 (1987): 157–60.

[57] Zhang Yi, "Ligen zhihou de Meiguo zhengju," *Meiguo yanjiu*, no. 3 (1987): 37–58.

gan gap" arising. In 1987 he did not foresee any suitable replacements for Reagan, but he concluded that the tone and substance of the national political agenda had shifted so significantly to the right that "the next government's policies will also be relatively conservative." The conservatives, Zhang argued, "had developed from a fringe faction into an orthodox faction that rules America today, a change that might be called world-shaking. Furthermore, conservative thought will continue to be the main current in American politics after Reagan, and the conservatives will continue to control the American political scene."[58]

The Role of Congress

Along with a growing awareness of the electorate and varying schools of thought in the American polity, the non-Marxists have also discovered Congress. With a couple of important exceptions, however, their understanding of the principle of the separation of powers, Congress's multiple roles in the policy process, the structure of Congress, and the importance of constituencies in a representative democracy is not very sophisticated.

The inordinate attention paid to the executive branch by the statists, as detailed above, results in mirror imagery whereby many Chinese Americanists perceive the executive as omnipotent. As a result, they either do not understand or do not take seriously the separation of powers or representative democracy. As will be seen, there are precious few pluralists who have studied the Congress in any detail, and therefore their analyses must be viewed against the backdrop of executive-centric analyses. According to the former American ambassador to China, Arthur Hummel, Jr., the Chinese government's handling of several cases in bilateral Sino-American relations—the Hu Na asylum case, the Huguang Railway Bonds case, and the Taiwan Relations Act, the Pell Amendment, entry into the Asian Development Bank, Northwest Orient Airlines servicing both Taiwan and mainland China—may reflect the omnipotent view of the executive branch as put forth by the statists. In each case Chinese leaders appealed directly to the president to eliminate the problem in question by executive fiat. Each case has been a learning process for the Chinese whereby, after seeing the president's limited authority under the separation of powers, these grievances were ultimately addressed to the appropriate bureau and branch of the U.S. govern-

[58] Ibid., p. 57.

ment. No matter how much Chinese leaders and Foreign Ministry officials have learned from these and other instances, according to a former senior American official, "They still have a very poor sense of our decentralized political process and separation of powers. . . . None of these individuals can put themselves in the place of a U.S. decision maker. They lack the sociological-anthropological training necessary for them to transcend their own system and view the United States as an American would."[59]

The Chinese Embassy in Washington has gradually come to understand the value of monitoring Capitol Hill and now allocates several staff from its political section to monitor congressional hearings, resolutions, publications, and so forth.[60] According to leading Chinese officials, however, these embassy efforts to monitor the executive and legislative branches are limited to issues bearing directly on Sino-American relations.[61] This focus precludes a full appreciation of the congressional role in the political process, executive-legislative bargaining, and coalition building on Capitol Hill. To learn more about the role of Congress, the America desk of the Foreign Ministry, CASS's America Institute, the Foreign Ministry's Institute of International Studies, and the State Council's Institute of Contemporary International Relations have all sent staff to the United States in recent years.

These efforts have not, however, resulted in a dramatic increase in writings about Congress. Considering that the previous baseline was virtually nil, those publications that have appeared represent a net increase in quantity if not quality. While no books specifically on Congress have been published in China, all main textbooks on U.S. politics do provide a fairly objective and detailed treatment of the structure of Congress and its constitutionally mandated roles. They give little sense, however, of how Congress actually functions.[62] There is no real analysis of the principles of "advise and consent" or "check and balance" and how they become operative, nor do these texts go beyond a structural description of the committee system. The periodical literature on Congress is less structurally oriented and

[59] Interview, Beijing, March 29, 1985.

[60] Interview with Chinese Embassy official, January 30, 1986.

[61] Interview with Zhang Wenjin and Ji Chaozhu at the Chinese Foreign Ministry, June 26, 1985, substantiated in discussions with numerous embassy personnel responsible for congressional affairs.

[62] Shen Zongling, *Meiguo zhengzhi zhidu* (Beijing: Shangwu yinshuguan, 1984): pp. 76–93; Cao Shaolian, *Meiguo zhengzhi zhidu shi*, pp. 118–47; Yang Baihua, *Zibenzhuyi guojia zhengzhi zhidu*, pp. 120–201; Fudan daxue guoji zhengzhixi zibenzhuyi guojia zhengzhi yanjiushi bianxie, *Meiguo: geguo shouce congshu*, pp. 96–100; Fudan daxue zibenzhuyi guojia jingji yanjiusuo bian, *Meiguo zhengfu jigou*, pp. 129–42.

more concerned with the legislative process and executive-legislative relations. Of particular interest is Congress's role in foreign policy, whether it be via appropriations, treaties, hearings, resolutions, or confirmation of officials. Several America Watchers have noted the increasingly independent role of Congress in the foreign policy process since the Vietnam War.[63] Congressional factional alignments are also a subject of increasing interest. One study by two America specialists at the Institute of Contemporary International Relations identified an emerging bipartisan "moderate's alliance" against "Democratic neoliberals" and "Republican neorightists" in the ninety-ninth Congress.[64]

Even in the few analyses of the separation of powers that have been written in recent years, the statists maintain an executive-dominant view of Congress and the judiciary. These analyses are most evident in the writings of America Watchers at the CASS's America Institute, Law Institute, and Institute of World Economy and Politics, and at the Law Institute of the Shanghai Academy of Social Sciences. The legal scholars in these institutes recognize that the Constitution grants different rights and responsibilities to each branch of government,[65] but the statists maintain that the president and executive branch dominates the political process. As a key piece of evidence to bolster this belief, the statists cite the June 1983 Supreme Court decision invalidating the "legislative veto" (lifa foujue).[66] CASS Americanist Zhang Yi (whose writings generally fall into the pluralist camp) found that during the 1970s Congress started to attach veto clauses to a large number of laws—eventually totaling some two hundred—including the 1973 War Powers Act, 1974 Budget and Funds Withold-

[63] Zhuang Qubing, "Meiguo guohui he liangdang zhidu," Shijie zhishi, no. 3 (1979): 14–16; Li Xiguang, "Meiguo zongtong he guohui de guanxi," Zhongguo qingnian bao, February 7, 1981, p. 2; Zhang Yebai, "Meiguo waijiao juece de tedian," Meiguo yanjiu, no. 4 (1987): 52–71; and Zhang Yebai, "Cong jingji yinsu kan Meiguo waijiao," paper presented at the Chongqing Conference on Political Implications of World Economic Trends, October 1984.

[64] Zhao Shenggan and Liu Zhigen, "Meiguo Dijiujiuju guohui de tedian jiqi dui Ligen zhengce de yingxiang," Xiandai guoji guanxi, no. 9 (1985): 20–24.

[65] See Zhongguo shehui kexueyuan faxue yanjiusuo, Ying-Mei xingfa xingshi susongfa gailun (Beijing: Zhongguo shehui kexue chubanshe, 1984); Shanghai shehui kexueyuan faxue yanjiusuo, Geguo falu gaikuang (Shanghai: Zhishi chubanshe, 1983).

[66] Wu Zhenying, "Lifa foujue de yici zhuanzhe," Meiguo yanjiu cankao ziliao, no. 1 (1985): 32–37; Wen Yang and Huang Deqian, "Meiguo zongtongzhi de yanbian," Meiguo yanjiu cankao ziliao, no. 2 (1985): 15–24; Li Daokui and Lin Xiaoyun, "Meiguo zhengzhi zhidu de fenquan yuanzi," Meiguo yanjiu cankao ziliao, no. 1 (1985): 17–24; Ren Yue, "Meiguo zuigao fayuan dui zongtong quanli suochi lichang," Meiguo yanjiu cankao ziliao, no. 12 (1985): 54–57; Wang Ping, "Meiguo sanquan fenli yu zhijue fenxi," Shijie jingji yu zhengzhi neican, no. 4 (1984): 49–53.

ing Control Law, 1975 International Development and Food Aid Act, 1976 Foreign Aid Act, and 1976 National Emergency Act, all of which became invalid as a result of the Supreme Court ruling.[67] On this basis Zhang Yi concluded that the "resurrection of Congress" in the wake of the Vietnam War and Watergate had by the end of the 1970s given way to a reassertion of the power of the executive branch. In a separate article on the Supreme Court and the Constitution, in which he examined numerous landmark cases, Zhang Yi found that the Court had done much to ensure First Amendment rights.[68]

Elsewhere Zhang Yi's writings reveal a considerable understanding of Congress. As part of his American politics program at the University of Virginia, Zhang worked on Capitol Hill. He may now be considered China's leading specialist on the U.S. Congress. In a significant analysis of Congress entitled "Why Congress?" Zhang stated that this was a question that many Chinese America Watchers had come to ask themselves as they examined cases of limited executive power. He argued that asking "why Congress" was equivalent to asking "why democracy." Zhang then proceeded to introduce his readers to one of the most thorough expositions of the concept of representational democracy ever published in a Chinese periodical. In doing so, he couched his analysis in historical terms. To do so in contemporary terms may have been too provocative given the political climate in China following the Tiananmen massacre. Perhaps Zhang's article was already in the pipeline before the events of June 4, 1989, but it nonetheless reveals a depth of understanding of Congress and American democracy unusual among China's America Watchers.

While the non-Marxists' scope of inquiry has broadened to Congress, it has not extended to examining congressional constituencies. As will be seen in the next section, other than analyses of regional monopoly groups, think tanks, and lobbies, little attention has been paid to politics outside of Washington, D.C. Studies of state and local government are particularly spartan. Aside from some media attention to Reagan's "New Federalism," only a few serious scholarly studies exist on relations among the federal, state, and local governments. Li Daokui, the former chief of the domestic politics section of the CASS's America Institute, spent a year in the United States conducting research on federalism and is writing a book on the subject.

[67] Zhang Yi, "The Origin and Development of the Power Struggle Between the White House and Congress in the United States," *Renmin ribao*, August 25, 1983, *FBIS-CHI*, August 26, 1983, B3–4.

[68] Zhang Yi, "Zuigao fayuan yu Meiguo xianfa fazhan," *Meiguo yanjiu*, no. 4 (1987): 18–35.

In 1983 Li Changdao of Fudan University published two articles on the subject.[69] In these articles, Li expresses the view that over time the federal government has inexorably encroached upon the autonomy guaranteed to states and local governments by the Constitution. He believes this trend is "the inevitable outcome of the development of state-monopoly capitalism."[70] A 1984 Master's thesis on U.S. federalism by an America Watcher in the International Politics Department at Fudan University stands in contrast to Li's image of increased centralization.[71] On the contrary, Gai Zheya stressed the autonomy of states and the balanced relationship between center and locale. Gai termed this system "cooperative federalism," as opposed to Li's image that American federalism is becoming a "unitary system."

Thus, the pluralists began in the late 1980s to study Congress. Other than a few scholars such as Zhang Yi, however, most have difficulty grasping the representational linkages and the checks that Congress exerts on executive power. As will be seen in the next chapter in the context of the America Watchers' perceptions of Sino-American relations, many view Congress as highly intrusive in other nations' domestic affairs.

Nongovernmental Actors in the Policy Process

It is in the intermediate realm of nongovernment actors that the America Watchers of the Marxist and non-Marxist schools find common ground. During the 1980s the America Watchers came to recognize that actors other than government organs contribute to the policy process. Analysts in both schools essentially have a conspiratorial view of the policy process in the United States whereby nongovernmental forces behind the scenes compete to manipulate government policies. Both focus attention on think tanks, foundations, associations, political action committees, and a wide range of special-interest lobbies. The Marxists, as would be expected, see these actors as agents of monopoly capital. The non-Marxists tend to focus on the policy positions advocated by these organizations, but they also look at their linkages with both government and financial backers. Besides somewhat different emphases, America Watchers in both schools

[69] Li Changdao, "Meiguo lianbang zhongyang he zhou de guanxi," *Zhengzhi yu falu*, no. 2 (1984): 39–41; "Meiguo difang zhengfu," *Zhengzhi yu falu*, no. 2 (1985): 23–25.

[70] Li Changdao, "Meiguo lianbang zhongyang he zhou de guanxi," p. 41.

[71] Gai Zheya, "Lun Meiguo de lianbangzhi he lianbangzhuyi," Master's thesis, Fudan University, November 1984.

consider nongovernmental organizations as influential and important actors in both the domestic and foreign policy process.

In his *History of the American Political System*, Cao Shaolian discusses seven ways that monopoly financial groups influence American politics. The first way is to bankroll the major parties and candidates at the federal, state, and local levels. The leading caituan pay particular attention to infiltrating party organizations and political action committees, paying off their "chieftains," and insuring that their candidates are nominated. Professor Cao says nothing of campaign financing laws, the state delegate selection and caucus systems, and other mechanisms designed to prevent such boardroom manipulation of the electoral process. This view, as will be seen in the next section, is very much in line with the Marxists' overall depiction of American elections as false exercises that simply perpetuate the rule of the bourgeoisie.

Second, as was described above, the caituan exert their influence through placing their personnel in key positions in the executive, legislative, and judicial branches. Lenin's dictum "today a minister, tomorrow a banker; today a banker, tomorrow a minister" is verified in the American "revolving-door syndrome." All administrations contain such monopoly representatives, but Professor Cao estimated that it reached its height during the Eisenhower years when, in 1955, 150 of the top 272 officials in the executive branch were placed there by the major monopolies. Nor are Congress and the judiciary immune to this phenomenon in Cao's estimation. Congressmen and judges are directly selected by the monopolies. Congressional whips and party seniors are all subject to monopoly influence, either directly or through special-interest groups.

Lobbies are thus the third major means for caituan to exert their influence. In addition to the vast array of special-interest groups, organizations such as the Chamber of Commerce and National Association of Manufacturers work behind the scenes (*beihou*) to draft "antilabor" legislation (such as the Taft-Hartley Act) on behalf of the bourgeoisie.

The fourth method is to create foundations that finance projects abroad that would otherwise appear to be a conflict of interest, and to fund research institutes that write policy papers favorable to caituan interests. The Ford and Rockefeller financial groups have long been active in such undertakings, but Professor Cao believes that in recent years the "Texas petroleum clique" and "West Coast war industries clique" have become more active.

Fifth, the monopolies convene special conferences to advance and publicize their policies. Such meetings bring monopoly representatives and government officials face-to-face in a secret environment for conspiratorial policy planning. For example, the Marshall Plan and Truman Doctrine grew out of such a secret conference in 1945 attended by sixty-six representatives of the Rockefeller, Morgan, and Dupont caituan. The Marshall Plan thus became a means to reap huge profits for these monopolists from the ashes of European destruction, not a humanitarian effort for postwar reconstruction. The Bretton Woods meeting, out of which grew the postwar international monetary structure, is cited as another example of such a meeting.

Control of the media is the sixth mechanism through which caituan influence American politics. According to Professor Cao, all major newspapers, wire services, magazines, television networks, and film companies are controlled by one or more of the leading monopoly groups and consequently serve as mouthpieces for them. The *New York Times* has, over the years, been an organ of the Harrimans, Morgans, and Rockefellers. All Hearst papers represent the interests of the California caituan, and to some degree those of the Morgans and Rockefellers. The Scripps-Howard chain belongs to the Morgans, while the Knight-Ridder chain is in the hands of the "Midwest commodities clique" and National Association of Manufacturers. *U.S. News & World Report* is a Rockefeller organ, while *Time* and *Newsweek* represent Morgan and Du Pont respectively. The Associated Press and United Press International are owned by the Morgan group. Reporters, columnists, and editors who work for these syndicated chains "must publish news and opinions identical with the interests of their respective monopoly groups, and if a news story deals directly with one of these groups before publishing it they must first seek instructions from the secret 'committee of twelve' which has representatives from each group." The three major television networks are similarly controlled: ABC by Morgan, CBS by Rockefeller, and NBC by Du Pont. Finally, the "eight big Hollywood film companies" are controlled by monopolies and, since the Kennedy administration, have carefully scripted movies to "advance the government's global strategy and strengthen foreign propaganda."[72] One wonders if Steven Spielberg is aware that he is a monopolist tool?

The seventh way in which Professor Cao sees the monopolies influencing politics is through education. Primary, secondary, and college education are all deeply shaped by the ruling monopoly bourgeoisie in his view. School principals and university presidents "must all be figures who the monopolies trust; . . . teachers and students alike must be loyal to the government, support its current pol-

---

[72] Cao Shaolian, *Meiguo zhengzhi zhidu shi*, pp. 235, 237.

icies, and believe in the superiority of capitalism."[73] Because foundations, which are themselves monopoly agents, dispatch their "agents" to become principals, directors of executive committees, and chairmen of the boards of trustees, teachers can be hired and fired on the basis of their allegiance to monopoly interests. It does not sound as though Professor Cao has been on many American campuses.

Professor Cao's explanation of these seven ways in which the caituan influence and control American politics is one of the most systematic expositions of monopoly influence over nongovernmental actors written by a Marxist America Watcher. Most other studies, particularly those by non-Marxists, analyze each of these organizations in a piecemeal fashion.

Virtually every major American think tank (sixiangku), foundation (jijinhui), and foreign policy association (waijiao xuehui) has been scrutinized by the America Watchers in recent years. Invariably, Chinese analysts attempt to pigeon-hole these organizations as beholden to one or another caituan, political party, and policy disposition.

For example, veteran America Watcher Zhuang Qubing of the Institute of International Studies claimed that the Committee on the Present Danger is staffed by individuals who have close ties to the California and Midwest defense industries, hence their advocacy of an arms buildup.[74] The Council on Foreign Relations and Trilateral Commission are believed to be funded and staffed by the Rockefeller caituan, which has multinational financial interests via Chase Manhattan Bank and other holdings, and hence are the primary advocates and architects of a globalist foreign policy that places relatively less importance on East-West relations and instead emphasizes trilateral and global issues.[75] America specialists at the Institute of Contemporary International Relations and Institute of World Economics and Politics at CASS argue that the American Enterprise Institute (AEI) is funded largely by the Texas oil clique and the Bechtel Corporation, both of which have substantial interests in the Middle East, and hence argued the Arab world's case in American policy councils during the Reagan administration through their "agents" Vice-President Bush, Secretary of State Shultz, and Secretary of Defense Weinberger.[76] Georgetown University's Center for Strategic and Interna-

---

[73] Ibid., p. 238.

[74] Zhuang Qubing, "Meiguo de yingpai yu gezipai," *Shijie zhishi*, no. 13 (1980): 4.

[75] Zhi Ying, "Meiguo duiwai guanxi weiyuanhui," *Shijie zhishi*, no. 13 (1979): 15; Zhuang Qubing, "Meiguo zhengfu beihou de sandong weiyuanhui," *Shijie zhishi*, no. 13 (1979): 13–15.

[76] Wu Tianyou and Fu Xi, "Wei Ligen chumou huace de sixiangku," *Xiandai guoji*

tional Studies is said by a leading New China News Agency correspondent to have the same financial backing and policy disposition toward the Middle East as AEI, but because of its simultaneous ties to Wall Street (Rockefeller and Morgan caituan) it is thought to be more concerned with U.S.-Soviet "contention" than AEI.[77] Many America Watchers share the view that the Hoover Institution is the main think tank for California caituan bankers, defense industrialists, and conservatives, and along with the Heritage Foundation, Stanford Research Institute, and Institute for Contemporary Studies, the leading contributor of officials and policies to the Reagan administration.[78] Analysts at the CASS's America Institute assert that the Brookings Institution primarily serves the Democrats, while the RAND Corporation leans toward the Republicans.[79] There is widespread agreement among America Watchers that the Trilateral Commission and Council on Foreign Relations are organs through which the Rockefellers direct American foreign policy. Dozens of other think tanks, foundations, and associations have been similarly analyzed in the periodical press.

The definitive work on this subject is the study *Meiguo zhongyao sixiangku* (Important American think tanks) compiled by analysts at the Institute of Contemporary International Relations.[80] This neibu 450-page volume describes in great detail the personnel, publications, functions, and alleged policy influence of sixty U.S. research institutes, foreign policy–related associations, and foundations. The authors view these organizations as the key source of personnel and policy positions for every administration, and as such are the main mechanism through which monopoly financial groups influence U.S. domestic politics and foreign policy. As table 5.1 indicates, each institute, association, or foundation is linked to one or more caituan through funding, personnel, selection of research topics, and advocacy of policy positions. The table reveals how the authors identify the affiliations of thirty such organizations.

---

guanxi, no. 1 (1982): 55–64; Li Shipei, "Beiketeer gongsi," *Xiandai guoji guanxi*, no. 3 (1983): 57–58; Ren Yi, "Mei xinren guowuqing," *Shijie zhishi*, no. 14 (1982): 18; "Meiguo guowuqing Shuerci," *Shijie jingji yu zhengzhi neican*, no. 9 (1982): 63–65; "Meiguo guofangbuzhang Wenbuoge," *Shijie jingji yu zhengzhi neican*, no. 11 (1983): 61–63.

[77] Yu Enguang, "Yuce helai yingxiang zhengce," *Liaowang*, no. 17 (1984): 34–36; Wu Tianyou and Fu Xi, "Wei Ligen chumou huace de sixiangku."

[78] Hu Zhengqing, "Ligen yikao de sixiangku," *Shijie zhishi*, no. 15 (1986): 8–9; Wu Tianyou and Fu Xi, "Wei Ligen chumou huace de sixiangku."

[79] Ning Li, "Meiguo sixiangku dui zhengzhi de yingxiang," *Meiguo yanjiu cankao ziliao*, no. 4 (1985): 14–17.

[80] Wu Tianyou and Fu Xi, *Meiguo zhongyao sixiangku* (Beijing: Shishi chubanshe, 1982).

Table 5.1
Affiliation of U.S. Think Tanks

Organization	Affiliation
Brookings Institution	Democratic party's exile government and liberal faction
American Enterprise Institute	Republican party's exile government and shadow cabinet; "conservative faction"; Morgan financial group
Hoover Institution	Republican party's shadow government; "right wing"; California, Rockefeller, but mainly Morgan financial group
Institute for Contemporary Conservative Studies	"Reagan's brain trust"; western financial group
Institute for Policy Studies	"Main left-wing think tank of the liberal faction"
Center for the Study of Democratic Institutions	Liberal faction of Democratic party
Foreign Policy Research Institute	Cold war; conservative; eastern and midwestern financial groups
Institute for Foreign Policy Analysis	Conservative faction of the Republican party; eastern and midwestern financial groups
National Strategy Information Center	Cold war; conservative; ties to intelligence community
U.S. Strategy Institute	"Reactionary militarists" and hard-line scholars
Arms Control Association	Détente faction
Georgetown University Center for Strategic and International Studies	Cold war; conservative; hard-line; Rockefeller financial group and "petroleum faction"
Columbia University Research Institute on International Change	Anti-Communist; Rockefeller financial group
Harvard University Center for International Affairs	Conservative; Rockefeller financial group
University of California, Berkeley, Institute of International Studies	Western and Rockefeller financial groups; Ford and Luce foundations

Table 5.1 (*cont.*)

The Rand Corporation	"America's most comprehensive strategic research organ"; ties to Republican party, western financial group, and intelligence agencies
The Hudson Institute	Conservative; eastern financial group; Defense Department
SRI International	Hard-line; Rockefeller and western financial groups
Institute for Defense Analysis	"Militarist"; CIA and Defense Department
Trilateral Commission	Anti-Soviet; Rockefeller and twenty other leading financial groups in United States, Japan, and Europe
Council on Foreign Relations	"Superpower braintrust"; "invisible government"; eastern financial group
The Atlantic Council	Anti-Soviet; shadow government; eastern financial group
Committee on the Present Danger	Militarist; hard-line; anti-Soviet; eastern and midwestern financial groups
Ford Foundation	"Supports research for the left and right"; eastern and midwestern financial groups
Carnegie Endowment for International Peace	Eastern financial group, mainly Rockefeller
The Heritage Foundation	"Extremely conservative," new-right; southern and western financial groups
Foreign Policy Association	Eastern financial group, especially Rockefeller and Morgan
Potomac Associates	Eastern financial group, mainly Rockefeller
The American Universities Field Staff	Rockefeller and Morgan financial groups
The Stanley Foundation	Liberal faction, midwestern financial group

Source: Wu Tianyou and Fu Xi, *Meiguo zhongyao sixiangku.*

If there is a difference between Marxist and non-Marxist School analyses of these organizations it is that the former pay relatively more attention to caituan connections, while the latter write more about the substantive research in, and policy recommendations of, these institutions. Either way, they are now recognized by the America Watchers as very important actors in American political life.

Special-interest lobbies are other nongovernment actors that have drawn increased attention from both Marxists and non-Marxists in recent years.[81] The Marxists portray organizations such as the National Association of Manufacturers, Business Roundtable, and U.S. Chamber of Commerce as advancing the interests of the entire monopoly bourgeoisie, while specific caituan hire individual lobbyists to promote their special interests.

The non-Marxists now recognize that lobbies not sponsored by monopolies exist that genuinely promote the interests of their constituents in the populace at large, for example, the American Farm Bureau Federation, AFL-CIO and other trade unions, NAACP, NOW, Consumer Federation of America, National Council of Churches, American Legion, National Education Association, and prolife groups. While the America Watchers have long paid attention to the Taiwan lobby,[82] they are now conducting research on other foreign interest groups that try to influence U.S. foreign policy (Arabs, Israelis, South Koreans, Japanese, South Africans). They also explore the nefarious means of lobbying: ABSCAM, the Park scandal, the savings and loan scandal, and the exploits of Congressman Wilbur Mills were all dutifully reported in the Chinese press.

Former CASS America Institute deputy director and CASS vice-president Li Shouqi was one of the first America Watchers to be sent to the United States for the expressed purpose of studying the role of interest groups in the political process. Li's research focused on the impact of interest groups on Congress. Li found that interest groups are a key mechanism of "political participation in the United States that exemplifies pluralism."[83] Interest groups perform three functions according to Li: they represent societal interests to politicians; they provide expertise to politicians; and they offer a diversification of po-

---

[81] See, for example, Song Mingjiang, "Meiguo yiyuan de zuohouke," *Shijie zhishi,* no. 8 (1979): 16–17; Xu Binghe, "New Trends in Lobbying Activities in the United States," *Guangming ribao,* January 19, 1983, in *FBIS-CHI,* February 1, 1983, B3; and Liu Zhigen, "Meiguo liyijituan de fazhan jiti dui zhengfu juece de yingxiang," *Shijie jingji yu zhengzhi neican,* no. 12 (1983): 35–39.

[82] Ren Yi, "Meiguo de Taiwanbang," *Shijie zhishi,* no. 3 (1981): 4–5; Li Jiaquan and Liu Xingxian, "Meiguo longduan ziben zai woguo Taiwan," *Xiandai guoji guanxi,* no. 2 (April 1982): 27–32.

[83] Li Shouqi, "Liyi jituan canzheng," *Meiguo yanjiu,* no. 4 (1989): 28–41.

litical power outside of the three branches of government. Li's analysis painted interest groups in a positive light, and, while he notes the necessity of finances to sustain lobbying activities, he makes no mention of ties to caituan.

Some America Watchers, notably professors Lu Xiaobo and Yang Baihua of the Foreign Affairs College in Beijing, have begun to explore the impact of lobbyists on the electoral process through analyzing political action committees (PACs).[84] In his widely used college textbook on the political systems of capitalist countries, Professor Yang designates PACs and other groups that actively lobby politicians as pressure groups (*yali jituan*), as distinguished from ordinary interest groups (*liyi jituan*) that operate in society at large, such as trade unions or religious organizations.[85] Others, like Lin Xiaoyun of the CASS America Institute, have looked into the increased use of political consultants by corporations as political risk analysts, by parties and candidates for polling and strategy purposes, by the media for expertise, by lobbies for contacts inside government, and by government for advice of various kinds.[86]

The Marxists point to these lobbying activities as proof of U.S. politics under state-monopoly capitalism, that is, the influence of monopolies on the state. The non-Marxists, however, tend not to pass such judgments. While they recognize that powerful financial interests lie behind many lobbies, they are content to note the rise of lobbies as a force in their own right in the political process and seek to explore the details of their activities without interpreting them in either a Stalinist or Leninist context.

Thus, both Marxist and non-Marxist School analysts have begun to discover the intermediate realm of political actors between monopolies and the state. Nongovernment actors are a burgeoning area of research on American politics in China, and it is this area that is likely to continue as the meeting ground of the Marxists and non-Marxists.

U.S. Electoral Politics

Concomitant with the study of broad political trends and groups, the pluralists have also focused their attention on U.S. political parties

[84] See, for example, Lu Xiaobo, "Zhengzhi xingdong weiyuanhui," *Shijie zhishi*, no. 19 (1984): 12–13.

[85] Yang Baihua, *Zibenzhuyi guojia zhengzhi zhidu* (Beijing: Shijie zhishi chubanshe, 1984).

[86] Lin Xiaoyun, "Zhengzhi zixun zhuanjia de jueqi," *Meiguo yanjiu cankao ziliao*, no. 7 (1985): 39–45.

and elections. While many in the Marxist School continue to articulate the image that elections are futile exercises because both parties are dominated by the monopoly bourgeoisie,[87] non-Marxists have questioned this assumption and now follow U.S. electoral politics very closely.

Since the Sino-American rapprochement of the early 1970s, Chinese media coverage of presidential elections and midterm Congressional elections has steadily increased in quantity and quality. This is evidenced in the analysis below of Chinese commentaries on the five presidential elections between 1972 and 1988.

Much of the non-Marxist commentary on American elections was written by NCNA journalists and research institute personnel in Beijing. This is not to say that Marxist interpretations do not appear in the Chinese press or academic publications. Indeed, much ink is spilled over trying to convince Chinese readers of the "real" nature of "bourgeois democracy." The issue of Western democracy is a difficult political issue for the Chinese authorities (witness the 1979 Democracy Wall and prodemocracy demonstrations of 1987 and 1989), and they go to great pains to point out the "false nature" of "sham democracy."

Marxist Perspectives on the Electoral System

Is the bourgeois "two-party system" the most democratic system as some people say? The answer is in fact negative. The bourgeois "two-party system" is a system in which two political parties, both representing the interests of the bourgeoisie, take turns in forming the government and putting into practice the system of class rule. . . . Regardless of how exciting the atmosphere of the elections between the two parties, a bourgeois cabinet will be formed and bourgeois policies followed. Under this kind of democratic system, the broad masses of working people are discriminated against and the only democratic right they are entitled to is to cast a vote every few years to decide which bourgeois party and people will assume the reins of government to rule over them. The bourgeois "two-party system" can never keep the working masses secure from exploitation, suppression, and slavery. Only if we completely abolish the "two-party system" and the entire bourgeois democratic system and replace them with

[87] While there are many examples of this in the periodical literature, an indicative book-length treatment is Chen Qiren, Wang Bangzuo, and Han Junjiu, *Meiguo liangdangzhi pouxi* (Beijing: Shangyue yinshuguan, 1984).

proletarian democracy in which the people can be the masters can we bring about a fundamental change in the people's status.[88]

This is the kind of commentary about democratic parties one would expect from one of the key organs of the Communist Party, the journal of the Central Party School. Until the mid-1980s this view was often echoed in the press. For example, in 1980 the other main organ of the Communist Party, the *People's Daily*, claimed that "under the capitalist system the general election is only a democratic right which protects capitalism, a tool for exercising capitalist rule."[89] The main newspaper in Shanghai opined, "The bourgeoisie's intention in promoting the two-party system is to maintain the political power of the bourgeois dictatorship. . . . The bourgeois two-party system is like a puppet show; no matter which puppet is on stage, it is always manipulated by someone in the background."[90]

University textbooks expound this Marxist interpretation as well. This is the case with two widely used political science textbooks by noted Chinese political scientists Zhao Baoxu of Peking University and Wang Bangzuo of Fudan University.[91] Both argue that since bourgeois countries are ruled by the monopoly bourgeoisie in the imperialist stage of development, it follows logically that elections are a means of perpetuating class rule by the bourgeoisie. Both books view political parties, politicians, and elections in capitalist countries as manipulated (*caozong*) by monopoly financial groups. In his basic text on the *History of the American Political System* and a companion article, Wuhan University professor Cao Shaolian makes the same argument that both major parties in the United States are pawns of monopoly financial groups, receive all their funds from them, select their candidates according to their wishes, and make policies that suit their interests.[92] Unquestionably the most comprehensive exposition of this kind of interpretation of the American electoral system is to be found in the volume *Analysis of the American Two-Party System* written by two professors from the International Politics Department at Fu-

[88] Guo Yongxian and Yan Zhimin, "Zenma liaojie zichanjieji liangdangzhi?" *Hongqi*, no. 11 (1981): 33–37.

[89] Zhang Qingfu, "Zibenzhuyi guojia de xuanju," *Renmin ribao*, June 9, 1980, p. 5.

[90] Yu Xianyu, "Thoughts on the 'Duel Between the Elephant and the Donkey'—On the Bourgeois Two-Party System," *Wen hui bao*, March 13, 1981, p. 3, FBIS-CHI, March 26, 1981, B3–4.

[91] Zhao Baoxu, ed., *Zhengzhixue gailun* (Beijing: Beijing daxue chubanshe, 1982): 160–75; Wang Bangzuo et al., *Zhengzhixue jiaocheng* (Henan: Renmin chubanshe, 1983): 261–75.

[92] Cao Shaolian, *Meiguo zhengzhi zhidu shi*, pp. 272–73; "Meiguo zongtong xuanju he youguande jige wenti," *Wuhan daxue xuebao*, no. 5 (1980): 73–78.

dan University and one from the History Department at Wuhan University.[93] This volume is an example par excellence of the subordination thesis. The Republican and Democratic parties are likened to the two hands of the monopoly bourgeoisie; both hands have their representatives in the executive and legislative branches, but they are ultimately attached to the same body—monopoly capital. The Marxists also analyze so-called third parties such as the Socialist Workers Party, the Communist Party of the USA, and various splinter groups.[94]

A few analyses argued that not all ruling parties in capitalist countries are necessarily front organizations only for the monopoly bourgeoisie. For example, one CASS scholar cited the British Labour Party as an example of a "bourgeois worker party."[95] But all Marxist analyses agree that the American two-party system represents the bourgeoisie:

> The United States and other capitalist countries have gone to great lengths to publicize the two-party system, describing the existence of an opposition party as the hallmark of democracy, insisting that there will be no democracy without opposition parties; with oppostion parties comes democracy. As a matter of fact, the two-party system is an effective tool to preserve the dictatorship of the bourgeoisie. To be blunt, the American presidential election means only choosing one of two agents selected by the monopoly bourgeoisie whether the people like him or not. This is the democratic right the American voters enjoy under the two-party system."[96]

Nor are such views confined to party organs, newspapers, and university textbooks. None other than the former ambassador of China to the United States, Chai Zemin, said in a 1987 interview:

> In the United States I found that democracy and freedom were flaunted everywhere. Some government heads and senior officials mentioned democracy and freedom whenever they spoke. It seems that the United

[93] Chen Qiren, Wang Bangzuo, and Han Junjiu, *Meiguo liangdangzhi puoxi.* In the polemic on imperialism Professor Chen articulated the subordination thesis.

[94] Li Shidong, "Meiguo shehuidang yu Makesizhuyi zai Meiguo de zhuanba," *Shijie lishi dongtai,* no. 4 (1983): 11–14; Hui Bo, "Dangdai Meiguo shehuizhuyi liupai jieshao," *Shijie jingji yu zhengzhi neican,* no. 12 (1982): 13–16; Huang Delu, "Jielun Meiguo de zhengdang zhidu," in Zhongguo zhengzhixuehui bian, *Zhengzhi yu zhengzhi kexue* (Beijing: Qunzhong chubanshe, 1981): 295–317; Lu Qichang, "Rise of 'Leftwing Social Democracy' Ideas in the United States," *Guangming ribao,* August 23, 1980, *FBIS-CHI,* September 9, 1980, B1.

[95] Zhang Juru, "Zichanjieji liangdangzhi zai dangdai," *Shijie jingji yu zhengzhi neican,* no. 4 (1984): 56.

[96] Chen Jun, "Meiguo xuanju," *Beijing ribao,* January 23, 1981, p. 3.

States is the most democratic country in the world. But what are the facts? . . . I found that some people can be elected president or congressmen just because they are supported and backed by many rich men with the necessary money. The entire election system is based on dollars. After taking office, they only serve the interests of, and seek benefits from, these groups. How much democracy and freedom can there be? The democratic system in the capitalist countries is, in essence, a ruling form of the bourgeoisie and only serves the capitalist private ownership system.[97]

And what does former ambassador Chai think of freedom of speech and press in the United States?

The United States has always flaunted its freedom of speech. On the surface, there is complete freedom of press in the United States, the large number of newspapers and magazines are always briskly arguing with each other. In fact, newspapers and magazines have standards for selecting or rejecting items to publish. For example, the Communist Party of the USA is a legal party, but what newspaper in the United States has ever published news about the CPUSA? American newspapers do not allow any propaganda or speeches that would change the capitalist system. All American newspapers and magazines represent the interests of financial groups.[98]

Unlike other Chinese ambassadors to the United States, Chai Zemin is not what would be described as an America specialist. He was picked for the post because of his political reliability. Chai was reportedly personally appointed by Mao's chosen successor Hua Guofeng.[99] In the years immediately after Mao's death, politics still took precedence over expertise. After Deng Xiaoping returned to power, America specialists in the Foreign Ministry again assumed the ambassadorship in Washington: Zhang Wenjin, Han Xu, and Zhu Qizhen.

These are brief examples from a vast body of literature of the Marxist interpretation of democracy, particularly its American variant. This line of analysis appears occasionally in the following comparison of Chinese analyses of five presidential elections, but it is notable that the majority of analyses of these elections presented in the Chinese press are not of a Marxist nature. Rather, they introduce readers to the ups and downs of election campaigns, issues debated between the candidates, voter preferences, and so forth.

[97] Zhu Minzhi, "Chai Zemin on Western Democracy," *Ban yue tan*, no. 4 (1987): 18–21, *FBIS-CHI*, March 19, 1987, B4–6.
[98] Ibid., B5.
[99] Interview with Foreign Ministry official, May 20, 1983.

Perspectives on American Presidential Elections, 1972–1988

THE 1972 ELECTION

As best as I can tell from surveying the relevant Chinese newspapers and periodicals, the Chinese media carried no accounts of the 1972 campaign. China was still in the throes of the Cultural Revolution, and only a handful of publications existed in 1972. NCNA merely reported Nixon's reelection on November 8 along with a brief discussion of the electoral college system.[100] An accompanying report filed in Beijing that day by Reuter correspondent James Pringle noted that "Senior Chinese officials said tonight that President Nixon's landslide victory came as 'no surprise.' "[101] The only other Chinese media report described Nixon's "reshuffling" of his cabinet following reelection.[102]

THE 1976 ELECTION

Reportage of the 1976 election was only marginally greater. The first report noted the nominees following the conventions: "After bitter inner-party struggles at their recent national conventions the two major U.S. bourgeois parties, the Democratic Party and Republican Party, have respectively elected their presidential and vice-presidential candidates."[103] There was no press coverage of the campaign thereafter. Following the election the People's Daily merely ran a fifteen-line story buried at the bottom of page 5 noting Jimmy Carter's election and the fact that Carter and Ford were the candidates of "the two major American bourgeois parties."[104] Following this announcement NCNA reported on Carter's cabinet nominees in December.[105]

The dearth of public media coverage of the 1972 and 1976 elections was probably offset by classified government studies, translations from the U.S. media carried in Cankao xiaoxi and Cankao ziliao, and analyses written by staff at the Chinese Liaison Office in Washington. The scant coverage of these two presidential elections is also partially attributable to three factors. First, much of the Chinese publish-

---

[100] See Xinhua International Service, November 8, 1972, FBIS-CHI, November 9, 1972, A1.

[101] James Pringle, "PRC Officials 'Not Surprised' by Election Result," FBIS-CHI, November 9, 1972, A1–2.

[102] Xinhua, December 16, 1972, FBIS-CHI, December 18, 1972, A1.

[103] Xinhua, August 20, 1976, FBIS-CHI, August 23, 1976, A15.

[104] See "AFP: People's Daily Notes Carter's Election," FBIS-CHI, November 5, 1976, A1; also see Xinhua, November 3, 1976, FBIS-CHI, November 4, 1976, A5.

[105] Xinhua, December 24, 1976, FBIS-CHI, December 27, 1976, A4.

ing industry that would have covered issues such as an American election was largely defunct during this period due to the lingering influence of the Cultural Revolution. Second, and concomitantly, most of the America Watchers who normally would monitor U.S. elections were still in political purgatory having been purged during the Cultural Revolution. Third, in the absence of diplomatic relations, New China News Agency was only permitted to post a small contingent of correspondents in the United States at the United Nations in New York. Together these conditions severely constrained coverage of U.S. elections prior to 1980, but following the normalization of relations coverage increased markedly and was notable for its descriptive, non-Marxist orientation.

THE 1980 ELECTION

New China News Agency correspondents newly posted in the United States in the wake of normalization took advantage of their new proximity to cover the U.S. presidential election in far greater detail and with more sophistication than ever before. At first, the main emphasis of their coverage was on the procedural aspects of the American electoral process, somewhat to the neglect of adequate coverage of the candidates and issues, but as the campaign progressed they focused more on the latter.

A full year before the election, these correspondents began to write of the brewing campaign. The first such dispatch appeared in a November 1979 issue of the popular journal World Affairs.[106] Yu Enguang described what he perceived to be four distinct phases of the American electoral process. The first phase starts about two years before the election when the leaders of the two parties begin informally to assess potential candidates' strengths and weaknesses. While conducting this assessment "inside the parties" (dangnei), they also use the device of public opinion polling (minyi ceyan) to ascertain who the public might prefer. The second phase begins about one year prior to the election when the two parties hold a series of straw votes, caucuses, and primaries in all the states across the country. This leads up to the party conventions, the third phase, when the final nominees for president and vice-president are chosen. The final phase is the fall campaign leading up to the November election.

This article then describes how national campaign committees are established (with state and local branches) that serve to raise funds and coordinate campaign activities. Successful candidates need "millions of dollars," Yu states, but he does not discuss campaign financ-

---

[106] Yu Enguang, "Qiutian de Meiguo zhenghai," Shijie zhishi, no. 22 (1979): 9–10.

ing laws. His description of the campaign process itself is straightfor-ward, although he tends to overemphasize the role of the convention and underemphasizes the primaries in the selection process. Selec-tion of final candidates is made, according to Yu, at the convention through the "intense struggle of internal party factions" (*dangneibu gepaixi de jiji douzheng*).[107] Although Yu's analysis tends to stress the role of elites over the public in the selection process, his report is nonetheless noteworthy for his effort to sketch out in nonideological terms for his readers the evolving process of an American campaign. Unlike the coverage of past elections, there was no mention in Yu's report of "sham democracy," a "bourgeois political system" with no difference between parties, financial groups, and their support for certain candidates, or other Marxist interpretations still prevalent in other forums. Some journalists were beginning to break out of the Marxist mold.

Another early commentary in the *People's Daily* was a little more prone to the traditional Marxist interpretation. Focusing on the cost of a presidential campaign, NCNA correspondent Zhang Yan claimed that "donations obviously depend on how strong your back-stage boss is." The enormous election cost "proves how incredible the myth is that in the United States a poor man can also be elected president." Despite this image of manipulative "backstage bosses," the author still did not view the two main parties as identical front organizations for the monopoly bourgeoisie. "Certainly we cannot say that no differences exist between these two parties whatsoever. Although they agree with each other on the fundamentals of defend-ing the capitalist social system, they may be different in approach and methods." Therefore following the campaign was not a moot process for that Chinese reporter, even though "it is imperative to have excellent stamina and determination, because it is long, tedious, and at times even boring." While Zhang Yan seemed to look forward to covering his first election campaign, for him "the most spectacular aspect of the campaign, more often than not, is not the policies and principles announced by the respective nominees, but the various scandals revealed when they mutually rake up each other's faults."[108]

As the 1980 campaign season moved through the winter and spring primary season, the Chinese print media kept readers in-formed of the rising and falling fortunes of different candidates. In January the contest for both parties' nominations appeared to be

---

[107] Ibid., p. 10.

[108] Zhang Yan, "Drums and Gongs Are Being Beaten for the U.S. Presidential Elec-tion," *Renmin ribao*, December 3, 1979, *FBIS-CHI*, December 7, 1979, B1–B2.

wide open.[109] But by April the *People's Daily* believed the field had narrowed to two candidates in each party—Reagan versus Anderson for the Republicans, and Carter versus Kennedy for the Democrats.[110] Why Bush was not considered a contender at this point is not clear.

Another April commentary in the *People's Daily* looked beyond the candidates at the issues. Despite the public's concern with the "Afghanistan incident" and the "U.S.-Iranian crisis," "election-year voters are primarily concerned with domestic issues which are of immediate interest to them." While all candidates were in agreement that inflation was "the No. 1 enemy, sharp differences exist on how to subdue this enemy." Some advocated tax cuts (Reagan), others advocated voluntary wage and price guidelines (Carter), others thought a six-month mandatory "freeze" on wages and prices was necessary (Kennedy). To deal with oil price hikes Carter thought a "windfall profits tax" was the answer; Anderson disagreed and argued for a fifty cent tax per gallon at the pump.[111]

By "super Tuesday" in June, the field had narrowed to Carter and Reagan, even though Anderson's candidacy continued. The bruising fight between Carter and Kennedy had not, however, left the Democrats united. Reagan's main problems were thought to be his age, lack of experience of working in Washington, and appropriate selection of a running mate, according to the *People's Daily*.[112]

A lengthy analysis by Hu Zhengqing, then director of the U.S. affairs research section of the Institute of International Studies, published as the lead article in a June cover story issue of *World Affairs*, examined the favorable and unfavorable factors for Carter and Reagan.[113] Despite the advantages of incumbency, Hu argued that Reagan's chances were better than Carter's, even though "some middle and petty bourgeois voters have also found Reagan's policies too extreme and hard to accept." The interesting thing about Hu's article is that having spent several pages dissecting the various policies of Carter and Reagan as a non-Marxist analyst would, he then switched hats and ended with a conclusion classically representative of the Marxist School:

[109] See, for example, Yan Ming, "Meiguo balingnian zongtong xuanju kailuole," *Shijie zhishi*, no. 2 (1980): 15–16.

[110] Xiao Xi, "People Contending for the White House Throne," *Renmin ribao*, April 4, 1980, *FBIS-CHI*, April 14, 1980, B1–2.

[111] Xiao Xi, "The U.S. Presidential Election and the Debates on Domestic Issues," *Renmin ribao*, April 1, 1980, *FBIS-CHI*, April 10, 1980, B3–5.

[112] Zhang Yan, "U.S. Presidential Election Campaign Enters a New Stage," *Renmin ribao*, June 7, 1980, *FBIS-CHI*, June 13, 1980, B1–3.

[113] Hu Zhengqing, "Meiguo zongtong jingxuan jujian minglanghua," *Shijie zhishi*, no. 11 (1980): 2–6.

When boiled down, the presidential election campaign in the United States is merely a struggle among different financial groups for control of the state machinery. Apart from confusing people's minds to win the voter's support, the fact that the candidates expose one another's past misdeeds during the election campaign has also demonstrated the different political advocations of different financial groups based on their own interests. . . . The eastern financial groups representing the "trilateral" advocations still occupy a ruling position in the United States. The western and southern financial groups that are now advocating the "new internationalism" once gained control of state power through Nixon toward the end of the 1960s and in the early 1970s. Under the pressure of the eastern financial groups, Nixon took the blame for the Watergate incident and resigned; the western and southern financial groups suffered a serious blow. At present, the western and southern financial groups are rallying their forces and making another attempt to support Reagan to enter the White House. The eastern financial groups are bound to do everything possible to obstruct this. . . . If Reagan really wants to win the presidency, he cannot ignore the support of the eastern financial groups. In addition, even if he really becomes president, his domestic and foreign policies must not deviate too far from the line of the eastern financial groups, or else it is possible that he will suffer the same fate as Nixon.[114]

Other articles about this time echoed the theme of monopoly financial groups operating behind the scenes. A *People's Daily* report claimed that candidates must have "financial support provided by monopoly groups to meet staggering campaign expenses."[115] Another article dealing expressly with campaign expenditures concluded, "Although presidential election campaign spending runs into the hundreds of millions, varied and colorful campaign activities still continue at a frenzied pace under the financial support of the big bosses of the monopoly capitalist groups."[116]

The specter of a strong showing by independent candidate John Anderson led reporter Zhang Yan to examine the provisions of the electoral college system for breaking the deadlock should no candidate win enough electoral college votes.[117] Should such a situation come to pass, Zhang discovered that the balance of seats held by

[114] Ibid., p. 6.

[115] "Cankao ziliao: Meiguo zongtong xuanju," *Renmin ribao*, March 21, 1980, p. 7.

[116] Da Gong, "Vying for the Throne with a Throw of a Hundred Million Dollars—Astonishing Expenditures for the U.S. Presidential Election Campaign," *Renmin ribao*, June 9, 1980, *FBIS-CHI*, June 25, 1980, B5.

[117] Zhang Yan, "What Is to be Done if the President Is Not Elected?" *Renmin ribao*, July 2, 1980, *FBIS-CHI*, July 3, 1980, B1–3.

each party in the House of Representatives would decide the election.

Dispatches from the party conventions focused on the pomp and circumstance: bands, balloons, music, speech-making, and so forth.[118] A dispatch from the Republican convention described the "self-intoxicating enthusiastic mood"; no real business was left to be done at the convention except adopting a party platform and selecting a vice-presidential candidate. As for the platform, "After the election the new president can very well forget the platform and do as he sees fit; therefore, the broad masses of American voters do not attach much attention to the platform." The choice of Reagan's running mate was not so pro forma, as "more than ten candidates engaged in an intensive behind-the-scenes struggle for this coveted position." Reagan's choice of Bush was viewed as a concession to the "pressure from party moderates . . . in order to win over more votes in the U.S. Northeast and Midwest."[119]

Reports from the Democratic convention were more concerned with substance than style. The *People's Daily* told of the spirited confrontation between the Carter and Kennedy factions in the party.[120] Carter may have emerged the party's candidate, but he was a wounded one. The party was badly divided and would have to regain its momentum before the November election if it had any hope of holding office.

Dispatches during September claimed that the election was too close to call.[121] Anderson remained in the race, but for all ostensible purposes it was deemed a two-man race between Carter and Reagan.

In an attempt to ferret out the issues that would influence the voters, NCNA correspondents went out into the country to talk with the "man in the street." *People's Daily* correspondent Zhang Yan spoke

---

[118] I recall Chinese television airing these visual images to amused Chinese viewers during the summer of 1980.

[119] Wang Fei, "Gonghedang daibiaodahui zai Detelu," *Renmin ribao*, July 19, 1980, p. 7.

[120] See, for example, Wang Fei, "It Is a Forgone Conclusion that Carter Will Be Nominated the Democratic Presidential Candidate—The 'Dump Carter' Movement within the Democratic Party Is Foiled and Kennedy Withdraws from the Contest for Nomination," *Renmin ribao*, August 13, 1980, *FBIS-CHI*, August 14, 1980, B1–2; Wang Fei and Zhang Yan, "The Tense, Seething Democratic Convention," *Renmin ribao*, August 16, 1980, *FBIS-CHI*, August 19, 1980, B2–4.

[121] See, for example, Wang Fei, "The U.S. Presidential Election Campaign Enters a Tense Stage," *Renmin ribao*, September 17, 1980, *FBIS-CHI*, September 18, 1980, B2–4; Peng Di and Yu Enguang, "It Is Difficult to Predict the Prospects of the U.S. General Election," Xinhua Domestic Service, September 30, 1980, *FBIS-CHI*, October 2, 1980, B1–2.

with blacks, Hispanics, Jews, and middle-class whites.[122] He learned that the economy, social welfare, and foreign affairs were the key issues on the minds of voters, but that many were not satisfied with the programs of any candidate. Wu Jin, though, found that a new conservatism and patriotism was sweeping the United States.[123] Both correspondents felt that these sentiments favored Reagan.

As election day approached, *People's Daily* correspondents in the United States still found the election unpredictable.[124] Reagan's landslide victory therefore left them hard put for explanations. Wang Fei's explanation was typical of the immediate interpretation: "Reagan's victory reflects the deep frustration and dissatisfaction of U.S. voters with the emergence of economic crisis at home and the decline of U.S. international prestige. They want a change and hope that a new leadership will turn the tide."[125] As the weeks passed, other analyses appeared that attributed Reagan's victory to more fundamental shifts in the electorate. Hu Zhengqing of the Institute of International Studies, for example, attributed it to the "rising tide of conservatism."[126]

In sum, the America Watchers did an admirable job of covering and interpreting the 1980 election, the first they witnessed firsthand. The print media, notably the *People's Daily*, were particularly active throughout the election year. Importantly, coverage of this election marks the beginning of a basic transition in analytical perspective among the America Watchers from dominance of the Marxist to the non-Marxist School. This watershed must be largely attributed to the coverage by the news media reporting directly from the United States, and relying heavily upon interpretations in the American press for their stories. By the 1984 election, the Chinese government's intelligence and research establishment would be more fully rehabilitated and would contribute to strengthening the non-Marxists' hand vis-à-vis the Marxists.

[122] Zhang Yan, "What Are the American Voters Thinking About?" *Renmin ribao*, October 7, 1980, *FBIS-CHI*, October 9, 1980, B3–5.

[123] Wu Jin, "Meiguo gongzhong ruhe duide zheici daxuan," *Shijie zhishi*, no. 21 (1980): 16–17.

[124] Wang Fei, "On the Eve of the Decisive Battle of the U.S. General Election," *Renmin ribao*, October 23, 1980, *FBIS-CHI*, October 24, 1980, B1–2; Peng Di, "The Final Dash," Xinhua, November 1, 1980, *FBIS-CHI*, November 3, 1980, B1–2; Zhang Yan, "The Last Several Shots of the U.S. Presidential Elections," *Renmin ribao*, November 3, 1980, *FBIS-CHI*, November 4, 1980, B2–3.

[125] Wang Fei, "Preliminary Analysis of the U.S. Presidential Election Results," *Renmin ribao*, November 6, 1980, *FBIS-CHI*, November 6, 1980, B1–2. For this line of reasoning also see Peng Di and Yu Enguang, "What the Landslide U.S. Election Demonstrates," Xinhua, November 11, 1980, *FBIS-CHI*, November 12, 1980, B1–2.

[126] Hu Zhengqing, "Meiguo daxuanhou de zhengzhi qifen," *Shijie zhishi*, no. 1 (1981): 8–9.

The increased sophistication and detailed analyses of the pluralist component of the non-Marxist School is very evident in the 1984 election, when the candidates, campaign issues, platforms, and constituencies were closely monitored from the primaries through the conventions to the November election and inauguration.[127] NCNA correspondents published the bulk of these analyses, but research institute personnel also wrote more interpretive analyses. University scholars tended to describe the procedural aspects of the electoral system, while at the same time articulating the Marxists' interpretations of elections as false exercises in democracy because of their manipulation by the monopoly bourgeoisie. While the improved quantity and quality of election coverage by the non-Marxists is itself noteworthy for its improved detail and objectivity, discussion of the democratic principles underlying the American electoral system remains relatively scant and critical.

Chinese coverage of the 1984 presidential election started early. More than a full year before the voters went to the polls the print media began to assess the potential candidates and campaign issues. The earliest such assessment ran in the *People's Daily* on October 7, 1983.[128] In this dispatch from Washington, reporter Zhang Liang noted several salient features. First, competition within the Democratic Party had already narrowed to a two-man race—Mondale versus Glenn. The unusually early endorsements of Mondale by the AFL-CIO and National Education Association gave him the early edge for the nomination. Second, Jesse Jackson's potential candidacy was noteworthy for its symbolic value, although he stood no real chance of gaining the nomination. Third, the resurgent economy benefited Reagan's chances of reelection, but his policy of "arms expansion" did not. "What is it that the voters are taking greatest interest in at present? When this reporter asked some Americans this question, almost all of them replied: 'the economy and peace.' " Despite an economy on the rebound, Zhang Liang found that Reagan's policy of cutting social welfare programs had made "the broad masses of workers and women, as well as the poor and blacks, the main supporters of the Democratic Party." Moreover, "many are ap-

[127] See Harald W. Jacobson, *Chinese Commentary on the 1984 Presidential Election* (Washington, D.C.: United States Information Agency Research Report, December 1984); David Shambaugh, *Coverage of the United States in Key Chinese Periodicals During 1984*, pp. 41–45.

[128] Zhang Liang, "Meiguo daxuannian qiande jingxuan huodong," *Renmin ribao*, October 7, 1983, p. 7.

prehensive about Reagan's military and foreign policies." On this basis Zhang predicted that going into the election year "rivalries in the U.S. campaign will become more and more acute with each passing day."

Zhang's colleague in the Washington bureau, Yu Enguang, took a similar tack in another *People's Daily* commentary at the end of October. Yu told his readers of the intense struggle between Mondale and Glenn. Mondale had enjoyed a "golden October," having won straw votes in Maine and Iowa. But the release of the film *The Right Stuff* had boosted Glenn's popularity, thus leading Yu to the astute observation that "the real [Glenn] and the celluloid [Glenn] are working in coordination" (*zhenjia gelun huxiang huying*). Glenn appeared to be taking the "middle road," while Mondale represented the "traditional liberal faction of the Democratic Party."[129]

A November 1983 commentary in *China Youth News* presented the race as a "tripod" (*sanjiao*)—that is, a contest among Reagan, Mondale, and Glenn—but did not rule out the emergence of a "dark-horse" (*heima*).[130] The author argued that the peculiar vulnerabilities of all three candidates made it a fluid situation ripe for change.

Pan Tongwen of the Institute of International Studies, and one of China's leading specialists on U.S. domestic politics, disagreed with this assessment in a January 1984 article in *World Affairs*.[131] Mr. Pan predicted Reagan's victory on the basis of a resurgent economy and the public relations advantages of incumbency.

In March, eight months before the election, America Watchers at the Institute of Contemporary International Relations published an article entitled "Forecasting the 1984 Presidential Election."[132] The authors predicted Reagan's landslide victory. They pointed to the influence of "moderate conservatives and policies" in the Reagan administration, which was mandated by Reagan's reelection bid. The Democrats had tried to enlist "southern conservatives" and "new conservatives" into the traditional New Deal coalition but had failed in this effort. Because these groups were essentially "middle class," the Reagan-engineered economic recovery benefited them most, and Reagan could therefore count on their support. The Democrats were

[129] Yu Enguang, "Shi yue de Meiguo zhengtan," *Renmin ribao*, October 31, 1983, p. 6.

[130] Yuan Ding, "The Posture of a Tripod—the Opening Scene of the U.S. Presidential Election Campaign," *Zhongguo qingnian bao*, November 12, 1983, *FBIS-CHI*, November 22, 1983, B1–3.

[131] Pan Tongwen, "Meiguo guonei xingshi," *Shijie zhishi*, no. 1 (1984): 6–7.

[132] Liu Zhigen and Geng Huichang, "Yijiubasinian Meiguo daxuan xingshi zhanwang," *Xiandai guoji guanxi*, no. 6 (March 1984): 7–10.

seen as too faction-ridden and lacking in an attractive candidate or platform.

Thus one sees early in the election year a significant difference of opinion existing among the non-Marxists. Those analysts at the Institute of International Studies and Institute of Contemporary International Relations had already predicted Reagan's victory, while those journalists reporting from the United States saw a more fluid and competitive situation.

This cleavage among the non-Marxists may be attributable to the fact that professional role influences analytical perspective. That is, China's leadership had quite probably asked these intelligence organs for hard predictions of the outcome of the November election in order to shape China's America policy and lobbying activities accordingly.[133] President Reagan cum candidate Reagan was, in fact, due to pay a state visit to China in April. The Chinese government was not unaware of the implications of this visit for his reelection chances and hence probably sought an early reading from the IIS and ICIR. The lavish welcome accorded the president may well have been based on his presumed reelection. Contrary to the predictions made by these institutes' staff, NCNA journalists were more interested in providing a mass readership with a sense of the unfolding election process. Moreover, the journalists' dispatches from the United States revealed a heavy reliance on American media analyses.

The sudden emergence of Gary Hart during the February primaries took all America Watchers by surprise and lent credence to the journalists' perspective. Who was this newcomer, and what did he stand for? One *People's Daily* analysis attributed Hart's rise to the generational shift in the electorate.[134] Those between the ages of thirty and forty-four shared Hart's search for "new ideas" that were different from a revamped "New Deal," "New Frontier," or "New Federalism."

As the primaries rolled into the spring and Jesse Jackson's candidacy gained some momentum, NCNA correspondents began to assess his "new direction" (*xin fangxiang*).[135] They discovered that Jackson's platform varied a great deal from that of Mondale or Hart by advocating "cutting defense expenditure; raising taxes; increasing

---

[133] My visits to these institutes during the late fall and winter of 1983–84 often turned into discussion sessions on the election. America Watchers at these institutes seemed almost singularly obsessed with the election.

[134] Zhang Yunwen, "Hate de yi juntu qi shuoming le shenma?" *Renmin ribao*, March 17, 1984, p. 7.

[135] See, for example, Zhang Liang, "Jiekexun de jingxuan huodong jichi yingxiang," *Renmin ribao*, May 5, 1984, p. 6.

spending for social welfare and education; supporting equal rights for all; urging defense burden sharing with European and Asian allies; advocating a nuclear freeze; opposing the deployment of the MX missile, B-1 bomber, chemical and space weapons; halting aid to El Salvador; establishing a direct dialogue with the PLO; imposing strict sanctions against South Africa, etc."[136] These correspondents recognized that a black candidate running on such a platform stood little chance of winning the nomination, but his candidacy nevertheless appealed to them politically because of Jackson's anti-establishment rhetoric.

The *People's Daily* sent correspondents to both the Democratic and Republican conventions during the summer. Zhang Yunwen's dispatch from the Democratic convention focused on Mondale's forging a national coalition through a multidirectional (*duobianxing*) platform, and the selection of Geraldine Ferraro as a running mate.[137] Zhang Liang's dispatch from the Republican convention analyzed the "ultraconservative" platform of the Republicans and singled out the plank on Sino-American relations for special criticism:

> Although the platform speaks of continuing to develop ties with the PRC, it crudely interferes in China's internal affairs by openly expressing "concern" for Taiwan's security and pledging support and overall implementation of the "Taiwan Relations Act." The platform also advocates "self-determination" for Hong Kong. Such crude interference in China's internal affairs and phraseology violating China's sovereignty cannot but arouse the serious concern and anger of the Chinese people.[138]

As the campaign moved out of the conventions and into the fall runup to election day, other periodicals increased their coverage. The influential weekly newsmagazine *Liaowang* paid little attention to the early stages of the campaign, but its coverage picked up following the party conventions. It ran five feature articles, four of which were straightforward analyses of the candidates, party platforms, contested issues, constituencies, and so forth. One of these articles, by veteran America Watcher and NCNA correspondent Peng Di, was more of an attempt to introduce readers to the U.S. electoral process and its pros and cons. Peng Di counted the principle of "one man, one vote," the secret ballot, party discipline, conventions, financial disclosure laws, public debates among the candidates, and the cam-

---

[136] Ibid.

[137] Zhang Yunwen, "Meiguo daxuan zhengshi lakai zhanmu," *Renmin ribao*, September 12, 1984, p. 7.

[138] Zhang Liang, "Wei Ligen jingxuan zuo zhunbei de gonghedang daibiaodahui," *Renmin ribao*, August 25, 1984, p. 7.

paign hustings among the plusses of the American electoral system. The importance of television, the length of the campaign process, the exorbitant financial expenditures, the inordinate influence of interest groups and monopoly financial cliques, and the monopoly of power by the two major parties, Peng thought, were all drawbacks of the U.S. electoral system. In evaluating the prospects for the 1984 election, Peng concluded that a fundamental realignment of political power had taken place whereby such a conservative consensus existed that there were no real differences in the platforms of the two parties and candidates, and that the U.S. political system had, in fact, become one of "one party, two factions" (*yi dang liang pai*).[139]

The other *Liaowang* articles provided much more detail of the campaign issues. They were in essential agreement that the economy was the primary issue of importance to American voters, and its robust state would serve Reagan well. All articles, in fact, predicted a Reagan victory. CASS America Institute economist Zhao Gui compared the two candidates' stands on the budget deficit, interest rates, tax policy, the foreign debt repayment crisis, the defense budget, unemployment, inflation, structural and geographic shifts in U.S. industry, and so forth.[140] Other articles in the series focused on foreign policy issues like Central America, U.S.-Soviet relations, "Star Wars," the Middle East, and terrorism. Ferraro was viewed as a mixed blessing for Mondale; she helped him in the East but not in the Midwest or South.[141] The ERA, the abortion issue, and women's discontent with the "axing" of social welfare expenditures were predicted to stimulate a greater women's voting turnout than men. *Liaowang* commentators disagreed on whether Mondale could keep the traditional New Deal coalition together, but by disaggregating the Democratic Party's constituencies to discuss the aged, minorities, trade unions, women, and so on, these analysts demonstrated more discriminating analysis than merely writing it all off to monopoly financial cliques.

As the campaign entered its final week, *People's Daily* correspondent Zhang Yunwen told his readers of Reagan's comfortable lead

[139] Peng Di, "Tantan Meiguo daxuan," *Liaowang*, no. 46 (1984): 36–38.

[140] Zhao Gui, "Cong jingji qingkuang kan Meiguo jinnian daxuan," *Liaowang*, no. 37 (1984): 28–29.

[141] Several America Watchers also expressed the view that Ferraro's nomination was of great symbolic importance and marked a turning point for the role of women in American politics. See, for example, Wu Zhenying, "Meiguo diyige fuzongtong houxuanren Feilaluo," *Meiguo yanjiu cankao ziliao*, no. 9 (1984): 38–41; "Juezhu zhong de Meiguo liangdang zongtong houxuanren," *Shijie jingji yu zhengzhi neican*, no. 10 (1984): 56–63; Li Zongyang, "Ferraro, a Strong Woman in the U.S. Political Arena," *Ban yue tan*, no. 15 (1984): 58–59, in *FBIS-CHI*, August 30, 1984, B1.

and Mondale's attempt to "reverse the tide and score the most un-expected political victory since 1948." "The battle for the big Sun Belt states" had intensified; both candidates had "thrown a lot of man-power and money there."[142]

Postelection analyses varied. *Liaowang* attributed Mondale's loss to the fact that he "had no new ideas," and Reagan's victory was said to be a product of "a good domestic economic situation," "a strong defense policy," and "conservatism's ascendance over liberalism."[143] An article in *Semi-Monthly Talks* agreed that a strong economy and defense policy had been decisive in the American public's decision to vote for Reagan.[144] An article in the journal of the CASS's America Institute noted that the voting turnout of 59.1 percent was the fourth highest during the twentieth century, which was testimony to Rea-gan's popularity.[145] Another postelection wrapup in *World Affairs* at-tributed Reagan's victory to three main factors: a healthy economy, a decline in the appeal of "New Deal liberalism," and an "alliance" among the eastern, southern, and western financial groups.[146] The *World Economic Herald* offered a more sanguine analysis of the state of the U.S. economy in the wake of Reagan's victory. It predicted that the record budget deficit would continue to offset any achievements throughout Reagan's second term.[147]

Jesse Jackson's 1984 candidacy sparked a number of articles about the increased social and economic standing of American blacks and their new importance in American politics. These stood in stark con-trast with the previously dominant image of the economic exploita-tion and political ostracism of blacks.[148] To be sure, the Chinese me-dia still run many articles about black impoverishment and racism in the United States, but the portrayal of the political status of blacks has changed. As Li Daokui (director of the domestic politics research section of the CASS's America Institute until his retirement in 1986) argued in one article, the focus of the "black movement" in the

---

[142] Zhang Yunwen, "Jinru zuihou yizhou de Meiguo daxuan," *Renmin ribao*, Novem-ber 1, 1984, p. 6.

[143] Peng Di, "Tantan Meiguo daxuan."

[144] Zhang Yunwen, "Cong Ligen dangxuan kan Meiguo," *Ban yue tan*, no. 22 (1984): 56–57.

[145] "Meiguo dangxuan zongtong suo huoxuan minpiaoshu zhi dianxuan minrenshu zhong de xiaoshu," *Meiguo yanjiu cankao ziliao*, no. 12 (1984): 46–48.

[146] Mei Zheng, "Meiguo daxuan jieguo fenxi," *Shijie zhishi*, no. 23 (1984): 4–5.

[147] Jing Xing, "Ligen zaixuanhou kan Meiguo jingji," *Shijie jingji daobao*, November 12, 1984, pp. 1, 4.

[148] See, for example, "Zhongguo renmin jiefang jun 52977 budui lilunzu he Nankai daxue lishixi Meiguo shi yanjiushi ji 72 ju bufen gong-nong-bing xueyuan," *Meiguo heiren jiefang yundong jianshi* (Beijing: Renmin chubanshe, 1977).

United States has evolved from seeking civil rights to seeking political power.[149] Civil rights have essentially been achieved, many blacks have entered the middle class and hold college degrees, and they now seek "equal political status" with whites, according to Li.

From the coverage in national periodicals and newspapers, Chinese readers gained a fairly comprehensive picture of the candidates and the issues in the 1984 presidential election. But they did not receive much explanation of the American electoral system or process aside from sketchy descriptions of the primaries, conventions, and debates. Much of this coverage was of the postconvention period. Readers were therefore not informed of how one becomes a candidate and mobilizes a constituency, the election laws governing candidacy and financial contributions, preprimary state and local caucuses, the primaries themselves, the electoral college system, convention delegate selection, the role of public opinion polling, platform writing, and so forth. There was no coverage of state, local, judicial, or congressional elections; the focus was entirely on the presidential race. While the Chinese press did do a good job of discussing the major campaign issues in the final stages of the presidential campaign, no attention was paid to issues that arose earlier in the primaries, state elections, or local bond issues.

Because much of this coverage was piecemeal, no systematic introductions to the electoral process itself were published in the periodical press, thus leaving readers to fit together pieces of a puzzle of which they did not know the original shape. More important, not only was the electoral system and process not clearly explained to the average Chinese reader, but the underlying democratic premises that guide that process were never spelled out. Nonetheless, the periodical press deserves high marks for the amount and sophistication of coverage it did present. It was a vast improvement over previous years.[150] Above all, it represents the pluralists' increasing importance in the print media.

THE 1988 ELECTION

Coverage of the 1988 election paralleled that of 1984. Very little Marxist commentary appeared in the Chinese press, and most attention was focused on the postprimary period. The nominating conventions were covered thoroughly, as were the party platforms, presidential debates, and run-up to election day.

---

[149] Li Daokui, "Meiguo heiren yundong de fazhan," *Liaowang*, no. 7 (1984): 29–30.

[150] Also see Julian Baum, "China's Press Gets High Marks for Marx-less U.S. Election Coverage," *The Christian Science Monitor*, September 24, 1984, p. 13.

At the end of the primary season Pan Tongwen, arguably China's leading authority on U.S. domestic politics, assessed the electorate's mood. Pan argued that the political center of gravity prevailed in the primaries as extreme elements of both parties lost out to the moderates. Bush was able to defeat Dole, Robertson, and Kemp because, "Aside from having the richest campaign fund, the best organization, and basking in Reagan's glory, the main reason behind Bush's easy triumph over all his rivals lies in the fact that he is not too much of an extremist or a radical, and is politically a moderate conservative."[151] In explaining the Democratic primaries, Pan Tongwen noted the limited appeal of Gephardt, Simon, and Gore but was intrigued by the "Jessie Jackson phenomenon." Jackson, Pan thought, had struck "responsive chords" among the voters with his antidrug, anti-unemployment, and antidefense policies, and through his support for a comprehensive national health system and "equal pay for equal work" had been able to broaden his "Rainbow Coalition" beyond black and poor voters to women and the middle class. But, in the end, being black and offering "radical" proposals unacceptable to many voters hindered Jackson from overtaking Michael Dukakis. Pan went on to discuss how Bush and Dukakis were perceived among voters. Pan judged Bush's major weakness as being perceived a "yes man, weak and indecisive." Dukakis looked to be a formidable candidate, but his inexperience in foreign affairs was deemed to be a significant shortcoming. Pan concluded that the 1988 race would be a very close one, and he sensed a certain restiveness in the mood of the electorate that might enable Dukakis to do as John F. Kennedy had done in 1960. Pan thus compared Bush to Nixon as sitting vice-presidents who were as much hampered by their office as helped by it.

The Chinese print media ran few articles during the summer leading up to the August conventions. As in their coverage of the 1980 and 1984 elections, Chinese press interest picked up markedly between the conventions and election day. During the 1988 election year the United States Information Agency arranged and paid for several Chinese correspondents to visit the United States to experience the campaign election. One such reporter for *Guangming ribao*, the intellectuals' newspaper, was struck by the apparent apathy he encountered. In an early July article Wu Xiaomin recalled for his readers a random sample that he had undertaken on the streets of Washington:

[151] Pan Tongwen, "Jinnian de Meiguo zongtong xuanju," *Guoji wenti yanjiu*, no. 3 (1988): 33.

This reporter randomly interviewed several passers-by in Washington. When asked about her opinion on the election, an elderly black woman did not seem to care much, except that she was disappointed at the failure of black leader Jackson to become the Democratic candidate. When a young white man hurriedly walked past, this reporter asked him to predict who would be the next president. This young man simply shrugged and did not say anything. The several other passers-by interviewed were not too "excited" about the presidential election. In Washington, one cannot see any posters or signs and the atmosphere is quiet. This is in sharp contrast to the lengthy articles, forecasts, criticisms, and attacks in the mass media. Tranquil and yet turbulent, this is what the United States is like in an election year.[152]

Reporter Wu went on to discuss the importance of economic issues to voters, but in the end came to the classic Marxist conclusion that, "In the final analysis, the contention between the two parties is in substance contention between various monopoly groups."[153]

The New China News Agency sent a team of reporters to Atlanta and New Orleans to cover the Democratic and Republican conventions respectively. Reports from the Democratic convention centered on the Dukakis-Jackson "power struggle."[154] They judged that the lack of unanimity among Democrats would impair their chances for the White House. Reports on the Republican convention zeroed in on "the storm over Quayle." Chinese readers were dutifully informed about vice-presidential nominee Dan Quayle's alleged draft-dodging and extramarital sexual liaisons.[155]

Following the conventions, several dispatches assessed the chances of Dukakis and Bush. One in *Guangming ribao*, citing polls and the appeal of Dukakis's integrity, gave Dukakis the upper hand.[156] One in the *People's Daily* by veteran America hand Zhang Yunwen agreed that Bush was vulnerable because of voter discontent about the economy, because he was perceived as the "loyal assistant" of Reagan, and because he was not popular among women vot-

[152] Wu Xiaomin, "Can the Democrats Regain the U.S. Presidential Throne?" *Guangming ribao*, July 6, 1988, p. 4, *FBIS-CHI*, July 19, 1988, p. 4.

[153] Ibid.

[154] See, for example, Bao Guangren, "Atlanta Prepares a Jump for Democrats to White House," *Xinhua*, July 17, 1988, *FBIS-CHI*, July 19, 1988, pp. 4–5; "Roundup: Jackson, Dukakis Struggle for Control of Convention," *Xinhua*, ibid., pp. 5–6.

[155] See Zhang Liang, "The Storm over Quayle," *Renmin ribao*, August 24, 1988, p. 6, *FBIS-CHI*, August 29, 1988, pp. 1–2; Bao Guangren, "Roundup: Bush's New Trouble," *Xinhua*, August 24, 1988, *FBIS-CHI*, August 25, 1988, pp. 11–12.

[156] Wang Deming, "New Situation in U.S. Presidential Elections," *Guangming ribao*, August 16, 1988, p. 4, *FBIS-CHI*, August 25, 1988, pp. 12–13.

ers, who now outnumber male voters by ten million.[157] Other dispatches focused on the campaign issues. NCNA Washington bureau chief and long-time America Watcher Li Yanning thought that Bush's incumbency was a distinct advantage since the United States had enjoyed sixty-eight months of sustained production growth, an unemployment rate down to a fourteen-year low, a steady inflation rate, and the U.S.-Soviet détente all added up to "peace and prosperity."[158] Others took a more geographic approach and argued that the weighted voting of the electoral college system meant that the election would be fought—and won—in California, Texas, Florida, Indiana, New York, Pennsylvania, and Illinois. NCNA correspondent Bao Guangren argued that the Democrats "need to make a significant dent" in the West, which holds 111 electoral votes; Bush's selection of Quayle and Dukakis's selection of Bentsen were direct reflections of their attempts to gain the 137 and 177 electoral votes in the Midwest and South respectively; and Bush's attacks on Dukakis's "Massachusetts miracle" were meant to undercut the Democrat's "stronghold" in the East.[159]

The Democratic Party also invited a twelve-person Chinese delegation to observe the Atlanta convention. Upon returning to China, delegation leader Gu Ming, vice-chairman of the National People's Congress Standing Committee Law Committee, gave an interesting interview in which he listed his observations and offered views on the relevance of American-style democracy for China:

> In the past, China has been uninterested in the presidential election campaigns in capitalist countries and just called them "farces." However, this is not the opinion of the first election study delegation in its report to the state leaders. . . . Compared with other capitalist countries, bourgeois democracy in the United States is rather thorough. This was reflected in the country's presidential elections. . . . China can learn from some methods and forms in the U.S. presidential election. For example, there should be a higher degree of openness in the election of leaders at various levels. The candidates should make themselves well-known by meeting the public directly, telling the public of their personal backgrounds, previous contri-

---

[157] Zhang Yunwen, "Aspiring to Win Another Term of Four Years—the Keynote of the U.S. Republican Convention," *Renmin ribao*, August 20, 1988, p. 6, *FBIS-CHI*, August 24, 1988, pp. 4–5.

[158] Li Yanning, "Battle for the White House Now Fought at Close Quarters," *Liaowang*, August 29, 1988, pp. 26–27, *FBIS-CHI*, September 6, 1988, pp. 6–7.

[159] Bao Guangren, "Roundup: U.S. Presidential Race Heads for Official Kickoff," *Xinhua*, September 2, 1988, *FBIS-CHI*, September 9, 1988, p. 10.

butions, and "political platforms" to subject themselves to the supervision of the people.[160]

The Chinese press covered the presidential debates well. The two presidential candidates were seen as splitting their two debates, while Senator Lloyd Bentsen was thought to have won the vice-presidential debate.[161]

As the campaign entered its final stages, the Chinese media began to give Bush the edge. Citing various U.S. opinion polls and media reports, NCNA correspondents reported to their readers that Bush had been able to capitalize on a "presidential image," strong economic indicators, a popular foreign policy based on "strength," distance from "Irangate," and above all had succeeded in depicting Dukakis as a traditional liberal with no foreign affairs experience.[162]

Bush's victory stimulated a number of postelection analyses of the factors that enabled an incumbent vice-president to win the presidency on his own for the first time since 1839. America Watcher Li Yanning attributed Bush's victory to four factors: a buoyant economy; improved U.S.-Soviet relations; Bush's emphasis on social issues of crime, (no) taxes, gun control, school prayer, and the pledge of allegiance; and the "negative campaign" run against Dukakis's liberalism.[163] The People's Daily attributed Dukakis's "failure to ascend the throne" to the fact that "he was never able to effectively capture the majority of votes from the postwar generations of young and middle-aged Americans, especially those Democrats who had supported Reagan. This is the fundamental reason why the lead he enjoyed after his nomination in Atlanta ebbed away and eventually disappeared."[164]

The beginning of Bush's term in office also occasioned a number of asessments of the problems he confronted and his choice of admin-

[160] "NPC's Gu Ming Views Upcoming U.S. Election," *Zhongguo xinwenshe*, September 8, 1988, *FBIS-CHI*, September 12, 1988, pp. 7–8.

[161] See, for example, Yue Dun, "The Situation of the U.S. General Election since the Debate on Television," *Gongren ribao*, October 18, 1988, p. 2, *FBIS-CHI*, October 26, 1988, pp. 4–5.

[162] See Bao Guangren, "The Possibility of Bush Becoming the Master of the White House Is Increasing," *Liaowang*, October 24, 1988, *FBIS-CHI*, October 25, 1988, pp. 7–9; Li Yanning, "Final Sprint Turns White-Hot Between Bush and Dukakis," *Xinhua*, November 6, 1988, *FBIS-CHI*, November 9, 1988, p. 2; Jing Xianfa, "A Battle Determining Who Will Be the Master of the White House," *Renmin ribao*, November 7, 1988, p. 6, *FBIS-CHI*, November 9, 1988, p. 3.

[163] Li Yanning, "Why Did Bush Win," *Xinhua*, November 8, 1988, *FBIS-CHI*, November 10, 1988, p. 7.

[164] Jing Xianfa, "The Election of the New U.S. President and the Prospects," *Renmin ribao*, November 10, 1988, p. 6, *FBIS-CHI*, November 14, 1988, pp. 4–5.

istration officials. The national debt, federal deficit, trade deficit, a Democratic Congress, continued rivalry with the Soviet Union despite détente, Central America, trade frictions with Japan, and the Middle East were mentioned as the key problems facing Bush upon assuming office.[165] In cataloguing the "challenges facing the Bush administration," Institute of International Studies America specialist Pan Tongwen argued that Bush would not be able to enjoy a honeymoon with Congress on domestic issues because of the budget deficit, but his room for maneuver in foreign affairs would be greater.[166] Pan predicted that while NATO and the U.S.-Japan alliance will continue to anchor American foreign policy, the Bush administration could be expected to give relatively less attention to East-West relations and more to Third World issues. Further, Pan felt that while Bush would continue the Reagan doctrine of "supporting freedom fighters," there may be a new emphasis on negotiated settlements of Third World conflicts.

The *People's Daily*, *World Affairs*, and the *Economic Daily* all gave Bush generally high marks for his selection of a "moderate," "pragmatic," and "experienced" cabinet.[167] With the exceptions of White House Chief of Staff Sununu, Council of Economic Advisors Chairman Boskin, and Secretary of Commerce Mosbacher, all senior appointees were noted for their prior federal government experience. Secretary of State–designate James Baker was singled out for particular praise despite his lack of experience in foreign affairs.[168]

Thus, it can be seen that the learning curve in Chinese understanding and coverage of U.S. presidential elections continued through the 1988 election. Coverage was complete from the primaries through the inauguration, although particularly concentrated on the postconvention phase. The campaign issues were thoroughly examined and the candidate's positions contrasted, the candidate's characters were assessed, their geographic power bases were noted, interparty conflicts

---

[165] Shi Lujia, "The Opportunities and Challenges Facing Bush," *Ban yue tan*, December 10, 1988, pp. 54–56, *FBIS-CHI*, January 10, 1989, pp. 13–15; also see Wu Jin, "President Bush's Political Honeymoon," *Liaowang*, February 20, 1989, p. 24, *FBIS-CHI*, February 28, 1989, pp. 6–7.

[166] Pan Tongwen, "Bushi zhengfu mianlin de tiaozhan," *Guoji wenti yanjiu*, no. 1 (1989): 17.

[167] Chen Gong, "Bush: Getting Out of Reagan's Shadow," *Renmin ribao*, February 23, 1989, p. 3, *FBIS-CHI*, February 24, 1989, p. 8; Xin Peihe, "President Bush Will Demonstrate His Talents," *Shijie zhishi*, no. 3 (1989): 16–17, *FBIS-CHI*, February 17, 1989: 3–5; Li Dongdong, "Thoughts Induced by the Change of Masters of the White House," *Jingji ribao*, January 16, 1989, *FBIS-CHI*, January 25, 1989, p. 5.

[168] Tong Wen and Hui Xin, "James Baker III—'Political Wizard' of the United States," *Shijie zhishi*, no. 24 (1988): 22–23, *FBIS-CHI*, January 26, 1989, pp. 6–8.

were analyzed and the candidate's advisors scrutinized, voter preferences were sampled, the delegate selection process was described, public opinion polls and U.S. media coverage were monitored and cited, and so on. All in all, China's America Watchers should again receive high marks for their coverage of the 1988 elections. As in 1984, they presented a large amount of coverage to the Chinese public, and, importantly, this coverage was non-Marxist and nonideological in its tone and substance. The facts were presented in a straightforward manner.

Summary

I have presented in this chapter a spectrum of views on a range of issues concerning the America Watchers' perceptions of American politics. As in previous chapters, it is apparent that these perceptions cleave into two principal schools of analysis, Marxist and non-Marxist.

Not surprisingly, the Marxists' image of American politics proceeds from an analysis of the role of monopoly capitalist financial groups (*longduan caituan*). As was the case in chapters 2 and 3, the Marxists' views divided along Stalinist and Leninist lines. Both groups went to great lengths to trace the connections between big business and banking and the U.S. government, but the Stalinists argued the "subordination thesis" that specific monopolies control specific administrations, while the Leninists saw the connections as more fluid and complex—the "unification thesis."

The perceptions of the non-Marxists divide not so much by degree of opinion as by unit of analysis. That is, the opinion group whose analyses are preoccupied with the executive branch of the federal government has been labeled "statist." A second opinion group cast their analytical net more broadly to encompass a wide range of political actors that included Congress, particular segments of the population, a variety of organizations, and trends in political and social thought among the electorate. This opinion group has been designated "pluralist."

Nongovernmental actors now command a great deal of attention from both Marxists and non-Marxists, that there is something of a convergence of opinion (or at least a convergence of attention) paid to these groups by America Watchers in both schools. Finally, case studies of Chinese coverage of five presidential elections from 1972 through 1988 show that the quantity of coverage has increased dramatically while the quality of anlaysis has also improved steadily.

Further, since the 1980 campaign few Marxist interpretations have been published, and the non-Marxists—particularly comprising New China News Agency journalists—have dominated the coverage.

In short, the Marxists' articulated perceptions of the American political process can be described as a rational actor model insofar as they believe political actions in the United States are taken on the basis of the rational calculation of benefiting the financial interests of the monopoly bourgeoisie. They perceive a political system of oligarchical class rule that allows for competition between monopoly financial groups for control of a unitary state. In contrast, the non-Marxists' articulated perceptions of American politics represent a multiple actor model based on the interaction of many groups inside and outside of government that compete to influence an autonomous state. These differences are briefly summarized in table 5.2.

Table 5.2
Perceptions of American Politics

Issue	Marxist School	Non-Marxist School
The state	Instrument of class rule by bourgeoisie; subordinate to, or coalesced with, the monopoly financial groups; target of competition among these groups; unitary actor	Autonomous political actor; target of competition among nongovernmental actors; fragmented bureaucratic and factional actor; subject to separation of powers; a primary actor in politics
Monopoly capitalist groups	United in finance capital oligarchy, but competitive between groups; divided along familial and regional lines; the dominant economic and political actor	Existent but peripheral to political process; fragmented and competitive
Nonmonopoly classes	Impotent in political process; middle class nonexistent; proletariat impoverished and potentially militant	Active in political process, via both parties and lobbies; large middle class; proletariat poor but politically participative

Table 5.2 (*cont.*)

Elections	Irrelevant exercises; manipulated by monopoly capitalist groups	Genuine exercises in participatory democracy; reflect contention of various political actors
Political parties	Agents of monopoly capitalist groups; no real difference between parties	Representative of societal interests; philosophical and policy differences exist between parties
Nongovernment institutions and interest groups	Agents of monopoly capitalist groups; source of personnel and policies for government	Source of government personnel and policy; some represent constituents' social interests; autonomous actors in political process
Liberals and conservatives	Invalid depiction of U.S. political spectrum; both represent monopoly bourgeoisie	Valid distinction; both groups are composed of various subgroups
Political system	Class-dominated by monopoly bourgeoisie	Pluralistic; state-centric
Model of political process	Marxist-Leninist rational-actor model based on oligarchical class rule, allowing for competition between monopoly groups for control of a unitary state	Multiple-actor model based on interaction of many groups inside and outside of government that compete for influence of an autonomous state

Six

American Foreign Policy

THROUGHOUT the preceding analyses of the American economy, society, and polity China's America Watchers have articulated two dominant images, Marxist and non-Marxist. These schools are apparent in the America Watchers' analyses of American foreign policy as well. The Marxists see U.S. foreign policy in a classic Leninist sense—imperialistic—while the non-Marxists perceive American foreign policy as ad hoc, driven by multiple interests and bilateral relationships, and essentially reacting to forces beyond its control. But in addition to Marxist and non-Marxist perspectives, in this chapter a new strain of commentary emerges—a normative strain derivative from the historical experience of modern China (and the lessons drawn therefrom) for fashioning a world free of "hegemony."[1] Here, the Marxists and non-Marxists find common ground. In this view, America acts rationally and coherently in pursuit of the singular goal of extending its hegemonic influence throughout the world. The philosophical origins of contemporary Chinese concepts of hegemony were discussed in chapter 2.

This chapter, like those before it, is organized to present contrasting images. Emphasis is placed on the three issues the America Watchers see as most pertinent and about which they write the most: (1) U.S. policies toward the Soviet Union, (2) the developing world, and (3) China. The America Watchers' perceptions of the domestic sources of U.S. foreign policy were discussed in the previous chapter; thus, this chapter is exclusively limited to examining the America Watchers' image of the conduct of American foreign policy behavior abroad.

Marxist Perspectives on American Foreign Policy

The Marxists, not surprisingly, analyze U.S. foreign policy in a classic Leninist sense. Based on Lenin's *Imperialism, the Highest Stage of Capitalism*, the Marxists believe the main motive force behind U.S. foreign policy are monopoly capitalists who seek ever-higher profits and

---

[1] "Hegemonism—the Ability in International Relations to Exercise Controlling Power," *Xiandai hanyu cidian* (Beijing: Shangwu yinshuguan, 1979), p. 18.

ever-expanding areas of control abroad. The primary focus of this line of analysis is economic, the principal actors are monopoly capitalists and their multinational corporations, and the main geographical targets of an "imperialist" U.S. foreign policy are the developing countries. The arms race is also attributed to the profit-hungry defense industrialists under conditions of state-monopoly capitalism. Chapter 3 discussed how the Marxists believe that American imperialism began in the nineteenth century and that the "Open Door" policy, the Spanish-American War, and the two world wars were all examples of the U.S. monopoly capitalists' search to secure new markets, ever-higher profits, and an outlet for war production. Chapter 5 showed how the Marxists believe that the monopoly capitalists have consistently been able to place their representatives in important positions in the U.S. government (including the White House) and leading private-sector think tanks and lobbying organizations, and that they have therefore been able to manipulate U.S. foreign policy in directions consummate with their economic interests. Table 5.1 and the accompanying discussion detailed these links.

The export of capital by U.S. multinational corporations has been viewed as the main manifestation of an imperialist foreign policy. Even government programs such as the Marshall Plan and Alliance for Progress are said to have been a "cloak" for multinationals to gain a foothold abroad.[2] Institutions such as the Overseas Private Investment Corporation (OPIC) and the Export-Import Bank are seen as mere manifestations of state-monopoly capitalism in the foreign policy realm, and international organizations such as the World Bank, International Monetary Fund, OECD, and GATT are also viewed as "tools" (*gongju*) in the hands of U.S. monopoly capitalists and their multinationals.[3] A book on American multinational corporations considers them to be the "invading instrument of neocolonialism."[4]

No corner of the globe is immune from penetration by American multinationals. The monopoly financial groups' investments are widely dispersed. According to one of many such analyses:

Viewing the layout of U.S. multinational corporations, the manufacturing industry of the Morgan financial group is dispersed mainly over Western Europe, Japan, and Southeast Asia, while its oil company [Continental Pe-

---

[2] See, for example, Shanghai guoji wenti yanjiusuo, *Xiandai Meiguo jingji wenti jianlun* (Shanghai: Renmin chubanshe, 1981), p. 147.

[3] Ibid., p. 148.

[4] Jilin daxue jingjixi shijie jingji jiaoyanshi, *Meiguo kuaguo gongsi—xin zhimindi de qinlue gongju* (Jilin: Renmin chubanshe, 1975). For a similar analysis by noted Marxist economist (and former president of Nankai University) Teng Weizao, see Nankai daxue jingji yanjiusuo shijie jingji yanjiushi, *Kuaguo gongsi pouxi* (Tianjin: Renmin chubanshe, 1978).

troleum Corporation] has invested considerably in the Middle East, Africa, and Asia in recent years. The Rockefeller financial group's interests are also widely dispersed. At present, the Middle East and Latin America are used as its bases for extracting oil, and Western Europe, Latin America, Oceania, and Canada are the bases for its refineries and the chief market for its oil products. The Rockefeller financial group has also invested in the manufacturing industry of Western Europe. In a word, the overseas interests of the major American financial groups are overlapping and criss-crossed. They are all multinational and transregional financial groups.[5]

When the multinationals' investments are in danger of expropriation, the Central Intelligence Agency comes to the rescue. One source cites the examples of the CIA-sponsored overthrows of Guatemalan President Arbenz in 1954 on behalf of the "green monster" United Fruit Company, and of Chilean President Allende in 1971 on behalf of ITT and Kennecott Copper, and the installation of American puppet regimes in Liberia for Firestone Rubber Company and in Iran for many U.S. oil firms.[6] Another article analyzed the importance of covert action as a foreign policy tool for the United States, and on this basis argued that the CIA played an inordinately important role in U.S. foreign policy.[7]

Do U.S. multinationals contribute anything to developing countries? The answer from the Marxists is a resounding "no." Economists at Nankai University believe that "The United States is the world's greatest exploiter, and its multinational corporations are its agents of plunder. . . . Between 1950 and 1976, American multinational corporations plundered the Third World for $1.4 trillion."[8] A dispatch from New China News Agency was even more strident:

> For years the United States, known as the "dollar empire," has through its transnational companies and the world monetary institutions under its control implanted numerous "blood-sucking tubes" in the Third World countries. Through capital export in huge amounts, it has monopolized most of the production, marketing, and transport of petroleum and many mineral products of the Third World. As one of the biggest international

[5] Zhang Jialin, "Meiguo longduan caituan shili he zuhe de ruogan bianhua," *Shijie jingji*, no. 9 (1980): 29.

[6] Nankai daxue zhengzhi jingjixi shijie jingji jiaoyanshi, *Zhanhou diguozhuyi jingji jige wenti* (Tianjin: Renmin chubanshe, 1975), p. 32.

[7] Yang Yongyi, "Zhangyang qingbaoju yu Meiguo waijiao zhengce," *Meiguo yanjiu*, no. 3 (1989): 38–57.

[8] Lu Wei, "Meiguo kuaguo gongsi dui disan shijie de boxue he lueduo," *Shijie jingji*, no. 4 (1978): 40, 44. For similar analyses see Zhou Qingquan, "Meiguo kuoguo gongsi zai qishi niandai," *Shijie jingji*, no. 1 (1980): 22–28; Teng Weizao, "Kuaguo gongsi de guowai zhijie touzi," *Shijie jingji*, no. 6 (1982): 1–5.

exploiters, U.S. imperialism extracted super-profits of more than $29 billion through unequal trade with the Third World in the period from 1960 to 1973.[9]

What parts of the developing world are the main targets of such classic Leninist imperialism? The Marxists identify the Middle East, southern Africa, and Latin America as particularly attractive targets. These regions possess the natural resources that American multinationals most covet.

With the important exception of Taiwan, the Marxists do not write much about the penetration of American monopoly capital into Asia. However, they point to Taiwan as a case par excellence of American monopoly capital governing foreign policy. Many analyses point to the long-standing links between caituan and the "Taiwan lobby" (*Taiwan bang*). As one analysis in *Shijie zhishi* succinctly put it:

> The activities of the "Taiwan lobby" actually reflect the interests of certain U.S. monopoly groups that have close ties with Taiwan. The United States exploits the people of Taiwan by direct private investment, Import and Export Bank loans, trade, and other methods. . . . The U.S. monopoly groups reap huge profits from Taiwan every year, and they are unwilling to let Taiwan, their place of investment and commodity market, go easily.[10]

Other analyses claim that U.S. monopoly capital "controls" (*kongzhi*) Taiwan,[11] and that the Taiwan Relations Act passed in the wake of normalization of relations between the United States and the People's Republic was a means to continue such control.[12] According to a study published in the classified journal *Internal Reference Materials on World Economics and Politics*, continued American arms sales to Taiwan are an example of the "influence" (*yingxiang*) that the "West Coast war industries have over President Reagan and the White House."[13]

In the case of the Middle East and the Carter Doctrine, one *People's Daily* writer described the Persian Gulf as "a huge pool of oil."[14] "Oil

[9] Xinhuashe, "Economic Hegemony of Superpowers Assailed," *FBIS-CHI*, May 6, 1976, A2.

[10] Ren Yi, "Meiguo de 'Taiwan bang,' " *Shijie zhishi*, no. 3 (1981): 5.

[11] Li Jiaquan, "Waiguo longduan ziben dui Taiwan de kongzhi," *Jingji yanjiu*, no. 2 (1984): 66.

[12] Li Jiaquan and Liu Xingxian, "Meiguo longduan ziben zai woguo Taiwan," *Xiandai guoji guanxi*, no. 2 (1982): 27.

[13] Sun Xianjun, "Ligen shangtaihou Meiguo yu Taiwan sheng de jingji guanxi," *Shijie jingji yu zhengzhi neican*, no. 8 (1982): 43.

[14] Xiao Xi, "Carter's Persian Gulf Strategy," *Renmin ribao*, March 4, 1980, *FBIS-CHI*, March 7, 1980, B1.

has been the object of American monopoly capital since the U.S. oil companies first penetrated the Middle East in 1927,"[15] claims an analyst at the Afro-Asian Research Institute of Nanjing University, while another writer in the party journal *Hongqi* stated that "The Western countries, headed by the United States, consider the Middle East an important base of oil supply as well as a vast market for commodities and arms sales. They take gains or losses of Middle East oil resources as a matter of 'survival.' "[16]

Southern Africa also offers the United States oil and important mineral resources. "Without the American need for strategic natural resources, the South African puppet regime would have fallen long ago," stated one analyst.[17] "The American scramble for natural resources in regions like southern Africa is a distinguishing characteristic of postwar international relations," said another.[18]

Perhaps the Marxists' sharpest condemnation of U.S. imperialism is reserved for U.S. foreign policy toward Latin America. One review summed up U.S. policy toward the region over the last century this way: "The United States has used many methods to promote its neo-colonialist policy [in Latin America], such as propping up proxies, engineering military coups, establishing military and political cliques, and plundering and controlling Latin America by giving 'aid' and loans."[19] The article goes on to give a laundry list of U.S. interventions in the region (overt and covert). The Monroe Doctrine, "big-stick policy," "dollar diplomacy," the "good neighbor policy," "Alliance for Progress," Carter's "human rights policy," and so forth are all denounced as imperialist attempts to control America's "back-yard" (*beihou*). "As a result of U.S. oppression and exploitation," says another analyst at the Institute of International Studies in Beijing, "the people's struggle in Latin America has a strong nature of opposing the United States, with extensive support of the masses."[20]

The Marxists believe that Central America and the Caribbean have been virtual colonies of the United States. For example, "U.S. impe-

---

[15] Ma Xiuqing, "Wulun Zhongdong shiyou de shijie zhanlue diwei," *Shijie jingji*, no. 10 (1982): 21.

[16] Qian Jinxi, "Middle East Oil and the Scramble for It," *Hongqi*, no. 8 (1981), *FBIS-CHI*, May 22, 1981, I4.

[17] Zhang Zhiyi, "Nanbu Feizhou de kuangchan ziyuan yu Su-Mei zhizheng," *Shijie jingji*, no. 1 (1980): 34–49.

[18] He Ming and Liu Taisheng, "Meiguo yu quanqiuxing de kuangchan yuanliao zhengtou," ibid., p. 75.

[19] Li He, "Meiguo dui La-Meizhou zhengce de yanbian," *Shijie zhishi*, no. 15 (1984): 5.

[20] Xiao Yu, "Zhong Meizhou de nanti yu jingsi," *Guoji wenti yanjiu*, no. 4 (1983): 14–18.

rialism has always considered the Caribbean its inland sea and has controlled and plundered this area."[21] The Marxists attribute the region's importance to economic reasons, for example, the fact that the United States gets 80 percent of its bauxite and 40 percent of its imported petroleum, has an annual trade volume of $7 billion, and direct investments totaling $14.3 billion in the region.[22] Various analyses point to the strengthening unity among Caribbean states in the face of "imperialists, new and old colonialists, and the feudal comprador autocratic forces."[23] At the time of the passage of the Panama Canal treaties in 1978, veteran America Watcher Chen Youwei, writing under his usual pseudonym Si Mada, reviewed the U.S. legacy in Panama as follows:

> The history of this canal has been written with the tears and blood of the Panamanian people. Beneath the canal are the remains of 70,000 Panamanians. Along the banks of the canal, several generations of Panamanians have worked as slaves of the United States. For scores of years, officials from Washington actually controlled Panama, forty Panamanian presidents were changed like coats, and the tycoons of New York and Florida squeezed more than $45 billion in profits from this canal. They reduced the territory of Panama, raised the stars and stripes over the Canal Zone, and built U.S. military camps and bases, courts, banks, and churches. Many wealthy Yankees and their wives raced horses, fished, gambled, and lived a carefree life in this land of comfort, playing golf, dancing the tango, and drinking champagne. Their enjoyment was based on the sufferings and bitterness of the Panamanian people![24]

Nor is the developing world the only target of U.S. multinational investment. Analysts at the Shanghai Institute of International Studies note that one of the driving forces behind Soviet-American détente in the early 1970s was the chance to make a buck. In particular, IBM, Pepsi, and Union Carbide of the Morgan financial group, Caterpillar Tractor of the Citicorp financial group, Occidental Petroleum of the California financial group, Dresser Industries of the Texas financial group, and Chase Manhattan Bank of the Rockefeller financial group all advocated détente because of financial interests they

[21] "Dialogue on Current Events," Peking Domestic Service, December 9, 1977, FBIS-CHI, December 12, 1977, A3.

[22] See, for example, Sun Guowei, "Su-Mei Zhengduo de disige 'ridian,' " Shijie zhishi, no. 13 (1980): 11.

[23] Ibid., p. 10.

[24] Si Mada, "Mr. Senator's Old Imperial Annals," Renmin ribao, May 8, 1978, FBIS-CHI, May 11, 1978, A4.

had in Eastern Europe and the Soviet Union.[25] The author of this assessment, none other than veteran caituan-watcher Zhang Jialin, concludes, "To sum up, in analyzing U.S. foreign policy, the eastern Wall Street financial groups and their multinational corporations play the decisive (*zui zhuyao de*) role. It remains the starting point in policy making of the American ruling clique to protect the overseas investments of American monopolies and continue economic and political expansion all over the world."[26] Zhang Yebai of the CASS's Institute of American Studies agrees: "In a word, American national interests largely reflect the economic interests of its big businesses which play a major role in shaping U.S. foreign policy. . . . We should always keep in mind the diversity and complexity of American diplomacy, but we should not forget the influence of economics, for it is the fundamental factor."[27]

Many Marxist commentators point to the confrontation with the Soviet Union, militarization of the domestic economy, and the arms race as the only means to quench the thirst for profits of the monopoly capitalists. Cui Wei, a professor at Beijing Normal University, wrote in a lengthy article about the U.S. military-industrial complex:

> To defend and extend its interests, the U.S. monopoly capitalists, which had acquired exorbitant ill-gotten wealth, began to expand abroad after World War II. During the 1960s in particular, the U.S. monopoly capitalists began to contend with the Soviet Union for world hegemony and indulged heavily in the arms race. They suppressed the people internally and stimulated production to insure big monopoly profits, to slow down economic crises, and to maintain enormous military expenditures. As a result, the United States has become the capitalist country with the highest degree of national economic militarization. . . . The key feature of monopoly capitalism is that the state apparatus belongs to monopoly capital, and this feature is shown in the activities of the military-industrial complex. It is in such activities that a few financial tycoons make use of the state apparatus (military budget) to exploit the people and to make big profits.[28]

U.S. foreign aid is seen as another instrument of imperialist plunder. The same book carries a lengthy denunciation of American "aid" (*yuan*) to other countries as a "means of U.S. monopoly capital pen-

[25] Shanghai guoji wenti yanjiusuo, *Xiandai Meiguo jingji wenti jielun*, pp. 114–15.

[26] Ibid., pp. 115–16.

[27] Zhang Yebai, "The Impact of Economic Factors on American Foreign Policy," paper delivered to the Chongqing Conference on Political Implications of World Economic Trends, October 1984.

[28] Cui Wei, "Meiguo junshi—gongye zongheti yu guojia longduan zibenzhuyi," *Shijie jingji*, no. 8 (1980): 24, 29.

etrating their economies, plundering their resources, exploiting their workers, violating their sovereignty, turning them into neocolonies, and preventing them from joining the anti-imperialist struggle that is gaining strength by the day."[29] Analysts at the CASS's Institute of World Economics and Politics agree with this assessment. An article in the institute's journal *World Economics* put it this way:

> The United States' "aid to developing countries" is in fact an important means of effecting political control over, and economic infiltration into, the developing countries. In addition it represents an important part of the U.S. global strategy and struggle for world hegemony. Such "aid" more often than not stipulates that the receiving country fall under American military control or political sphere of rule, or that the country provide military bases for the United States. . . . Such "aid" thus makes the country receiving it more and more dependent on the United States in economic and political terms, even to the point of falling into heavy debt. . . . It is absolutely impossible that the United States will change its basic aims of providing "aid" to developing countries, in particular its aims of a very clearly aggressive and expansionist nature.[30]

The Marxists' critiques of U.S. imperialism in the developing world are part of their broader analysis of North-South relations and the inequitable international economic structure. They have been some of the strongest proponents of a "new international economic order." The following quotations from *Hongqi* and *Guoji wenti yanjiu* provide a flavor of how the Marxists view the existing international economic system and North-South relations:

> The world has divided into two opposite extremes since the 1870s when the transition from laissez-faire capitalism to monopoly capitalism occurred. By all sorts of economic and supra-economic means, monopoly capital has carried out aggression and expansion abroad, controlling most of the world's resources, markets and wealth and formed a minority of affluent imperialist countries. The vast number of colonies and semicolonies have been exploited, plundered, oppressed, and enslaved. They have become places for imperialism to invest, produce raw materials, and sell their products. . . . The colonialist and imperialist rule has resulted in an unequal and irrational old international economic order. The most essential and basic characteristic of this old order is the monopoly rule and ruth-

---

[29] Nankai daxue zhengzhi jingjixi shijie jingji jiaoyanshi, *Zhanhou diguozhuyi jingji jige wenti*, p. 33.

[30] Du Fangli, "Ligen zhengfu dui fazhan zhongguojia yuanzhu zhengce de bianhua," *Shijie jingji*, no. 9 (1982): 40–44. Also see Zhao Suisheng, "Shilun Meiguo dui fazhan zhongguojia de jingji yuanzhu," *Shijie jingji*, no. 10 (1981): 32–36.

less exploitation of international financial capital. . . . Imperialist monopoly capital still controls to a great extent the production of primary and manufactured products and the trade, finance, shipping and so on of many Asian, African, and Latin American countries for long periods after they have become independent.[31]

In essence, North-South economic relations consist of control, exploitation, and plunder of the developing countries by the developed countries. . . . Today, developed countries continue to a greater or lesser extent to control certain major economic sectors of the developing countries. The mineral and agricultural raw materials sectors have always been the areas most under the control of Western monopoly capital. Statistics show that in the 1970s, multinational corporations continued to control directly or indirectly 75–90 percent of the raw materials and metals of developing countries, and 30–40 percent of their agricultural raw materials. . . . The direct aim of the economic expansion of Western monopoly capital into developing countries is the extraction of super-monopoly profits. With the strengthening of private and state-monopoly capitalism in postwar advanced countries, the exploitative methods adopted by these countries have become even more ingenious and ruthless.[32]

And what do the Marxists say about American policy toward North-South relations? Zhang Ruizhang, an analyst at the Shanghai Institute of International Studies, states that "The United States is the greatest beneficiary of the old international economic system and thus any move against the old order is a move against U.S. interests, and for this reason the United States is the strongest defender of the old order and it constantly rejects the Third World's demands for the establishment of a new international economic order."[33] Hu Pan of the Foreign Ministry's Institute of International Studies agrees and pointedly takes the Reagan administration to task: "In its attempt to put the North-South dialogue under its control, the Reagan administration has adopted a negative attitude, dilatory tactics, and has worked hard to replace global negotiations with small-scale negotiations between specialized organizations under its manipulation, attempting to maintain its monopolistic position in the present international economic structure."[34]

[31] Dai Lunzhang and Wang Zichuan, "Guoji jingji lingyu de 'pojiu lixin' douzheng," *Hongqi*, no. 7 (1980): 44.

[32] Jiang Jianqing and Li Weiguo, "Nan-Bei jingji guanxi de shizhi," *Guoji wenti yanjiu*, no. 1 (1984): 17–19.

[33] Zhang Ruizhang, "Ligen zhengfu de Nan-Bei zhengce jiqi xiaoji yinxiang," *Shijie jingji*, no. 4 (1983): 32.

[34] Hu Pan, "Ligen zhengfu dui Nan-Bei guanxi de zhengce," *Shijie jingji*, no. 10 (1984): 49.

What do the Marxists think of the United States promoting the theory of interdependence? One radio commentary put it this way: "While trumpeting that interdependence is the core of maintaining an international order, it claims that the prosperity of the whole world must rely on its leadership. To call a spade a spade, it wants only to maintain its control, plunder, and exploitation of the developing countries."[35]

From the above examples it is evident that the Marxists' critique of American imperialism is fundamentally rooted in Lenin's prescriptive analysis discussed in chapter 2. It is an economic determinist line of analysis that views American monopoly capital and multinational corporations as the root of the inequitable world order. U.S. foreign policy thus serves caituan interests and profits. Under such conditions, all forces—particularly in the developing world—should be mobilized to combat U.S. imperialism (*Mei di*). This was the principal rationale for much of Maoist foreign policy.

When one examines the institutional affiliations of those Marxists who articulate an imperialist image of U.S. foreign policy, one finds that they are primarily located in universities. The only research institutes that contributed significantly to this camp were the CASS's Institute of World Economics and Politics and the Shanghai Institute of International Studies.

Non-Marxist Perspectives on American Foreign Policy

Unlike the Marxists, the non-Marxists do not see the United States acting on the world stage as a rational actor, and often not as a unitary actor either. To be sure, the non-Marxists see the United States as globally engaged with interests to protect all over the world, but they do not see U.S. behavior abroad as stemming from a singular definition of national interests, as the imperialist camp views commercial gain or the hegemonist camp perceives competition with the Soviet Union as the sole driving force behind U.S. conduct. Rather, the non-Marxists see the United States as having a multiplicity of interests that are defined in the context of this or that specific region, country, or domestic interest group. In short, the non-Marxists tend to view U.S. foreign policy as a series of disaggregated bilateral relationships.

Thus, the non-Marxists see a more variegated, ad hoc U.S. foreign policy. As such, the non-Marxist critique of U.S. foreign policy is,

---

[35] "The Superpowers Are the Upholders of the Old International Economic Order," *Peking Domestic Service*, August 1, 1976, *FBIS-CHI*, August 5, 1976, A1.

above all, an atheoretical one. It is largely descriptive—the United States did X here and Y there—but it is also at times analytical.

If anything, the non-Marxists see a dynamism in all bilateral relationships. That is, they see fluidity, and they are always looking for emerging tensions between the involved parties. Thus, they see elements of conflict and cooperation in most relationships but tend to emphasize the conflictual. This propensity probably owes itself to the dialectical method of analysis in which all Chinese intellectuals have been schooled.

Institutionally, the non-Marxists are mainly composed of New China News Agency journalists with a cohort from some military and civilian research institutes (mainly the Beijing Institute of International Strategic Studies, CASS's America Institute, IIS, and ICIR). Also, as noted in previous chapters, the non-Marxists did not really emerge until the 1980s. Thus, the analysis that follows focuses on the Reagan era. In this section, I limit examination of the non-Marxists' articulated images to the two subjects about which they write the most—U.S.-Soviet relations and U.S.-China relations. Certainly they do report on, and write analyses of, America's relations with other countries, but their interests lie mainly with U.S. relations with the Soviet Union and China.

U.S.-Soviet Relations

The non-Marxists follow the vicissitudes of the Soviet-American relationship very closely. Hardly an issue of leading Chinese newspapers and periodicals is published without some report of the latest round of arms talks, leadership statements, visiting dignitaries, policy pronouncements, and so forth. To chronicle all these events and writings over eighteen years falls well beyond the scope of this section and is not of great import given its generally descriptive quality. What is more interesting and possible is to summarize the elements of conflict and cooperation that the non-Marxists see in U.S. policy toward the Soviet Union. Until 1987 the non-Marxists did not see much of a cooperative element in the Soviet-American relationship; détente was a fiction in their view. Their image is a conflict model. From the non-Marxists' point of view, the major element of conflict and tension that the United States introduces into the superpower relationship is its contribution to the arms race. As will be shown, this conflict model began to change in the late 1980s as they began to view arms control in a more positive light.

U.S. arms procurement and deployments are monitored closely by the non-Marxists. After being posted to Washington in 1979, New China News Agency correspondents began to study the shift in U.S. nuclear targeting strategy as contained in Carter's Presidential Directive No. 59. Their dispatches reported to their readers that the U.S. strategy, should war break out, was now to "concentrate on destroying Soviet military forces and the defense installations of Soviet leaders, instead of focusing on the destruction of cities as in the past."[36] Wu Chu's report went on to say that this new "counterforce" strategy indicated that the Carter administration had "abandoned the concept of rapid escalation to all-out nuclear war" by accepting the idea that a "sustained, limited nuclear war that might last several weeks or even several months" could now be fought. The adoption of PD No. 59, in his view, also represented the victory of "actual war theory faction" over the "deterrence faction." Wu argued that the deterrence faction, which believes in mutual assured destruction, had held sway in the United States since McNamara was defense secretary, but since the mid-1970s the "counterforce school" led by Schlesinger had been gaining currency. He concluded that "the strategic concept of taking a hard line toward the Soviet Union now holds the upper hand in the argument between the two factions, hence there was no alternative but to abandon the obsolete strategy of MAD and accept the ideas of the anti-Soviet hardliners."[37] A report in *Worker's Daily*, however, saw the adoption of PD No. 59 as politically motivated. That is, in lieu of the presidential election campaign, "Carter, taking advantage of his office as president, anticipated Reagan by approving a new nuclear strategy based upon that advocated by Schlesinger, and his objective was to prevail over Reagan."[38] Thus, Carter was really trying to win over the conservatives.

The non-Marxists also argued that the Soviet invasion of Afghanistan had galvanized Carter's commitment to "readjust" U.S. military policies in light of an increased Soviet threat. An article in the *People's Daily* noted the U.S. intent to build a "three-in-one" nuclear force consisting of the MX mobile missile, new SLBMs to be launched from Trident I class submarines, and air-launched cruise missiles from B-52s. The same article chided the United States for trying to "cooperate" with the Soviets:

All U.S. restraints and concessions for seeking "cooperation" have failed to achieve the expected results. Instead, they have only weakened the

---

[36] Wu Chu, "Meiguo de xinde hezhanlue," *Renmin ribao*, August 23, 1980, p. 7.
[37] Ibid.
[38] Deng Yin, "On the New U.S. Nuclear Strategy towards the Soviet Union," *Gongren ribao*, September 30, 1980, JPRS 76883, November 25, 1980, p. 2.

United States and strengthened the Soviet Union. It is unprofitable to continue this one-way "cooperation" which has done harm to the United States. . . . Therefore, the Carter administration must revise its nuclear deterrent strategy, concentrate on developing the mobile defense capabilities of its naval and air forces, step up the modernization of its conventional forces, organize rapid deployment, and formulate a Persian Gulf strategy to meet the Soviet challenge more effectively in the 1980s.[39]

Such was the tenor of the times. It can be surmised that the Chinese were hoping the new relationship with the United States would provide them with a "free ride" by using the American military counterweight to the Soviet Union to augment their own security. This cost-effective strategy also helped to build bridges of shared interest with conservatives in the United States. Chinese rhetoric about containing the "polar bear" fell on receptive ears among hardliners in and out of the U.S. government during 1979–1980. China became a vociferous advocate of Western military preparedness in the face of "Soviet hegemonism," and a virtual adjunct member of NATO during these years.

However, the Chinese cheering from the sidelines for a U.S. defense buildup diminished after the Reagan administration took office. I see four principal reasons for this important shift from supporter to critic. First, the non-Marxists began to see the Soviet military threat as less pressing than in the late 1970s. Second, and relatedly, in their estimation the U.S. buildup itself now presented more of a threatening than stabilizing factor in the international arena. Third, and very important, the perception was growing that the United States was not a trustworthy partner because of its handling of the Taiwan question and other issues in the bilateral Sino-American relationship, principally technology transfer. Fourth, U.S. policies and actions in third areas (Central America, Middle East, Europe, Northeast Asia) were increasingly seen as aggravating conflicts in those regions rather than resolving them. The first, second, and fourth arguments gained currency in Beijing policy-making circles at this time because of the growing acceptance of the hegemonist critique of U.S. foreign policy.

The non-Marxists therefore reported on the Reagan defense buildup in great detail. In 1981 analysts at the the Institute of International Studies and Institute of Contemporary International Relations began to publish articles on the different elements of the Reagan plan. In one article IIS America Watcher Zhuang Qubing

---

[39] Jun Xiang, "Meiguo dui Su junshi zhengce de xin fazhan," *Renmin ribao*, March 25, 1980, p. 7.

explained how Reagan's decision to produce and stockpile the neutron bomb would not only help counter the Warsaw Pact superiority in conventional weapons, but "strengthen the U.S. position" in arms control talks.[40] Zhuang's colleague at IIS Jin Junhui wrote that the Reagan policy toward the USSR is one of "carrot and big stick with an emphasis on strengthening the hardness of the big stick."[41] To this end, Jin took note of the planned annual 7 percent real increase in the defense budget over five years totaling $1.5 trillion; a six-year, $18 billion plan to modernize strategic nuclear forces, including procurement of 110 MX missiles and 100 B-1 bombers; an unprecedented peacetime naval buildup; deployment of air and submarine-launched cruise missiles; recruitment of 200,000 new military personnel; development of the Rapid Deployment Force; and preparations to fight several wars simultaneously.[42] However, Wang Qianqi of the ICIR, writing in the fall of 1981, was dubious of the U.S. defense industry's ability to meet the planned buildup:

> The current state of the U.S. armament industry also is not suited to the requirements of rapid, large-scale increases in production. Following the conclusion of the Vietnam War, there was a reduction in the industrial base of America's national defense. Much of the machinery and equipment of the munitions factories is outdated; trained workers have been reduced; important raw materials are in short supply; the margin of increase in the production rate has declined; and delivery dates have been greatly extended.[43]

Insufficient production capacity was not the only potential impediment to the realization of the buildup plan. Congress and the public were also seen as standing in the way. *People's Daily* correspondent Zhang Dezhen monitored congressional deliberations over the best basing mode for the MX missile—mobile versus "dense pack"[44]—as well as the public "nuclear freeze" movement.[45] NCNA America Watcher Peng Di described Reagan's response to the antinuclear movement as "a snort of contempt."[46]

By 1983, particularly after the beginning of deployment of Pershing

[40] Zhuang Qubing, "Ligen de zhongzidan juece," *Shijie zhishi*, no. 18 (1981): 2–3.
[41] Jin Junhui, "Ligen zhengfu de duiwai zhengce," *Guoji wenti yanjiu*, no. 1 (1982): 5.
[42] Ibid., p. 4.
[43] Wang Qianqi, "Ligen zhengfu de junshi zhanlue," *Xiandai guoji guanxi*, no. 1 (1981): 24.
[44] Zhang Dezhen, "MX daodan miji bushu fang'an geqian," *Renmin ribao*, December 23, 1982, p. 7.
[45] Zhang Dezhen, "Dongjie hewuqi zhizheng," *Renmin ribao*, April 22, 1982, p. 7.
[46] Peng Di, "'Lun 'gai'—Ligen zhengfu de waijiao zhengce de xin zhongtai," *Liaowang*, no. 2 (1983): 32.

II IRBMs in Western Europe, many Chinese analysts believed that the military balance between the superpowers had been restored to "rough equivalence."[47] Analysts at the Institute of International Studies came to this conclusion based on the following assessment of strengths and weaknesses. In conventional forces, the United States was deemed superior in aircraft, large-scale surface ships, and anti-tank weaponry, but the Soviet Union had "superiority in numbers" in all other areas. In strategic nuclear forces, the Soviet Union has "greater numbers of warheads," but in terms of qualitative assessments the United States has the edge in targeting accuracy and bombers. In theater nuclear weapons, they thought that the U.S. deployment of Pershing II and cruise missiles would offset the Soviet SS-20 advantage. Finally, the United States was thought to have a distinct advantage in "long-range air and sea capacity" due to its extensive network of air and naval bases around the world.

In a separate evaluation of the Soviet-American military balance, another IIS researcher concluded that despite an accelerated arms race in which the "United States had taken the offensive . . . on the whole, the Soviet Union and the United States are in balance. Neither can use force to defeat the other, and neither can subject the other to its political demands."[48]

Shi Wuqing arrived at this conclusion after comprehensive consideration of a number of factors. In terms of total troops, Shi felt that the USSR held a 4:3 advantage, although the United States held a distinct advantage in combat readiness and worldwide deployments. The situation in strategic nuclear forces, Shi argued, was more complex. Neither side, Shi asserted, has a first-strike capability, but both have the ability to launch a counterattack after absorbing a first strike. The Soviets may have overall numerical superiority in their "nuclear offensive force," including equivalent megatonnage (EMT) in warheads, but the U.S. force has better targeting accuracy, higher mobility, and survivability potential. The Soviets have an advantage in hitting "soft targets such as cities," but the United States has better counterforce capability. Shi found the situation in theater nuclear

[47] See, for example, Xing Shugang, Li Yunhua, and Liu Yingna, "Changing Balance of Soviet-U.S. Power and Its Impact on the International Situation of the 1980s," *Guoji wenti yanjiu*, no. 1 (1983), in *Selected Articles of "International Studies," No. 1* (Beijing: China Translation and Publishing Corporation, 1985), p. 19. For a fine analysis of Chinese perceptions of the shifting U.S.-Soviet balance of power during this period, see Banning Garrett and Bonnie Glaser, *Chinese Estimates of the U.S.-Soviet Balance of Power*, Asia Program Occasional Paper no. 33 (Washington, D.C.: Woodrow Wilson International Center for Scholars, July 1988).

[48] Shi Wuqing, "Su-Mei junbei jingsai he junshi liliang duibi," *Guoji wenti yanjiu*, no. 1 (1985): 30.

forces "ambiguous" but reckoned the Americans would have the edge following deployment of Pershing II and cruise missiles in Western Europe. In conventional weaponry, Shi found Soviet ground force units basically superior in terms of total firepower. The Soviet air force held a lead numerically but not qualitatively, and the American navy was "much superior." All of these estimates and other factors taken together led Shi to conclude that not only do the two sides have overall equivalence, but "neither side has the technological superiority to tip the rough military balance."

Recognition of military parity between the superpowers was a key element in convincing many analysts that mutual deterrence was actually a valid concept, and that it made the outbreak of world war unlikely. As three leading strategic analysts at the Institute of Contemporary International Relations stated in an important article carried in *Shijie zhishi*: "Nuclear deterrence is playing a containing role in preventing the Soviet Union and the United States from risking the danger of launching a world war or a nuclear war."[49] This denial of the theory of the inevitability of war—which the Chinese had been arguing for years—was a remarkable theoretical and substantive breakthrough.

Wu Zhan, deputy director of the CASS's America Institute and one of China's leading specialists on nuclear weaponry (Wu is also a nuclear scientist who worked on China's nuclear program in the 1960s), concurred that nuclear deterrence (*heweishe*) had saved the postwar peace.[50] Not only had nuclear deterrence based on MAD contained the U.S.-Soviet struggle, Wu wrote, but so too has "extended deterrence" provided a nuclear umbrella for allies. Wu's article, probably the most extensive ever to appear on the subject in China, traced the evolution of American nuclear doctrine from the Second World War through the late 1980s. Wu introduced his readers to the concepts of assured survival, mutual assured destruction, balance of terror, damage limitation, flexible response, large-scale retaliation, passive defense (civilian shelters), anti–ballistic missile systems, counterforce and countervalue targeting, acceptable counterstrikes, minimum deterrence, "overkill," damage limitation, single integrated operational plan (SIOP), and so on.

While the non-Marxists were beginning to accept the theory of mutual deterrence based on equivalence, Zhang Jingyi of the CASS's America Institute, a leading military-strategic analyst, pointed out

[49] Zhou Jirong, Wang Baoqin, and Gu Guanfu, "Su-Mei zhengba taishi de bainhua yu qianjing," *Shijie zhishi*, no. 23 (1983): 2.
[50] Wu Zhan, "Heweishe," *Meiguo yanjiu*, no. 1 (1988): 35–49.

that the Americans were actually moving away from the concept of deterrence based on the doctrine of mutual assured destruction to more of a "war-fighting doctrine" at lower thresholds of combat (so-called low intensity conflict), hence the return of a "flexible response" strategy.[51] This development, Zhang thought, was destabilizing, dangerous, and would fuel the arms race even further. An article published by the America Institute in 1988 dissented from Zhang's view and argued instead that the United States had swapped MAD for a strategy of "assured survival."[52]

Other military analysts at the Beijing Institute of International Strategic Studies, an organization affiliated with the second intelligence division (er zu) of the PLA General Staff Department,[53] also took note of the new American emphasis on war fighting. Zong He claimed the Reagan administration had abandoned the Carter strategy of fighting "one and a half wars" in favor of confronting the Soviet Union "around the globe" (huanqiu).[54] In assessing the new U.S. "flexible response strategy," Sa Benwang argued that the United States was preparing to be able to fight a war at four different levels: nuclear war, large-scale conventional war, small-scale conventional war, and low-intensity conflict.[55] He went on to argue that the United States was trying to "exhaust" the Soviet Union in an arms race but was also trying to "push back" (tuihui) the Soviet Union. Third, Sa argued that the United States under Reagan was not only better prepared for war fighting, but more willing to employ force in the Third World. In another article Sa and a BIISS colleague argued that the United States now operated from a three-stage, multilayered deterrence strategy.[56] The first stage is "defense" that aims at preventing the enemy from executing his plan of attack through a combination of forward defense, rapid deployment, and flexible response. The second stage of "escalation" aims to stop the adversary's attack when forward defense fails through "partial war mobilization, strategic reinforcement,

---

[51] Zhang Jingyi, "Ligen zhengfu junshi zhanlue pouxi," Renmin ribao, May 5, 1983, p. 7; Zhang Jingyi and Song Jiuguang, "Cong 'chunweishe' dao 'shizhanweishe," Meiguo yanjiu, no. 4 (1988): 7–27.

[52] Yu Zhiyong, "Cong zhongdan tiaoyue kan Mei-Su zai junkong fangmian de xin bianhua," Meiguo yanjiu, no. 2 (1988): 135–43.

[53] For more on BIISS and other strategic research units, see my "China's National Security Research Bureaucracy," pp. 276–304.

[54] Zong He, "Cong junshi zhanlue kan Mei-Su zhengduo fangxiang," Shijie zhishi, no. 1 (1984): 5.

[55] Sa Benwang, "Ligen zhengfu de xin 'linghuo fanying' zhanlue," Shijie zhishi, no. 13 (1986): 2–4.

[56] Sa Benwang and Li Qinggong, "Meiguo junshi zhanlu xin fazhan," Guoji zhanlue yanjiu, no. 2 (1986): 10–13.

and the use of tactical nuclear weapons." The third stage is "retaliation," which aims at limiting further escalation through the threat of
using strategic nuclear and chemical weapons. This integrated strategy, Sa and Li argued, indicated the U.S. shift from a conventional
deterrent strategy based on mutual assured destruction to a new war-
fighting doctrine.

Finally, in the realm of the American contribution to the arms race,
the non-Marxists have devoted considerable energy to studying the
Strategic Defense Initiative (SDI), or Star Wars (*xingqiu dazhan*) as it is
uniformly referred to by Chinese. It took some time after President
Reagan's March 23, 1983, speech announcing the SDI program for
Chinese strategic analysts to focus on it. The *People's Daily* correspondent in Washington did take note of the speech and reported it in a
straightforward manner.[57] But it was not until May and July that Chinese commentary began to focus on the details of the program and
voice concerns over both its technological feasibility and its destabilizing effect on the nuclear balance.[58] By late summer 1983 the Chinese press took note of the deleterious effect SDI was having on the
arms control talks, but there is no evidence of systematic Chinese
study of SDI as a system, its role in U.S. defense strategy, or its implications for China until 1984. In the October issue of *Research in
International Studies*, two articles were published that were harbingers
of what would become China's official position on SDI.[59]

Zhuang Qubing's article is reportedly an unclassified version of a
report written at the request of then premier Zhao Ziyang.[60] Zhuang
concluded that a "leak-proof" deployment of SDI was not feasible,
that the system would greatly destabilize the military balance by providing the United States with a first-strike capability, and it would
contribute to the further acceleration of the arms race. Zhuang

[57] Zhang Liang, "U.S.-USSR Outer Space Contention Getting More and More
Fierce—Reagan Demands Development of New Antiballistic Missile System; Andro-
pov Warns U.S. against Seeking Military Superiority," *Renmin ribao*, March 29, 1983,
FBIS-CHI, March 31, 1983, A2.

[58] See Liu Qin, "Ligen xinde he zhanlue," *Shijie zhishi*, no. 9 (1983): 8–9; Si Mada,
"Xingqiu dazhan de menghuan yu xianshi," *Shijie zhishi*, no. 12 (1983): 10–11.

[59] For analyses of the evolution of Chinese thinking and policy on SDI see John
Garver, "China's Response to the Strategic Defense Initiative," *Asian Survey* (November 1986): 1220–39; Bonnie S. Glaser and Banning N. Garrett, "Chinese Perspectives
on the Strategic Defense Initiative," *Problems of Communism* (March–April 1986): 28–44;
James L. Huskey, "An Inside Chinese View of SDI," U.S. Information Agency Office
of Research *Report*, December 12, 1986; Alastair I. Johnston, *China and Arms Control:
Emerging Issues and Interests in the 1980s*, pp. 60–67.

[60] Zhuang Qubing, "Meiguo 'xingqiu dazhan' jihua," *Guoji wenti yanjiu*, no. 4 (1984):
24–31, 36.

thought the United States was "unrealistic" if it thought SDI could "force its opponent to retreat or even to knuckle under."

While Zhuang's article was more analytical than programmatic, an accompanying article by He Qizhi in the same issue addressed the legal aspects of controlling the "arms race in outer space."[61] As Alastair I. Johnston points out in his study of China's approach to arms control, with these articles China began to serve notice that "space had become the premier arms control issue for China."[62] Since then, the non-Marxists have continued to show interest in the technological aspects of SDI but also continue to be pessimistic about deployment possibilities and condemn the United States for stimulating a new and dangerous round in the arms race.

Do the non-Marxists see a cooperative dimension in arms control talks? It was not until President Reagan and General Secretary Gorbachev signed the Intermediate Nuclear Force (INF) Accord in 1987 that Chinese analysts began to express the view that superpower arms control efforts could help alleviate world tension.[63] Prior to that time, Chinese commentators viewed the arms control talks and efforts toward détente in general as disingenuous. The arms control negotiations were regularly denounced as mere exercises in maintaining the superpowers' monopoly of nuclear weapons, and détente was seen as an attempt to build a superpower "condominium" rather than a sincere attempt to reduce tensions.

Since 1987, however, the non-Marxists have been considerably more upbeat about U.S.-Soviet relations in general and arms control in particular. This is seen, for example, in the writings of nuclear expert Wu Zhan of the CASS's America Institute. Following the INF Accord, Wu Zhan wrote that deep cuts in nuclear arsenals were possible.[64] On this basis, Wu argued in another article, a sustainable détente between the superpowers was possible.[65] In early 1990 Wu predicted that a Strategic Arms Reduction (START) agreement was possible, as well as deep conventional force reductions within the CSCE (Conference on Security and Cooperation in Europe) process and the destruction of chemical weapons stocks.[66] The strategic arms

[61] He Qizhi, "Jiaqiang zhizhi waikong jingsai de falu cuoshi," pp. 32–34.

[62] Alastair I. Johnston, *China and Arms Control*, p. 64.

[63] See, for example, Yu Zhiyong, "Cong zhongdan tiaoyue kan Mei-Su junkong fangmian de xin bianhua."

[64] Wu Zhan, "Mei-Su zai zhanlue wuqishang de douzheng," *Meiguo yanjiu*, no. 1 (1987): 79–95.

[65] Wu Zhan, "Shijie heping yu caijun," *Meiguo yanjiu*, no. 1 (1989): 7–21.

[66] Wu Zhan, "Dangqian de junbei kongzhi tanpan," *Meiguo yanjiu*, no. 1 (1990): 58–73.

agreement reached at the June 1990 U.S.-Soviet summit and the No-vember 1990 Charter of Paris for a New Europe proved Wu correct.

Other analysts also reflected the new view of détente. In October 1988 senior foreign affairs specialist Huan Xiang predicted that due to superpower détente the world was entering "a fairly long-term stage of relative warmth."[67] Chen Qurong, deputy director of the In-stitute of Contemporary International Relations, argued that détente was due not to the efforts of the United States and Soviet Union but rather to pressure brought by the international community, including China.[68] Other commentators surmised that this new round of dé-tente was qualitatively different from previous détentes.[69] Chen Qimao, the director of the Shanghai Institute of International Studies, and his colleagues at SIIS argued that the détente inaugurated during 1988 would be viewed by history as a watershed year in international relations, and that superpower détente would result in progress to-ward the resolution of many regional conflicts.[70] Wang Shu, director of the Foreign Ministry's Institute of International Studies, opined that this trend of events constituted a "new international political or-der" in which "hegemonism and politics by alliance no longer work."[71]

Thus, the non-Marxists' perceptions of U.S. policy toward the So-viet Union were, until 1987, essentially conflictual. They saw inher-ent and irresolvable conflicts of interest between the two superpow-ers and perceived the United States as doing its fair share to aggravate the relationship and contribute to global tensions through the arms race. But beginning in 1987 a fundamental shift of opinion is evident among the non-Marxists. While continuing to see elements of contention, the emphasis in their analyses shifted to limited co-operation.

---

[67] Huan Xiang, "Huan Xiang Discusses State of World Affairs," *Guoji zhanwang*, no. 21 (1988), *JPRS-CAR-89-004*, January 11, 1989, p. 1.

[68] Chen Qurong, "Huanhe shitou kewang baochi, yao nandong taqian jin ye bu-chang," *Shijie zhishi*, no. 19 (1988): 4–5.

[69] See, for example, Li Yihu, "Guoji tixide zhongxin suzao," *Shijie zhishi*, no. 20 (1988): 6–7; Ji Yin, "Mei-Su zhouyan ding 21 shiji kangzhang de baowangqi," *Shijie zhishi*, no. 21 (1988): 2–4.

[70] Chen Qimao, "A New Stage of Relative Détente Has Emerged in World Affairs," *Guoji zhanwang*, no. 1 (1989): 3–6, *JPRS-CAR-89-032*, April 10, 1989, pp. 2–6; Zhang Jinrui, "World Military Trend in the Nineties," *Guoji zhanwang*, no. 5 (1989): 5–6, *JPRS-CAR-89-070*, July 6, 1989, pp. 1–3; "Shanghai Foreign Affairs Experts on Shifting World Power," *Shijie jingji daobao*, January 16, 1989, p. 7, *JPRS-CAR-89-027*, March 29, 1989, pp. 6–8.

[71] Wang Shu, "Pushing the Establishment of a New International Political Order," *Liaowang*, no. 3 (1989): 38, *JPRS-CAR-89-026*, March 27, 1989, pp. 5–6.

The Hegemonist Critique of American Foreign Policy

For America Watchers of this genre, geopolitics is primary. Their "level of analysis" is a global, systemic one. They believe that the two superpowers are the primary actors on the world stage, and all tension and conflict in the world is instigated or exacerbated by the competition for hegemony between the United States and the Soviet Union, both of whom seek global supremacy and world domination. As two leading strategic analysts at the China Institute of Contemporary International Relations put it, "Superpower contention has been the principal source of most turmoil and tension in postwar international relations. Originally it began as a rivalry and finally towards the end of the fifties escalated into a real confrontation for world domination with their tentacles spread out over the whole planet, and with an intensity that has often brought the world to the brink of global confrontation."[72] For a while during the 1960s some Chinese analysts of international relations believed the two superpowers were "colluding" for world hegemony, but since the fall of former defense minister Lin Biao in 1971 and throughout the period of this study, "contention" has been the dominant theme.[73]

Given this superpower contention, Chinese analysts do attempt to establish whether the United States or Soviet Union is waxing or waning in terms of overall power and threats to world peace. When one nation appears more threatening than the other, such as the Soviet Union appeared during the 1970s, then Chinese commentary attempts to mobilize a "united front" against the predominant hegemon. During this period, Chinese accusations of "U.S. hegemony" were relatively few but became predominant during the 1980s. I thus label this group of America Watchers the "hegemonists."

The analysis of American foreign policy that emerges in this context is one of the United States obsessed with maintaining global hegemony in the face of Soviet encroachments on its spheres of influence at a minimum, while reestablishing American "supremacy" is seen to be the real goal. The United States is seen as not content with a balance of power or strategic equivalence with the U.S.S.R. but

[72] Wang Baoqin and Li Zhongchen, "The Emergence of the Superpowers," in *As China Sees the World*, ed. Harish Kapur (London: Frances Pinter, 1987), p. 25.

[73] For evidence and analysis of the "collusion" theme and the competitive "contention" line of analysis during this period see Michael Pillsbury, *SALT on the Dragon* (Santa Monica: Rand Research Report P-5457, April 1975); and Thomas M. Gottlieb, *Chinese Foreign Policy Factionalism and the Origins of the Strategic Triangle* (Santa Monica: Rand Research Report R-1902-NA, November 1977).

seeks outright supremacy.[74] Consequently, all such analyses of the hegemonists take as their starting point this zero-sum competition with the Soviet Union. All U.S relationships with other countries and behavior in other regions of the world are seen as derivative of this competition.[75]

In recent years, the hegemonist critique of American foreign policy has gained predominance in Chinese foreign policy-making circles, as reflected in the fact that many of the individuals who articulate this view work in institutions concerned with intelligence analysis and advising the central leadership on international relations (primarily the Institute of International Studies and Institute of Contemporary International Relations). These analysts perceive superpower contention to be the most important variable in international relations; in their estimate, global prospects of war and peace hinge on this relationship.

The hegemonist critique of U.S. foreign policy became particularly salient during the Reagan administration. During the Carter years—particularly in the wake of the Soviet invasion of Afghanistan—Chinese analysts had been urging the United States to do more to check Soviet expansionism, but early into the Reagan presidency many analysts began to change their tune. One no longer read of the Soviet Union on the "offensive" and the United States on the "defensive" (*Sugong, Meishou*), but rather of two hegemons of relatively equal threat. One review of Reagan's foreign policy at the end of his first term put it this way:

> The Reagan administration's foreign policy, guided by a bipolar concept, aims at achieving superiority in a battle with the Soviet Union for global hegemony. It tries hard to check Soviet expansion and reinforce the role of the United States as the world's overlord. . . . Previously, Moscow was on the offensive while Washington took the defensive. Now they are in a strategic stalemate in which neither side is absolutely on the offensive or defensive.[76]

[74] See, for example, Xing Shugang, Li Yunhua, and Liu Yingna, "Su-Mei liliang duibi jiqi dui bashiniandai guoji jushi de yingxiang," *Guoji wenti yanjiu*, no. 1 (1983): 30.

[75] Perhaps the best example of the hegemonist critique is Wang Shuzhong et al., *Mei-Su zhengba zhanlue wenti* (Beijing: Guofang daxue chubanshe, 1988). This internal circulation (*neibu faxing*) volume, written principally by international relations specialists of the world politics research division of the CASS Institute of World Economics and Politics, attributes the entire history of postwar international relations to the U.S.-Soviet struggle for global hegemony.

[76] Jin Junhui, "Ligen zhengfu sinian waijiao fenxi," *Guoji wenti yanjiu*, no. 2 (1985): 24.

Concomitant with this shift in strategic perspective, official Chinese foreign policy pronouncements began to move away from fostering an anti-Soviet united front toward the "independent foreign policy" line that became official policy at the Twelfth Party Congress of 1982.[77]

The American policy of seeking hegemony is seen as particularly manifest in the context of its competition with the Soviet Union in third regions. The hegemonists' critique holds that regional tensions are not indigenous, but instead are a function of the hegemonist designs of the superpowers. A special *People's Daily* commentary put it starkly:

> Some people have spread a theory to the effect that almost all of today's disputes and conflicts occur in the Third World and that it is evident that the source of tension and danger of war lies in the contradictions between Third World countries, not in the rivalry between superpowers. This idea is a complete reversal of right and wrong. . . . In fact, the superpowers' shadow can always be seen behind Third World conflicts. Herein lies the incessant turmoil of these regions.[78]

U.S. hegemonist behavior in Europe, the Middle East, and Asia is particularly singled out for criticism.

EUROPE

Europe has always been viewed as the locus of superpower contention for hegemony. As Europe goes, so goes the world. As one commentator simply put it, "Europe is the strategic center of gravity in the Soviet-American struggle for hegemony."[79]

The hegemonists' critique of U.S. policies in Europe focuses almost exclusively on the military-strategic component of the superpower balance in the region. While they take the Soviet military threat to the Western alliance as very real, the hegemonists tend to view U.S. military deployments in Europe as attempts to maintain hegemony over the West European countries. In other words, they do not ac-

[77] For analyses of Chinese assessments of the United States and Soviet Union during this period, see Carol Lee Hamrin, "China Reassesses the Superpowers," *Pacific Affairs* (Summer 1983): 209–31; Banning Garrett and Bonnie Glaser, *War and Peace: The Views from Moscow and Beijing* (Berkeley: Institute of International Studies, University of California, 1984); Garrett and Glaser, *Chinese Estimates of the U.S.-Soviet Balance of Power*; Jonathan Pollack, *The Lessons of Coalition Politics: Sino-American Security Relations* (Santa Monica: The Rand Corporation, R-3133-AF, February 1984).

[78] Commentator, "Weichi shijie heping bixu fandui bachuanzhuyi," *Renmin ribao*, January 5, 1983, p. 6.

[79] Yang Xu, "Ou-Mei maodun pouxi," *Shijie zhishi*, no. 15 (1982): 3.

cept the theory of deterrence, but rather see the United States as seeking superiority instead of parity. Shan Shi of the Institute of International Studies articulated this perspective perfectly:

> Though the Reagan administration makes all sorts of claims that its aim is to maintain a military balance between East and West, its actual behavior, such as greatly increasing its military budget and intensifying research and development on new weaponry and deployment, demonstrates that its actual policy is to fight for military (and, in particular, nuclear) superiority. In the strategic thinking of the Reagan administration, only by achieving military superiority can the United States win the initiative in its struggle with the Soviet Union, strengthen its control over Western Europe, and secure its leading status in the West.[80]

The hegemonists thus see the efforts by the United States to rectify a perceived military imbalance in the European theater as destabilizing attempts to exercise unilateral control. They portrayed the 1983 deployment of Pershing II medium-range and cruise missiles in this light.[81]

The military balance in central Europe is not the only focus of the hegemonists' attention in the region. For example, *Guoji wenti yanjiu* ran an article in 1984 on the contention for naval hegemony in the Mediterranean. The article asserted that having inherited from France and Britain the position as "overlord of the Mediterranean Sea," the U.S. Sixth Fleet was now being challenged for "control" by the Soviets.[82] This article is one of many appearing around this time criticizing the U.S. naval buildup under Reagan (and then Secretary of the Navy John Lehman) as "gunboat diplomacy," "marine hegemony," or "supremacy of the seas."[83] As one analyst at the Institute of Contemporary International Relations put it, "As far as the United States is concerned, control over the oceans has a significance equal in importance to Soviet control over their land territories. In this respect, parity and reciprocity are meaningless words, the United States must possess 'naval superiority.' "[84]

[80] Shan Shi, "Dangqian Xi-Ou xingshi fazhan zhongde ruogan wenti," *Guoji wenti yanjiu*, no. 3 (1984): 21.

[81] For an analysis of coverage in the Chinese periodical press of this deployment see my *Coverage of the United States in Key Chinese Periodicals During 1984*, pp. 20–21.

[82] Xiao Ming, "Mei-Su zai dizhonghai de zhengduo ji yuqi ta youguan dizhonghai anquan de zhuchang," *Guoji wenti yanjiu*, no. 3 (1984): 37.

[83] See, for example, Su Dushi and Han Bin, "Mei-Su zhengduo hai jida," *Shijie zhishi*, no. 17 (1986): 14–15.

[84] Wang Qianqi, "Ligen zhengfu de junshi zhanlue," *Xiandai guoji guanxi*, no. 1 (1981): 23.

Prior to the 1990 Kuwait crisis, the hegemonist analysis of U.S. objectives in the Middle East concluded that the United States had a two-pronged policy: (1) denying the region to the Soviet Union and (2) support for Israel. As Zhang Dezhen of the CASS's Institute of World Economics and Politics has argued, "The major U.S. interest in the region is the prevention of Soviet expansion."[85] Zhang went on in his article to note that U.S. efforts in the Middle East during the Reagan administration were part of a global strategy to "roll back" Soviet gains made in the 1970s. Forging "strategic cooperation" with Israel and a "common strategy" with Persian Gulf states had been successful, Zhang thought, in blunting further Soviet adventurism in the wake of Afghanistan even if it had raised the ire of the people of the region. But Lu Xi of the Institute of Contemporary International Relations believes that "the rivalry between the United States and the Soviet Union has always been the root cause of turmoil in the Middle East," and he therefore sees the "contention for hegemony with the U.S.S.R." as the basis for U.S. policy in the region.[86] Lu claimed that the creation of the Rapid Deployment Force, the buildup of U.S. military facilities in the Gulf states and Indian Ocean, increased military assistance throughout the region, and attempts to exclude the U.S.S.R. from regional peace talks are all indicative of U.S. attempts to counter Soviet influence. In another article, written jointly with his colleague Ren Pinsheng, Lu and Ren also noted that the United States was trying to forge an "anti-Soviet strategic unity" in the region because the Middle East was the "weakest" of the "three strategic regions of vital interest to the United States (Western Europe, Middle East, and Northeast Asia)."[87]

The second main source of instability in the Middle East according to the hegemonists is American support for Israel, which they naturally view as an extension of the U.S. desire for hegemony in the region. All analysts are in agreement that without strong and unqualified support from the United States, Israel would not act with such impunity. Chinese analysts note U.S. backing for Israel in the 1967 and 1973 wars, the annexation of the Golan Heights, and the events leading up to the 1984 invasion of Lebanon. Such support has

[85] Zhang Dezhen, "Ligen zhengfu Zhongdong zhengce yanbian jiqi maodun," *Renmin ribao*, March 19, 1982, p. 6.
[86] Lu Xi, "Zhongdong xingshi: huigu yu liaowang," *Xiandai guoji guanxi*, no. 2 (1982): 12.
[87] Ren Pinsheng and Lu Xi, "Ligen zhengfu de zhongdong zhanlue," *Shijie zhishi*, no. 3 (1982): 5.

had its costs. "The United States has stood behind Israel's expansionist aggressive policies throughout, provoking popular anti-U.S. anger in the Arab world. By identifying with Israeli expansionism, the United States has in effect made itself the enemy of 150 million Arab people," claims Middle East expert Wan Guang.[88] In another article Wan Guang had a few words of advice for Washington: "American policies make life difficult for those who look toward Washington for a Middle East solution, forcing them to put distance between themselves and the United States. As long as the United States fails to correct its basic bias for Israel and rejects any fair and reasonable solution for Palestine and the Middle East, this weakness will continue to be a drawback in its new rivalry with the Soviet Union in the area."[89]

Other analysts take note of U.S. efforts to cultivate "conservative" Arab states in Egypt, Saudi Arabia, and the Gulf region, but always toward the ultimate goal of expanding its own hegemony in the region. Again Wan Guang minces no words: "It has always been the aim of the United States to undermine Arab nationalism. . . . Even as it works to improve relations with Arab nations and offers them economic and military aid, it [the United States] invariably tries to control them with an eye toward steering them into its own sphere of influence."[90]

ASIA

Outside of Europe and the Middle East, many Chinese analysts see Asia as the region of stepped-up military confrontation between the superpowers and the American quest for hegemony. Wang Baoqin of the Institute of Contemporary International Relations and one of China's leading strategic analysts argued that increased U.S. military presence in Asia is really a diversionary tactic to keep the Soviet Union occupied on two fronts. Said Wang in a 1984 article:

> The United States is pursuing a strategy of "flexible response on various fronts," attempting to concentrate its superior force in Asia, especially in Northeast Asia, so as to contain Soviet action in the Middle East and Europe by directly confronting the Soviet's Asian region. Even so, taking the

[88] Wan Guang, "U.S. Policies in the Middle East Are Inherently Self-Contradictory," *Xiandai guoji guanxi*, no. 2 (1986), *JPRS*-CPS-86-066, August 28, 1986, pp. 13–14.

[89] Wan Guang, "Mei-Su zhengduo Zhongdong de xin huihe," *Liaowang*, no. 42 (1984): 33.

[90] Wan Guang, "U.S. Policies in the Middle East Are Inherently Self-Contradictory," p. 10.

whole situation into consideration, the gains and losses in Europe are still the decisive factors in U.S.-Soviet contention for hegemony, and for a rather long period of time to come (for example, within this century), the strategic focus of both sides will not shift from Europe to Asia.[91]

Others believe that the U.S. buildup in Asia will be more long-standing. Writing in *Shijie zhishi*, Yuan Yuzhou pointed to the favorable points for attacking the Soviet Union's "weak flank" which Northeast Asia and the Northern Pacific offer the United States.[92] Another article noted that, should war break out, the United States intends to "bottle up" the Soviet Union in its coastal waters like a "turtle in a jar," thus exposing the Soviets to attack from "front and rear."[93] Wang Shuzhong, deputy director of the world politics research division of the CASS's Institute of World Economics and Politics, believes that the U.S. naval buildup in the Pacific and the intent to pursue a "two-ocean strategy" are the strongest indications of U.S. resolve to "slow the decline of U.S. hegemony in the Asia-Pacific region."[94]

Some leading experts on Asian security at the Institute of International Studies are less sanguine about the U.S. buildup in Asia. They see it as destabilizing and threatening.[95] One senior analyst at the institute even felt the need to warn the ASEAN countries to "maintain their vigilance against the United States."[96] In a similar commentary, journalistic pundit and senior America Watcher Peng Di warned of the threat of U.S. military action in the region:

> Although the Reagan administration has increased its military strength in the Asia-Pacific region, it has not taken any action as large-scale as its invasion of Grenada. This is not because the United States has another set of standards for conduct in this region. The only reason is that the opportunity for it to interfere directly has not yet appeared.[97]

In a speech to an internal meeting of Chinese international security specialists in 1982, senior foreign affairs adviser Huan Xiang levied

[91] Wang Baoqin, "Mei-Su de zhanlue zhongdian hui yixiang Yazhou ma?" *Shijie zhishi*, no. 21 (1984): 6.

[92] Yuan Yuzhou, "Wenzhong buwen de Yatai jushi," *Shijie zhishi*, no. 9 (1984): 3.

[93] Dong Xiang, "Su-Mei zai dongbei-Ya diqu de junshi duizhi," *Liaowang*, no. 15 (1984): 6–7.

[94] Wang Shuzhong, "Guanyu Meiguo zhanlue zhongdian wenti," *Shijie jingji yu zhengzhi neican*, no. 1 (1984): 39.

[95] Pei Monong, "Yazhou-Taipingyang diqu de xingshi he wenti," *Guoji wenti yanjiu*, no. 4 (1985): 12–14; Xie Wenqing, "Su-Mei zai ya-Tai diqu de junshi zhanlue," ibid., pp. 15–17.

[96] Tao Bingwei, "Ya-Tai diqu: zhengba yu fanba jiaozhi," *Shijie zhishi*, no. 2 (1984): 6.

[97] Peng Di, "Luetan Meiguo de 'baoshou' waijiao," *Liaowang*, no. 1 (1984): 42.

stinging criticisms of both American and Soviet roles in Asia. He criticized the United States for its "arrogance" in trying to create an "American world" at a maximum, or exerting "world leadership" at a minimum when, in fact, the United States is just a "superhegemonist."[98]

As would be expected, it is in the context of U.S.-Soviet competition that the hegemonists discuss American policy toward China. Unlike the Marxists, who argue that it is U.S. monopoly capital's financial interests in Taiwan that govern U.S. policy toward the island (and hence toward China), the hegemonists see the United States as trying to use China in its struggle against the Soviet Union. This perspective elicits condemnation from the hegemonists. The strategic factor in Sino-American relations is something that the America Watchers do not write openly about—at least not since the 1979–1980 period of the anti-Soviet united front. They limit their discussions— such as they exist—to classified publications. During the 1982–1984 period one such publication, *Shijie jingji yu zhengzhi meican* (Internal reference materials on world economics and politics), did carry several articles that criticized the United States for trying to use the "China factor" (*Zhongguo yinsu*) against the Soviet Union. One article charged the early Reagan administration (under Haig) with trying to "ally with China to oppose the Soviet Union" (*lian-Hua, kang-Su*).[99] Another claimed that "Since the 1970s the U.S. government has tried to play the 'China card' against the Soviet Union, and has also tried to play the 'Soviet card' and 'Taiwan card' against China. We are opposed to all such 'card playing.' "[100]

Other articles were less critical of a U.S.-China alignment against the Soviet Union. One article, written by America Watcher Ding Xinghao of the Shanghai Institute of International Studies, agreed that early in his first term Reagan was trying to "play the China card" against the Soviets—thus demonstrating continuity with his predecessors "Nixon, Ford, Carter, Brzezinski, Vance, and Haig," all of whom represent the "mainstream faction" (*zhupai*) of U.S. foreign policy, which takes an "international perspective" when viewing U.S.-China relations. But Ding argued that after Shultz became secretary of state, the United States no longer adhered to the concept of the "strategic triangle" (*sanjiao*) but rather had oriented its Asian pol-

[98] Huan Xiang, "Chaojidaguo yu Ya-tai diqu de heping yu anquan," *Shijie jingji yu zhengzhi neican*, no. 8 (1982): 1–2.

[99] Wang Baoqin and Xu Lei, "Ligen zhengfu de dui Su zhanlue," *Shijie jingji yu zhengzhi neican*, no. 11 (1982): 24.

[100] Wang Baoqin, Yan Yumei, and Liu Dacai, "Bashiniandai de Zhong, Mei, Su guanxi chutan," *Shijie jingji yu zhengzhi neican*, no. 10 (1983): 35.

icy toward Japan.[101] Ding went on to argue that "strategic factors" should continue to govern U.S.-China relations. He was not alone in this assessment. Others argued in the same journal that the Soviet threat to China remained and, despite U.S. policy toward Taiwan, the Americans had a positive role to play in augmenting Chinese security:

> At present the Soviet Union is still the major threat to our country, and it is still the major source of insecurity in the world. This point cannot but be reflected in our policy toward the United States and the Soviet Union. Under this condition, it is natural that Sino-American relations have reached a higher level than Sino-Soviet relations.[102]

Other analysts argued that as long as the U.S. China policy is guided by "anticommunism" (fangong) and attempts to "divide China" (fen Zhong) by practicing a "one China, one Taiwan" (yi Zhong, yi Tai) policy, China should not allow itself to be used as a "card."[103]

Returning to the U.S. Asia policy as a whole, many analysts explored whether the United States would be able to (re)establish its hegemonic control over Asia. All such analysts reject the possibility, principally for three reasons. First, there exist internal weaknesses in the United States that cannot sustain extensive overseas commitments. Second, there is essential parity between the superpowers in the region, and the Soviet Union will never permit the United States to gain the upper hand. Third, most nations reject bipolarity and refuse to become aligned with one of the superpowers.[104]

TOWARD A NEW INTERNATIONAL POLITICAL ORDER

In the estimate of many Chinese international relations specialists, the world has become multipolar and less susceptible to meddling by the superpowers and their establishment of hegemony. This perspective has been evident since the "theory of the three worlds" was first enunciated in the 1970s, but it gained currency again in the mid-1980s:

[101] Ding Xinghao, "Mei-Su kangheng Zhong-Meiguo rukekan 'Zhongguo yinsu.' " Shijie jingji yu zhengzhi neican, no. 2 (1983): 23.

[102] She Ge, "Dui Zhong-Su-Mei guanxizhong kugan zhanlue celue yuanze de tantao," Shijie jingji yu zhengzhi neican, no. 4 (1984): 5.

[103] Wang Shuzhong, "Mei-Su zhengba zhongde Meiguo dui Hua zhanlue," Shijie jingji yu zhengzhi neican, no. 3 (1983): 6, 8–9.

[104] See, for example, Chen Qimao, "Changing Asian-Pacific Patterns—Preliminary Exploration of the Establishment of a New International Political Order in the Asia-Pacific Region," Guoji zhanwang, no. 11 (1989): 3–7, JPRS-CAR-89-103, October 17, 1989, pp. 1–6.

The time that the United States and the Soviet Union could dominate and monopolize world affairs is over. The affairs of various regions and nations can only be decided by the nations and people concerned. A multipolar world is arising.[105]

More and more countries have adopted an independent foreign policy, and the democratization trend of relations between states is becoming more prominent. Now more and more countries in the world, including the allies of the two superpowers, have adopted an independent foreign policy under the general demand for peace and development and in light of their own conditions and interests, and thus no longer take orders from the two superpowers. Therefore, it is more difficult for the two superpowers to achieve their schemes to control, direct, and dominate the world.[106]

The U.S. strategic objective of regaining world hegemony will not be realized within Reagan's term of office. . . . From the angle of U.S. history, this effort represents an effort to stage a comeback to regain world hegemony, which was once shaken. However, the development of the world situation in the decades since World War II have made it impossible for the United States to enjoy the absolute world hegemony it enjoyed in the early postwar years.[107]

The polarized system is on the decline, but the United States and Soviet Union are not reconciled to giving up their hegemonic position. They are vehemently trying to uphold and strengthen the polarized system.[108]

These quotations (selected from among many) not only illustrate the hegemonists' assessment of the pluralization of world politics and the resulting effect on the superpowers' inability to "divide and conquer" the world, but also reveal approval of this development. As indicated in chapter 2, the hegemonist critique is very much rooted in a distaste for the big bullying the weak. From the mid-nineteenth to the mid-twentieth century, the Chinese were themselves victims of such a Darwinian state of international relations, and today they are attempting to lead the global condemnation of such hegemonist behavior. Most Chinese analysts find "power politics" abhorrent. One of the most articulate and hard-hitting critiques of "power politics" (*quanli zhengzhi*) can be found in an article by Chen Qurong of the Institute of Contemporary International Relations:

[105] Zhang Wuwei, "Mei-Su diqu zhengduo de xin qushi," *Guoji wenti yanjiu*, no. 4 (1986): 25.

[106] Li Dai and Zhou Yang, "Wulun dangdai de zhanzheng yu heping wenti," *Guoji wenti yanjiu*, no. 3 (1986): 5.

[107] Wan Guang, "Meiguo zaixiu zhanlue," *Liaowang*, no. 18 (1986): 29.

[108] Wan Guang, "Shijie duoyanghua de fazhan qushi," *Liaowang*, no. 11 (1987): 33.

Power politics is the attempt by one nation, relying on its political, economic, and especially its military capabilities, to rule or dominate another
nation. There are several basic precepts to power politics: first is the obsession with power, that is, the insane pursuit of "world supremacy" in international relations, the quest to establish an authoritative relation of
dominance and obedience between nations or races. Second, it is the obsession with military power, a propensity to use force, or threaten to use
force in international relations; it is the belief that crucial contemporary
problems are not solved by resolutions or majority votes, but by iron and
blood. Third, it is the obsession with the logic of "might makes right," and
the belief that sheer size, strength, and wealth give one the right to bully,
oppress, and cheat; and in order to achieve one's goals, one can abandon
principles, trustworthiness, and integrity. Fourth, power politics also has
a set of "power patterns," like "empire," "sphere of influence," "league,"
"axis," "buffer zones," and "satellite nations." Those who pursue power
politics adopt these patterns to establish and maintain their dominance
over other nations. The decline of power politics signifies the gradual loss
of the "utility" of the above precepts and patterns in international relations. It has become increasingly difficult to dominate, control, or influence another country by ways of imperialism, colonialism, and hegemonism.[109]

This lengthy quotation is indicative of the worldview underlying the
hegemonist critique of U.S. foreign policy. America Watchers of this
persuasion are preoccupied with power politics even if they abhor it.
They may hope to, and indeed already do, see indications of the
breakdown of bipolarity, but their focus remains the superpower
contention for global hegemony.

Perceptions of American China Policy

The hegemonist critique of American foreign policy is also clearly evident in the America Watchers' perceptions of American policy toward China. On this issue one sees the Marxist and non-Marxist perspectives converge. The common denominator is nationalism.
America Watchers in both schools are, in the end, Chinese national-
ists; and as such they both view U.S.-China relations in light of China's national interests and historical experience. High on the agenda
of national interest is the reunification of Taiwan with the China
mainland. With a few exceptions of articulated perceptions of the Tai-

[109] Chen Qurong, "Guoji guanxi minzhuhua yu shijie heping," *Xiandai guoji guanxi*,
no. 3 (1986): 1–9.

wan issue that link U.S. policy to monopoly capital's financial interest on the island, one does not see much evidence of a distinctly Marxist perspective on Sino-American relations since 1972. Rather, both Marxist and non-Marxist schools view U.S. policy largely in terms of infringement on Chinese national sovereignty.

From the perspective of the Chinese Communists, American support for the Guomindang government—both on the mainland and after it fled to Taiwan in 1949—has always been a key issue in the Sino-American relationship. From their perspective the absorption of Taiwan into the People's Republic is the last unfinished chapter in the Chinese civil war. Therefore, in what for the American side was very adroit language in the Shanghai Communiqué of 1972, the People's Republic took as U.S. accession to their long-standing claim over Taiwan: "the United States acknowledges that all Chinese on either side of the Taiwan Strait maintain there is but one China and that Taiwan is part of China. The United States does not challenge that position."[110] The first of these two sentences was also inserted into the Communiqué on the Establishment of Diplomatic Relations of December 15, 1978.[111] While the Chinese translation of this and other key phrases in these documents was accurate,[112] differences in interpretation of what this meant for China's suzerainty over Taiwan were readily apparent in the attendant unilateral statements of each government. The Chinese interpretation was quite evident in the following:

> As is known to all, the Government of the People's Republic of China is the sole legal government of China and Taiwan is a part of China. The question of Taiwan was the crucial issue obstructing the normalization of relations between China and the United States. It has now been resolved between the two countries in the spirit of the Shanghai Communiqué and through their joint efforts. . . . As for the way of bringing Taiwan back into the embrace of the motherland and reunifying the country, it is entirely China's internal affair.[113]

[110] The English text of the Shanghai Communiqué can be found as Appendix I in Richard H. Solomon, ed., *The China Factor* (Englewood Cliffs: Prentice-Hall, 1981): 296–300.

[111] Ibid., p. 301.

[112] I have compared the terminology in the English and Chinese texts and have found that, linguistically, the Chinese versions are direct translations and accurate portrayals of the inference of the English terms. Thus, the Chinese differences in interpretation exist over adherence to the *spirit* of the terminology, while the Americans tend to be much more legalistic by pointing out the policy leeway inherent in the ambiguity of the terminology in the texts. For the Chinese texts of these documents, see Li Changru and Shi Lujia, eds., *Zhong-Mei guanxi erbainian* (Beijing: Xinhua chubanshe, 1984).

[113] Solomon, ed., *The China Factor*, p. 304.

The Chinese government had served notice that the Taiwan issue was a matter of sovereignty and principle. This set the tenor of commentary by the America Watchers of both schools for the future.

Within a matter of days after the normalization of relations, an authoritative "commentator" article in the Communist Party's theoretical journal *Hongqi* emphasized the importance of these principles in Sino-American relations and warned of the need for strict adherence to them if the relationship were to progress:

> Based on these very principles, our government and that of the United States issued the Shanghai Communiqué seven years ago. It is also on the basis of these very principles that the two governments have now removed the obstacles to normalization of relations and established diplomatic relations. Continuous observance of these principles in the future can further help develop the relations between China and the United States.[114]

Other commentaries echoed similar notes of caution despite being positive in overall tone. The coverage of Deng Xiaoping's state visit to America was extensive and effusive. Through the medium of television, ordinary Chinese were given their first visual glimpse of the United States in thirty years. The United States and China had entered the "honeymoon" phase of their new relationship. It was not to last long.

As the United States Congress began to write legislation that would serve to guide the new "unofficial" relationship with "the people of Taiwan," known as the Taiwan Relations Act (TRA) when passed in April 1979, the Chinese press began to issue warnings. An authoritative commentator's article in the widely read periodical *Ban yue tan* (Semi-monthly talks) stated firmly:

> The Taiwan question involves China's sovereign rights. How can we allow ourselves to be manipulated on the major question of sovereignty? The Chinese people will definitely not allow this. Taiwan is a part of China. This is a question of principle and was stated in the joint communiqué when China and the United States established diplomatic relations. . . . China and the United States have established diplomatic relations and their relations have developed. The Chinese people are happy about this. They sincerely hope that these relations can be further developed on the basis of the principles stipulated in the Shanghai communiqué and the communiqué on the establishment of diplomatic relations between China and the United States.[115]

[114] Commentator, "A Major Event Favorable to World Peace," *Hongqi*, no. 1 (1979), *JPRS* 73074, March 23, 1979, p. 126.

[115] Commentator, "Refuting Several Fallacies of Certain Personages in the United States," *Ban yue tan*, no. 3 (1981): 16–17, *FBIS-CHI*, March 12, 1981, B2.

A year-end review of the state of Sino-American relations after one year sounded a similar warning. "The U.S. Congress has adopted the 'Taiwan Relations Act,' while some groups and individuals in that country still cling to the 'two China' concept. This is in violation of the principles laid down in the joint communiqué on the establishment of diplomatic relations and is to the detriment of the political foundation of the normalization."[116]

The next major round of protest from the Chinese side came after the June 1980 announcement that the United States had approved a $280 million arms package for Taiwan. The Chinese press became increasingly strident. One New China News Agency commentator stated bluntly:

> It is obvious that the continued and increased arms sales by the U.S. government to Taiwan constitute a breach of the principles embodied in the agreement of diplomatic relations between China and the United States and are harmful to the development of Sino-U.S. relations in a normal way. The Chinese people certainly could not remain indifferent toward such a move. . . . It is obvious that the U.S. arms supply to the Taiwan authorities is completely different than the maintenance of normal commercial relations with the people in Taiwan. . . . It is the strong demand of the Chinese people that the U.S. government stop forthwith its arms sales to Taiwan. They are watching developments in the United States with close attention.[117]

The next flareup resulted from the 1980 presidential election. Republican candidate Reagan's discussion of upgrading U.S diplomatic relations with the "Republic of China" to an official basis caused great consternation in Beijing and provoked a wave of critical commentary in the Chinese press throughout the summer. Not only did this invective hammer away at Reagan and other "doubledealers,"[118] it also again sharply criticized the Taiwan Relations Act as a violation of the principles guiding the relationship and an infringement on China's sovereignty. A *People's Daily* "commentator" put it this way:

> It is known to all that the "Taiwan Relations Act" is nothing but a domestic law of the United States. It can in no way serve as a legal basis for handling U.S.-China relations. It should be pointed out that many parts of the Act, including its claim to reserving the United States' right to continue inter-

[116] Zhou Cipu, "A Year After the Establishment of Sino-U.S. Diplomatic Relations," *Xinhua, FBIS-CHI,* December 31, 1979, B4.

[117] Commentator, "Do No Harm to Sino-U.S. Relations," *Xinhua,* June 20, 1980, *FBIS-CHI,* June 23, 1980, B2–3.

[118] See, for example, Wang Fei, "Who Will Benefit?" *Renmin ribao,* June 23, 1980, *FBIS-CHI,* June 25, 1980, B2–3.

fering in the Taiwan problem, run counter to the fundamental principles of the communiqué on the establishment of diplomatic relations between China and the United States. Therefore, the Chinese government has more than once made clear its solemn stance against the Act and demanded that the United States have the overall interests of Sino-U.S. relations in mind and strictly abide by the principles of the Sino-U.S. agreement and truly respect China's sovereignty and territorial integrity—a norm governing relations between states.[119]

An article in *China Youth Daily* echoed this editorial two days later: "This is a question of principle involving China's territorial integrity and national sovereignty, and is the firm and unshakable stand of the Chinese government and the Chinese people. This principle leaves no room for compromise."[120]

The dispatch of Reagan's running mate, and former China emissary, George Bush to Beijing to calm the fears of China's leaders did not work. The critical commentary continued as the election drew nearer. Both the *People's Daily* and *World Affairs* published tough warnings on the eve of the November election against any change in diplomatic status for Taiwan and called for the repeal of the Taiwan Relations Act.[121] With Reagan's election, the warnings continued, particularly as individuals (such as Richard Allen and Ray Cline) who were considered potential cabinet officials continued to call for an upgrading of ties with Taiwan.[122]

Throughout Reagan's first year in office the Chinese press continued to criticize the Taiwan Relations Act. The warnings became more emotionally charged and strident. It was no longer just a matter of principle, legality, and sovereignty, but increasingly a matter of national pride—"hurting the feelings of one billion Chinese people."[123] Some articles argued there was no "moral basis" for arms sales to Taiwan, since the United States seemed to have no problem "aban-

[119] Commentator, "Whither Does Reagan Intend to Lead the Sino-American Relationship?" *Renmin ribao*, August 28, 1980, *FBIS-CHI*, August 28, 1980, B1.

[120] Zhuang Zong, "A Question of Principle Leaving No Room for Compromise," *Zhongguo qingnian bao*, August 30, 1980, *JPRS* 76858, November 21, 1980, p. 1.

[121] Commentator, "An Inadvisable Move," *Renmin ribao*, October 9, 1980, *FBIS-CHI*, October 9, 1980, B1–2; Wen Fu, "Sunhai Zhong-mei guanxi de Meiguo 'yu Taiwan guanxifa,' " *Shijie zhishi*, no. 21 (1980): 14–15.

[122] See, for example, Lu Yan, "Those Who Show No Understanding of the Times Will Surely Meet with a Rebuff," *Renmin ribao*, December 5, 1980, *FBIS-CHI*, December 9, 1980, B1; Kuang Ming, "Ray Cline and People Like Him Must Not Miscalculate," *Guangming ribao*, January 18, 1981, *FBIS-CHI*, February 3, 1981, B2–3; Ren Ming, "Cline Talks Nonsense," *Renmin ribao*, January 9, 1981, *FBIS-CHI*, January 12, 1981, B3–4.

[123] Among many such articles, see, for example, Chen Zu, "Meiguo de 'yu Taiwan guanxifa,' " *Guangming ribao*, May 31, 1981, p. 3.

doning old friends such as Syngman Rhee and the Shah of Iran."[124] Others thought it was indicative of the "superpower complex" that drove Americans to interfere compulsively in the affairs of others.[125] Veteran America Watcher Peng Di, who articulated this perspective, also had a flare for the dramatic in describing how the Taiwan Relations Act "hangs suspended over the heads of the Chinese people like Damocles' sword in Greek mythology."[126] Others felt it showed a "declining power" trying to hold onto its remaining overseas possessions.[127] In evaluating the argument of a "security" justification, another extensive review of the TRA by analysts at the Institute of International Studies disputed the claim that Taiwan needed "defensive" weapons because "everyone knows that the local Taiwan administration is obtaining American weapons for the purpose of resisting the Chinese central authorities."[128] In an article published in the U.S. journal *Foreign Affairs*, Huan Xiang also dismissed, in turn, all of these "reasons" for continued arms sales, and came to the conclusion that

> Evidently, none of these explanations has touched the crux of the question. In reality, there probably is a basic guideline among a number of Americans, that is, to obstruct China's reunification, to keep Taiwan in the U.S. sphere of influence and to use it to hold China in check. This antiquated sphere-of-influence theory should never be used in Sino-U.S. relations. It is sheer power politics, and is both unwise and unrealistic, and to keep various checks around a country in the hope that this would prevent it from growing too big and independent, from becoming a "potential enemy," and would keep it perpetually under one's control.[129]

By the end of 1981 the Chinese began to take some solace in their campaign against the TRA and arms sales because they detected a "domestic debate" in the United States over the arms sales issue. The *People's Daily* took note of the public support given to China's position by such Americans as Jerome Cohen, Christopher Phillips, A. Doak Barnett, Zbigniew Brzezinski, and Leonard Unger.[130] The

---

[124] Hua Xiu, "The Limp U.S. Policy towards China—Further Comment on the Question of Selling Arms to Taiwan," *Liaowang*, no. 4 (1981), *FBIS-CHI*, August 6, 1981, B1.

[125] Peng Di, "The Superpower Complex," B3–6.

[126] Ibid., B4.

[127] Mu Guangren, "The Current U.S. Policy towards China," *Ban yue tan*, no. 16 (1981), *FBIS-CHI*, September 11, 1981, B1–2.

[128] Zhuang Qubing, Zhang Hongzeng, and Pan Tongwen, "Ping Meiguo de 'yu Taiwan guanxifa,' " *Guoji wenti yanjiu*, no. 1 (1983): 23.

[129] Huan Xiang, "On Sino-U.S. Relations," *Foreign Affairs* (Fall 1981): 47.

[130] Yuan Xianlu, "Tong Taiwan chushou wuqi wenti Meiguo guonei fenxi qilun," *Renmin ribao*, December 18, 1981, p. 7.

America Watchers particularly took heart in the publication of Barnett's study *The FX Decision*, which counseled against selling Taiwan an upgraded jet fighter.[131]

But this positive development did not make the hegemonists back off from pressing their case. On the last day of the year another authoritative "commentator" article in the *People's Daily* sounded the sovereignty theme again:

> What China requires from the United States on the Taiwan issue is that it should properly respect China's sovereignty and territorial integrity and not interfere in China's internal affairs. This is the most elementary requirement of a sovereign state. For a century the Chinese people made bloody sacrifices, advancing wave upon wave, in fighting for their national independence and sovereignty. Today, the Chinese people have stood up, and they resolutely will not tolerate any foreign country's intentions to violate China's sovereignty, carve up its territory, and interfere in its internal affairs. This is a major question that involves the national emotions of one billion Chinese people. . . . In these circumstances, if the United States goes on selling arms to Taiwan, persistently violates China's sovereignty, and hinders its peaceful reunification, it is perfectly reasonable to ask: What designs does the United States in fact harbor on China's territory of Taiwan? Should it or should it not be called hegemonism if the United States ignores the principles of international relations, violates the sovereignty of other countries, and interferes in their internal affairs in this way?[132]

Despite the harsh critique contained in this key editorial, and with an important caveat about governing "principles," the article also contained a new and important clause: "This means that in accordance with the principles of international relations and the communiqué on the establishment of Sino-American relations, the United States should properly respect China's sovereignty and should not interfere in its internal affairs and should not sell arms to Taiwan. Under the premise of recognizing this principle, *both sides can hold consultations on ways to solve this problem* (emphasis added)."[133] In other words, as long as the United States was willing to come to the bargaining table with these "principles" (concessions) in mind, China was willing to negotiate.

Negotiations did indeed take place during the first half of 1982,

---

[131] Sha Dawei, "Americans Voice Opposition to Arms Sales to Taiwan," *Renmin ribao*, December 22, 1981, *FBIS-CHI*, December 22, 1981, B1.

[132] Commentator, "China Resolutely Opposes Foreign Arms Sales to Taiwan," *Renmin ribao*, December 31, 1981, *FBIS-CHI*, December 31, 1981, B1.

[133] Ibid., B2.

resulting in the important joint communiqué of August 17. As the negotiations proceeded, the Chinese commentators continued their diatribes—perhaps as diplomatic posturing. In April, a key "commentator" article (reportedly written by Xue Mouhong) entitled "Where Lies the Crux of Sino-American Relations?" was published in the influential journal *Guoji wenti yanjiu* (International studies). It warned of "retrogression" in U.S.-China relations because of the Taiwan arms sales problem. The article sounded a somber warning:

> Whether or not Sino-American relations will retrogress depends on whether or not the United States will earnestly respect China's sovereignty and make up its mind to solve the question of selling arms to Taiwan. . . . We have ample patience and flexibility. However, there is a limit to our forebearance, and we will also never barter away our principles. The situation in which Sino-American relations are seriously threatened at present is entirely created by the United States. . . . Relations between the two countries today are at a crossroads. While the Chinese side is striving for good prospects, it is also prepared for a bad ending.[134]

The Chinese press promptly reiterated the theme that U.S.-China relations were at a turning point and affixed all blame on the American side. A short while later an article in *Semi-Monthly Talks*, for example, in reporting on the visits of Vice-President Bush and Senate majority leader Baker, said the following:

> Sino-U.S. relations are now at a crossroad. Whether they will progress or retrogress has become one of the most important topics attracting worldwide attention. Bush and Baker came to China at this critical juncture to discuss the relations between the two countries with the Chinese leaders. Just as people expected, their visits did not effect any breakthrough in Sino-American relations, and the Taiwan problem is still a stumbling block hindering the progress of the relations between the two countries. . . . The Taiwan problem is created by the United States itself.[135]

Then, in July, as the negotiations between the two governments were nearing a climax, *International Studies* published another hard-hitting article. Written by Zi Zhongyun, and ostensibly a historical study of American policy toward China during 1948–1950, the article's implications for the present were clear. Zi concluded her study of how the United States made the wrong choice in 1949 with a warning for the present:

[134] Commentator, "Zhong-Mei guanxi de zhengjie hezai?" *Guoji wenti yanjiu*, no. 2 (1982): 6, 7.

[135] Zhou Cipu, "Fazhan Zhong-Mei guanxi de zhang'ai zai nali?" *Ban yue tan*, no. 13 (1982): 12.

Frankly speaking, the fact that there still remains a "Taiwan issue" in the relations between China and the United States is the consequence of the imperialistic, expansionist policy on the part of the United States. . . . How Sino-American relations develop in the future depends on whether U.S. policy makers will awaken to the irresistible law of learning from historical experience, throw off their heavy burden, and catch up with the tide of the times.[136]

Though known as a tough critic of American policy toward Taiwan, Zi does point up the operative assumption in the minds of many America Watchers that since the United States made a "mistake" by siding with the Guomindang during the Chinese civil war and in 1949, it ought to rectify that mistake by cutting off Taiwan. They view U.S. policy toward China and Taiwan in zero-sum terms and conclude that the U.S. recognition of the People's Republic of China as the sole legal government in the Shanghai Communiqué and normalization accords is proof positive that the United States had tacitly admitted the previous mistake. What galls them is that this tacit admission is not matched by rectifying the mistake through breaking contact with Taiwan, but on the contrary perpetuating the unresolved civil war. At the heart of their anger is the feeling of helplessness in the face of a big power that is once again manipulating and partitioning China.

On August 17, 1982, the Joint Communiqué on the Question of U.S. Arms Sales to Taiwan was issued. Among the key passages were the following:

Respect for each other's sovereignty and territorial integrity and non-interference in each other's internal affairs constitute the fundamental principles guiding U.S.-China relations. . . . The United States Government attaches great importance to its relations with China, and reiterates that it has no intention of infringing on Chinese sovereignty and territorial integrity, or interfering in China's internal affairs, or pursuing a policy of "two Chinas" or "one China, one Taiwan." . . . Having in mind the foregoing statements of both sides, the United States Government states that it does not seek to carry out a long-term policy of arms sales to Taiwan, that its arms sales to Taiwan will not exceed, either in qualitative or in quantitative terms, the level of those supplied in recent years since the establishment of diplomatic relations between the United States and China, and that it intends to reduce gradually its sales of arms to Taiwan, leading over a period of time to a final resolution. In so stating, the United States acknowl-

[136] Zi Zhongyun, "Lishi de kao'an: Xin Zhongguo dansheng qianhou Meiguo de dui Tai zhengce," *Guoji wenti yanjiu*, no. 3 (1982): 41.

edges China's consistent position regarding the thorough settlement of this issue.[137]

The ink was hardly dry on the communiqué when the *People's Daily* issued the following warning to the United States:

> The problem now is that the United States must be as good as its word and take practical measures to solve the problem of selling arms to Taiwan. . . . The issuance of the Sino-U.S. joint communiqué has broken the deadlock between the two countries in solving the problem of arms sales to Taiwan, but this does not mean that the problem has been completely solved. The dark cloud that has blurred the prospects of Sino-U.S. relations has not been completely swept away. . . . It is still necessary to point out that the fundamental obstacle to the development of Sino-American relations is the U.S. "Taiwan Relations Act."[138]

Follow-up articles in September criticized various "anti-China elements" in Congress and the Republican right wing for trying to undermine implementation of the communiqué.[139] These criticisms continued into 1983.[140] The Chinese press, for example, unleashed a salvo of expected criticism of the November 1983 Senate Foreign Relations Committee resolution on the "future of Taiwan."[141]

The reciprocal exchange of state visits between then Premier Zhao Ziyang and President Reagan in 1984 restored some of the momentum to bilateral relations. But the Chinese press commentary during both visits, particularly that of NCNA Washington bureau chief Peng Di, remained highly critical and took every opportunity to attack the Taiwan Relations Act.[142] In addition, during Reagan's visit to China the Chinese made it known that they believed the United States had not lived up to the 1982 communiqué. Then Vice-Foreign Minister and Director of the Foreign Ministry's Bureau of American and Oce-

---

[137] See the text contained in Richard Solomon, *Chinese Political Negotiating Behavior* (Santa Monica: The Rand Corporation, 1985), pp. 25–26.

[138] Editorial, "Strictly Observe the Agreement and Overcome Obstructions," *Renmin ribao*, August 17, 1982, *FBIS-CHI*, August 17, 1982, B5.

[139] See, for example, Zhuang Qubing and Pan Tongwen, "Zhong-Mei lianhe gongbao fabiao yihou," *Shijie zhishi*, no. 18 (1982): 2.

[140] See, for example, Peng Di, "Meiguo dui Hua zhengce hefa hecong?" *Liaowang*, no. 26 (1983): 8–9.

[141] Commentator, "How Can China Tolerate Others Interfering in Its Internal Affairs?" *Renmin ribao*, November 20, 1983, *FBIS-CHI*, November 21, 1983, B2–3; Commentator, "Zhong-Mei guanxi fazhan zhongde yiduan nipai," *Renmin ribao*, November 14, 1983, p. 5; Editorial, "Gross Interference in China's Internal Affairs," *China Daily*, November 15, 1983, p. 4.

[142] For examples of this commentary see my *Coverage of the United States in Key Chinese Periodicals During 1984*, pp. 7–13.

anic Affairs Zhu Qizhen (later Chinese ambassador to the United States) told American television viewers in an interview, "In our opinion the United States has not honored its commitments in the August 17 Joint Communiqué in some aspects. For instance, in terms of quantity, the United States has gone far beyond the obligation they have assumed in the Joint Communiqué."[143]

In September 1984 Li Shenzhi, director of the CASS's America Institute, published an article in the *People's Daily* reviewing the development of Sino-American relations. It was generally an upbeat account but still took the United States to task for "encroaching on China's sovereignty, interfering in China's internal affairs, and hurting China's national feelings."[144]

Since 1985, however, Chinese criticism of American policy toward Taiwan—arms sales and the TRA—dropped off considerably. Of course one finds the odd article, but generally speaking since the Joint Communiqué and exchange of state visits in 1984 the volume and intensity of such criticisms dropped off noticeably. To be sure, other issues came onto the bilateral agenda (trade, technology transfer, Tibet, human rights, and the various issues associated with the Tiananmen massacre) that the Chinese have criticized, but the Taiwan issue enjoyed a respite during this period. This is probably due to the fact that arms sales did indeed begin to decline in quantity, if not quality. China's America Watchers also probably began to accept the fact that the Taiwan Relations Act would not be repealed.

With Taiwan relegated to the back burner of the America Watchers' agenda, commentary on the U.S.-China relations and American China policy from 1986 to 1989 was primarily devoted to analyzing various aspects of the relationship and monitoring high-level exchanges between the two countries.

The year 1987 was deemed a bad year for Sino-American relations as the hegemonist critique of U.S. policy gained momentum. None other than Huan Xiang published a blistering attack on American "wanton interference in China's internal affairs" during 1987 that introduced "unstable factors" into the relationship. Huan cited six examples of U.S. "interference" during 1987: (1) U.S. congressional support for the "Taiwan Independence Movement"; (2) congressional opposition to China's birth control policies; (3) the invitation from the U.S. Congress to the Dalai Lama, who intended to "split China"; (4) congressional criticism of China for selling Silkworm mis-

---

[143] Text of interview with Zhu Qizhen, ABC News, April 26, 1984.

[144] Li Shenzhi, "Zhong-Mei guanxi de zhongyao zhuanxi," *Renmin ribao*, September 29, 1984, p. 7.

siles to Iran, which, Huan claimed, was never done "directly"; (5) the "political blackmail" of the Congress in holding up technology transfers to China; (6) passing of "anti-China" bills in the Congress condemning China for persecuting intellectuals, not respecting freedom of speech and the press, and stealing technological secrets. Huan deemed these six issues as "wanton interference in China's internal affairs" and "rude political blackmail against China. In brief, these are an obvious demonstration of hegemonism." Obviously, Huan singled out Congress as particularly guilty of such hegemonist behavior. But Congress was not alone in Huan's estimate: "In my opinion a certain number of American statesmen and people of the press circles have indeed a very strong sense of great-nation chauvinism and think that the United States has all the truth and strength in the world at its disposal. . . . These people proceed in everything from U.S. interests, but they do not understand and are unwilling to understand the legitimate interests of other countries. This will certainly have a negative effect on Sino-U.S. relations." Huan concluded his diatribe by setting out four conditions necessary if retrogression of relations was not to occur: (1) increased mutual respect; (2) improved mutual understanding; (3) removing ideological bias from state relations; and (4) building on past achievements. Huan's prognosis, in the end, was not optimistic.[145]

In 1988 the America Watchers viewed Sino-American relations in a more positive light. In July Secretary of State Shultz paid an official visit to Beijing, which was covered extensively and positively in the Chinese press. Criticism of the United States was muted, and the commentary pointed to the satisfactory development of relations in the decade since normalization.[146]

The ten-year anniversary occasioned an outpouring of articles on Sino-American relations. The CASS's Institute of American Studies (IAS) convened a symposium to commemorate the event and to coincide with the founding of the Chinese Association of American Studies. The symposium was an unprecedented congregation of China's leading America Watchers. It resulted in publication of the volume *Zhong-Mei guanxi shinian* (Ten years of Sino-American relations), the first book of its kind written by Chinese to appear in China.[147]

Institute of American Studies Director Zi Zhongyun opened the

[145] Huan Xiang, "Sino-U.S. Relations Over the Past Year," *Liaowang*, no. 2 (1988): 22–23, *FBIS-CHI*, January 15, 1988, pp. 2–5.
[146] See the coverage in *FBIS-CHI*, July 14, 15, 18, and 19, 1988.
[147] Zhongguo shehui kexueyuan Meiguo yanjiusuo he Zhonghua Meiguo xuehui, eds., *Zhong-Mei guanxi shinian* (Beijing: Shangye yinshuguan, 1989).

symposium and the volume in her characteristic blunt and critical style. Her contribution—translated as "The Confluence of Interests: The Basis of State Relations"—is an example par excellence of the hegemonist school of thought underlying the America Watchers' view of American foreign policy, and China policy in particular. Zi began with a rendition of the five principles of peaceful coexistence that, she believes, should guide the relationship. Zi took note of the fact that China has attached more importance to the five principles than has the United States. Why?

> because in modern history relations between China and the big powers were rarely established on an equal basis. The purpose of the Chinese in carrying out a bloody battle for several generations was to end our national humiliation, and to safeguard our sovereignty and territorial integrity. . . . In the postwar period, the United States interfered once in the civil war in China. Later it pursued a policy of isolating, imposing a blockade on, and cutting apart China. China believes that it was a victim in previous Sino-U.S. relations.[148]

Madame Zi then proceeded to analyze the strategic, economic, and cultural exchange dimensions of U.S.-China relations. She dwelled at length on the latter and accused the United States of launching another "cultural invasion": "As far as the United States is concerned it has the idea of, intentionally or unintentionally, imposing its value concepts on others, and that of the 'American center.' "[149] Zi's critique of the U.S. China policy has always stood at the most conservative and critical end of the spectrum. She has, over the years, been at the forefront of criticizing American policy toward Taiwan, takes every opportunity to denounce U.S. interference in China's internal affairs, and in her own writings about U.S. diplomacy is unrelenting in her critique of U.S. attempts to impose its will on the world. She is a leading and typical example of the hegemonist opinion group within the America-watching community.

Li Shenzhi, Zi's predecessor as director of the Institute of American Studies, also spoke at the symposium. Li has been a personal adviser on the United States to Zhou Enlai, Deng Xiaoping, and Zhao Ziyang. As discussed in the introduction, Li single-handedly built the institute from its inception in 1979 and has played a major role in the America-watching community ever since. In his speech, Li also harped on the Taiwan issue, referring to it as a "thorn in the side" of

---

[148] Ibid., p. 21; also published in *Meiguo yanjiu*, no. 2 (1989): 16–36, and *Renmin ribao*, December 30, 1988, p. 7, *FBIS-CHI*, January 10, 1989, pp. 6–12.

[149] *Zhong-Mei guanxi shinian*, p. 33.

Sino-American relations. "Until it is solved, it will always be the number one obstacle that must be removed," Li stated.[150]

The other twenty-three papers presented at the symposium examined various aspects of the Sino-American relationship. IAS strategic specialist Zhang Jingyi wrote on the changing nature of the strategic relationship between the United States and China.[151] Zhang argued essentially that despite the changing nature of the Soviet threat to both countries, parallel strategic interests remained for both nations with respect to third areas (Northeast Asia, Southeast Asia, Taiwan, and the Middle East) and intrinsically in bilateral relations. On this basis Zhang felt that the strategic dimension would continue to play an important role in the relationship, although diminished from previous years.

Seasoned America Watcher Zhuang Qubing of the Institute of International Studies looked more closely at the "Soviet factor" (*Sulian yinsu*) in American China policy.[152] Zhuang agreed with Zhang Jingyi that the strategic (Soviet) factor would diminish in importance in coming years, and as such American China policy could be expected to rest more on bilateral interests. But, Zhuang maintained, it was precisely the Soviet factor that drove the United States to broaden the relationship with China from one of purely strategic cooperation that characterized the early years. Zhuang cited U.S. technology transfer policy toward China, the expansion of economic cooperation (particularly the facilitation of international lending), and the expansion of military ties as evidence of the role that the Soviet factor played in U.S. China policy.

Beijing Institute of International Strategic Studies America Watcher Liu Pei picked up on the latter point in his paper on "security relations" between the United States and China.[153] Liu detailed the range of arms transfers, dual-use technology sales, confidence-building measures, and consultations between the American and Chinese military establishments. Despite the impressive developments in this realm of relations, Liu thought that security cooperation would be limited in the future because of the limited absorptive capacity on the

[150] As reported in Qin Lang, "Li Shenzhi Believes that Sino-American Relations Have a Broader Basis for Relations Than Ten Years Ago," *Zhongguo xinwenshe*, December 18, 1988, *FBIS-CHI*, December 21, 1988, p. 3.

[151] Zhang Jingyi, "Zhong-Mei guanxi zhongde anquan yinsu: Huigu yu zhanwang," *Zhong-Mei guanxi shinian*, pp. 38–52.

[152] Zhuang Qubing, "Meiguo dui Hua zhengce zhongde Sulian yinsu," ibid., pp. 66–81.

[153] Liu Pei, "Zhong-Mei jianjiao yilai de liangguo anquan guanxi," ibid., pp. 53–65.

Chinese military establishment, the relatively low priority given to military modernization in China, and the declining Soviet threat.

IAS America Watcher He Di wrote on the role of the Taiwan issue from 1979 to 1989.[154] He argued that the United States and China had learned to manage the Taiwan problem effectively, and that the 1982 Joint Communiqué was a basis of effective compromise. He felt that since the normalization of relations, the United States had "basically ended the history of interfering in China's internal affairs." This view is at variance with many other America Watchers, notably institute director Zi Zhongyun. Nonetheless, He Di put forward the view that the United States still operated a "dual policy" with respect to Taiwan and the mainland, and that this represented "official diplomacy in essence."

Beijing University America Watcher Wang Jisi contributed a paper on the relationship between American diplomatic thought and American China policy.[155] Wang argued in this and a later article[156] that the traditions of both "realism" and "idealism" have guided American China policy over the years. For Professor Wang perceptions are an important variable in assessing international relations in general and Sino-American relations in particular. Together with his Beijing University colleague Yuan Ming, Wang is the only America Watcher to have paid attention to this factor in the relationship.[157]

Wang Jisi argued that from the Truman through the Johnson administrations the United States based its China policy on "idealism," and as such badly misperceived China and missed opportunities for a rapprochement based on shared interests. Kissinger and Nixon, however, were hard-headed "realists" who grasped the potential of U.S.-China relations in a world of shifting balance of power. President Carter, according to Wang, was an idealist who viewed China in more traditional missionary terms, but National Security Adviser Brzezinski balanced Carter's zeal through his realism. President Reagan was an idealist at the outset of his administration while Secretary of State Haig was thought to be a realist. Wang attributed Haig's resignation in part to this clash with his boss. Eventually, however, Reagan came around to a more realistic assessment of China. In conclusion, Wang thought that both strands of diplomacy bore within them

[154] He Di, "Mei-Tai guanxi shinian," ibid., pp. 82–109.

[155] Wang Jisi, "Meiguo waijiao sixiang chuantong yu dui Hua zhengce," ibid., pp. 130–62.

[156] Wang Jisi, "Idealism, Realism: The Weave of U.S. China Policy," *Beijing Review*, no. 3 (1989): 10–14.

[157] Also, see Yuan Ming, "Luelun Zhongguo zai Meiguo de yinxiang," *Meiguo yanjiu*, no. 1 (1989): 35–49.

potential problems for American China policy. The realist school viewed China too myopically, overstressing the strategic factor and the "China card," while the idealists sought to impose the American system and values on China.

IAS America Watcher Zhang Yi contributed an interesting paper to the symposium on the role of Congress in American China policy.[158] Interestingly, like Wang Jisi, Zhang Yi found that idealism and realism were reflected in congressional China policy. The idealists, Zhang argued, were anti-Communists and anti-China elements who let ideology guide their approach to China policy. It was this group, Zhang felt, who were responsible for raising human rights concerns, Tibet, China's birth control program, and so forth. On the other side of the aisle were realists who had done much for expanding Sino-American relations through passing various legislation, including OPIC funding, most-favored-nation trade status, and the nuclear agreement, and had encouraged the relaxation of export control' restrictions. Both groups, however, have acted as Taiwan's guarantor since the passage of the Taiwan Relations Act.

IAS America Watcher Zhang Yuehong contributed an interesting paper evaluating U.S press coverage of China and Chinese press coverage of the United States during the ten years since normalization of relations.[159] Zhang gave Chinese journalists high marks for their coverage of the United States. Zhang observed, as noted in this study, that most NCNA reports are straightforward descriptions of events. He attributed this to the fact that "Chinese reporters think a factual report without imposing a prejudiced view (good or bad) will help [Chinese] readers understand the United States." American correspondents in China did not receive as high marks from Zhang because they tended to play up the negative aspects of reform. Zhang felt that journalists from both sides were subject to cultural bias. In terms of total coverage, Zhang's research revealed that in the *People's Daily* the United States ranks first in foreign coverage, while in the *New York Times* China ranks fifth of all countries. Zhang concluded with a plea for more accurate reporting and perceptions; only on this basis did he feel the relationship could continue to expand.

The America Watchers' perceptions of the United States during 1989 were dominated by two events: the state visit by President Bush to China in February and the American role in the "counterrevolutionary rebellion" of April–June.

[158] Zhang Yi, "Meiguo guohui yu Zhong-Mei jianjiao shinian," *Zhong-Mei guanxi shinian*, pp. 110–29.
[159] Zhang Yuehong, "Zhong-Mei xinwen jiaoliu xinwen," ibid., pp. 288–307.

Bush's visit itself was amply covered in the domestic press. The president was welcomed as an "old friend of China" dating to his days as chief of the Liaison Office during the 1970s, and his meetings with Chinese officials were given full coverage. The Chinese press, however, seemed to seize upon the meeting with then Communist Party General Secretary Zhao Ziyang. This was not for protocol reasons alone. Indeed, one suspects NCNA was instructed to replay Zhao's remarks widely. Rarely is the actual dialogue of such meetings revealed in the Chinese press. Why this time? The answer is because Zhao scolded Bush for American meddling in Chinese affairs. The hegemonist critique had percolated up through the system to even the broad-minded Zhao Ziyang. Zhao, during his tenure as premier and general secretary, had been the Chinese leadership's leading advocate of Sino-American relations and in fact had often pushed the relationship forward when his more conservative-minded colleagues had wished to restrict it. Zhao's statements to Bush, therefore, must be seen in the context of the behind-the-scenes political struggle then being waged in the Chinese leadership over the future of the reform agenda—particularly political reform. Zhao was clearly on the defensive at this time vis-à-vis the conservatives, and Bush's visit was therefore an opportunity for him to demonstrate his nationalistic credentials and thereby buy himself some room for maneuver on other issues.

Zhao told Bush that

> Some people in the American media like to be depicted as being close to those Chinese who are advocating importation of a political system from the West, including the United States, in an attempt to influence the U.S government's current and future China policy. . . . Therefore, the fact that certain persons in American society support those Chinese who are not satisfied with the Chinese government will be detrimental not only to China's political stability and to the progress of its reform, but also to Sino-American friendship.[160]

The postvisit coverage also stressed the theme of American meddling in China's internal affairs.[161] The only exception was an article by Zhuang Qubing surveying American policy toward China since 1972. As something of a swan song before going into retirement, Zhuang's

[160] Zhang Liang, "When Meeting With Bush, Zhao Ziyang Stresses that China Will Not Copy Other Countries' Systems and that Reform Can Only Be Promoted Gradually and in a Practical Way," *Renmin ribao*, February 27, 1989, p. 1, *FBIS-CHI*, February 27, 1989, p. 23.

[161] See Xin Peihe, "Yici bi zhengshi fangwen hai zhongyao de gongzuo fangwen," *Shijie zhishi*, no. 6 (1989): 6–7.

analysis was both detailed and upbeat. While noting existing grievances between the two countries, but in a distinctly low-key fashion, Zhuang concluded that the "common interests and needs of the two countries, and the trends of the times, will surely make the United States develop its China policy in a direction favorable to the people of the two countries."[162]

Zhuang's prediction was not to be borne out. The prodemocracy demonstrations during April–May 1989 across China—but concentrated in Tiananmen Square—and the political fallout from the People's Liberation Army's suppression of the demonstrations had a major negative impact on Sino-American relations. Deng Xiaoping held the United States partially responsible for fomenting the demonstrations and contributing to their sustenance. "Frankly speaking, the United States was involved too deeply in the turmoil and counterrevolutionary rebellion that occured in Beijing not long ago," Deng told former President Nixon in October 1989. This, Deng told Nixon, had brought Sino-U.S. relations to a "stalemate."[163]

Deng's assessment stimulated an outpouring of anti-American invective not seen in the Chinese media since the period prior to rapprochement. This critical invective again exemplified the hegemonist critique of the United States. Congress was singled out for particular criticism. The criticism by Liu Huaqiu, vice–foreign minister in charge of American affairs, was typical in this regard. Liu called in U.S. Ambassador Lilley for official protests on several occasions during the fall of 1989 and spring of 1990. On one occasion he informed Lilley:

> I am instructed to express our utmost indignation and lodge a strong protest with the U.S. government against the hegemonist act of the U.S. Congress which, basing its legislation on rumors, has willfully trampled on the basic norms governing international relations and has wantonly interfered in China's internal affairs. . . . Certain U.S. congressmen, addicted to bias and disregarding the realities, have readopted the amendment on sanctions against China. This can only reveal their stubborn anti-China position and their true nature of pushing power politics. . . . The U.S. government ought to have met its commitments under the successive Sino-U.S. joint communiqués and promptly stopped the U.S. Congress from adopting anti-China bills again and again in contravention of the above principles and grossly interfering in China's internal affairs. The U.S. govern-

[162] Zhuang Qubing, "1972 nian yilai Meiguo dui Hua zhengce de huigu yu liaowang," *Guoji wenti yanjiu*, no. 2 (1989): 15–24. The quotation is from p. 23.

[163] As quoted in Daniel Southerland, "Deng Says U.S. Involved in Democracy Movement," *Washington Post*, November 1, 1989.

ment has an unshirkable responsibility for the unbridled anti-China waves stirred up by the U.S. Congress.[164]

The U.S. Department of State's annual human rights report took the Chinese government to task for the use of armed force to suppress the demonstrations as well as the postmassacre political persecution. This report also drew sharp criticism from the Chinese Foreign Ministry and again typified the hegemonists' critique:

> The U.S. government smears the Chinese government on a series of issues that are purely China's internal affairs. The principle of noninterference in the internal affairs of other countries is a basic code of international law. What right does the U.S. government have to make irresponsible remarks about and flagrantly interfere in China's internal affairs? Where does the U.S. government want to lead Sino-U.S. relations with such an act that serves to undermine the bilateral relations and harm the feelings of the Chinese people? The repeated acts of grossly interfering in China's internal affairs by the U.S. government are but expressions of out-and-out hegemonism and power politics.[165]

China's National People's Congress, meeting in February 1990, also chastised the United States for the sanctions imposed after the June 4 crackdown:

> The short-sighted anti-China act of certain members of the U.S. Congress . . . will only prompt the Chinese people to deepen their understanding of the nature of hegemonism and power politics. . . . We would like to advise these members of the U.S. Congress to sober up and look ahead so as to free themselves from indulgence in arrogance, prejudice, and lack of reason and, taking account of the overall and long-term interests of Sino-U.S. relations, to change over to a new way and stop their wanton interference in the internal affairs of other countries.[166]

These official views of U.S. hegemonist interference were also echoed by the America Watchers in the post-Tiananmen period. Many criticized the United States for the policy of "peaceful evolution" whereby the United States attempts to subvert the socialist system in

[164] Xinhua News Agency, "China Protests against Amendment on Sanctions Passed by U.S. Congress," BBC *Summary of World Broadcasts—Far East*, February 3, 1990, A1/1.

[165] Xinhua News Agency, "China Expresses 'Extremely Furious Indignation' Over U.S. Human Rights Report," BBC *Summary of World Broadcasts—Far East*, February 23, 1990, A1/1.

[166] Xinhua News Agency, "China's NPC and CPPCC Protest Against U.S. Congress Sanctions Amendment," BBC *Summary of World Broadcasts—Far East*, February 6, 1990, A1/1.

China by peaceful means. The policy of "peaceful evolution" supposedly began with John Foster Dulles, according to hardliner Huo Shiliang of the CASS's America Institute, but has accelerated since the normalization of relations.[167] A colleague of Huo's at the America Institute went further:

> Before June 4 China considered the United States as a trustworthy and friendly country, but since June 4 the United States has become the main source of instability in China. Peaceful evolution is the main threat to China's stability today. The ideological struggle will be the most important factor in future Sino-American relations. The U.S. will again become the major threat to China, but not a military one. The Taiwan problem will remain important, but the ideological struggle—particularly peaceful evolution—will be primary.[168]

Former ambassador to the United States Zhang Wenjin agrees that it is the ideological and cultural sphere that is most troubling: "During the present time the United States is trying to export its values to China and is trying to impose its will."[169]

America Watchers at the Institute of International Studies hold similar views of an ideological struggle with the United States. Said one, "There is a conflict between two ideologies in U.S.-China relations. State-to-state relations should not be ideological, but based on the principle of noninterference in internal affairs. The United States is attempting to make China a capitalist country. American hegemonic behavior is one of the central aspects of American foreign policy since World War II. Its core is to sacrifice other's national interests for its own."[170] An IIS colleague agreed: "The most important factor is mutual respect for the social systems of both countries. On the pretext of human rights the United States has gone too far in trying to impose its own image on China. The root cause of this is the missionary/Messianic impulse, a superiority complex, which is deep-rooted in U.S. foreign policy. . . . We are for exchange but not the imposition of one's views on the other. We admire academic cooperation and open-door exchanges, but not the imposition of values on China."[171]

Thus, one sees in the America Watchers' perceptions of U.S. China policy a preoccupation with preserving cultural integrity and what

---

[167] Huo Shiliang, "Lun Dulousi de heping zhexue jichi heping biange shuo," *Meiguo yanjiu*, no. 1 (1990): 7–36.

[168] Interview at the CASS Institute of American Studies, May 7, 1990.

[169] Interview with Zhang Wenjin in Beijing, May 16, 1990.

[170] Interview at the Institute of International Studies, May 18, 1990.

[171] Ibid.

they perceive to be China's state sovereignty. When it comes to assessing American China policy, most America Watchers find themselves in agreement with the hegemonist critique of U.S. foreign policy more generally.

Summary

This chapter has indicated the articulation of both Marxist and non-Marxist perceptions of American foreign policy, but also a third strand of opinion that is not evident in the America Watchers' perceptions of the U.S. economy, society, and polity—hegemonism. As seen in chapter 2, the hegemonist critique is rooted in both the traditional Chinese philosophy of governance and modern Chinese historical experience. This perspective is reflective of China's desire to maintain sovereignty and not be dictated to by foreign powers, but it also represents a certain worldview of proper interstate relations. It clashes directly with American assumptions of the universality of human rights, the interdependence of nations, and the appeal of democracy. As long as China remains a socialist state, this clash of values will persist, and Sino-American relations will reflect the resultant tensions.

Seven

Conclusion

IN THE INTRODUCTION I raised several core questions that this study sought to answer: Who are China's America Watchers? What perceptions of the United States did they articulate between 1972 and 1990 and how did these change over time? Why do the America Watchers articulate the perceptions they do?

In this concluding chapter I will summarize my principal findings with respect to the first three of these questions of inquiry. In the second section I will consider some possible explanations for the fourth issue—accounting for perceptions. I will conclude with some general observations on the significance of the America Watchers' perceptions for Sino-American relations.

Principal Findings

The America Watchers

This study has examined the articulated perceptions of a large sample of a total community of China's approximately six hundred to seven hundred professional America Watchers who work in the central government bureaucracy, research institutes, journalism, or universities. These individuals' main profession is to analyze the United States and interpret it for China's concerned elite and mass public, although some are also practitioners involved in helping to make and implement China's America policies.

This community of America Watchers has really taken shape since 1979, in the aftermath of the normalization of relations between the United States and People's Republic of China and the Third Plenum of the Eleventh Congress of the Chinese Communist Party, which brought Deng Xiaoping and his reformist policies—including the opening to the outside world—to the fore. This community is constantly growing. In 1972, the starting point for this study, the active America Watchers numbered only a small fraction of what they did in 1990, but now their ranks continue to swell by the year. The institutional loci of America watching has expanded along with the personnel. In the Introduction I noted that virtually every central government ministry now has a United States analysis section, and many ministries can call upon a plethora of affiliated research institutes for expertise. The New China News Agency now maintains a large contingent of correspondents in the United States who file regular dispatches in the Chinese domestic media. The study of the United States has also expanded in universities, where many departments now teach courses on the United States, and at least fifteen Centers of American Studies have been established on campuses across China. Finally, professional associations have been formed in China to bring together specialists on American history, literature, and the economy. In December 1988, on the ten-year anniversary of the establishment of diplomatic relations, the Chinese Association for American Studies was inaugurated, based at the Institute of American Studies of the Chinese Academy of Social Sciences, home to the largest critical mass of Americanists in China.

America watching, in short, has become a growth industry in China. This study has extensively sampled the perceptions articulated by these four cohorts of the America-watching community. Below I will explore how their perceptions have varied by sector and professional role.

During this period—particularly since 1979—most America Watchers have had the opportunity to visit the United States, many for a year or more. Some have been sent by the Chinese government, but much of the visitation has been facilitated by American sponsors—government and nongovernment alike. It has been a conscious policy of the American government, national exchange organizations, foundations, and private groups to expose Chinese America specialists to the United States firsthand so as to improve mutual understanding, facilitate more empirical accuracy in their reports to the Chinese leaders and public, and influence to some extent the direction of reform in China. It has been an American national effort to win Chinese hearts and minds. Later in this chapter I will consider the implications of the latter effort for Sino-American relations more broadly, but suffice it to note here that this study has provided demonstrable proof of the success of the former efforts.

Substance and Variation in Articulated Images

From 1972 to 1990 the America Watchers advanced a spectrum of views on the U.S. economy, society, polity, and foreign policy. These articulated perceptions have evolved over time, but throughout they have clustered into two rival schools of interpretation—Marxist and non-Marxist. A shift in the center of gravity in this spectrum from the former to the latter occurred between 1972 and 1990, with non-Marxist analyses becoming more prevalent over time. Nonetheless, it has not been a zero-sum transformation. That is, although the non-Marxist school was not much in evidence at the outset of this study (1972), the Marxist School remained very much in evidence at its conclusion (1990). This is significant testimony to the sustenance of the Marxist-Leninist worldview in China and its application to analyzing specific countries such as the United States.

More refined clusters of perceptions were also identified within each school. In the Marxist School there exists a more determinist and Stalinist line of interpretation, for whom the structure of classes in advanced capitalist countries (such as the United States) is paramount. To them, all activities in both the economic "base" and the political "superstructure" are a function of the disposition of economic class power—which is dominated by the financial oligarchy within the monopoly bourgeoisie. This stratum, in the view of the Stalinists, dominates and controls the economic, social, and political life of the nation, and dictates its foreign policy. This line of analysis is seen, respectively, in chapters 3 through 6. The Stalinists are institutionally based primarily in universities—notably Wuhan University, Nankai University in Tianjin, and Fudan University in Shanghai—but also have a handful of representatives in the journalistic and research institute communities.

A second opinion group, the Leninists, also employ Marxist categories of analysis but are much less deterministic in their analyses. They invoke Lenin by name in challenging and revising the more dogmatic Stalinist interpretations. This group has their adherents in universities and the Central Party School, but they are anchored in the Institute of World Economics and Politics at the Chinese Academy of Social Sciences. They dispute the Stalinist interpretation of state-monopoly capitalism and instead invoke Lenin by arguing that the political superstructure is not a direct function of the economic base, but is rather one of "coalescence." They maintain that the monopoly bourgeoisie is an important actor in countries like the United States, but they argue that the state enjoys relative autonomy in policy making. Under such conditions the American economy has demonstrated resilience, and the working class is no longer "absolutely impoverished" as the Stalinists argue. Besides, argue the Leninists, the monopoly bourgeoisie in the United States has become progressively dispersed since World War II to the point where it is no longer possible to link events in the domestic political arena or foreign policy directly to the machinations of one or another "monopoly financial group."

This realization was hammered out in the polemics over the efficacy of Lenin's theory of imperialism and Stalin's interpretation of state-monopoly capitalism waged among Chinese ideologists between 1978 and 1984. These doctrinal debates are analyzed in chapter 2 and are offered as poignant examples of the changing role of orthodox ideology in post-Mao China. While these debates are important in doctrinal terms and were passionately argued by loyal adherents to this orthodoxy, the polemics simultaneously served two other functions. First, they theoretically justified the policy of rapprochement and peaceful coexistence with the United States. They believed that since imperialism demonstrated continued "life" and the state exhibited "autonomy" from the monopoly bourgeoisie, having relations with the imperialist U.S. government was therefore not a sellout of proletarian values since imperialism was not in danger of "dying" and the government did not necessarily represent Wall Street and other oligarchical interests. Second, by coming to these twin conclusions about imperialism and state-monopoly capitalism, respectively, the analytical door was opened to explore the reasons for imperialism's robust health as well as the inner workings of the capitalist polity, economy, and society.

These debates within the Marxist School are significant in that they were an important step from left to right on the spectrum of the America Watchers' perceptions of U.S. domestic affairs. Once the Leninists had asserted that the state exhibited autonomy of political action, the door was opened to analyses of the inner workings of the U.S. government unencumbered by explanations of manipulation by the monopoly bourgeoisie. Similarly, in analyzing the American economy the Leninists took a less gloomy view of the periodic "crises" that afflict the U.S. economy and ipso facto are thought to result in the collapse of the capitalist system. Instead, they noted the apparent ability of the U.S. economy to rebound from such "crises" and renew itself. This led them to the conclusion that capitalism's "general crisis" as predicted by Stalin could be postponed, and that American imperialism was not in danger of "dying" anytime soon. Moreover, interimperialist war was not deemed an imminent possibility either.

Considered together, these are fundamental shifts in the Marxist worldview, albeit by degree. These were significant changes for the America Watchers and Chinese Marxists, but they were not new departures in international Marxist circles. On the contrary, these are no longer pressing or debatable issues among Marxists around the world. Marxists today are more worried about the moribund nature of socialism, the collapse of centrally planned economies, the erosion of communist ideals amid the crisis of social alienation that grips what is left of the socialist camp, and the meaning of having lost the cold war.

Chinese Marxists, on the other hand, remain mired in debates of literally four decades ago. I noted in the introduction and chapter 2 the fascinating and important discovery that the issues debated and conclusions reached in the Chinese polemics on imperialism and state-monopoly capitalism during 1978–1984 were virtually identical to those argued by Varga against Stalin in 1950–1952 and reached by Soviet Americanists and analysts of capitalism during the Khrushchev era. One reason for this was the exposure that some Chinese theorists had to Varga and specialists in his Institute of International Relations and World Economy during the 1950s. These Chinese theorists, many in the CASS's Institute of World Economics and Politics, led the way in advocating Vargaesque interpretations cloaked in the name of Lenin during the early 1980s.

In contrast to their Marxist counterparts, the non-Marxists are characterized by their atheoretical analyses of the United States. Their analyses are largely piecemeal and descriptive. There are within the non-Marxist School, however, varying clusters of opinion. One group, the "statists," picks up where the Leninists left off. In analyzing American politics and the making of U.S. foreign policy, they focus their attention on the federal government, particularly the executive branch. They try to identify institutional, factional, and personal cleavages. On occasion they take account of Congress, but their primary focus of analysis is on the various organs of the executive branch. The statists can be found primarily in the central government bureaucracy (notably the Foreign Ministry), among New China News Agency journalists, and in research institutes—most notably the Institute of Contemporary International Relations and Shanghai Institute of International Studies.

By contrast, a second identifiable opinion group within the non-Marxist school are the "pluralists." Their analytical scope knows no boundaries. The pluralists take into account a broad range of economic, social, and political actors. Some of these actors are institutional, such as the Congress; some are organizational, such as interest groups and think tanks; and some are simply bodies of opinion in the American body politic. For the pluralists, policy making is the product of multiple inputs that vary across issue areas, and politics itself exists in a pluralistic environment. In other words, they recognize the democratic process and describe it as such. The pluralists are primarily located in professional research institutes—particularly the CASS's Institute of American Studies and the Institute of International Studies—but also in the journalistic community.

Chapters 3, 4, and 5 traced and analyzed the America Watchers' perceptions of the American economy, society, and political system respectively. In all three cases both the Marxist and non-Marxist tendencies of analysis were discernible. They were also apparent in chapter 6, on American foreign policy. The Marxists made their case for an imperialist foreign policy driven by the profit motive. They traced the ties of big business and financial interests to U.S. behavior abroad in a classic Leninist fashion. The various coercive abilities at the disposal of the U.S. government, notably covert use of the CIA and overt use of the military, were employed to advance the financial interests of the big bourgeoisie and their agents in government. The discussion in chapter 5 concerning nongovernmental actors in the policy process also showed clearly the linkages between domestic financial interests and foreign policy behavior abroad.

Chapter 6 also discussed the non-Marxist interpretation of U.S. foreign policy. Consistent with their analyses of domestic policy in the United States, the non-Marxists tended to view American behavior abroad in an ad hoc and descriptive manner. This line of analysis tended to view American foreign policy as a series of disaggregated bilateral relationships. It also tended to be most evident in the articulated perceptions of journalists and central government America Watchers (especially the Foreign Ministry). Chapters 5 and 6 both revealed evidence of statist and pluralist explanations of the domestic sources of U.S. foreign policy. For example, the statists perceive that the State Department, Defense Department, National Security Council, and their principal staff members all compete with each other in the formulation of policy, and the pluralists argue that various think tanks, foundations, university institutes, conservatives and liberals, hawks and doves, hardliners and softliners, advocates of the cold war versus détente, and so forth all sought to influence American foreign policy.

But chapter 6 uncovered a significant new departure from the Marxist/non-Marxist dichotomy so evident throughout the study of domestic American affairs. Rather than seeing a variegated foreign policy (as the non-Marxists) or a profit-driven foreign policy (as the Marxists), this new strand of analysis viewed American foreign policy as the pursuit of global hegemony. For America Watchers articulating this image—and the majority cluster in this camp—all American actions abroad are derivative of the U.S. quest for global hegemony. Some see this quest for hegemony as derivative from

U.S. competition with the Soviet Union for such supremacy, while others see it as driven by a combination of factors in the American historical experience and national psyche—what veteran America Watcher, journalist, and pundit Peng Di referred to as the "superpower complex." The hegemonist critique of American foreign policy is very apparent in the America Watcher's perceptions of American policy and behavior toward China. The United States, in the view of many, is bent on manipulating China for its own strategic purposes, wantonly interfering in its internal affairs irrespective of Chinese national dignity and sovereignty, and trying to transform China in its own vision.

These, then, are the principal findings of this study with respect to the substance of the America Watchers' perceptions of the United States. In sum, there is an essential cleavage between Marxist and non-Marxist interpretations, but a growing sophistication and plurality of views are advanced over time. In the end, however, it must be said that the depth of understanding of the United States among these America Watchers remains very shallow. Progress has been made, to be sure, but on the whole the America Watchers do not understand the United States very well. Many of them are burdened by the Marxist belief system, image structures, and categories of analysis. They suffer from a great deal of cognitive dissonance and simply look for evidence to confirm their preconceived images of how the United States functions. Others are so nationalistic in their views of hegemony that they too are blinded from recognizing more nuanced and variegated policies and behavior. Even the so-called non-Marxists, who come the closest to understanding the United States in objective terms, suffer from a lack of sociological perspective that would enable them to understand process and plurality better. At the root of these misperceptions is the fact that the America Watchers are Chinese and bring all the attendant cultural, sociological, political, and historical baggage to bear on their analyses of the United States.

Accounting for Perceptions

Although I have primarily been concerned in this study with tracking the substance of the America Watchers' articulated perceptions over time, categorizing them, and showing their variation, I have secondarily been concerned with accounting for their variation. That is, why do the America Watchers articulate the perceptions they do?

One can only speculate about the sources of the America Watchers' perceptions. While some biographical data exist for the America

Watchers, it is too fragmentary for an empirically sound and extensive quantitative analysis on which to base a convincing sociological and social-psychological explanation. In the ideal world, one would want to identify precisely several key socializing variables such as locale of rearing, schooling, family and peer groups, Communist Party indoctrination, exposure to Americans and other nationalities, travel to the United States, and so on. Then one would want to control for some variables and see how they covary with respect to articulated perceptions. To attain such data, extensive and systematic interviewing and questionnaire sampling under controlled conditions would be necessary if rigorous empirical standards were to be maintained.

In my doctoral dissertation, I attempted to analyze some of these factors.[1] Based on biographical data for 162 America Watchers, most of which derived from curriculum vitae submitted to sponsoring U.S. scholarly exchange organizations,[2] I was able to offer some tentative explanations about the individual sources of the America Watchers' perceptions. These are summarized below.

Exposure to the United States

Exposure to the United States definitely influences the America Watchers' interpretations in a non-Marxist direction. Most America Watchers have now been to the United States for extended periods. But equally important is the fact that this correlates positively with age. That is, younger America Watchers are more prone to articulate non-Marxist perceptions of the United States as a result of exposure to it. The older an America Watcher is, the more tenaciously they cling to previously held beliefs (as measured by the articulation of published perceptions before and after visiting the United States).

This confirms a basic tenet of cognitive dissonance, namely, that after the age of about thirty one tends to look for evidence confirming one's core beliefs and rejects contradictory evidence, because dissonance is psychologically uncomfortable. This theory was sustained by this study, as younger America Watchers who had articulated Marxist perceptions prior to visiting the United States tended to articulate non-Marxist views after return (if they returned) while those

[1] See my "China's America Watchers' Images of the United States, 1972–1986," Ph.D. dissertation, University of Michigan, 1988.

[2] I wish to thank the Ford Foundation, Henry Luce Foundation, National Committee on U.S.-China Relations, and Committee on Scholarly Communication with the People's Republic of China for making available these data.

over thirty tended to articulate the same perceptions before and after firsthand exposure to the United States. It was a rare case, such as Zhang Jialin, of an older America Watcher who had his Marxist views challenged by the reality he saw in the United States and changed his views accordingly. Thus, as one would expect, exposure to the United States increases understanding and generally contributes to non-Marxist perceptions—particularly for younger individuals.

Professional Role

Professional role is also a very important source of the America Watchers' perceptions. Professional role means that people are conditioned by their organizational environments. Professional role conditions one's view of the world insofar as different occupations introduce different perceptual screening mechanisms related to one's role in society. Fundamental to this idea is the recognition that different institutions have differing organizational missions, and an individual's perceptions are significantly shaped by both the specific organizational mission of the particular institution for which he or she works and the professional role that institution performs in society more generally. The foundations of this idea derive from organizational theory. I discussed in the introduction some of the ways in which this body of theory informs the analysis of this study, taking note of the maxim that "where one stands is where one sits."

Defined by professional role, the America Watchers perform different functions in Chinese society. True, they all interpret the United States for their fellow countrymen, and to some extent this binds them together professionally, but they work for different types of institutions that perform differing social roles. Four broad institutional categories can be identified.

Those America Watchers who work in the central government bureaucracy, particularly in the Foreign Ministry, perform the dual professional roles of managing the logistical details of China's relations with the United States and advising senior Chinese leaders and policy makers about the United States. They are therefore simultaneously policy makers, policy implementers, policy advocates, and advisers to other policy makers. To perform these professional roles to the best of their ability, they must have the most accurate information possible about the United States on which to base their decisions and advise others. Ideologically imbued interpretations generally obscure such accurate interpretation of information and do not serve well as the intellectual basis to guide important policy decisions. Intelligence analysis is supposed to be value-free; all policy makers need the facts so as to inform rational decisions. Chinese policy makers are no different. Interviews with them confirm that they do not think and debate policy issues in ideological terms.

This study found that America Watchers working in policy-making positions in the central government bureaucracy and affiliated intelligence organs tended to articulate straightforward, descriptive, non-Marxist perceptions of the United States and world affairs of a quite detailed and relatively sophisticated nature. This is not to say that the policy maker or leader concerned does not have his own set of perceptual proclivities, including ideological biases, but the professional role of the America specialist in the central bureaucracy is to give the generalist policy maker "the facts." As Aberbach, Putnam, and Rockman have found in Western democracies, Kingdon in the United States, and Halpern and Lieberthal and Oksenberg in the case of China, specialists perform other roles in the policy process in addition to contributing facts and their judgments on the technical feasibility of alternative policy courses.[3] They articulate and mediate others' interests. Their participation in the policy process is therefore multifaceted, the roles they play are complex, and the influence they exert on policy outcomes vary. But since the consequences of their actions affect so many others, they seek the maximum objective information possible on which to base their decisions—even if those judgments are not optimal.

Thus, policy makers must rely on subordinates, advisers, and a large intelligence apparatus. In China, as noted above, many America Watchers who work in professional research institutes perform the professional role of intelligence analyst. Their writings land on the desks of ministers, state councillors, and party and state leaders in the Zhongnanhai. They also orally brief leaders on occasion, accompany them on trips to the United States, and attend meetings with visiting American dignitaries. America Watchers in three civilian research institutes apparently perform this professional role most regularly: the Institute of Contemporary International Relations, Institute of International Studies, and the Institute of American Studies at the CASS. Although the latter maintains bona fide scholarly cre-

---

[3] See Joel Aberbach et al., *Bureaucrats and Politicians in Western Democracies* (Cambridge: Harvard University Press, 1981); John W. Kingdon, *Agendas, Alternatives, and Public Policies* (Boston: Little, Brown, 1984); Nina P. Halpern, "Economic Specialists and the Making of Chinese Economic Policy, 1955–1983," Ph.D. dissertation, University of Michigan, 1985; Kenneth Lieberthal and Michel Oksenberg, *Policy Making in China*. I also wish to thank Nina Halpern for sharpening my sense of varying professional roles that specialists play in different political systems.

These perspectives on the importance of professional role shed light on the specific perceptions witnessed in this study. Perceptions are not articulated in a vacuum. They are conditioned and strongly shaped by the professional roles of the perceiver.

Other factors are also important. In addition to exposure to the United States and professional role, four other factors appear to influence the America Watchers' perceptions: research materials; the domestic political climate; the state of Sino-American relations; and culture.

Research Sources

How do America Watchers go about their job? On what do they base their perceptions? How do they research their articles and reports? These may be obvious questions, but the answers are illuminating.

Essentially there are three types of data used by the America Watchers: documentary, oral, and visual. Since the normalization of relations, the America Watchers have at their disposal tremendously increased access to sources of all three types.

Of the documentary type, they can use American books, periodicals, newspapers, and government documents. A survey that I conducted for the U.S. Information Agency turned up 668 translated books about the United States that were published in Chinese during the decade 1977–1987.[7] In addition, as this study has demonstrated, there is a growing body of literature written by Chinese about the United States that fellow America Watchers can draw upon. During the same period, I found that 107 titles were published by Chinese.[8] It is interesting to note that these figures vary somewhat from a survey conducted by CASS America Institute Director Zi Zhongyun. Zi's survey determined that for the period 1971–1986, there were 116 books written by Chinese and 580 translated titles about America published in China.[9]

Similarly, the America Watchers draw upon both American and Chinese periodicals and newspapers. Many American periodicals can now be purchased (with foreign currency) in China, and most libraries used by America Watchers subscribe to them. As has been quite evident from the data used in this study, many Chinese periodicals and newspapers regularly carry translated items on the United

[7] See my *Books on America in the People's Republic of China, 1977–1987* (Washington, D.C.: U.S. Information Agency, 1988).

[8] Ibid.

[9] See Zi Zhongyun, "Zhongguo de Meiguo yanjiu," *Meiguo yanjiu*, no. 1 (1987): 16.

States.[10] American newspapers are more scarce in China, as many libraries deem subscriptions too expensive. (The CASS's America Institute, for example, had to let its subscription to the *New York Times* lapse due to the prohibitive cost.) Many American newspaper dispatches are, however, translated daily in the internal-circulation *Reference News* and the more highly classified *Reference Materials*. The latter is probably the single most important source of information about the United States for China's political elite.[11]

Perhaps the most important fact about the use of American periodicals and newspapers is not only that they are extensively used— as this is to be expected of any specialist attempting to research a foreign country—but that they are reproduced, sometimes verbatim, by the America Watchers for the domestic audience. The majority of NCNA, *People's Daily* and other dispatches filed from the United States are derived from American sources. This is a very significant finding in that it produces a mirror-image effect: Chinese readers are reading regurgitated American press analyses. The increased amount of non-Marxist, descriptive analyses written by Chinese journalists reflects the very fact that these dispatches are based on American analyses. As the NCNA Washington bureau chief told me on the day of the 1987 Iowa caucuses when I asked how he was going to compile his report, "I will go back to the office, read the wire service dispatches this evening and the major newspapers tomorrow morning."[12] Perhaps this is no different from how any journalist plies his or her trade, but it points up the mirror imagery conveyed by Chinese journalists to the reading public. Interviews with scores of institute researchers and central government bureaucrats, who also have access to such sources, indicate that they often base their analyses and judgments on the same. Academic America Watchers in China have considerably less access to U.S. periodicals and newspapers, and it shows in their articulated images.

Finally, U.S. government publications offer an additional, and increasingly important, source of information on the United States. The Chinese embassy in Washington acquires innumerable congressional committee reports and often sends them back to research institutes in China (cursory surveys of research institute libraries makes one wonder, however, about the amount they are actually used). Importantly, Chinese scholars are making increasing use of archival mate-

---

[10] See my *Coverage of the United States in Key Chinese Periodicals During 1984.*

[11] Michael Schoenhals makes the same point in his "Elite Information in China," *Problems of Communism* (September–October 1985): 65–71.

[12] Interview with Li Yanning, April 1987, Washington, D.C.

rials at presidential libraries in the United States. As a result, there is an increased empiricism among some Americanists as their analyses are more often footnoted with primary sources.

Oral sources of information about the United States essentially derive from contacts with Americans in China and the United States. It is reasonable to estimate that the America Watchers have more contact with Americans than perhaps any other segment of the Chinese intelligentsia. A constant stream of Americans flows through the professional research institutes and American studies centers on Chinese campuses, and the America Watchers travel frequently to the United States. As is the case with American scholars in China, the America Watchers are making increased use of oral interviews in their research on the United States.

Visual sources can be described as both human and electronic. On the human level, the America Watchers can both observe Americans in China and, much more important, see the United States with their own eyes. The latter is a vitally important source for the America Watchers. The highly anecdotal nature of many of their writings vividly conveys the impact that their personal encounters have had on their interpretations of the United States. As witnessed in chapter 4, many Americanists readily cite visits to American homes, farms, factories, hospitals, and urban neighborhoods as evidence in their writings on American society.

The point is that the America Watchers' perceptions of the United States now convey a firsthand feel for the country not previously evident. One of the things they have discovered is that many of the stereotypes they had been brought up to believe about "Old Gold Mountain" or "American imperialism" are challenged by visual realities: the streets are not paved with gold, nor is it a society on the verge of revolution.

Electronic visual images also have an impact on their perceptions. Many Chinese who come to the United States spend hours watching television, and the perceptions they form are strongly conditioned by this medium. Similarly, American satellite news feeds and other programs are now carried daily on Chinese television (not to mention the hundreds of millions of Voice of America listeners), and American movies increasingly play to packed houses in Chinese theaters.

Taken together, these three forms—documentary, oral, and visual—constitute both the primary data sources used in the America Watchers' research and the broader environment of inputs shaping the total milieu in which the America Watchers perceive the United States.

The Domestic Political Climate

In a nation such as China, politics, as Mao once put it, "is in command." Politics no longer intrudes as pervasively on people's lives as it did during Mao's day, but the political climate under Deng Xiaoping has continued to have a definite impact on all intellectuals—America Watchers included. This impact has been varied.

On a broad level it must be said that the political liberalization that China enjoyed under Deng's aegis during the 1980s contributed a great deal to the development of the American studies. Deng opened diplomatic relations with the United States and gave his blessing to the rapid expansion of contact between the two countries. Deng's second would-be successor, Zhao Ziyang, was given the policy portfolio within the Chinese leadership for overseeing the Sino-American relationship during the 1980s, and Zhao personally relied upon select America hands for advice. Deng's first hand-picked successor, Hu Yaobang, was also instrumental in the "rehabilitation" of numerous Americanists who had remained "capped" from the Anti-Rightist Campaign of 1957 or had been victims of the Cultural Revolution. These rehabilitations swelled the ranks of the America Watchers with individuals trained in American missionary schools prior to 1949, who were fluent in English and had an understanding of the United States based on prerevolution contact. As noted in the introduction, many of these individuals had grown up together, been schooled together at institutions like Yanjing University, or had worked together during the 1940s and 1950s. There existed a certain camaraderie among this first generation of Americanists, just as there appears to be one forming now among the generation being trained in the United States during the 1980s and 1990s.

From 1979 to 1989 the Deng Xiaoping–led reformist leadership took various measures to enlist the intelligentsia in the modernization program and create a research environment more conducive to intellectual inquiry. The epistemological task was to change the way intellectuals thought and conducted their research. In a very real sense, this necessitated unlearning many of the epistemological lessons learned since 1949. When the People's Daily proclaimed in a major editorial on May 12, 1978, that "practice is the sole criterion of truth," the Deng regime had made its first official step toward accepting empiricism as the epistemological guide to research. By implication, dogmatic interpretations of ideological doctrines were no longer to serve as a guide to "truth" in research.[13] The very notion that there could be a single "truth" was challenged.

This regime-induced attempt at normative intellectual change, essentially replacing deduction with induction, significantly affected the America Watchers. Very simply, it has meant that there is no longer a "correct" view of the United States. This is one of the major findings of this study. Prior to the Third Plenum and the ensuant normalization of diplomatic relations with the United States—which brought the non-Marxist cohort of the America-watching community to the fore—there was such a thing as a standard, singular, state-set interpretation of the United States in China. This interpretation was that of the Marxist School, particularly the Stalinist camp within it. The main storyline of this study is the replacement of this dominant and singular image of the United States by competing and variegated perceptions.

Just as politics under Deng contributed to the blossoming of America watching in China, so too did it intrude several times on the work of the Americanists. Censorship remained a fact of life throughout this period despite the liberalization noted above. Sometimes the censorship was more extreme and exerted from above—notably during the 1983 Anti–Spiritual Pollution Campaign, the 1987 Anti–Bourgeois Liberalization campaign, and the 1989–1990 Anti–Peaceful Evolution Movement—but in more normal times individual Americanists exerted self-censorship. This meant that some would continually test the limits of the permissible. Short of the outright advocacy of American-style democracy much was tolerated, as the emergence of the pluralist camp of the non-Marxists reflects. During these campaigns, however, the bolder Americanists tended to stop writing and publishing, and more orthodox Marxist articles appeared.

Thus, in a general sense, the systemic political changes brought about by the Dengist reform program helped to create the environment for the rapid development of American studies in China. Conversely, the reemergence of more orthodox and totalitarian leaders since the crushing of the 1989 prodemocracy movement cast a cloud over the field of American studies just as it did over Sino-American relations more generally. "We don't write anymore, and if we do we just keep it in the drawer," said one leading Americanist in the CASS's America Institute in the wake of the Tiananmen massacre.[14]

---

[13] For an analysis of the "criterion of truth" and related campaigns, see Brantly Womack, "Politics and Epistemology Since Mao," *China Quarterly* (December 1979): 768–92.

[14] Interview at the Institute of American Studies, CASS, January 26, 1990.

The IAS came under intense political pressure during the post-Tiananmen investigations.

The Impact of Sino-American Relations

This is a clear, if somewhat extreme, example of how the Sino-American relationship has also served to influence the America Watchers' articulated perceptions of the United States. With this exception, broadly speaking I have not found evidence that the state of Sino-American relations has adversely affected the America Watchers' perceptions of the United States. That is, during periods when bilateral relations were strained, a parallel negative shift in the coverage of the United States is not apparent. Coverage of U.S. domestic affairs and foreign policy continued without any significant alteration of tone or substance. This is not to say that negative commentary did not appear; to the contrary, one of the major findings of this study is that many America Watchers remained highly critical and negative throughout the period considered.

Where one does notice a shift is in coverage of Sino-American relations. The discussion of the America Watchers' perceptions of U.S.-China relations presented in chapter 6 did show an increase in negative and critical commentary of American China policy during periods of strain in the relationship, but this negativism did not seem to carry over readily into other realms of coverage. This increase may be attributed to two factors. First, published articles were often meant as diplomatic signals, and second, central control over the publishing domain can be reactivated at any time.

Thus, one can conclude that while the America Watchers are subject to censorship (much of it self-censorship), they are not necessarily a barometer of Sino-American relations. Their writings on U.S. China policy do occasionally reflect diplomatic and political concerns, but for the most part they write what they want. Interviews and private discussions with well over one hundred Americanists, and several years of living in China, convince me that during noncrisis periods these individuals are not subject to the censorship and political manipulation often assumed abroad.[15]

[15] The fact that Gilbert Rozman found this to be the case for Chinese Sovietologists may have more to do with the sensitivity of the subject area at the time and should not be extrapolated more broadly to include other international affairs specialists. See Rozman, *The Chinese Debate on Soviet Socialism.*

Cultural Differences

Culture is the sixth and final—but critically important—factor that conditions the broader intellectual milieu shaping the America Watchers' perceptions. For more than two hundred years, ever since the United States and China first came into direct contact, America Watchers have existed in China. This study has thus looked at the revival of a group of "cultural intermediaries" specializing in American affairs.[16] In historical terms, this group carries forward a tradition of interpretation and intermediation that developed during the Qing dynasty when "understanding the barbarians in order to control them" became a vocation among Chinese scholar-officials. The Qing state established a special bureau for dealing with the United States and Europe, designated "Barbarian Affairs" (yi wu), and those literati who staffed it were among the first to articulate distinct images of the United States. This tradition flowered during the Republican period and then fell increasingly out of favor after 1949. It has now been revived.

Certainly perceptions evolve over time, but throughout this century of interpretation of the United States, one dominant theme has been evident in these individuals' images of America: ambivalence. Historians Michael Hunt and Jerome Chen and philosopher Tu Wei-ming have tracked this theme over a long period of time.[17] This ambivalence is fundamentally rooted in two factors: China's quest for modernity, and the different value systems held by Americans and Chinese. Both of these are enormous issues and are worthy of major studies unto themselves, but their fundamental importance in placing this study in context demands brief elaboration.

America Watchers are intellectuals. Historically, many Chinese intellectuals did not perceive the United States merely as an abstract entity or a large and powerful nation on the opposite side of the Pacific Ocean that warranted their attention by virtue of sheer presence. Rather, they viewed it in light of its relevance to their own nation's prolonged national crisis and search for "wealth and power," terri-

[16] I thank Michael Hunt for focusing my attention on this issue.

[17] See Michael Hunt, The Making of a Special Relationship: The United States and China to 1914 (New York: Columbia University Press, 1983); Hunt, "Themes in Traditional and Modern Chinese Images of America," in Mutual Images and U.S.-China Relations (Washington, D.C.: Occasional Paper no. 32 of the Asia Program of the Woodrow Wilson International Center for Scholars, June 1988); Jerome Chen, China and the West: Society and Culture, 1815–1937 (London: Hutchinson, 1979); Tu Wei-ming, "Chinese Perceptions of America," in Dragon and Eagle, ed. Robert B. Oxnam and Michel C. Oksenberg (New York: Basic Books, 1978), pp. 87–106.

torial unity and integrity, national dignity, and international respect. Over time, many Chinese intellectuals and elites have evaluated the United States primarily on the basis of what it did to facilitate or hinder the realization of these goals.[18] It can be argued that, to a significant extent, China's America policy has fluctuated in accordance with this evaluation. The more the United States was prepared to contribute to the attainment of these goals, the more positive these Chinese intellectuals' and elites' images of it became, and concomitantly, the more cooperative a partner China was for the United States. Conversely, when the United States was perceived as either directly or indirectly frustrating the realization of these ambitions, it was perceived as China's enemy. Over the last two centuries, the United States has thus been an object of alternating amity and enmity for both the governments and intellectuals of China. A consistent equilibrium of constructive relations between the two countries has been elusive as mutual images have swung through successive love-hate cycles.

Thus, on the one hand, these image cycles are rooted in a deeper ambivalence about the West as both model and threat. The key intellectual, economic, political, cultural, and spiritual attributes of Western nations—including the United States—have been both the object of emulation and rejection over time.

On the other hand, these fluctuant images are rooted in the differing value systems in Chinese and American society. As Donald Munro, Tu Wei-ming, Andrew Nathan, and Lucian Pye have all described in their writings,[19] there exist fundamental differences in the basic beliefs about the nature of man and society that make it difficult for Chinese to understand and appreciate the liberal premises and principles underlying the pluralistic way that the American society, polity, and economy function. Certain core values and principles of Western liberalism are fundamentally alien to the Chinese philosophical tradition, and Chinese intellectuals—Marxists and non-Marxists

[18] This section draws upon my "Anti-Americanism in China," *Annals of the American Academy of Political and Social Science* 497 (May 1988): 142–56. For a discussion of China's perceptions of America in this context (one of the few), see Yuan Ming, "Dui dangqian Zhongguo dalu zhishifenzi kan Meiguo de jidian sikao," *Meiguo yanjiu*, no. 2 (1989): 72–87, and Yuan Ming, "Chinese Intellectuals and the United States: The Dilemma of Individualism vs. Patriotism," *Asian Survey* (July 1989): 645–54.

[19] Donald Munro, *The Concept of Man in Early China* (Stanford: Stanford University Press, 1969), and *The Concept of Man in Contemporary China* (Ann Arbor: University of Michigan Press, 1977); Tu Wei-ming, "Chinese Perceptions of America"; Andrew J. Nathan, *Chinese Democracy* (Berkeley: University of California Press, 1985); Lucian W. Pye, *Asian Power and Politics: The Cultural Dimensions of Authority* (Cambridge: Harvard University Press, 1985), chapter 7.

alike—have long had trouble grasping their essence and intended meaning.

For example, the Chinese perception of the individual as an inexorable part of an extended network of obligatory human relationships (*guanxi*), and the concomitant subjugation of individual desires to the collective will, is quite different from the American belief in the dignity and importance of the individual in its own right. Indeed, Benjamin Schwartz makes the point in his biography of Yan Fu (one of China's first intellectuals systematically to study Western liberal thought) that Yan's translations of Mill, Spencer, Huxley, and others led him to distort the values of democracy, liberty, and progress to mean that the rights of the individual should not be strengthened vis-à-vis the state, but should rather be channeled to strengthen the state itself! Similarly, no clear distinction between the public and private self has ever been fully elaborated in traditional Chinese philosophy, although the Daoist penchant for withdrawal and eremitism is frequently the subject matter of Chinese painting and literature. The very idea that civil and economic behavior should be codified and regulated by the external authority of the state (through the judiciary) strikes many Chinese as odd and unnecessary given Confucian traditions of civic duty. A true separation of powers is also without precedent in Chinese political history. Interest groups, lobbies, and the self-designated watchdog role the press plays in monitoring and criticizing government behavior strikes many Chinese as odd, as does the adversarial relationship that intellectuals seem to relish having with the state.

Essentially, it therefore seems that Chinese perceptions of the United States are fundamentally confounded by the strong American commitment to pluralism in politics, economic organization, and social structure. The coexistence of many conflicting channels of political participation, economic opportunity, and social mobility is fundamentally different from the Chinese preference for clearly structured roles and functions in society. Chinese fear of "disorder" (*luan*) also lends itself to interpretations of American pluralism as a sign of the disintegration of the social order rather than as an expression of the internal dynamism of the system. Thus, for reasons of political culture, many Chinese do not generally view pluralism as having intrinsic merit.

It is for this reason that many America Watchers appear to encounter difficulty in fully grasping American pluralism. Indeed, there is strong evidence of pluralist interpretations of the American economy, society, and political system, and to a much lesser degree in foreign policy, but these analyses are characterized by their descriptive nature. That is, they simply describe a broad range of actors in American society and in this sense perceive a pluralistic environment, but they do not understand pluralism qua system as Americans would, nor do they portray pluralistic behavior in a positive light. Most see American pluralism as a sign of weakness rather than strength.

Implications for Sino-American Relations

What does this study imply for Sino-American relations? This study has sought to probe beneath the surface of bilateral nation-state interaction to understand the intellectual milieu in which China's America policy is made. To be precise, it has sought to explore the specific perceptions of the United States articulated by a cadre of China's America Watchers. Since access to the top political elite who make policy in China (America policy included) is next to impossible, I thought it useful to study their advisers. Through examining this cohort of specialists (who Robert Putnam refers to as the "influential elite"[20]) and their articulated perceptions of the United States, I believed that one could come to a different, and hopefully deeper, understanding of the Sino-American relationship than is evident from examining purely behavioral interactions. By looking at this echelon of specialists and their perceptions I hope to have illuminated the interpretive prism through which the United States is viewed in China, and therefore the context in which China's America policy is made. This study was premised on the belief that behavior is a function of perception.

What has been learned of importance to Sino-American relations? First, different opinion groups exist within China's America watching community, and only a fraction of this community—those in the central government bureaucracy and affiliated research institutes— have any real input into China's America policy. Journalists and university academics tend to inform public audiences, while those working in ministries and institutes inform the elite. The elite also has access to translations of the American press via the classified *Cankao ziliao*, which tends to reinforce the non-Marxist images that the Americanists in the bureaucracy and institutes provide in their analyses of the United States.

Thus, the first finding of significance is that Chinese government

[20] Robert Putnam, *The Comparative Study of Political Elites* (Englewood Cliffs: Prentice-Hall, 1976), p. 11.

leaders and policy makers have access to information and intelligence of very detailed nature. Much of this interpretation reflects mirror imagery as it is based on American sources and portrayals of the United States. How Chinese policy makers themselves interpret this material is quite another matter, but if what has been witnessed emanating from the nonclassified and classified journals of the Institute of International Studies, Institute of Contemporary International Relations, CASS's America Institute, Shanghai Institute of International Studies, Beijing Institute of International Strategic Studies, National Defense University, Academy of Military Sciences, and the like is any indication of how China's leaders think about the United States, then there are grounds to conclude that policy toward the United States is made on a relatively well-informed basis.

Second, one sees in the America Watchers' interpretations of U.S. foreign policy—particularly Sino-American relations—a strong prejudice toward viewing the United States as a hegemonic power driven by the desire for world conquest. This is certainly not the way most Americans—leaders and public alike—view their nation's international behavior, but it does coincide with the views of many in other parts of the world. To view the United States as an aggressive and arrogant power that throws its economic and military might around the globe is hardly unique to the Chinese. This view, when juxtaposed in the context of modern Chinese history, leads one to the conclusion that no matter how well Chinese leaders understand the internal workings of the United States, its external behavior worldwide (and particularly toward China) will always be viewed with a great deal of suspicion. Given their historical experience and this perception of American hegemony, Chinese leaders simply do not trust American motives. They fear American manipulation of China in international strategic terms, exploitation in economic terms, and subversion in political and ideological terms. From the Chinese official perspective, therefore, cooperation between the two countries must be tactical since essential shared interests are relatively few, the two nations' political systems are fundamentally different and the United States is perceived as harboring aggressive designs on China.[21]

Negative Chinese commentary about the United States did not begin after the Tiananmen massacre. This study is dramatic proof that during the entire period since rapprochement, the Chinese have continued a constant and unremitting barrage of critical commentary of

[21] For elaboration of the problems in Sino-American cooperation see Harry Harding and David Shambaugh, "Patterns of Cooperation in the Foreign Relations of Modern China," in Harding ed., *China's Cooperative Relations*, forthcoming.

the United States. American policy makers were simply deluding themselves to think that China had become a "friend" or quasi-ally.

For much of the Chinese intelligentsia and millions of Chinese youth, however, the United States serves as a model. This is testimony not only to the appeal of the United States, but to the growth of knowledge about the United States in China—in no small part due to the efforts of the America Watchers. Yet, many pro-American Chinese intellectuals are quick to condemn the United States for what they perceive as hegemonic behavior and interference in China's internal affairs. How can this be? The answer lies in China's modern historical experience.

National disunity and impotence in the face of imperialist aggression for more than a century has left an indelible mark on the Chinese national psyche that Americans should not underestimate. Chinese denunciations of U.S. imperialism, hegemonism, great power chauvinism, interference in the internal affairs, and so on should not be read on the American side as propagandistic posturing. As seen in chapter 6, it is a serious intellectual critique as well as a statement of national interest. If the United States continues to delude itself with a series of ill-grounded stereotypes about China and fails to grasp the thrust of the Chinese critique of the United States shown in this study, the all too familiar love-hate cycle will continue to characterize Sino-American relations.

For its part, the Chinese government cannot continue to live under the illusion that sovereignty is immutable. Rather than come to terms with the realities of global interdependence of the late twentieth century, Chinese leaders apparently think they are living in a world of the Westphalian state system of old. They fail to grasp the simple fact that what goes on inside China's borders is the world's business. This includes the realm of language. Talk is not cheap; it should carry a price. If China felt it legitimate to criticize Japan for the way Japanese history texts portrayed China and the Second World War, so too does the United States have a legitimate right to complain about the types of portrayals of the United States seen in this study.

The import of this discussion is that there continues to exist a large "perception gap" in U.S.-China relations. Both sides are imbued with severe cases of cognitive dissonance, wishful thinking, stereotypical imagery, misinformation, and misperception. Granted, since 1972 mutual understanding has improved considerably as a result of direct contact between the two countries. This study is testimony to this fact with respect to China. But much still needs to be done if real mutual understanding and respect are to become realities.

Without more accurate perceptions, Sino-American relations will forever be plagued by falsely heightened and unfulfilled expectations followed by disillusionment and recriminations, potentially leading to wider conflicts. This repetitive pattern means that Sino-American relations will forever fluctuate, never finding a proper equilibrium. Given the size, strength, and importance of the United States and China in world affairs, unstable Sino-American relations are a dangerous omen for both countries and for the world.

Thus, the fluctuant characteristic of Sino-American relations noted at the outset of this study continues to hold true today. Fluctuating Sino-American relations reflect the continuing ambivalent images that the United States and China hold of each other. For the Chinese, the United States remains a Beautiful Imperialist.

Name Index

Subject Index

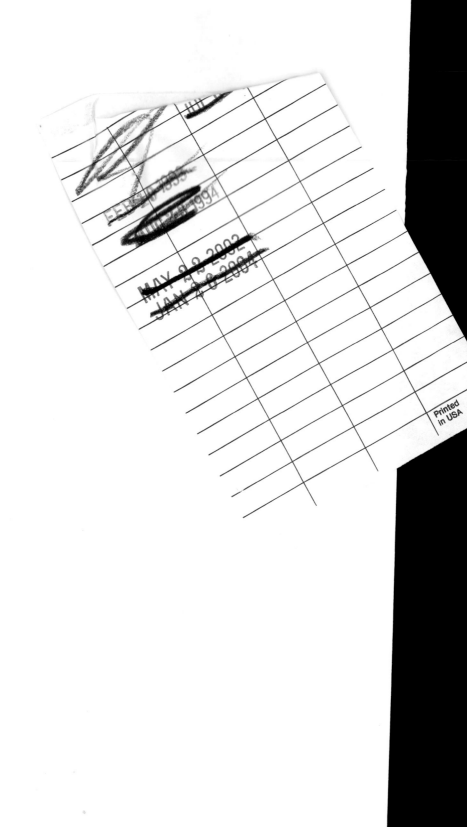